PSYCHOLOGY AND
HISTORICAL INTERPRETATION

Edited by

WILLIAM McKINLEY RUNYAN .
University of California, Berkeley

New York Oxford
OXFORD UNIVERSITY PRESS
1988

Oxford University Press

Oxford New York Toronto
Delhi Bombay Calcutta Madras Karachi
Petaling Jaya Singapore Hong Kong Tokyo
Nairobi Dar es Salaam Cape Town
Melbourne Auckland

and associated companies in
Berlin Ibadan

Copyright © 1988 by Oxford University Press, Inc.

Published by Oxford University Press, Inc.,
200 Madison Avenue, New York, New York 10016

Oxford is a registered trademark of Oxford University Press

Library of Congress Cataloging-in-Publication Data
Psychology and historical interpretation.
  Bibliography: p.   Includes index.
  1. Psychohistory. 2. History—Psychological aspects.
3. Personality and history. 4. Psychology—Methodology. I. Runyan, William McKinley.
D16.16.P87 1988   901′.9   87–25708
ISBN 0–19–505327–3
ISBN 0–19–505328–1

"A Historical and Conceptual Background to Psychohistory," "Alternatives to Psychoanalytic
Psychobiography," and "Reconceptualizing the Relationships Between History and Psychology"
copyright © 1988 by William McKinley Runyan.
"A Stalin Biographer's Memoir" from INTROSPECTION IN BIOGRAPHY, edited by S. Baron
and C. Pletsch, published by The Analytic Press, Inc. Copyright © 1985 by The Analytic Press,
Inc. Reprinted by permission.
"Alice James: A Family Romance" copyright © 1987 by Jean Strouse.

Printing (last digit): 9 8 7 6 5 4 3 2 1

Printed in the United States of America
on acid-free paper

For Elizabeth and William A. Runyan
and John F. Runyan
With Affection and Appreciation

Preface

This volume explores the uses of psychoanalytic and nonanalytic psychology in historical interpretation. What contributions can psychology make toward understanding the flow of historical events, the course of individual lives, or stability and change in social structures over time? To what extent is psychology useful, or perhaps even necessary, for understanding phenomena such as the career of Joseph Stalin, the experience of women in the nineteenth century, or the behavior of Nazis and Holocaust victims during World War II? Most simply and most generally: What kinds of psychology can be used, in what ways, for analyzing what range of historical phenomena?

The book begins with a historical and conceptual introduction to the field of psychohistory, discussing contributions to psychohistory from seven different disciplinary traditions, the institutional development of the field with the growth of publications and professional organizations, and several key intellectual debates that underlie the troubled relations between history and psychology. The central portion of the book consists of chapters on the uses of psychology in historical interpretation written by distinguished contributors with backgrounds in history, psychoanalysis, political science, literature, and psychology. Their topics range from case studies in biography and psychology, to relations between classic psychoanalytic theory and history, to applications of ego psychology and object relations theory in history. Additional topics include the analysis of subjectivity in history, the adequacy of psychoanalytic theory, and the uses of nonpsychoanalytic psychology in biography and history. The conclusion attempts to provide a more comprehensive conceptual framework for psychohistory, one that outlines its differentiated internal structure and that suggests its relationships with adjacent disciplines such as psychological anthropology, historical sociology, and political psychology.

When I initially agreed to edit this book, I thought that my previous work in psychobiography would make it relatively easy to provide a brief historical and conceptual background to psychohistory and to analyze common themes linking the individual chapters. What a piece of cake. But it did not quite turn out that way. Never have I investigated an area that required such extensive reanalysis of my earlier beliefs and assumptions. The more I attempted to systematically think through the conceptual and methodological relationships between history and psychology, the more confusing things became. Prior conceptual frameworks just didn't hold up, like weakened floor boards collapsing when too much weight is put on them. It was alternately exhilarating and depressing, moving from apparent insight, to confusion and despair, to glimpses of order at a deeper or more general level, until reaching a more stable formulation of the issues. This synthesis, which is sketched in the conclusion, may not be the final one, but it stands up to the range of substantive problems it has thus far been tested against, and feels substantially more comprehensive and secure than its predecessors.

This book has been a long time in the making, and I would like to express my appreciation to a number of people and institutions that helped along the way. First, I'd like to thank the Stanford University History Department and the Stanford Humanities Center, which sponsored the conference on "History and Psychology: Recent Studies in the Family, Biography, and Theory," May 7 to 9, 1982, which led to the initial preparation of papers included in this volume. With thanks to Peter Stansky, Chair of the History Department, and Ian Watt, Director of the Humanities Center, the conference was supported by the Munro Fund of the History Department and by the Humanities Center, with the assistance of the Hewlett Foundation and the Center for Teaching and Learning. In particular, I am deeply indebted to Nathan G. Hale, Jr., who was primarily responsible for planning and organizing the conference and also for suggesting that I edit this volume. I still think he should have been the editor. I would also like to thank Robert S. Wallerstein, who, in spite of earlier arrangements with another press, graciously allowed me to pursue possibilities of publishing with Oxford University Press.

I agreed to edit this volume late in 1984, and much of the work on the introduction and conclusion was pursued on a sabbatical year in 1985–86. I would like to thank Robert Jervis of the Center for War and Peace Studies, Columbia University, for his hospitality during the fall semester, and Lawrence Kohlberg, late of the Center for Moral Development and Education, Harvard University, for his hospitality during the spring and summer. As I was preoccupied with questions about the relationships between history and psychology, a sabbatical year provided an ideal opportunity for many discussions of the issues. Specifically, I'd like to thank Jerome Bruner and his seminar on "Forms of Narrative Elaboration" at the New School for Social Research; Ira Roseman for his friendship and conversations; and Arthur M. Schlesinger, Jr., who was kind enough to make available the transcript for a conference on psychohistory that he had organized at the Graduate Center of the City University of New York in 1971. He and several others suggested that an earlier version of the conclusion was probably too abstract, which I have tried to address by analyzing an interconnected set of examples from the Nazi era. At Harvard University, my thanks go out to the late and deeply missed Larry Kohlberg; to the friendly atmosphere provided by members of the Center for Moral Development and Education; and for stimulating conversations on these topics with Robert LeVine, Mary Vogel, Ting Lei, Lee Mintz, Howard Gardner, and Sheldon White.

I would also like to thank a number of colleagues at the University of California at Berkeley and elsewhere for their helpful reactions to and suggestions on earlier drafts of the introductory and concluding chapters, including Gerald Mendelsohn and members of his personality proseminar, Kenneth Craik, Philip Tetlock, Setsuo Mizuno, Nathan Hale, Jerome Wakefield, and members of the Society for Personology for discussing a related paper at their June 1987 meeting. Bruce Mazlish provided some helpful information over the telephone and by letter. I am particularly grateful to Bertram J. Cohler and Peter Loewenberg for their thoughtful critiques of the introductory and concluding chapters. My thanks also go to Kathy Vergeer for her unfailing help in typing and re-typing drafts of chapters, and to Betsy Locke for her work on the quantitative analyses of the growth of literature in psychohistory. I feel fortunate in having found such a supportive and congenial work environment as that provided at Berkeley in the School of Social Welfare under Dean Harry Specht and the Institute of Personality Assessment and Research, directed by Kenneth Craik.

I am pleased that Oxford University Press will be publishing the volume and want to thank Shelley Reinhardt for her valued editorial support of this project and this author, Irene Pavitt for her careful copy-editing, and Catherine Clements for her help with the many details of production. My hope is that the volume's historical, substantive, and theoretical discussions will serve to advance the debate about the problems and potentials of psychohistory.

Berkeley, California   W. M. R.
February 1988

Contents

Part III: Conclusion and Future Directions

Contributors

KENNETH H. CRAIK is Professor of Psychology and Director of the Institute of Personality Assessment and Research at the University of California, Berkeley, where he received his Ph.D. in 1964. He is author of over eighty publications in the fields of personality psychology, political psychology, and environmental psychology, including reports of studies on the personalities of political party leaders. He is author of *Perceiving Environmental Quality* (co-editor with E. H. Zube) and *Personality and the Environment* (co-editor with G. E. McKechnie), and founding co-editor of the *Journal of Environmental Psychology*.

FREDERICK CREWS, Professor of English, University of California, Berkeley, received his Ph.D. at Princeton in 1958. He is the author of, among other works, *E. M. Forster: The Perils of Humanism, The Pooh Perplex, The Sins of the Fathers: Hawthorne's Psychological Themes, The Random House Handbook, Out of My System, Skeptical Engagements,* and (with Sandra Schor) *The Borzoi Handbook for Writers.*

ALEXANDER DALLIN is professor of history and political science at Stanford University. He is the author of a number of books and articles on Soviet affairs and Soviet-American relations and previously served as director of the Russian Institute at Columbia University. He is currently president of the International Committee for Soviet and East European Studies.

PETER GAY, Sterling Professor of History at Yale University, received his Ph.D. in Public Law and Government at Columbia University. He has taught at Columbia and been at Yale since 1969. He is the author, among other works, of *The Enlightenment,* 2 vols.; *Style in History; Freud, Jews and Other Germans; Freud for Historians; The Bourgeois Experience, Victoria to Freud:* Vol. I, *Education of the Senses,* and Vol. II, *The Tender Passion;* and *Freud: A Life for Our Time.*

PETER LOEWENBERG, Professor of History, University of California, Los Angeles, was born in Hamburg. He received his Ph.D. at Berkeley. He also has a Ph.D. in Psychoanalysis from the Southern California Psychoanalytic Institute where he is on the faculty. He is Board Certified in Psychoanalysis and integrates the career of University historian and research psychoanalyst with a clinical practice. He is the author of over one hundred papers on German and Austrian history, European cultural and intellectual history, psychohistory, and of *Decoding the Past: The Psychohistorical Approach* (1983, 1985).

PETER PARET, Andrew W. Mellon Professor in the Humanities, Institute for Advanced Study, Princeton, received his Ph.D. at the University of London. He is the author of several works on German history, among them *Clausewitz and the State* and *The Berlin Secession.* Among books he has edited is the English translation of a classic of psychoanalytic pedagogy by his stepfather, Siegfried Bernfeld, *Sisyphus or the Limits of Education.*

WILLIAM McKINLEY RUNYAN received his Ph.D. in Clinical Psychology and Public Practice from Harvard University in 1975, and is currently Associate Professor, School of Social Welfare, and Associate Research Psychologist, Institute of Personality Assessment and Research, at the University of California, Berkeley. A winner of the Henry A. Murray Award for contributions to personality psychology, he is the author of *Life Histories and Psychobiography: Explorations in Theory and Method* (1982).

JEAN STROUSE is the author of *Alice James, A Biography* (1980), which won the Bancroft Prize in American History and Diplomacy in 1981. She edited *Women & Analysis, Dialogues on Psychoanalytic Views of Femininity* (1974) and is currently working on a biography of J. Pierpont Morgan. She graduated from Radcliffe College in 1967 and has published articles or reviews in The New York Review of Books, The New Yorker, The New York Times Book Review, and Newsweek.

ROBERT C. TUCKER, Professor of Politics, Emeritus, Princeton University, received his Ph.D. at Harvard University in 1958. He is former director of Princeton's Russian Studies Program and a current vice president of the International Society of Political Psychology. He is the author of, among other works, *Philosophy and Myth in Karl Marx, The Soviet Political Mind, The Marxian Revolutionary Idea, Stalin as Revolutionary: A Study in History and Personality, Politics as Leadership,* and *Political Culture and Leadership in Soviet Russia: From Lenin to Gorbachev.*

ROBERT S. WALLERSTEIN, Professor and former Chairman, Department of Psychiatry at the University of California School of Medicine, received his M.D. from Columbia University College of Physicians and Surgeons, his psychiatric training at The Menninger School of Psychiatry, and his psychoanalytic training at the Topeka Institute for Psychoanalysis. He is a Training and Supervising Analyst at the San Francisco Psychoanalytic Institute, a past president of the American Psychoanalytic Association, and the current president of the International Psycho-Analytic Association. His most recent book is *Forty-two Lives in Treatment: A Study of Psychoanalysis and Psychotherapy.*

FRED WEINSTEIN, Professor of History, State University of New York, Stony Brook, received his Ph.D. at the University of California, Berkeley, in 1962. He serves currently as the Chairman of the Board of Editors of the *Psychohistory Review;* as a member of the Board of Advisors of the *Psychoanalytic Review;* and as a Special Member, Membership Corporation, National Psychological Association for Psychoanalysis. He is the author of *The Dynamics of Nazism* and, with Gerald M. Platt, of *Psychoanalytic Sociology* and *The Wish To Be Free.*

Introduction

A Historical and Conceptual Background to Psychohistory

William McKinley Runyan

There is an underlying tension between the disciplines of history and psychology. The story of their relations in psychohistory is not simply one of cooperation and recognition of mutual interests, but also one of suspicion, misunderstanding, and occasional flashes of hostility. This tension is evident not only in shrill critiques of the accomplishments and potential of psychohistory (Barzun, 1974; Stannard, 1980), but also resonates at a deeper level of significant divergence in intellectual aims and assumptions, formidable institutional barriers to collaborative training and practice, and even temperamental differences between those attracted to history or psychology. There is, in short, a "deep gap between the history-minded and the social-science-minded" (Bruner, 1983, p. 189).

The conceptual logic for utilizing psychology in historical analysis seems unassailable. History is concerned with the study of human action and experience in circumstances in the past; psychology is the scientific study of human behavior and experience. Ergo, psychology could usefully be employed in analyzing the psychological component of historical events and processes, rather than relying solely on implicit and common-sense psychological assumptions. There is, however, a substantial gap between abstract promise and actual performance, as discussed by many historians surveying their discipline (Breisach, 1983, pp. 341–347; Handlin, 1979, pp. 14–15, 270–279; Marwick, 1981, pp. 111–115; Stone, 1981, pp. 40–41, 220–229).

Oscar Handlin (1979), for example, grants that the techniques and concepts of psychology may be useful to historians, but that "it is far easier, however, to make than to implement such suggestions, for more is required than a simple plastering over of gaps in the evidence with patches of theory" (p. 14) and those efforts to treat the data of the past with psychology, such as Elkins's (1959) study of the "Sambo" personality of American slaves or Freud and Bullitt's psychobiography of Woodrow Wilson "have not commanded confidence" (p. 14).

Lawrence Stone (1981) states, "I just do not think that such things as the extermination of six million Jews can be explained by the alleged fact that Hitler's mother was killed by treatment given her by a Jewish doctor in an attempt to cure her cancer of the breast; or that Luther's defiance of the Roman church can be explained by the brutal way he was treated by his father or by his chronic constipation" (p. 220). Much psychohistorical work to date "has been disappointing, partly because of the flimsiness of the evidence of childhood experience, partly because of the speculative nature of the causal links with adult behavior, partly because of the neglect of the influence of the great processes of historical change in religion, economics, politics, society, and so on" (pp. 220–221). Finally, in one of the more intemperate critiques of the whole field of psychohistory, Stannard (1980) charges that "from the earliest endeavors to write psychohistory to those of the present, individual writings of would-be psychohistorians have consistently been characterized by a cavalier attitude toward fact, a contorted attitude toward logic, an irresponsible attitude toward theory validation, and a myopic attitude toward cultural difference and anachronism" (p. 147).

Indications of the tensions between history and psychology are discernible not only in published critiques of the field, but also in visceral negative reactions by many historians and psychologists to work in psychohistory, and in institutional barriers to collaborative training and practice. Some understanding of this intellectual, personal, and institutional background is necessary in order to understand the current embattled status of psychohistory. Later sections of this chapter briefly discuss the history of the relationships between psychology and history, and examine several of the intellectual debates affecting the course of work in this field.

Ever since the pioneering work of Freud in *Leonardo da Vinci and a Memory of His Childhood* (1910/1957), through Erikson's *Young Man Luther* (1958) and *Gandhi's Truth* (1969), which launched the modern phase of the field, to the literally thousands of publications produced in the past quarter-century, the use of psychology in history has been beset by controversy. Disputes have centered around a number of questions: What kinds of evidence are needed for psychohistorical interpretation, and can the historian have access to such information without "putting the person on the couch"? Are psychohistorical analyses inevitably reductionistic, whether in slighting external social, economic, and cultural forces; in focusing on pathology rather than strengths; or in attributing too much influence to early childhood experience while ignoring later determinants of personality and behavior? Is it legitimate to apply a psychological theory developed in turn-of-the-century Vienna to people in other cultures or historical periods? What influence does childhood experience have on adult personality and behavior? To what extent should the historian draw on psychoanalysis, neoanalytic theories, and/or other branches of psychological theory? Finally, what criteria and procedures are there for critically evaluating proposed psychohistorical interpretations?

This methodological ferment was the background against which the papers in this volume were prepared. The chapters take a variety of different approaches, from substantive discussions of specific psychobiographical interpretations and the process of constructing them (Robert Tucker on Stalin and Jean Strouse on Alice James), to reviews of the utilization of neo-Freudian and non-Freudian theory in psychohistory (Peter Loewenberg and William Runyan), to critiques of and commentaries on other papers (Alexander Dallin and Peter Paret), to discussions of the status of psychoanalytic theory or methodological issues affecting the field as a whole (Peter Gay, Robert Wallerstein, Fred Weinstein, Frederick Crews and Kenneth Craik). Reflecting the necessarily interdisciplinary character of work in this field, the contributors come from a wide range of backgrounds, with primary affiliations with history, political science, psychoanalysis, psychology, and literature.

This introductory chapter gives a brief overview of the other chapters. This is followed by a selective historical sketch of the development of relationships between history and psychology, by a quantitative analysis of the growth of literature in psychohistory, and by a discussion of the degree of institutionalization of the field. The final section analyzes several fundamental intellectual debates that have a continuing impact on the relationships between history and psychology.

Preview of Chapters

Part I is organized around two psychobiographical case studies, one a study of Joseph Stalin utilizing the neoanalytic theories of Karen

Horney, and the other a psychoanalytically informed study of Alice James, the younger sister of William and Henry James.

In Chapter 2, Robert Tucker details the circumstances surrounding the course of his analysis of Stalin's personality in light of Horney's theory of an "idealized self." Tucker argues that the personality cult surrounding Stalin was not just passively tolerated, but rather was supported by Stalin as a prop to his neurotically inflated vision of himself as the greatest genius of Russian and world history. The paper provides an unusually open statement about the personal and emotional relationship of an author with his subject; the Stalin regime prevented Tucker and his Russian wife from leaving the Soviet Union, and Tucker frankly admits that he came to loathe Stalin the more he studied him. The question is thus forcefully raised of whether such emotional involvement inhibits responsible scholarship or, if properly channeled, can enhance it.

In Chapter 3, Soviet expert Alexander Dallin, in commenting on Tucker's piece, raises several basic interpretive questions, such as the importance of Stalin's identification with Lenin, the relationship between rational and irrational factors in shaping Stalin's policies, and the relative importance of intuition and evidence in assessing interpretations of Stalin's personality.

In Chapter 4, Jean Strouse discusses the relationship between psychoanalysis and biography through her study of Alice James, "a cranky, hysterical neurasthenic who essentially forced the people she cared about to take care of her by having spectacular nervous breakdowns and becoming a professional invalid" (p. 90). Strouse emphasizes the fundamental importance of artfulness, empathy, and intuition in writing a good biography, and then asks what additional contribution psychoanalytic theory can make. After several years of research, Strouse found herself wanting to take care of Alice James, to rescue her from her unhappy years of invalidism. This personal response was used to recognize something important about Alice James—that she wanted to be taken care of and that, given her remarkable mind and latent talents, she wanted to be perceived as someone whose life should have turned out better. Analysis of the psychological undercurrents of this relatively obscure life can illuminate larger issues about nineteenth-century family life, particularly in regard to the restricted roles and opportunities of women.

The chapters in Part II bear on the uses of psychoanalysis and psychology in psychohistory. The chapters move from the application of classic psychoanalytic theory (Gay and Paret), to the use of ego psychological and object relations theory in history (Loewenberg and

Wallerstein), to a discussion of subjectivity in psychoanalytic interpretation (Weinstein), to a critique of psychoanalysis (Crews), and, finally, to examples of nonpsychoanalytic and general personality assessment approaches to psychobiography (Craik and Runyan).

In chapter 5, Peter Gay argues that psychoanalysis and history have an affinity in that both are sciences of the past—psychoanalysis concerned primarily with memories of the individual past, and history with memories of the public past. A central category for both history and psychoanalysis is that of "experience," experience resulting from an encounter of mind with world, from an "uninterrupted traffic between what the world imposes and the self receives and reshapes" (p. 109). Because experiences have both conscious and unconscious dimensions, psychoanalysis becomes a valuable tool for historians in exploring the subsurface dimensions of experience and in developing a more comprehensive analysis of the individual and collective past. Gay illustrates this multidimensional approach to history with examples of sexual and aggressive material in an early memory of Freud, oedipal and pre-oedipal dimensions in Charles Dickens's novels, the "rescue fantasies" of William Gladstone and other Victorians toward prostitutes, and the Victorians' half-veiled interest in nudes. Rather than being reductionistic, psychoanalysis, if properly employed, has the potential of enriching the historian's understanding of the interplay between rational and irrational dimensions of past experience.

In his commentary on Professor Gay's paper, Peter Paret finds himself largely in agreement about affinities between psychoanalysis and history, yet also cites several dissimilarities between them. For example, interpretation in psychoanalytic therapy is concerned not primarily with intellectual understanding, as it is in history, but with bringing about changes in the analysand's functioning and well-being. While psychoanalysis may be a valuable auxiliary instrument for the historian, Paret argues that any particular methodology, whether psychoanalytic or quantitative, is less decisive for the historian than are sympathy, intelligence, and imagination. George Lefebvre's classic study *The Great Fear of 1789* (1932/1982) was most effective in revealing the feelings and behavior of the French peasants who were frightened in July 1789 by rumors that they were going to be attacked by criminals hired by the aristocracy, but Lefebvre conveyed this understanding without any formal psychological analysis. While psychoanalysis can be immensely useful to historians, it is perhaps best seen as one research instrument among many, invaluable in some areas of study, yet secondary to the historian's intelligence and sensitivity.

Peter Loewenberg, in Chapter 7, discusses changes in the *kinds* of psychoanalytic theory used in psychohistory, charting a shift from the application of classic libidinal-drive models to the more recent use of ego psychological and object relations theories. The strengths and weaknesses of the instinctual-drive approaches to psychohistory are illustrated with a discussion of Fawn Brodie's *Richard Nixon: The Shaping of His Character* (1981). In an analysis of the extensive psychobiographical literature on Adolf Hitler, Loewenberg points out the limitations of reductionistic interpretations that explain only Hitler's weaknesses and overlook the considerable adaptive capacities that allowed him to obtain and wield power. Since the psychohistorical research on Hitler is so extensive, it provides an excellent arena in which to examine the relative contributions of different theoretical orientations within psychohistory. A second major theme of Loewenberg's chapter is the use of "countertransference," or the historian's subjective reaction to his or her material, not as something to be avoided, but as a source of insight. The value of utilizing the historian's subjectivity is illustrated in studies of Leon Trotsky, Léon Blum, Gustav Landauer, and the American Civil War. Finally, Loewenberg discusses the utility of object relations theory in psychohistory, as in the work of John Demos on witchcraft and of Judith Hughes on relations between British and German statesmen preceding the outbreak of World War I.

Robert Wallerstein, in his discussion of Loewenberg's chapter, raises the question of why psychohistory has had such a slow and uneven development to date. In spite of the logic of a marriage between history and psychoanalysis, stemming from their common concern with constructing narrative explanations of developments over time, problems arise in maintaining the integrity of phenomena central to each discipline and in curbing the tendencies that each discipline may have to eliminate the other. Wallerstein and Smelser (1969) have argued for the importance of developing a "complementary articulation" between adjacent disciplines, in which the simplifying assumptions that each discipline makes about phenomena beyond its borders are gradually modified and made more realistically complex. Wallerstein notes that each discipline can be a generation behind in the theories that it borrows from other fields. Loewenberg has reviewed the contributions of more recent ego psychological and object relations theories to psychohistory, and Wallerstein suggests that these more recent theories effectively supplement rather than replace the earlier drive models. As a future task for psychohistory, Wallerstein argues for the importance of developing more sophisticated bridging concepts between the individual and the sociohistorical context (a topic that is addressed in the concluding chapter).

Fred Weinstein, in Chapter 9, analyzes the problems involved in interpreting subjectivity in history, or in interpreting the perceptions, feelings, motivations, and intentions of historical agents. The inadequacies of purely "objective" historical accounts force us to deal with problems in interpreting subjectivity and with questions about appropriate criteria for assessing such interpretations. Weinstein discusses the current blurred boundaries between history and fiction, as novelists increasingly use historical material and historians draw on fictional techniques in exploring the subjective worlds of their subjects. Although psychoanalytic theory is typically used in psychohistorical studies, Weinstein acknowledges a number of serious problems with Freudian theory, but points out that psychohistory is not dependent on psychoanalysis alone and that regardless of the fate of psychoanalysis, problems of interpreting subjectivity in history will remain. He proposes that statements about subjectivity be made in terms of three criteria: (1) that events be written about in two languages, the language of the actors and the language of our theories; (2) that descriptions of action be consistent with what actually happened, in the sense of including the perspectives on the world and on experience of the actors involved; and (3) that the dynamically and socially *heterogeneous* composition of groups be taken into account. There may well be problems with current theories of subjectivity, including psychoanalytic theory, but the analysis of subjectivity is unavoidable for historians, and the only feasible solution is the development of stronger theories.

In his commentary on Professor Weinstein's paper, Frederick Crews argues that the central issue is not really the problem of subjectivity in history, but rather the intellectual standing of psychoanalysis. Crews, a former Freudian, believes that psychoanalytic theory is fundamentally defective, and thus does not provide an adequate foundation for psychohistory. Crews reviews a number of criticisms of psychoanalytic theory noted by Weinstein, such as that Freud's propositions about drives, psychic energy, and affect lead away from historical understanding; that beliefs in the unity of unconscious perception are unwarranted; that psychoanalysis tends to collapse heterogeneous tendencies and strivings into shared ones; and that there are no solutions to historical problems or sociological problems (except perhaps biographical ones) in psychoanalytic terms.

Crews states that had Weinstein built his whole paper around these criticisms of Freud, "I could have reduced my critique to a single sentence of praise" (p. 190). Weinstein, however, has also made a number of points defending psychoanalysis, such as that its weaknesses are shared with other social science theories, that it is more likely that academic psychology will develop some kind of theory consistent with psychoanalysis than that psychoanalysis will disappear, and that psychoanalytic concepts of unconscious mental activity and repression can prove useful to historians in interpreting subjectivity. Crews, in his inimitable style, argues that each of these points is unconvincing. Crews also reviews the three criteria that Weinstein has proposed for addressing problems in subjectivity, and finds the first two inadequate and only the third, of attending to heterogeneity, as "unexceptionable." Crews critiques Weinstein's use of the concept of "verification," by which Weinstein means supplying relevant documentation, and argues that it is all too easy to find supporting evidence for almost any assertion. More rigorous criteria for assessing a theory or hypothesis are tests of its predicted factual consequences and of its plausibility relative to rival theories or hypotheses. Crews concludes with a recommendation that we continue to study subjectivity, but, preferably, unencumbered by psychoanalysis.

Kenneth Craik, in Chapter 11, argues that psychoanalysis is only one tradition within contemporary personality psychology and that an examination of the relationships between personality psychology and historical inquiry is much broader than an analysis of the relationships between psychoanalysis and history. Moving away from problems in psychoanalyzing historical figures, Craik focuses instead on the fundamental issue of systematically *describing* the personalities of historical figures, and indicates its similarity to the core issue in personality assessment of how best to describe persons. He breaks down the descriptive process into three analytically distinguishable components: (1) the assembling of source material or information about the subjects; (2) the background and qualifications of the raters, whether informed experts or those relying on the assembled source materials; and (3) the format used in recording descriptions, ranging from free-response descriptions, as in narrative character sketches, to more structured instruments, such as rating scales.

Craik reviews a number of studies that systematically describe the personalities of historical figures, and then proposes a collaborative project for describing the personalities of the 343 men who served as members of the Continental Congress from 1774 to 1789. Such a project is related to the traditional historiographic enterprise of "prosopography," or collective biography, as exemplified in Sir Lewis Namier's study of members of the House of Commons in the late eighteenth century, although such studies typically focus on sociodemographic factors including family of origin, place of residence, economic interests, education, occupation, and religion. When asked what "Namierizing history" meant, Namier replied that "it means finding out who the guys were." Craik's argument is that applying systematic methods of personality assessment to historical figures can add a valuable dimension to "finding out who the guys [and gals] were."

In Chapter 12, I attempt to survey the contributions of nonanalytic psychology to psychobiography. This is preceded by a brief examination of several basic questions that have been raised about psychoanalytic psychobiography, such as the adequacy of available evidence, problems of reductionism and historical reconstruction, the causal influence of early experience on adult behavior, and the multiplicity of psychoanalytic interpretations. This last issue is illustrated through an examination of the variety of psychoanalytic explanations that have been proposed as to why Vincent Van Gogh cut off the lower half of his left ear and gave it to a prostitute. My survey of the contributions of other branches of personality, developmental, and social psychology to psychobiography yielded a range of examples, including selected applications of social learning theory, trait-factor approaches, phenomenological–existential theory, social cognition, and adult developmental psychology. The yield from other psychological approaches was, though, surprisingly meager, which led to an examination of the relative merits of psychoanalytic and nonanalytic approaches to psychobiography.

The concluding chapter attempts to outline a broader conceptual foundation for work in psychohistory. The argument, in brief, is that history can usefully be conceptualized as being composed of six system levels that interact over time: the history of persons (or aggregates of persons), groups, organizations, institutions, sociocultural systems, and international relationships. The problem of relating psychology to history is understanding how psychological structures, elements, and processes within persons and collectivities of persons are involved in the maintenance and transformation of groups, organizations, institutions, sociocultural systems, and international relationships over time, and, in turn, how each of these system levels is involved in shaping psychological structures, elements, and processes. The uses of psychology in analyzing each of the six system levels from persons up through organizations, institutions, and international relations are illustrated with a set of interconnected examples from Nazi-era psychohistory.

The relationships between psychological processes and these other system levels are analyzed within sociology, anthropology, and political science (and, to some extent, in economics, linguistics, and demography) in subfields such as social structure and personality, psychological anthropology, and political psychology. The relationships between psychology and history are not only direct ones, but also those mediated by contributions from the aggregate-level social sciences of sociology, anthropology, and political science. In many cases, the field is appropriately conceived not solely as "psychohistory," but rather as "psychosocial history," with an analytic focus on the reciprocal interplay between psychology, biography, social structure, and history.

Historical Sketch of Psychohistory

The history of psychohistory and psychobiography has often been told (for example, Africa, 1979; Barnes, 1925; Gedo, 1972; Hoffman, 1982, 1984; Lifton with Strozier, 1984; Mack, 1971; Manuel, 1972; Mazlish, 1977; Strozier and Offer, 1985) and need not be repeated in detail here. After briefly describing several major stages and traditions in the history of the field, this section will provide a relatively detailed quantitative analysis of the growth of publications in psychohistory. This is followed by a discussion of the increasing institutionalization of the field, as indicated by a rise in the number of conferences, professional organizations, specialty journals, academic courses, and dissertations in the field.

The history of psychohistory is traditionally defined as beginning with Freud's study *Leonardo da Vinci and a Memory of His Childhood* (1910/1957), which was followed by his historical and anthropological studies *Totem and Taboo* (1912/1953), *Group Psychology and the Analysis of the Ego* (1921/1955), *The Future of an Illusion* (1927/1961), *Civilization and Its Discontents* (1930/1961), and *Moses and Monotheism* (1939/1964), as well as a number of shorter pieces on Dostoevsky, Goethe, war, and other topics. One other book-length contribution wtih Freud's name on it, published posthumously, is Freud and Bullitt's (1967) psychological study of Woodrow Wilson, although the literary style of the work strongly suggests that Freud wrote little more than the introduction (Erikson, 1975). A sample of other early psychoanalytic psychobiographies includes analyses of Shakespeare as revealed through Hamlet (Jones, 1910), of the artist Giovanni Segantini (Abraham, 1911/1955), of Richard Wagner (Graf, 1911), and of Amenhotep IV (Abraham, 1912/1935). A number of these earliest psychobiographical studies are summarized in Dooley's "Psychoanalytic Studies of Genius" (1916) and discussed in Barnes (1919) and Fearing (1927).

Less frequently, histories of the field contain a discussion of pre-Freudian contributions to psychologically informed history. Manuel (1972), for instance, begins his discussion of the use of psychology in history with Giambattista Vico (1688–1744) and his *New Science* (1725), and traces the story through Michelet, Herder, Hegel, and Dilthey before reaching Freud. Strozier and Offer (1985, Chapter 2) discuss the biblical story of Joseph and Plutarch's *Lives* as examples of early psychological studies of leaders, although these works would fall outside a definition of psychohistory as the application of a systematic psychology.

Perhaps the most detailed discussion of pre-Freudian psychohistory is still that of Harry Elmer Barnes in *Psychology and History* (1925); he reviews the contributions of a number of workers who left no direct legacy and are little cited now, such as Wilhelm Wundt's folk psychology (which has been overshadowed by his pioneering work in experimental psychology) and that of his colleague at Leipzig, the historian Karl Lamprecht, who argued that history should define itself as collective psychology and who provided a schematic and controversial conception of stages in the sociopsychological evolution of Western civilization.

Professor James Harvey Robinson taught an influential course on intellectual history at Columbia University in the early decades of the twentieth century, and his arguments in a *New History* (1912), for the greater use of the social sciences encouraged a number of his students and those influenced by him (including Barnes) to utilize psychology in historical and biographical analysis (see Garraty, 1954; Ross, 1974). In the 1920s and 1930s, much of the work that applied psychoanalysis to history was reductionistic and unsatisfactory and was widely criticized.

The rise of Hitler and National Socialism led to an increased willingness to consider irrational forces in history and biography, and provided material for a stream of psychobiographical and psychohistorical works, beginning during World War II with a psychobiographical study of Hitler commissioned by the Office of Strategic Services (Langer, 1972) and picking up steam in the 1960s and 1970s (see reviews in Cocks, 1979, 1986; Fox, 1979; Gatzke, 1973; Hoffman, 1982; Kren and Rappoport, 1980; Loewenberg, 1975).

The modern period of psychohistory is frequently identified as beginning in 1958, the year of publication of Erik Erikson's *Young Man Luther: A Study in Psychoanalysis and History* and of William L. Langer's presidential address to the American Historical Association. In his paper "The Next Assignment," Langer urged his colleagues to deepen their historical understanding through use of the concepts and findings of modern depth psychology. Erikson's book was hailed by many as the first persuasive psychohistorical study (although not without later critiques, as in Johnson et al., 1977) and is still perhaps the single best-known work in the field.

Among those influenced by Erikson were Robert Jay Lifton (with Olson, 1974), in his studies of "shared themes" and of groups of men and women sharing similar experiences, such as survivors of the atomic bomb dropped on Hiroshima (1967), Vietnam veterans (1973), or Nazi doctors (1986); Robert Coles (1967), in his study of children facing the crisis of integration; and Kenneth Keniston (1965, 1968), in his analyses of alienated or politically committed American youth.

Key contributions within group psychohistory were psychological studies of colonial childhood and its consequences (Demos, 1970; Greven, 1970), which were followed by many other studies of the history of the family and of the life course (for example, Demos, 1986; Elder, 1974; Hareven, 1978; Hareven and Adams, 1982; Rabb and Rotberg, 1971).

The field of psychohistory has not developed within one unified and coherent stream, but has evolved within several partially independent traditions and lines of influence. These semiautonomous subtraditions cluster in part within traditional disciplinary boundaries, with the relevant groups including those in psychoanalysis and psychiatry, history, political science, academic psychology, literature, the deMause group, and an assortment of others with backgrounds in religion, education, the humanities, and so on. At this point in our historical sketch of the discipline, several contributions may usefully be viewed in light of these disciplinary traditions.

These disciplinary traditions, or loosely ordered streams of work, are identifiable by patterns of formal education and subsequent employment, by student-teacher contacts, by personal contacts and networks, by primary professional affiliation, and, to a lesser extent, by previous works cited, journals published in, and subsequent lines of influence.

Consider, for example, the publication in 1956 of Alexander George and Juliette George's *Woodrow Wilson and Colonel House: A Personality Study*. This work originated in a paper prepared in 1941 by Alexander George for a graduate course, "Personality and Politics," taught by Nathan Leites at the University of Chicago, and was indebted to the theories and personal encouragement of Harold Lasswell, also at Chicago. Thus the book fell within a tradition of psychological analyses of politics, going back at least to Lasswell's *Psychopathology and Politics* (1930). Subsequently, the Georges' book has been central within the political science community, often cited as perhaps the most effective political psychobiography (see Elms, 1976; Freidländer, 1978; Greenstein, 1975), while it is cited substantially less frequently by psychoanalysts, psychiatrists, and literary scholars. Recently, the work has again become prominent with a debate over the relative merits of psychodynamic and medical explanations of Woodrow Wilson's personality and behavior (Weinstein, Anderson, and Link, 1978; Post et al., 1983; George et al., 1984).

There is, in any case, a tradition of work within political science applying psychology to political phenomena that contributes substantially to the broader field of psychohistory. This tradition includes the work of Harold Lasswell (1930, 1948); Alexander and Juliette George; Robert Lane (1972) and those in the political psychology program at Yale; Jeanne Knutson, with her editing of the *Handbook of Political Psychology* (1973) and her organization of the International Society of Political Psychology in 1977; Arnold Rogow, with his study of America's first Secretary of Defense, *James Forrestal: A Study of Personality, Politics, and Policy* (1963); Fred Greenstein on political socialization (1965) and *Personality and Politics* (1975); Betty Glad, with psychobiographical studies of Jimmy Carter (1980) and others; Elizabeth Marvick on *The Young Richelieu* (1983); Irving Janis (1982), with his studies of psychological and group factors affecting the decision making of political leaders; Stanley Renshon, with *Psychological Needs and Political Behavior* (1974); Lloyd Etheredge (1978), on psychological influences on American foreign-policy decisions; Robert Jervis, with his comprehensive *Perception and Misperception in International Politics* (1976); and many others who have contributed to political psychology (see reviews in Cocks, 1986; Davies, 1980; Elms, 1976, 1984; Glad, 1973; Greenstein, 1975).

A second partly autonomous tradition contributing to psychobiography and psychohistory is the work of those academic psychologists influenced by Henry Murray, Gordon Allport, Robert White, and others at Harvard in the 1930s and 1940s. Earlier academic psychologists had been involved in psychological interpretations of biography or history, such as Morton Prince's *Psychology of the Kaiser: A Study of His Sentiments and His Obsession* (1915) and "Roosevelt as Analyzed by the New Psychology" (1912), and G. Stanley Hall's *Jesus, the Christ, in the Light of Psychology* (1917), but these were isolated works that fell on infertile soil, leaving no enduring legacy. The group around Murray and others at the Harvard Psychological Clinic has been described in some detail by Levinson (1981), Sanford (1980), and White (1981), all of whom were active in or influenced by that tradition.

Among academic psychologists who have published contributions to psychohistory or psychobiography, many of whom have had some connection with the Harvard Psychological Clinic, are Robert White (1972, 1975); Silvan Tomkins (1965), with his emphasis on affect theory and script theory; David C. McClelland (1961), in his studies of the influence of achievement motivation and economic development in different cultures and historical periods, and his research on power motivation (1975); Alan Elms, with psychobiographical studies of Freud (1980), Skinner (1981), Allport (1972), and others; James W. Anderson, with methodological writings on psychohistory (1981a) and on William James (1981b); Faye Crosby on methodological issues (1979; Crosby and Crosby, 1981); Dean Simonton on quantitative archival studies in *Genius, Creativity, and Leadership* (1984); Stolorow and Atwood (1979) on personality theorists; and a good many others, although the total number of psychologists contributing to this field seems smaller than that from history, political science, or psychoanalysis. One group of academic psychologists contributing to this field that is particularly apparent to me from my own association with it is at the Institute of Personality Assessment and Research, University of California, Berkeley, with psychobiographical or psychohistorical studies by its director, Kenneth Craik (Historical Figures Assessment Collaborative, 1977); Gerald Mendelsohn (1978–79, 1985), Ravenna Helson (1984–85); Philip Tetlock (Tetlock, Crosby, and Crosby, 1981); and myself (Runyan, 1981, 1982a, 1982b, 1988).

Among psychoanalysts and psychiatrists, in addition to the work of Freud, Erikson, Lifton, and others discussed earlier, those making notable contributions in recent years include John Mack (1976), with his study of T. E. Lawrence; Erik Erikson, with his later study of Gandhi (1969) and other writings (for example, 1975, 1987); a study of the field by a task force of the American Psychiatric Association (1976); Margaret Brenman-Gibson (1981) on the playwright Clifford Odets; and psychiatrist Vamik Volkan with historian Norman Itkowitz (1985) on Kemal Ataturk. One group of psychoanalysts particularly active in psychohistory is connected with the Institute for Psychoanalysis in Chicago, including John Gedo (1972, 1983), George Moraitis, who has collaborated with a number of biographers and historians (Baron and Pletsch, 1985), and George Pollock (Moraitis and Pollock, 1987). Charles Strozier, a historian and former editor of the *Psychohistory Re-*

view, also had long-term connections with the Chicago group (Strozier, 1982; Strozier and Offer, 1985) before moving to New York in 1986.

A fourth group is clustered around Lloyd deMause and his Institute for Psychohistory in New York, the International Psychohistorical Association, and the *Journal of Psychohistory.* This cluster includes David Beisel, Caspar Schmidt, and Henry Ebel, and has been quite active in the past decade. While many academics are extremely critical of the logic and reasoning of at least some of the work done by this group (for a sample of the more vitriolic criticism, see deMause, 1982, pp. 300–301), it has received a good deal of public attention and is, to the regret of many other psychohistorians, often seen as representative of the field as a whole. The *Journal of Psychohistory* contains some well-done articles and reviews, but so many deeply flawed ones that it has been a public relations embarrassment for the wider field of psychohistory (which is better represented in the *Psychohistory Review* and *Political Psychology*). A sample of their work is contained in deMause's *Foundations of Psychohistory* (1982), deMause and Ebel's *Jimmy Carter and American Fantasy* (1977), and deMause's *Reagan's America* (1984).

To turn to the world of academic historians, a sample of the most distinguished or influential contributions made in recent years would include Fred Weinstein's theoretical elucidation of relationships among history, sociology, and psychoanalysis (Weinstein and Platt, 1973) and his *Dynamics of Nazism* (1980); Peter Loewenberg's classic article "The Psychohistorical Origins of the Nazi Youth Cohort" (1971), his review of psychohistory for Kammen's survey of the state of the historical discipline (1980), and his book *Decoding the Past: The Psychohistorical Approach* (1983); Bruce Mazlish's psychobiographical studies of, among others, Richard Nixon (1972/1973) and James and John Stuart Mill (1975); Robert Waite's (1977) psychobiography of Adolf Hitler; Saul Friedländer's *History and Psychoanalysis* (1978); Cushing Strout's psychobiographical and psychohistorical studies in *The Veracious Imagination* (1981); John Demos's (1982) synthesis of biographical, psychological, sociological, and historical approaches in analyzing witchcraft in early New England; critiques of the field by Jacques Barzun (1974) and David Stannard (1980); Charles Strozier's utilization of Kohut's self-psychology in a study of Lincoln (1982) and in an edited collection of psychohistorical approaches to the leader (Strozier and Offer, 1985); Philip Pomper's (1985) analysis of the structural principles of development of mind and history used by five leading psychohistorians; William Gilmore's (1984) comprehensive research bibliography of psychohistory and psychobiography; and Peter Gay's psychohistorical study of Victorian culture, psyche, and sexuality, *The Bourgeois Experience: Victoria to Freud: Vol. I. Education of the Senses* (1984), and his defense of the use of Freudian theory in history (1985). The field of psychohistory has been defined in part through the publication of readers, and several of the most important collections edited or co-edited by historians are those by Mazlish (1963, 1971), Kren and Rappoport (1976), Brugger (1981), and Cocks and Crosby (1987). Of the many readers edited by non-historians one of the more influential ones was done by Lifton with Olson (1974).

Within the discipline of history, one group that potentially might make some use of psychology is the *Annales* group in France. Beginning with the publication of *Annales* in 1929 by Marc Bloch and Lucien Febvre, there was an interest in uniting history with the social sciences and a concern with *mentalités,* or with the range of thought and emotional experience in a group, as one of the components of a more comprehensive approach to history. Although Bloch occasionally mentioned the importance of psychological factors in methodological statements, psychology was never a significant part of his substantive work. Febvre had a much greater interest in the study of *mentalités,* but a limited knowledge of psychoanalysis (Marvick, 1985) and a strong conviction (at least during part of his career) that contemporary psychology is of no value in understanding the radically different psychology of persons who lived in the past. In Febvre's (1938/1976) view, it is a "psychological anachronism" to apply present psychology to history, and "it is obvious that we shall be unable to accept for the historical period in question any of the descriptions or statements made by psychologists of today working on the basis of data provided for them by our own age" (p. 9).

The evolution of views on the use of psychology within the *Annales* school is a complex affair, influenced by the Durkheimian anti-individualistic tradition in France, the personal experiences and professional associations of individual historians, and the changes in their individual views over time (see Bizière, 1983; Burguière, 1982; Marvick, 1985; Ratcliffe, 1980); but in general, the *Annales* tradition has had only a minimal interest in the use of psychology, with far more attention paid to alliances with geography, demography, economics, and anthropology. There are indications of a revival of interest in *mentalités* and of the psychological experiences of individuals and groups (Stone, 1981), with current historians of *mentalités* interested in sexuality, conviviality (as in ritual and festivals), and the lives of marginal citizens such as the poor, vagrants, criminals, and prostitutes (Bizière, 1983). However, this increased interest in the emotions and experiences of people in the past is typically *not* pursued with the aid of any systematic psychology, but rather with informal or intuitive psychological assumptions. If psychoanalysis or academic psychology is ever a significant influence in the *Annales* school, it will be a thing of the future, rather than the past or the present.

A sixth tradition, which will only be mentioned here, is that of literary psychobiography. Eminent examples of this genre include Leon Edel's five-volume study of Henry James (1953–72/1985), Walter Jackson Bate's biography of Samuel Johnson (1977), Frederick Crews's study of Nathaniel Hawthorne (1966), Jean Strouse's biography of Alice James (1980), and a large number of other works (see the extensive bibliography in Kiell, 1982). A seventh and final category includes all those with training and employment in other fields, including sociology, anthropology, religion, education, social work, musicology, the history of science, and others who contribute to psychohistory.

To summarize, this section has argued that the history of work in psychohistory and psychobiography can usefully be analyzed in terms of developments within seven or so partially autonomous traditions, each corresponding roughly to a particular discipline or profession. Contributions to psychobiography or psychohistory were discussed within the areas of political science, academic psychology, psychoanalysis and psychiatry, the deMause group, history, literary psychobiography, and, finally, a miscellaneous category including all other contributors. These traditions are, of course, not wholly independent of one another, yet still, many individual works can be identified as belonging more closely to one or two of these traditions than to the others. Current work in psychohistory is dispersed across a diverse range of disciplines, and the structure of the field may be better represented as a set of partially autonomous streams of work rather than as a single tightly organized tradition.

A Quantitative Analysis of the Growth of Literature in Psychohistory

The most succinct way of presenting the history and growth of the field of psychohistory is through a quantitative analysis of the increase in publications over time (Runyan, 1987).[1] A rough quantitative assessment of the number of articles, books, and dissertations on psychohistory

1. I would like to thank Betsy Locke for her exceptionally helpful work on the quantitative analyses and associated tables.

and psychobiography from before 1920 to 1980 is presented in Figure 1.1.

These figures are derived from a quantitative analysis of 1,723 items in William Gilmore's extremely useful *Psychohistorical Inquiry: A Comprehensive Research Bibliography* (1984).[2] This bibliography, which contains more than 4,000 items, was intended to provide a relatively comprehensive list of English-language publications in psychohistory through 1981, as well as selected studies in other languages, with a substantive focus on methodology and on American and European studies. The bibliography includes a section on The Life Cycle, including historical works on childhood, adulthood, old age, and death—works that bear on the history of the life cycle, but not necessarily on psychohistory in the sense of the use of psychology in historical analysis. Thus my analyses excluded these items and are based on 1,723 items in the psychohistory and psychobiography categories. An additional 400 or so methodological items in psychohistory from Gilmore's bibliography will be discussed later. Other definitions of the scope of psychohistory and other procedures for locating citations may, of course, yield somewhat different results, but it is hoped that the analyses discussed here provide at least rough indicators of trends in the literature, and can be a starting point for other quantitative analyses of the development of the field.

Figure 1.1 indicates that the number of publications (including dissertations) was at a fairly constant low level through the 1950s, with a gradual increase in the 1960s and a sharp increase in dissertations,

2. Gilmore identifies his sources in constructing this bibliography as earlier bibliographies in psychohistory and related fields; his own bibliographical contributions to the *Psychohistory Review* and items encountered as co-editor of the *Psychohistory Review* and the *GUPH Newsletter;* a card file from bibliographer Normal Kiell; a systematic search of citations in *Psychological Abstracts, Sociological Abstracts, Abstracts in Anthropology, Dissertation Abstracts, America: History and Life,* and *Historical Abstracts;* and a search of the contents of the *History of Childhood Quarterly, Journal of Psychohistory,* the *Psychohistory Review,* the *I.P.A. Bulletin,* the *GUPH Newsletter,* and the *Journal of Interdisciplinary History.* The search yielded more than 4,000 items, which Gilmore classified according to geographical area, historical period, and the three topical categories of general psychohistorical studies, studies of stages of the life cycle, and psychobiographical studies of individuals. Studies of the life cycle included items such as *Antiques of American Childhood* and *A Critical History of Children's Literature,* which bear on the history of the life cycle, although not on psychohistory defined as the explicit use of psychology in historical analysis. Thus, my analysis excludes these items on the life cycle, and is based on an analysis of all items within the psychohistory and psychobiography categories. Undoubtedly, some relevant items were also excluded from my analyses, so the quantitative estimates are on the conservative side. Finally, Gilmore's bibliography contains items that appeared through the end of 1981, but my analysis indicates that the listings for 1980 and 1981 are quite incomplete, so I analyzed studies done through the end of 1979.

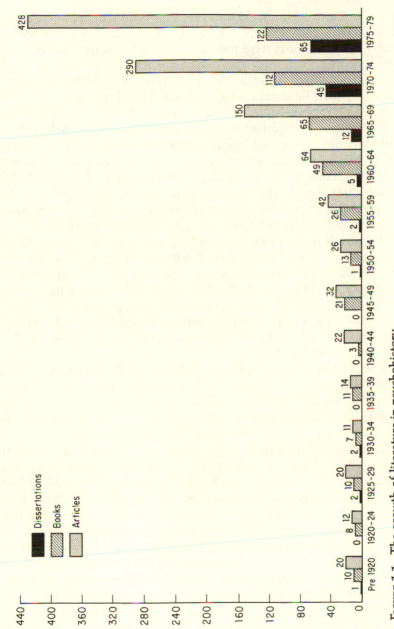

FIGURE 1.1. The growth of literature in psychohistory.

books, and articles in the 1970s. The right-hand column indicates that between 1975 and 1979, 428 articles (including chapters and book reviews) and 122 books were published, and 65 dissertations were completed.

A pattern consisting of a highest number of articles, followed by books, followed by dissertations, held without exception in each of the time periods from 1975 to 1979 back through before 1920. The number of dissertations is important as an indicator of the extent to which psychohistory has been institutionally accepted within universities, and also as a harbinger of future growth in the field. In these figures, there were 110 dissertations in the 1970s, compared with a total of 28 before 1970. A far greater number of graduate students are working in psychohistory and psychobiography, which suggests that the number of psychohistorical books and articles in future years should continue to rise.

The growth in the number of doctoral dissertations in psychohistory can be compared with the growth of doctoral dissertations in history as a whole. Across all areas of history, there was an increase from 201 dissertations in 1958 to 862 dissertations in 1978, or more than 4 times as many dissertations (Darnton, 1980). In psychohistory for approximately the same time period, there was an increase from 2 dissertations between 1955 and 1959 to 65 dissertations between 1975 and 1979, or more than 30 times as many.

In all history dissertations from 1968 to 1978, there was a growth from 754 to 862 dissertations, or an increase of 14 percent. In psychohistory for approximately the same time period, there was an increase from 12 dissertations between 1965 and 1969 to 65 dissertations between 1975 and 1979, or more than a 500 percent increase.

To compare psychohistory with several other subfields of history, the number of dissertations in political history declined by approximately 20 percent from 1968 to 1978 (252 in 1968 to 204 in 1978), and the number of dissertations in intellectual history remained relatively stable between 1968 and 1978 (approximately 72 in 1968 and 76 in 1978). The number of dissertations in other growth areas, such as labor history, black history, and history of women and the family, increased from 2 to 3½ times from 1968 to 1978 (Darnton, 1980). In contrast, during the same time period there was more than a fivefold increase in the number of dissertations in psychohistory, with 12 dissertations between 1965 and 1969 and 65 dissertations between 1975 and 1979. These calculations may be fairly rough estimates, but the general point is that the number of dissertations has been increasing more rapidly in psychohistory than in history as a whole; than in more established areas, such as political and intellectual history; or even in other growth areas, such as labor, black, and women's and family history.

The growth in the number of publications is also reflected in Table 1.1, which gives the total number of publications (books, articles, and dissertations) per five-year period, broken down by geographical subject area. Table 1.1 reveals a relatively constant low level of publication from before 1920 through 1944, with approximately 20 to 30 total publications per five-year period, a gradual increase from 1945 through the 1950s (perhaps sparked by the attention to Nazi Germany), and an accelerating increase from 1960 through the 1970s.

Of all 1,723 publications from before 1920 through 1979, 1,062, or 62 percent, appeared between 1970 and 1979. In other words, more than three-fifths of all studies were published in the last decade. Within the most recent 15 years, from 1965 to 1979, there were 1,289 publications, or 75 percent of the total.

Table 1.1 also indicates the relative emphasis within English-language psychohistorical publications on the United States, or on Europe and the Soviet Union (abbreviated in the tables as Europe), compared with the Third World (defined here as the rest of the world). It is clear that studies of Europe (and the Soviet Union) and the United States constitute the bulk of English-language psychohistorical works, with Europe being the subject of slightly more studies than the United States in every time period. Summed over all time periods, the total number of studies of the United States is 665, or 39 percent of the total; of Europe and the Soviet Union, 897, or 52 percent of the total; and of the Third World, 161, or 9 percent of the total.

This general overview of the growth of publications in psychohistory can be broken down more finely. Table 1.2 indicates the number of dissertations, articles, and books within psychohistory and psychobiography on subjects in the United States, Europe, and the Third World by five-year time period. With this more detailed chart, readers can investigate questions of their own interest about the history of psychohistorical literature. To direct attention to one feature of this table, it can be seen in the far-right-hand column of the bottom row that there was a total of 135 dissertations, 457 books, and 1,131 articles during this time period. Thus there are more than twice as many articles as books, and more than three times as many books as dissertations.

What about the claim frequently made that the field of psychohistory is dominated by psychobiographical studies of individuals? At least as indicated by this analysis of the literature, that statement does not hold up. A comparison of the number of psychobiographical versus group

TABLE 1.1. Books, Articles, and Dissertations by Geographical Subject Area

	Pre-1920	1920-24	1925-29	1930-34	1935-39	1940-44	1945-49	1950-54	1955-59	1960-64	1965-69	1970-74	1975-79	Total
United States	5	7	7	6	5	9	13	12	26	41	86	183	265	665
Europe	25	12	13	11	19	14	34	24	40	63	118	221	303	897
Third World	1	1	12	3	1	2	6	4	4	14	23	43	47	161
Total	**31**	**20**	**32**	**20**	**25**	**25**	**53**	**40**	**70**	**118**	**227**	**447**	**615**	**1723**

psychohistorical works on subjects in the United States or Europe and the Soviet Union was abstracted from Table 1.2 and is highlighted in Table 1.3. Examining the totals in the far-right-hand column, the number of group psychohistorical works on subjects in the United States is 428, compared with 237 psychobiographical studies. For Europe and the Soviet Union, group psychohistorical works outnumber psychobiographical studies by 517 to 380. Summed over the United States and Europe and the Soviet Union, group psychohistorical works outnumber psychobiographical studies by 945 to 617, or approximately 50 percent more psychohistorical than psychobiographical studies. The greater frequency of psychohistorical over psychobiographical studies holds within books, articles, and dissertations.

In addition to the 1,723 substantive studies analyzed in Table 1.2, Gilmore lists 417 methodological or theoretical studies written through 1979 under the title, "Models; Approaches; and Methods." The majority are from a Freudian or psychodynamic viewpoint, with 43 from an Eriksonian approach and 21 following the "psychogenic" approach of deMause and his colleagues. The rate of publications on models and methodology has also increased dramatically, from 2 published before 1920, 6 in the 1920s, 11 in the 1930s, 17 in the 1940s, 33 in the 1950s, 91 in the 1960s, to—the biggest jump—257 in the 1970s. In the 1970s, 98 of these studies were published between 1970 and 1974, with another 159 in the second half of the decade. There are also 26 readers, overviews, and bibliographies up through 1979, with another 6 since 1979.

In summary, the current rate of substantive publications in psychohistory as assessed from Gilmore's bibliography indicates that from 1970 through 1979, there was (in addition to more than 200 methodological publications) a total of 718 articles, 237 books, and 110 dissertations, yielding an average of more than 70 articles per year, 20 books per year, and 10 dissertations per year, which suggests the difficulty of keeping up with the field. If current trends continue, as the increasing number of dissertations suggests they will, the number of publications within psychohistory and psychobiography will continue to rise. In retrospect, this may be seen as a golden age, when it was relatively easy to keep up with the flow of literature in the field.

Institutionalization

The proliferation of publications in psychohistory has been accompanied by, and in part made possible by, an increasing institutionalization of

TABLE 1.2. Dissertations, Articles, and Books in Psychohistory

	Pre-1920	1920–24	1925–29	1930–34	1935–39	1940–44
United States Psychohistory						
Dissertations	0	0	1	0	0	0
Articles	1	1	0	3	1	5
Books	3	0	0	0	2	2
Total	**4**	**1**	**1**	**3**	**3**	**7**
United States Psychobiography						
Dissertations	0	0	0	0	0	0
Articles	1	2	2	2	2	2
Books	0	4	4	1	0	0
Total	**1**	**6**	**6**	**3**	**2**	**2**
Europe Psychohistory						
Dissertations	0	0	0	1	0	0
Articles	0	5	2	4	3	9
Books	3	2	2	2	3	1
Total	**3**	**7**	**4**	**7**	**6**	**10**
Europe Psychobiography						
Dissertations	1	0	1	0	0	0
Articles	17	4	5	1	7	4
Books	4	1	3	3	6	0
Total	**22**	**5**	**9**	**4**	**13**	**4**
Third World						
Dissertations	0	0	0	1	0	0
Articles	1	0	11	1	1	2
Books	0	1	1	1	0	0
Total	**1**	**1**	**12**	**3**	**1**	**2**
Total: All categories and geographical areas						
Dissertations	1	0	2	2	0	0
Articles	20	12	20	11	14	22
Books	10	8	10	7	11	3
Total	**31**	**20**	**32**	**20**	**25**	**25**

1945–49	1950–54	1955–59	1960–64	1965–69	1970–74	1975–79	Total
0	1	1	3	6	18	29	59
8	4	8	10	27	71	104	243
3	3	7	11	16	38	41	126
11	**8**	**16**	**24**	**49**	**127**	**174**	**428**
0	0	1	0	0	7	18	26
1	2	7	12	30	30	58	151
1	2	2	5	7	19	15	60
2	**4**	**10**	**17**	**37**	**56**	**91**	**237**
0	0	0	1	2	13	10	27
11	12	10	20	45	91	130	342
7	6	14	18	24	24	42	148
18	**18**	**24**	**39**	**71**	**128**	**182**	**517**
0	0	0	1	4	5	5	17
9	5	13	15	31	67	102	280
7	1	3	8	12	21	14	83
16	**6**	**16**	**24**	**47**	**93**	**121**	**380**
0	0	0	0	0	2	3	6
3	3	4	7	17	31	34	115
3	1	0	7	6	10	10	40
6	**4**	**4**	**14**	**23**	**43**	**47**	**161**
0	1	2	5	12	45	65	135
32	26	42	64	150	290	428	113
21	13	26	49	65	112	122	457
53	**40**	**70**	**118**	**227**	**447**	**615**	**1723**

TABLE 1.3. Publications in Group Psychohistory and Psychobiography

Group Psychohistory

	Pre-1920	1920–24	1925–29	1930–34	1935–39	1940–44	1945–49	1950–54	1955–59	1960–64	1965–69	1970–74	1975–79	Totals
United States	4	1	1	3	3	7	11	8	16	24	49	127	174	428
Europe	3	7	4	7	6	10	18	18	24	39	71	128	182	517
Total	**7**	**8**	**5**	**10**	**9**	**17**	**29**	**26**	**40**	**63**	**120**	**255**	**356**	**945**

Psychobiography

	Pre-1920	1920–24	1925–29	1930–34	1935–39	1940–44	1945–49	1950–54	1955–59	1960–64	1965–69	1970–74	1975–79	Totals
United States	1	6	6	3	2	2	2	4	10	17	37	56	91	237
Europe	22	5	9	4	13	4	16	6	16	24	47	93	121	380
Total	**23**	**11**	**15**	**7**	**15**	**6**	**18**	**10**	**26**	**41**	**84**	**149**	**212**	**617**

the field, particularly since the early 1970s. Throughout the history of the field, one can see a growing degree of institutionalization, from pioneers working in relative isolation, through the formation of networks of peers and the organization of conferences, to the establishment of professional organizations and publication outlets in which psychohistory is a central rather than a peripheral concern. There has also been a modest degree of academic institutionalization of the field, through the establishment of courses, the writing of dissertations, and the possibility of specializing within this area.

To illustrate this process of institutionalization, one can conceptually distinguish six aspects of it, each aspect temporally overlapping with and affecting the others. The process of institutionalization can be visualized as progressing (1) from the original lone worker at his or her desk, without a surrounding network of colleagues working on similar problems and without a prior tradition to draw on (although in psychohistory, it is difficult to identify such a pure "state of nature," since even the original pioneers had at least some minimal external support, such as Freud from the Vienna Psychoanalytic Society by the time he was working on *Leonardo da Vinci and a Memory of His Childhood* in 1910, Alexander George beginning his work on Woodrow Wilson in a course on personality in politics with Nathan Leites in 1941 at the University of Chicago, or Erik Erikson working in the context of the psychoanalytic community while writing *Young Man Luther* at Austen Riggs in the 1950s); (2) to the establishment of informal contacts, discussion, correspondence, and exchange of manuscripts; (3) to the organization of single conferences or conventions, such as the conference on psychohistory at the City University of New York, organized by Arthur Schlesinger, Jr., and held in April 1971; the conference "Psychohistory—Present State and Future Prospect," organized by William J. Gilmore and held at Stockton State College, New Jersey, in October 1976; the Adelphi Conference on Psychohistory honoring Erik Erikson, held in October 1977; the conference on history and psychoanalysis emphasizing the work of Heinz Kohut, organized by Charles Strozier and Daniel Offer, and held at Michael Reese Hospital in Chicago in June 1979; the conference "The Psychology of Biography," organized by Samuel Baron and Carl Pletsch, and held at Chapel Hill, North Carolina, in November 1981; and the conference "History and Psychology: Recent Studies in the Family, Biography, and Theory," organized by Nathan Hale, Jr., and held at Stanford University in May 1982, which provided the background for this volume; (4) to groups meeting on a regular basis, such as the Wellfleet Group, organized by Robert Jay Lifton and meeting on

Cape Cod since 1966; the Los Angeles Interdisciplinary Psychoanalytic Study Group, which met regularly from 1966 to 1970 and included Alexander L. George, Peter Loewenberg, E. Victor Wolfenstein, Fawn Brodie, and Robert Dorn, and an interdisciplinary study group meeting at UCLA since 1984, including Robert Dallek, Peter Loewenberg, Elizabeth Marvick, Victor Wolfenstein, and others; the Group for Applied Psychoanalysis in Cambridge, Massachusetts, which met from 1965 to the early 1980s; and the Group for Applied Psychoanalysis at Cornell University; (5) to the establishment of formal professional organizations and societies, which may lead to the founding of journals and publication outlets, from Freud's Vienna Psychoanalytic Society in 1908 (emerging out of the Psychological Wednesday Society, formed by Freud in 1902); through the Group for the Use of Psychology in History, an affiliate of the American Historical Association that was organized by Richard Schoenwald and inaugurated in 1972, the same year in which it started its own newsletter, the *GUPH Newsletter,* changing into the *Psychohistory Review* in 1975, and edited from 1973 to 1986 by Charles Strozier (Strozier, 1986); the establishment by Lloyd deMause of the Institute for Psychohistory in 1972, the International Psychohistorical Association in 1976, the *Journal of Psychohistory* (changing to that name in 1976, after being called the *History of Childhood Quarterly* since its founding in 1973), and the Psychohistory Press, which publishes its own books in the field; to the foundation by Jeanne Knutson of the International Society of Political Psychology in 1977 and the launching of its journal, *Political Psychology,* in 1979; (6) and, finally, to academic institutionalization of the field, including the establishment of courses, the production of dissertations in psychohistory, and employment possibilities. In spite of the rapid growth in publications and other facets of institutionalization, the academic institutionalization of psychohistory has been very partial to date. It should be noted that it is possible to have substantial professional and intellectual development of a field, with little or no penetration of academic institutions (Shils, 1972). As for the number of courses offered in psychohistory, Mazlish (1966) stated in 1966 that only he and Erikson taught psychohistory courses at that time, but a little over a decade later (Mazlish, 1977), more than 200 courses in psychohistory were listed in college and university catalogues in the United States. This estimate of 200 courses has been repeated in other publications (Kren, 1977; Lawton, 1978; Lifton with Strozier, 1984), but another current survey of course offerings would be of value.

Another indicator of the growth of psychohistory within academia, and of the extent to which it is being pursued by younger generations of scholars, is the number of doctoral dissertations, which reflects both the interests of students and the extent to which faculty members are willing to serve as chairpersons and committee persons on dissertations in this area.

I made a computerized search of *Dissertation Abstracts* from its beginning through 1984 to identify all dissertations that have the term *psychobiography, psychobiographical, psychohistory,* or *psychohistorical* in their titles or abstracts. This search of *Dissertation Abstracts* yielded a total of 60 items, with 41 dissertations describing themselves as psychohistorical and 19 as psychobiographical. If the abstract indicated that the topic is discussed in a peripheral way—for example, that a psychobiographical approach would not be pursued in the dissertation—the item was deleted, leaving a total of 56 dissertations. This is unquestionably a subset of all dissertations in the field, since many psychobiographical or psychohistorical dissertations do not include those specific words in their title or abstract. For example, UCLA has produced at least 7 dissertations in psychohistory, only one of which has the word *psychohistorical* in the title. Gilmore's (1984) bibliography yielded a total of 135 dissertations through 1979 under the sections of psychohistory and psychobiography, not including those on the life cycle. My search was more limited in scope, but also more up to date, in that it covered the literature up through 1984.

Each dissertation in *Dissertation Abstracts* is classified as belonging to a primary field or discipline. I would have expected a substantial proportion of dissertations in psychohistory or psychobiography to be associated with the field of history, but only five of these 56 dissertations were listed with their primary descriptor as history. One might quarrel with the classification of particular dissertations, and a different classification procedure might well yield different results, but given the nature and limitations of this coding scheme, the distribution across fields was as follows: psychology, 29; literature, 11; history, 5; education, 4; political science, 3; religion, 3; and 1 each for economics, fine arts, American studies, and sociology. If nothing else, this distribution suggests the interdisciplinary spread of those engaged in psychohistory.

A second issue is the distribution of dissertations across universities. Are there a few key universities with influential professors who are responsible for producing a disproportionate share of dissertations in this field, as has been true in several other subfields of history (Kammen, 1980)? Clifford Geertz (1983) has noted an "exile from Eden syndrome" (p. 159), in which a high proportion of doctorates in a discipline are awarded at a few elite universities, and graduating students then move down the academic prestige ladder, or away from the center to more peripheral institutions. I do not have information on the career lines of those writing dissertations in psychohistory, but are the bulk of dissertations in psychohistory produced by a few central universities?

As indicated by this search strategy, the dissertations in psychohistory and psychobiography are widely scattered around the country, with the most common pattern being a single dissertation from a given university. Universities having more than one dissertation describing itself as psychohistorical or psychobiographical were University of Chicago, with 3; Adelphi University, 2; Northwestern University, 2; University of Tennessee, 2; United States International University, 2; Yale University, 2; Yeshiva University, 2; University of Alberta, Canada, 2; and, surprisingly, having the most in the country, the California School of Professional Psychology, Berkeley, 7.[3]

In short, there seems to be a remarkable degree of decentralization in the production of doctoral dissertations in psychohistory. One possible interpretation is that although the field may be gradually becoming an *intellectual* discipline, with a defined set of problems and approaches, it has not yet become an *academic* discipline, with well-defined and well-organized academic training programs (see Shils, 1972). Although a few universities have more systematic training in psychohistory (for example, UCLA and Kansas State University), the bulk of dissertations are apparently being produced by single interested students in conjunction with one or more sympathetic faculty members at institutions scattered across the country.

The two earliest dissertations using the word *psychohistory* or *psychobiography* in the title or abstract were those by Alan Lichtenstein at Indiana University in 1971, "T. N. Granovskii and the Roots of the Politics of Enlightenment, 1813–1844: A Psychohistorical Inquiry," and by

3. Universities with one dissertation each that describes itself as psychohistorical or psychobiographical were Boston University; Brown University; California Institute of Asian Studies; California School of Professional Psychology, Los Angeles; Carnegie-Mellon University; Columbia University; Cornell University; Harvard University; Indiana University; Loyola University, Chicago; Michigan State University; North Texas State University; Northwestern University; Ohio State University; Rutgers University, Graduate School of Applied and Professional Psychology; Saint Mary's Seminary and University; Southern Baptist Theological Seminary; State University of New York, Buffalo; State University of New York, Stony Brook; Union for Experimental Colleges and Universities; University of California, Berkeley; University of California, Los Angeles; University of Iowa; University of Minnesota; University of Pennsylvania; University of Pittsburgh; University of Wisconsin, Madison; Wayne State University; and, outside the United States, the Caribbean Center for Advanced Studies, Puerto Rico; University of British Columbia; and University of Toronto.

Alvin Ramsey at Harvard in 1973, "A Psychohistorical Analysis of Afro-American Identity: Theory, Hypotheses, Methods for Investigation."

The peak years for production of dissertations in this area were 1976, with 7, and 1983, with 10. During the 1970s, there were 27 dissertations describing themselves as psychohistorical or psychobiographical, and in the first half of the 1980s (1980–84), there were 28, so the rate of production approximately doubled.

In conclusion, it should be remembered that this discussion includes only a subset of dissertations in the field, those explicitly describing themselves as psychohistorical or psychobiographical, and that the results may be somewhat different for the complete set of dissertations in psychohistory. In the following sections, we will examine several basic intellectual issues that have influenced the growth of the field and its limited degree of institutionalization.

Antibiographical Trends Within Historiography

One theme cutting across a number of schools of historiography is a distrust of biography, or a distrust of an overemphasis on individuals. "The spirit of the modern period, with its new respect for collectivism, with its hatred of all individualism, has cried out with great conviction: 'It is not heroes, the few, who make history; it is groups, classes, peoples, races'" (Huizinga, 1934, quoted in Stern, 1972, p. 299). As history moved beyond its initial focus on political, diplomatic, and military affairs ("drum and trumpet history") to a broader concern with economic, intellectual, social, ecological, and demographic history, there has been an increasing uneasiness about what is perceived as an overemphasis on individuals in traditional historiography.

This theme underlies many of the debates about psychohistory (and particularly about psychobiography), and it has pervasive implications for the extent to which psychology may or may not be useful to historians. Whatever else psychology does, it studies motivational, cognitive, affective, and behavioral processes of individuals. If persons have no place in history, then psychology has no place in history. Conversely, if individuals (and detailed biographical studies of individuals) have a place within history, then the prospects of fruitfully using psychology in history are considerably brighter.

The nature and persuasiveness of these antibiographical arguments are worth examining, as they have significant implications for one's beliefs about the relevance of psychology for history. A discussion of anti-biographical trends within historiography is certainly *not* to claim that all historians are uninterested in the study of individual lives, since many of the best biographies have been written by historians and there is an increasing interest in historical studies of the family and of the life course (Demos, 1986; Elder, 1974, 1985; Hareven, 1978, 1982; Hareven and Adams, 1982).

However, influential antibiographical beliefs are shared by a substantial number of historians across different schools of historiography, as in the work of many Marxist, *Annales,* structuralist, and quantitative social historians. The intent of this section is to review a number of expressions of these antibiographical beliefs within different branches of historiography, to disentangle several of their components, and to critically evaluate them with the intent of better understanding the relationships between history and psychology.

According to Marx, for example, social relations and their transformation have priority over the study of individuals. "Society does not consist of individuals, but expresses the sum of interrelations, the relations within which these individuals stand" (Marx, 1857–58/1978, p. 247), and "the human essence is no abstraction inherent in each single individual. In its reality it is the ensemble of the social relations" (Marx, 1845/1978, p. 145). The apparent influence of "great men" on the course of history is illusory, as the course of history is governed by economic necessity. "That such and such a man and precisely that man arises at a particular time in a particular country is, of course, pure chance. But cut him out and there will be a demand for a substitute, and this substitute will be found. . . . If a Napoleon had been lacking, another would have filled the place" (Engels, 1894/1978, pp. 767–768).

Although notably heterogeneous, much of Marxist thought has been antagonistic to the study of individuals and their psychological processes. In summarizing some of these views (and subsequently arguing against them), Lucien Sève (1978) states that first, from the perspective of historical materialism, in which consciousness is a product of the material world and of social life, the analysis of objective social life and economic relations takes precedence over the psychological analysis of human subjectivity. Second, scientific socialism is concerned with studying the masses, and the psychological investigation of individuals is subordinate to this.

Within the *Annales* tradition, beginning in France in 1929 with the publication of the journal *Annales* by Marc Bloch and Lucien Febvre, there has often not been much enthusiasm for biography, particularly in the second generation as Fernand Braudel became a dominant figure (Bizière, 1983; Burguière, 1982; Ratcliffe, 1980). Biography was seen as encapsulating much that was defective in the older tradition of political history, against which *Annales* scholars were reacting—that is, "it was elitist, narrative, short-term, superficial, atomized, and abstracted the individual from his context" (Ratcliffe, 1980, p. 559). In 1972, a leading *Annales* historian, Emmanuel Le Roy Ladurie, stated that "present-day historiography, with its preference for the quantifiable, the statistical and the structural, has been obliged to suppress in order to survive. In the last decades it has virtually condemned to death the narrative history of events and the individual biography" (quoted in Stone, 1981, p. 96). (As we shall see later, this view has subsequently been modified.)

Skepticism about the intensive study of individual lives is shared by a number of quantitative social historians, who believe that the study of individuals is "elitist," is nonrepresentative, is anecdotal rather than systematic, and does not deal with the everyday experience of ordinary men and women.

Structural linguistics has also influenced historiography and the general intellectual climate, in part through anthropology and the work of Claude Lévi-Strauss. Its emphasis is on synchronic study of language systems and a search for universal linguistic structures that shape human thought and action. "In this scheme human beings disappeared as acting, deciding, and decisive individuals. All research was now directed toward finding the invisible, impersonal, and timeless structures—the keys to human behavior" (Breisach, 1983, p. 374).

One final illustration of antibiographical sentiments, which does not even require translation, can be presented in the original French: "De tous les genres historiographiques, la biographie est le plus futile, le plus paresseux, le plus arrogant, le plus réactionnaire et le plus irrationnel" (Romano, 1982, p. 43).

What are some of the sources of this antipathy toward biography? There are a number of strands of the argument against biography, which I will attempt to disentangle so that each can be exposed to the light of day and assessed independently. The intent is to initiate a dialogue leading to a defensible position about the study of persons and their psychological processes within historiography.

Many historians look askance at biography because they associate it with a crude "Great Man" theory of history, which overemphasizes the influence of prominent individuals on the course of history, while neglecting the role of populations and the operation of massive economic, cultural, religious, and social structural processes. The classic statement of the "Great Man" view is by Thomas Carlyle (1840/1972) who wrote that

> Universal History, the history of what man has accomplished in this world, is at bottom the history of the Great Men who have worked here. They were the leaders of men, these great ones; the modelers, patterns, and in a wide sense creators, of whatsoever the general mass of men contrived to do or to attain; all things that we see standing accomplished in the world are properly the outer material results, the practical realisation and embodiment of Thoughts that dwelt in the Great Men sent into the world: the soul of the whole world's history, it may justly be considered, were the history of these. (p. 101)

It should be clear that in-depth studies of individuals need not be based on this crude theory of history. One can write and read biographies as studies of the perceptions, beliefs, actions, and experiences of individuals, even if it is assumed that individuals had *no* historical influence and were no more than passive perceivers and experiencers of large-scale impersonal historical forces and processes. A biography of Alice James (Strouse, 1980) need not assume that she was a World-Historical figure.

With the assumption that individuals had no influence at all, would biography then be an entirely separate genre, outside the walls of history? No, not if one believes that studying the human meaning or significance of economic, social, political, ecological, and technological changes is part of the historical enterprise.

A more sophisticated stance is to search for the conditions under which individual actors (along with economic, political, social, religious, and other factors) do or do not influence historical events. This is the stance taken in a number of sophisticated biographical studies, which analyze both individual and institutional factors, such as John Mack's study of T. E. Lawrence (1976), Robert Tucker on Stalin (1973), Waite on Hitler (1977), the Georges on Wilson (1956/1964), and the recent debate on the effect of Kaiser Wilhelm on World War I (Röhl and Sombart, 1982).

An instructive analysis of the influence of individuals in history is still Sidney Hook's *The Hero in History* (1943), which attempts "to work out some generalization of the types of situations and conditions in which we can justifiably attribute or deny causal influence to outstanding personalities" (p. xiv). In an analysis of the historical influence of Lenin, Hook persuasively argues that the Russian Revolution had an important influence on the political, cultural, and economic life of the world; that the revolution was not inevitable; that other revolutionary leaders, such as Zinoviev, Kamenev, or Trotsky, would not have been effective substitutes for Lenin; and that Lenin's leadership was crucial to the success of the revolution. Whether or not one agrees with the conclusion of Hook's analysis, he demonstrates the level of detail and subtlety of argument needed to assert or deny claims about the causal influence of an individual on the course of historical events.

A more recent critique of the determinist view that individuals never make a difference in the course of history is presented in Arthur Schlesinger's *Cycles of American History* (1986), which argues that if one applies historical determinism to specific historical episodes, "the results are self-convicting" (p. 421). With figures as diverse as Napoleon, Shakespeare, Winston Churchill, Franklin Roosevelt, Lenin, or Hitler, claims that particular individuals make no difference in the course of history are simply unconvincing.

A second strand of the antibiography position is that the study of individuals is "elitist." The argument is that biographies focus too much attention on kings, queens, political and military leaders, and the privileged, while ignoring the experience of the masses, the oppressed, and ordinary men and women.

One can agree that it is virtuous to get away from an exclusive focus on the elite and to learn more about the oppressed, the inarticulate, and those groups of persons too often neglected in history as well as by society. However, the social class issue should not be confused with the level of aggregation question, which conceptually is an entirely independent issue.

One can do detailed biographical studies of individuals from the social elite, the middle class, or the poorest or most oppressed groups, as is indicated by the substantial and growing number of biographical and autobiographical studies of criminals, drug addicts, psychotic killers, black and Puerto Rican ghetto dwellers, marginal anthropological informants, and so on (Bennett, 1981; Langness and Frank, 1981). Conversely, one can do large-scale quantitative studies not only of anonymous masses, but also of the elite, such as members of Parliament (Namier, 1957) or eminent political, military, and cultural leaders (Simonton, 1984).

In sum, an interest in the experience of ordinary men and women is not an adequate reason for preferring quantitative to biographical studies, since both kinds of analysis can be done and need to be done for all social groups.

Whether a study is "elitist" or not depends not just on the persons being studied, but also on the interpretation offered. Is every study of an elite individual "elitist"? What about debunking biographies, which reveal the misuse of power and privilege, such as Robert Caro's detailed critical studies of Robert Moses (1974) and Lyndon Johnson (1982)? Whether a study is "elitist" or not depends not solely upon the subject, but also upon interpretations given and how the individual is related to his or her social, political, and historical context.

In short, it is naïve to argue that a particular level of analysis in itself is "elitist." It is no more persuasive to argue that the study of individuals is "elitist" than it is to argue that quantitative studies are inherently "progressive," or egalitarian. There is no substitute for individual, group, and population studies of the entire range of social groups and classes.

A third strand of the antibiographical argument is that it is reductionistic to take a biographical approach to history or to operate on "the assumption that history was the sum of the biographies of a limited number of dominant individuals" (Handlin, 1979, p. 267). Jared Sparks, launching a dictionary of American biography in the nineteenth century, suggested that since social, cultural, and political progress is so dependent on a few eminent individuals, a biographical collection of distinguished Americans "would embrace a perfect history of the country" (quoted in Handlin, 1979, p. 267). In the twentieth century, this view became increasingly untenable as historians have turned their attention to large-scale impersonal forces shaping economic, political, and social institutions.

It is, unquestionably, simplistic to claim that "History = Biography" or that history can be reduced to nothing more than the aggregation of individual biographies, since this leaves out the impact of ecological and demographic factors, ignores the evolution of economic, political, religious, educational, and other institutions, and neglects the complex interactions between institutions and social groups.

It is, however, equally reductionistic to claim that an understanding of individual persons and their psychological processes has nothing to contribute to an analysis of the history of groups, social movements, institutions, and nations. Only a dogmatic reductionism would maintain that the personality and life of Hitler had nothing to do with the course of World War II; of Lenin, with the Russian Revolution; of Gandhi, with India's struggle with the British; or of Martin Luther King, Jr., with the civil rights movement. Regardless of the trends of intellectual fashion, it is just as reductionistic to exclude the role of individuals and their psychological processes in historical analysis, as it was to naïvely overemphasize them in the nineteenth century.

A fourth strand of the antibiographical argument, which appears not just in history, but in sociology, anthropology, and psychology as well, is that it is hard to know if any single individual is "representative" of some larger group or population. For many purposes, this issue of "representativeness" is irrelevant because one is often interested in studying individuals who are *not* representative, who because of position, chance, or personal characteristics have unusual interest for us or had an unusually great influence on the course of history. Questions about the representativeness of an Alexander the Great, a Joan of Arc, a Vincent Van Gogh, or an Adolf Hitler are not to the point.

When biographical analysis is used for portraying the experience of a particular historical group, such as American slaves, assembly-line workers, or women in nineteenth-century France, it is often helpful to use a set of biographical sketches to illustrate the diversity of life experiences of those within the group. Analysis of a number of lives can reveal the ways in which a historical period or event was differentially perceived, experienced, and interpreted by a variety of persons in different social locations (Runyan, 1986). For portraying the experience of a group, the representativeness of individuals *is* an important issue, but given the internal heterogeneity of most groups, quantitative group studies are often usefully supplemented with measures of dispersion and with a set of individual portraits.

Two additional strands of the antibiographical argument may be briefly mentioned. A fifth is the view among some historians that biography is too easy a genre, the objection being that biography is "a lazy and easy form, having an obvious shape based on the birth, development, and death of the subject of the biography" (Marwick, 1981, p. 223) and that the biographer could escape the archival complexities of most historical research by working primarily with the collected papers of the subject (Handlin, 1979, p. 268). There undoubtedly are superficial biographies that are quickly and easily written, but a serious biography is extraordinarily difficult to do well (as acknowledged by both Marwick and Handlin), requiring consultation with a great range of sources, extensive knowledge of the subject's social-historical world and arena of professional activity, psychological knowledge for interpreting personality and behavior, and literary skill in presenting the whole. The complexity of these problems is indicated in the extensive literature on the art and science of biography (Bowen, 1969; Clifford, 1962, 1970; Edel, 1984; Garraty, 1957; Pachter, 1979; Runyan, 1982a).

A sixth issue, which sometimes distresses historians, is that biography as a genre is too popular compared with other forms of historiography.

It tends to pander to public interest in the personal, the gossipy, and the sensational, while diverting attention away from deeper historical analyses. One can empathize with the frustrations of historians who see their own laborious analyses of underlying social and institutional forces neglected by the public in favor of cheap and sensational biographies. "The failure of the public to appreciate the professional historical expert—as it appreciated both the popular historian and the scientific expert—rankled deeply" (Higham, 1983, p. 78).

To summarize, antibiographical sentiments can be found in a number of branches of contemporary historiography, including Marxist, *Annales,* structuralist, and quantitative social historians. A number of analytically separable strands of these views were distinguished and critically evaluated, including the views that biographical studies are based on a "Great Man" theory of history, that they are elitist, that they assume history can be reduced to the sum of individual biographies, that individuals are not representative of a larger group, and that the analysis of individual lives is intellectually lazy and panders to a public interest in personality, while diverting attention from deeper historical processes.

To simplify the history of the debate about the place of individuals and psychological processes within history, one can analytically distinguish three separate positions, each partially overlapping in time and each still alive in some quarters and in contention with the others. These three viewpoints, in rough sequential order, are (1) a naïve overemphasis on the role of prominent individuals in influencing and representing the course of historical events; (2) a rejection of the study of individuals, in favor of larger structures, whether in the form of modes of production, class relationships, demographic and ecological processes, or quantitative studies of social groups; and (3) a search for ways of reintegrating individuals and their psychological processes into analyses of their reciprocal causal relationships with broader economic, demographic, and institutional forces.

The movement beyond antibiographical approaches, seeking to integrate individuals into broader historical patterns, is not restricted to any single school, but cuts across branches of historiography and is reflected in general overviews of the field. For example, Lucien Sève (1978) reviews and critiques a number of the common Marxist objections to the study of individual psychology, and attempts to develop a theory of personality and of biography consistent with Marxist theory, while associates of the *Annales* school, long ambivalent about biography, increasingly argue that studies of individual subjective experience can make contributions to a total history (for example, Bizière, 1983; Ratcliffe, 1980; Stone, 1981).

A synthesis of individual and structural levels of analysis is argued for by a variety of commentators on contemporary historiography. After surveying the history of Western historiography from ancient through modern developments, Breisach (1983) argues that a principal issue is the need to avoid extremes marked by "the chaos of individuals or by the timeless and ahistorical silence of structures" (p. 408). The extreme of expunging the individual element for the sake of quantitative scientific studies of structure is parodied by Chiari (1975) as follows. With the human element, "there is always a residuum of uniqueness which does not fit the abstractions and generalizations in which the scientist would like to enclose it. The human being is thus difficult to handle; the best solution, of course, is to suppress him, or to declare that he no longer exists. In this way, science could really take over and work out theories no human element could contradict" (quoted in Plummer, 1983, p. 1). In Breisach's (1983) view, historians over the past half-century have been torn by a "dichotomy between the realm of the individual's world of purposes, intentions, and acts of will and the concept of a binding order with an all-encompassing structure" (p. 410). Historians must, in his view, pursue the most difficult option of analyzing an order in which the influence of impersonal structures and forces is intertwined with the choices and actions of at least partly free and morally responsible individuals.

Oscar Handlin (1979) uses a theatrical metaphor to represent the relationships between individuals and their sociohistorical contexts. While individuals are shaped by their times, they may also have a "discernible influence" on the course of subsequent events: "The individual takes part in a drama that began long before the birth, that goes on long after the death, of any player. Entering for a brief turn on a scene already set, a stage already crowded, and with the action already in progress, each person confronts a situation that already exists, the product of long preparation. . . . But to some degree, all are free—to move, to alter the wandering of others, even to reshape bits of the set. . . . Institutions that are the results of complex historic forces determine the situation. But the situation does not determine the reaction to it" (pp. 275–276).

One of the most widely known statements on the transition from a focus on structures to one on persons-in-structures is in Lawrence Stone's essay on the return of narrative (Stone, 1981). Stone suggests that historians of *mentalités,* concerned with using narrative methods in the pursuit of subjective experience, mind sets, and intimate personal behavior, are currently challenging the quantitatively oriented social historians, who focus on impersonal structures. Stone argues that, "There are signs of change in the central issue in history from the circumstances surrounding man to man in circumstances; in the problems studied from the economic and demographic to the cultural and emotional; in the prime sources of influence from sociology, economics, and demography to anthropology and psychology; in the subject matter from the group to the individual; in the explanatory models of historical change from the stratified and monocausal to the interconnected and multicausal . . ." (p. 96).

The interconnections among these different levels of analysis is usefully characterized by Bernard Bailyn (1982) as a tension between manifest history and latent history. *Manifest* history depicts the story of events that contemporaries were aware of, that were perceived as important at the time, even if the actual causes and determining factors were "buried below the level of contemporaries' understanding" (p. 9). In contrast, *latent* history is the story of underlying events and processes that people at the time were partially or wholly unaware of, that they did not consciously struggle over, and that may or may not have been recorded in documentation of the time. Underlying shifts in demographic patterns, in agricultural conditions, in income distribution, in church membership, and in living arrangements may all have important consequences for people, yet may not have been in their awareness at the time, and discovered only centuries later through historical research. These underlying, or latent, events "form a new landscape—a landscape like that of the ocean floor, assumed to have existed in some vague way by people struggling at the surface of the waves but never seen before as actual rocks, ravines, and cliffs" (pp. 10–11).

An important agenda for contemporary historiography is exploring the relationships between these latent and manifest levels, between underlying structures and more easily visible actions and experiences. As expressed by Bailyn (1982), "the essence and drama of history lie precisely in the active and continuous relationships between the underlying conditions that set the boundaries of human existence and the everyday problems with which people consciously struggle. The goal of history is not to separate out events of these different dimensions at a particular point in time, but to show their continuous interaction in an evolving story. The drama of people struggling with the conditions that confine them through the cycles of limited life spans is the heart of all living history" (p. 5).

To summarize, a central challenge for contemporary historiography is to explore the relationships between manifest and latent events, between human agency and structural constraint, and between the psychological processes of individuals and groups and the maintenance and change of social structures and institutions. Far from being a peripheral or dispensable development within historiography, a psychologically informed history is crucial for addressing these issues.

Antiparticularism and Levels of Generality in Psychology

A key intellectual issue that divides the disciplines of history and psychology is their respective positions on the search for particularity or generality. To put the matter in simplest form, history is concerned with the description and interpretation of particular sequences of historical events and processes, while the science of psychology is concerned with a search for general theories about the mind, experience, and behavior. A classic formulation of this distinction is that history is an "idiographic" discipline, concerned with interpreting specific events and processes, while psychology is a "nomothetic" discipline, concerned with searching for general laws (Allport, 1962; Windelband, 1904). This emphasis on a search for general theories rather than the study of particulars applies particularly to academic psychology, which will be the focus of the following discussion, as psychoanalysis has always had an interest in the interpretation of particular cases as well as in general theory.

These distinctions between nomothetic and idiographic disciplines are, of course, rough simplifications (with a number of exceptions to be discussed later), but there is still a clear difference between history and psychology in their underlying assumptions and in the *bulk* of their practice. The two disciplines differ in their aims, methods, and typical products in that historians aim to understand the histories of particular nations, institutions, or events, depend on methods of collecting and interpreting vast amounts of particularistic information, and traditionally present their research in the form of narrative accounts, while academic psychologists aspire to develop general theories, use quantitative and experimental methods designed to test theoretical conjectures, and present their work in the form of empirical tests of explicit hypotheses.

The discipline of psychology is devoted to the search for generalizations about psychological structures, elements, and processes within the domains of cognition, sensation and perception, biopsychology, and developmental, personality, abnormal, and social psychology. As expressed by Levy (1970), the goal of psychology is "the development of generalizations of ever increasing scope, so that greater and greater varieties of phenomena may be explained by them, larger and larger numbers of questions answered by them, and broader and broader reaching predictions and decisions based upon them" (p. 5).

Psychologists are typically *not* concerned with the study of psychological processes of particular individuals in particular historical circumstances, since the study of single cases is seen primarily as a springboard for developing more general ideas and hypotheses. For example, from the study of historical particulars, such as that of Kitty Genovese, who was murdered near a railroad station in Queens without any of thirty-eight bystanders who heard her screams doing anything to help, the psychologist moves to general questions about the relationships among variables that affect the likelihood of bystander intervention (Latané and Darley, 1970). As expressed by Allport (1962), "We recognize the single case as a useful source of hunches—and that is about all. We pursue our acquaintance with Bill long enough to derive some hypothesis, and then spring like a gazelle into the realm of abstraction" (p. 406).

The study of particular historical cases or events is seen as a source of hypotheses that then need to be tested with "more rigorous" correlational and experimental methods. It is important to note, however, that there is a shift in the level of generality of the causal hypothesis. It is no longer a hypothesis about the relationship among factors in a particular case, but rather a more general hypothesis about the causal relationships among classes of variables, such as factors that influence bystander intervention, the persuasiveness of communications, or obedience to authority.

Psychologists are often socialized into a way of viewing the world in which questions about historical particulars are rendered invisible on the intellectual landscape (or if not invisible, at least peripheral). Specific historical incidents may be used to raise a general causal question, but with a few exceptions (for example, Cronbach, 1975; Gergen, 1973, 1982), sustained inquiry into the interpretation of psychological structures and processes in particular historical circumstances tends not to be pursued, or even identified as a worthy objective.

I sometimes ask psychologists whether they are aware of work that applies their theories or research findings to particular historical events or periods. The response is often one of puzzlement or bewilderment. What would be the point of doing that? If these findings are general, presumably they would apply anywhere, anytime. Why bother trying to apply them to partly known historical circumstances, in which the data are fragmentary, the observations uncontrolled, and the causal variables confounded? From this point of view, there *is* no great value in attempting to study particular historical events or circumstances, as the possibility of rigorously testing general causal hypotheses is usually much greater in controlled experimental settings.

In brief, the view of many psychologists is that the naturalistic study of particular persons or groups in particular social-historical circumstances is not useful if one cannot generalize from it; is valuable primarily as a source of more general hypotheses, which then need to be tested with other, more rigorous methods; and is problematic in that observations are often fragmentary, causal variables are confounded, and general causal questions can be more rigorously investigated under controlled experimental conditions than through the cloudy mirror of history. A number of these beliefs can be grouped together under the label of "antiparticularism," which includes all those beliefs and assumptions downgrading the importance of studying social and historical particularities.

The relative indifference of psychologists to the study of historical issues is indicated in at least two ways: (1) a lack of involvement of most psychologists in work on the use of psychology in interpreting particular historical events and processes (as the bulk of work in psychohistory and psychobiography is done by those from other disciplines), and (2) a lack of concern of most psychologists for testing the transhistorical generality or specificity of their theories. There seems to be far greater interest in the transsituational, cross-subject, and cross-cultural generality of theories than in their transhistorical generality.

A Continuum of Levels of Generality

I will argue that psychology and history can be related more effectively than they have been in the past if we think of a *continuum* of levels of generality, ranging from the most particular and idiographic, through concepts and theories of moderate or context-bound generality, to the most general and universal. I have argued elsewhere (Runyan, 1982a, 1983) that psychology needs to be concerned with at least three different levels of generality, seeking to learn (1) what is true of all human beings; (2) what is true of groups of human beings, distinguished by sex, race, social class, culture, historical period, and the like; and (3) what is true of individual human beings in particular social and historical contexts. The beliefs and assumptions identified earlier as composing antiparticularism tend to imply that the *important* issues are deep and general ones, while the study of particularities and context-bounded regularities is relatively superficial and unimportant. I submit that it is of both theoretical and practical importance to explore the entire continuum of levels of generality in psychological and social phenomena, and to pursue the difficult and elusive questions of their interpenetration.

In the famous "social psychology as history" debate (Gergen, 1973, Schlenker, 1974; Manis et al., 1976; Gergen, 1982), Gergen drew attention to a number of factors that limit the establishment of general laws in the social sciences, such as that facts and the relationships among them are constantly changing over historical time and that the process and results of inquiry may reflexively alter the social relationships under investigation as people change their behavior as a result of advances in knowledge. On the other side, critics such as Schlenker argued that there are greater transcultural and transhistorical regularities than Gergen recognized, that the reflexive effects of social science knowledge could be predicted or studied as regularities in themselves, and that a few general processes could be found underlying and producing the apparent diversity of human behavior. I will not attempt to resolve that debate here, but rather suggest that it is useful to consider a continuum of levels of generality and to analyze the historical processes that produce, maintain, and change different levels of generality.

There is a continuum of levels of generality not only in the relationships among elements or variables, but also in all the analytic units in the human-social-historical world, including the elements themselves, processes, causal relationships, correlational relationships, meanings, interactions among systems, and the temporal trajectory of systems and processes.

Over time, evolutionary processes produce, maintain, transform, and make extinct each particular level of generality. The processes produce some elements or components that are of quite wide generality, such as atoms; other entities of moderate generality, such as feudalism, slavery, or capitalism; and yet other things that are remarkably specific and idiographic, such as Lincoln's Gettysburg Address or the career of Joseph Stalin. The essential notion is that there is a whole continuum of levels of generality, that they change over time, and that it is important to understand each level of generality and their interrelationships.

From the perspective of a continuum of levels of generality, there is a certain *primacy* in the historical perspective, in that it is more encompassing than the social scientific perspective. Psychology and the other social sciences are devoted to a search for regularities in the world—to developing quantitative measurements, finding correlations, building models of underlying structures and processes, developing general theories of change, and discovering causal relationships that hold across space and time. These are profoundly important tasks, but they are restricted in scope in that they are focused on the search for order and regularity in the world.

Historical inquiry is broader in scope, in that in investigating the flow of humanly important events and experiences, it must attend not only to the ordered, structured, and lawlike aspects of human and social reality, but also to the disorderly, the particular, the idiosyncratic, the transient, and the random.

History is the medium within which the kinds of order, regularity, comparability, and generality sought by the social sciences are formed, maintained, transformed, and extinguished. The historical process is the medium within which phenomenal order is born, lives, and dies. The social sciences study islands of structure and stability within seas of historical change.

Different research methods, or different strategies of knowledge seeking, are appropriate for revealing different aspects of this unfolding world. Narrative and descriptive–interpretive methods are best suited for representing particular entities and processes over time, while scientific generalization-seeking methods are best suited for searching for order, regularity, structures, and underlying causal processes that hold across space and time. The very possibility of the social scientific enterprise being successful is dependent on the degrees of homogeneity, order, and transtemporal stability which are present in this unfolding historical process.

The success of each research strategy, the historical and the scientific, will depend on the kind of world we are living in. If the world is, in fact, highly structured, with stable and regular relationships among elements and entities, then, to that extent, the scientific program of searching for broad-ranging generalizations can be highly successful. (Perhaps one reason the physical sciences are more successful than the social sciences is that the physical world does have more of these characteristics than the social world.) On the other hand, to the extent that the social world is disorderly, emergent, and heterogeneous, with elements, structures, processes, and meanings changing over time in unpredictable ways, then the historians' knowledge-seeking strategies will be relatively more effective. There is, in short, a relationship between the underlying degrees and types of order in the world and the fruitfulness of different knowledge-seeking strategies.

The vision of an ordered, structured world can be called a Model I view of the world, and the vision of an emergent, disorderly, ever-changing universe as a Model II view of the world. What kind of world do we, in fact, live in? The answer to this is not immediately apparent, but can gradually emerge through the process of applying various knowledge-seeking strategies and examining their outcomes. My own reading of the evidence suggests that we live in a Mixed Model World, with some features of order, homogeneity, and temporal stability, and other features of a disorderly world, with great heterogeneity, temporal instability, changes in relationships, and the operation of random factors. If we do live in such a Mixed Model World, this suggests the utility of a combined social scientific and historical approach, with psychohistory as one such hybrid approach.

The prospects for effectively integrating scientific-psychological and historical modes of inquiry have improved somewhat in recent years. Traditionally, psychologists emphasized the search for generalizations, and historians concentrated on the description and interpretation of particular sequences of events, but there are signs that both disciplines are paying greater attention to a wider range of levels of generality.

Historians, particularly those interested in "scientific history," are showing greater interest in measurement, quantification, comparison, generalization, and the testing of explicit hypotheses (Fogel and Elton, 1983; Kousser, 1980; Tilly, 1978), while at least some psychologists are taking into account the historical context and the transhistorical generality of their theories. Over time, both historians and psychologists are coming to occupy a broader spectrum of positions on the continuum of levels of generality, historians working in from the particularistic end, and psychologists in from the generalizing end.

Among the indications that psychologists are paying greater attention to historical dimensions of psychological inquiry, six will be noted here: (1) the "social psychology as history" debate, discussed earlier, which focuses attention on the historically shifting patterns of social-psychological phenomena and on the possibly transformative effects of social inquiry itself; (2) work in life-span development and socialization, which demonstrates historical differences in the shape and pattern of life-span developmental processes for those born in different generations (Featherman and Lerner, 1985; McCluskey and Reese, 1984; Nesselroade and Baltes, 1974; Sørenson, Weinert, and Sherrod, 1986); (3)

the increasing involvement of psychologists with different aspects of narrative, such as narrative aspects of the self, of cognition and action, and of the life course (Bruner, 1986; Cohler, 1982; McAdams, 1985; Sarbin, 1986); (4) the repetition of sample surveys to study historical continuity and change in attitudes, behavior, and subjective well-being (Campbell, 1980; Veroff, Douvan, and Kulka, 1981); (5) evaluation research, with an increasing emphasis on qualitative, process-oriented, and historically oriented assessments of the effects of programs (Campbell, 1984; Cronbach, 1982; Light and Pillemer, 1984); and (6) empirical research on transhistorical regularities in factors influencing genius, creativity, and leadership (Simonton, 1984). Other areas might also be cited, such as studies of the historically influenced nature of forms of psychopathology such as hysteria or narcissism, research on changes in cognitive-developmental processes over time, and inquiry into changing patterns of personality and national character.

In spite of some trends toward greater convergence between history and psychology on the continuum of levels of generality, the different emphases, on theoretical generality in psychology and on understanding particular sequences of events in historiography, seem unlikely to disappear soon as one of the sources of tension between the two disciplines.

This section has argued that two significant dimensions affecting the relationships between history and psychology are an antibiographical impulse within historiography and antiparticularistic tendencies within psychology. Although both of these have understandable sources, when subject to critical evaluation, neither provides compelling reasons for not investigating the reciprocal causal relationships between the psychological processes of persons and changing social-historical circumstances. Although somewhat abstract, it is hoped that this discussion of background issues may be of use in analyzing the general relationships between history and psychology, and in thinking about specific issues emerging in the papers that follow.

Without further ado, I invite readers to plunge into the diverse viewpoints and examples discussed by the distinguished contributors to this volume. In spite of having attended the conference and heard versions of the papers read at that time, I was stimulated by, informed by, and occasionally provoked while reading the following chapters, and hope that readers will be as well.

References

Abraham, K. (1955). Giovanni Segantini: A psychoanalytic study. In *Clinical papers and essays*. New York: Basic Books. (Original work published 1911.)

Abraham, K. (1935). Amenhotep IV (Ikhnaton): A psychoanalytic contribution to the understanding of his personality and the monotheistic cult of Aton. *Psychoanalytic Quarterly, 4*, 537–549. (Original work published 1912.)

Africa, T. W. (1979). Psychohistory, ancient history, and Freud: The descent into Avernus. *Arethusa, 12*(1), 5–33.

Allport, G. W. (1962). The general and the unique in psychological science. *Journal of Personality, 30*, 405–422.

American Psychiatric Association, Report of the Task Force on Psychohistory. (1976). *The psychiatrist as psychohistorian.* Washington, D.C.: American Psychiatric Association.

Anderson, J. W. (1981a). The methodology of psychological biography. *Journal of Interdisciplinary History, 11*, 455–475.

Anderson, J. W. (1981b). Psychobiographical methodology: The case of William James. In L. Wheeler (Ed.), *Review of personality and social psychology* (Vol. 2). Beverly Hills, Calif.: Sage.

Bailyn, B. (1982). The challenge of modern historiography. *American Historical Review, 87*, 1–24.

Barnes, H. E. (1919). Psychology and history: Some reasons for predicting their more active cooperation in the future. *American Journal of Psychology, 30*, 337–376.

Barnes, H. E. (1925). *Psychology and history.* New York: Century.

Baron, S. H., and Pletsch, C. (Eds.). (1985). *Introspection in biography: The biographer's quest for self-awareness.* Hillsdale, N.J.: Analytic Press.

Barzun, J. (1974). *Clio and the doctors: Psycho-history, quanto-history and history.* Chicago: University of Chicago Press.

Bate, W. J. (1977). *Samuel Johnson.* New York: Harcourt Brace Jovanovich.

Bennett, J. (1981). *Oral history and delinquency: The rhetoric of criminology.* Chicago: University of Chicago Press.

Bizière, J. M. (1983). Psychohistory and histoire des mentalités. *Journal of Psychohistory, 11*(1), 89–109.

Bowen, C. D. (1969). *Biography: The craft and the calling.* Boston: Little, Brown.

Breisach, E. (1983). *Historiography: Ancient, medieval, and modern.* Chicago: University of Chicago Press.

Brenman-Gibson, M. (1981). *Clifford Odets, American playwright: The years from 1906 to 1940.* New York: Atheneum.

Brodie, F. (1981). *Richard Nixon: The shaping of his character.* New York: Norton.

Brugger, R. J. (Ed.). (1981). *Our selves/Our past: Psychological approaches to American history.* Baltimore: Johns Hopkins University Press.

Bruner, J. (1983). *In search of mind: Essays in autobiography.* New York: Harper & Row.

Bruner, J. (1986). *Actual minds, possible worlds.* Cambridge, Mass.: Harvard University Press.

Burguière, A. (1982). The fate of the history of mentalités in the Annales. *Comparative Studies in Society and History, 24,* 424–437.

Campbell, A. (1980). *Sense of well-being in America: Recent patterns and trends.* New York: McGraw-Hill.

Campbell, D. T. (1984). Can we be scientific in applied social science? In R. Conner et al. (Eds.), *Evaluation studies review annual* (Vol. 9), Beverly Hills, Calif.: Sage.

Carlyle, T. (1972). On heroes, hero-worship, and the heroic in history. Excerpts in F. Stern (Ed.), *The varieties of history* (2nd ed.). New York: Vintage Books. (Original Work Published 1840.)

Caro, R. (1974). *The power broker: Robert Moses and the fall of New York.* New York: Knopf.

Caro, R. (1982). *The years of Lyndon Johnson: The path to power.* New York: Vintage Books.

Chiari, J. (1975). *Twentieth-century French thought: From Bergson to Lévi-Strauss.* London: Elek.

Clifford, J. L. (Ed.). (1962). *Biography as an art.* New York: Oxford University Press.

Clifford, J. L. (1970). *From puzzles to portraits: Problems of a literary biographer.* Chapel Hill: University of North Carolina Press.

Cocks, G. (1979). The Hitler controversy. *Political Psychology, 1*(2), 67–81.

Cocks, G. (1986). Contributions of psychohistory to understanding politics. In M. Hermann (Ed.), *Political psychology.* San Francisco: Jossey-Bass.

Cocks, G., and Crosby, T. L. (Eds.). (1987). *Psycho/history: Readings in the method of psychology, psychoanalysis and history.* New Haven, Conn.: Yale University Press.

Cohler, B. J. (1982). Personal narrative and life course. In P. Baltes and O. Brim, Jr. (Eds.), *Life-span development and behavior* (Vol. 4). New York: Academic Press.

Coles, R. (1967). *Children of crisis: Vol 1. A study of courage and fear.* Boston: Atlantic–Little, Brown.

Crews, F. (1966). *The sins of the fathers: Hawthorne's psychological themes.* New York: Oxford University Press.

Cronbach, L. J. (1975). Beyond the two disciplines of scientific psychology. *American Psychologist, 30,* 116–127.

Cronbach, L. J. (1982). *Designing evaluations of educational and social programs.* San Francisco: Jossey-Bass.

Crosby, F. (1979). Evaluating psychohistorical explanations. *Psychohistory Review, 7*(4), 6–16.

Crosby, F., and Crosby, T. L. (1981). Psychobiography and psychohistory. In S. Long (Ed.), *Handbook of political behavior* (Vol. 1). New York: Plenum Press.

Darnton, R. (1980). Intellectual and cultural history. In M. Kammen (Ed.), *The past before us: Contemporary historical writing in the United States.* Ithaca, N.Y.: Cornell University Press.

Davies, A. F. (1980). *Skills, outlooks and passions: A psychoanalytic contribution to the study of politics.* Cambridge: Cambridge University Press.

deMause, L. (1982). *Foundations of psychohistory.* New York: Creative Roots.

deMause, L. (1984). *Reagan's America.* New York: Creative Roots.

deMause, L., and Ebel, H. (Eds.). (1977). *Jimmy Carter and American fantasy.* New York: Psychohistory Press.

Demos, J. (1970). *A little commonwealth: Family life in Plymouth Colony.* London: Oxford University Press.

Demos, J. (1982). *Entertaining Satan: Witchcraft and the culture of early New England.* New York: Oxford University Press.

Demos, J. (1986). *Past, present, and personal: The family and the life course in American history.* New York: Oxford University Press.

Dooley, L. (1916). Psychoanalytic studies of genius. *American Journal of Psychology, 27,* 363–416.

Edel, L. (1953–72). *Henry James* (5 vols.). Philadelphia: Lippincott.

Edel, L. (1984). *Writing lives: Principia biographica.* New York: Norton.

Edel, L. (1985). *Henry James: A Life* (rev. ed.). New York: Harper & Row.

Elder, G. H., Jr. (1974). *Children of the Great Depression.* Chicago: University of Chicago Press.

Elder, G. H., Jr., (Ed.). (1985). *Life course dynamics: Trajectories and transitions, 1968–1980.* Ithaca, N.Y.: Cornell University Press.

Elkins, S. (1959). *Slavery: A problem in American institutional and intellectual life.* Chicago: University of Chicago Press.

Elms, A. C. (1972). Allport, Freud and the clean little boy. *Psychoanalytic Review, 59,* 627–632.

Elms, A. C. (1976). *Personality in politics.* New York: Harcourt Brace Jovanovich.

Elms, A. C. (1980). Freud, Irma, Martha: Sex and marriage in the "Dream of Irma's injection." *Psychoanalytic Review, 67,* 83–109.

Elms, A. C. (1981). Skinner's dark year and Walden two. *American Psychologist, 36,* 470–479.

Elms, A. C. (1984). Psychology and political science. In M. Bornstein (Ed.), *Psychology and its allied disciplines: Vol. 2. The social sciences.* Hillsdale, N.J.: Erlbaum.

Engels, F. (1978). Letter to H. Starkenburg. In R. C. Tucker (Ed.), *The*

Marx–Engels Reader (2nd ed.). New York: Norton. (Original in 1894.)

Erikson, E. H. (1958). *Young man Luther: A study in psychoanalysis and history.* New York: Norton.

Erikson, E. H. (1969). *Gandhi's truth.* New York: Norton.

Erikson, E. H. (1975). *Life history and the historical moment.* New York: Norton.

Erikson, E. H. (1987). (Ed., S. Schlein). *A way of looking at things: Selected papers from 1930 to 1980.* New York: Norton.

Etheredge, L. S. (1978). *A world of men: The private sources of American foreign policy.* Cambridge, Mass.: MIT Press.

Fearing, F. (1927). Psychological studies of historical personalities. *Psychological Bulletin, 24,* 521–539.

Featherman, D. and Lerner, R. (1985). Ontogenesis and sociogenesis: Problematics for theory and research about development and socialization across the lifespan. *American Sociological Review, 50,* 659–676.

Febvre, L. (1976). History and psychology. In P. Burke (Ed.), *A new kind of history: From the writings of Lucien Febvre.* New York: Harper & Row. (Original work published 1938.)

Fogel, R. W., and Elton, G. R. (1983). *Which road to the past? Two views of history.* New Haven, Conn.: Yale University Press.

Fox, J. P. (1979). Adolf Hitler: The continuing debate. *International Affairs, 55*(2), 252–264.

Freud, S. (1957). *Leonardo da Vinci and a memory of his childhood.* In J. Strachey (Ed. and Trans.), *The standard edition of the complete psychological works of Sigmund Freud* (Vol. 11). London: Hogarth Press. (Original work published 1910.)

Freud, S. (1953). *Totem and taboo. Standard Edition,* Vol. 13. London: Hogarth Press. (Original work published 1912.)

Freud, S. (1955). *Group psychology and the analysis of the ego. Standard Edition,* Vol. 18. London: Hogarth Press. (Original work published 1921.)

Freud, S. (1961). *The future of an illusion. Standard Edition,* Vol. 21. London: Hogarth Press. (Original work published 1927.)

Freud, S. (1961). *Civilization and its discontents. Standard Edition,* Vol. 21. London: Hogarth Press. (Original work published 1930.)

Freud, S. (1964). *Moses and monotheism. Standard Edition,* Vol. 23. London: Hogarth Pres. (Original work published 1939.)

Freud, S., and Bullitt, W. C. (1967). *Thomas Woodrow Wilson: Twenty-eighth President of the United States. A psychological study.* Boston: Houghton Mifflin.

Friedländer, S. (1978). *History and psychoanalysis.* New York: Holmes and Meier.

Garraty, J. A. (1954). Preserved Smith, Ralph Volney Harlow, and psychology. *Journal of the History of Ideas, 15,* 456–465.

Garraty, J. A. (1957). *The nature of biography.* New York: Vintage Books.

Gatzke, H. W. (1973). Hitler and psychohistory. *American Historical Review, 78,* 394–401.

Gay, P. (1984). *The bourgeois experience: Victoria to Freud: Vol. 1. Education of the senses.* New York: Oxford University Press.

Gay, P. (1985). *Freud for historians.* New York: Oxford University Press.

Gedo, J. (1972). On the methodology of psychoanalytic biography. *Journal of the American Psychoanalytic Association, 20,* 638–649.

Gedo, J. (1983). *Portraits of the artist: Psychoanalysis of creativity and its vicissitudes.* New York: Guilford Press.

Geertz, C. (1983). *Local knowledge: Further essays in interpretive anthropology.* New York: Basic Books.

George, A. L., and George, J. L. (1964). *Woodrow Wilson and Colonel House: A personality study.* New York: Dover. (Original work published 1956.)

George, J. L. et al. (1984a). Issues in Wilson scholarship: References to early "strokes" in the papers of Woodrow Wilson. *Journal of American History, 70,* 845–853.

George, J. L. et al. (1984b). Communication. *Journal of American History, 70,* 945–956.

George, J. L. et al. (1984c). Letter to the Editor. *Journal of American History, 71,* 198–212.

Gergen, K. J. (1973). Social psychology as history. *Journal of Personality and Social Psychology, 26,* 309–320.

Gergen, K. J. (1982). *Toward transformation in social knowledge.* New York: Springer-Verlag.

Gilmore, W. J. (1984). *Psychohistorical inquiry: A comprehensive research bibliography.* New York: Garland.

Glad, B. (1973). Contributions of psychobiography. In J. Knutson (Ed.), *Handbook of political psychology.* San Francisco: Jossey-Bass.

Glad, B. (1980). *Jimmy Carter: In search of the great white house.* New York: Norton.

Graff, M. (1911). Richard Wagner in *The Flying Dutchman.* A contribution to the psychology of artistic creation (English translation), *Schriften zur angewandten Seelunkunde, 9,* 45 pages.

Greenstein, F. (1965). *Children and politics.* New Haven, Conn.: Yale University Press.

Greenstein, F. (1975). *Personality and politics: Problems of evidence, inference and conceptualization* (new ed.) New York: Norton.

Greven, P. J., Jr. (1970). *Four generations: Population, land, and family in colonial Andover, Massachusetts.* Ithaca, N.Y.: Cornell University Press.

Greven, P. J., Jr. (1977). *The Protestant temperament: Patterns of child-rearing, religious experience, and the self in early America.* New York: Meridian.

Hall, G. S. (1917). *Jesus, the Christ, in the light of psychology*. Garden City, N.Y.: Doubleday, Page.

Handlin, O. (1979). *Truth in history*. Cambridge, Mass.: Harvard University Press.

Hareven, T. K. (Ed.). (1978). *Transitions: The family and the life course in historical perspective*. New York: Academic Press.

Hareven, T. K. (1982). *Family time and industrial time*. Cambridge: Cambridge University Press.

Hareven, T. K., and Adams, K. J. (Eds.). (1982). *Aging and life course transitions: An interdisciplinary perspective*. New York: Guilford Press.

Helson, R. (1984–85). E. Nisbet's forty-first year. *Imagination, cognition, and personality, 4*, 53–68.

Higham, J. (1983). *History: Professional scholarship in America*. Baltimore: Johns Hopkins University Press.

Historical Figures Assessment Collaborative. (1977). Assessing historical figures: The use of observer-based personality descriptions. *Historical Methods Newsletters, 10*(2), 66–76.

Hoffman, L. E. (1982). Psychoanalytic interpretations of Adolf Hitler and Naziism, 1933–1945. A prelude to psychohistory. *Psychohistory Review, 11*(1), 68–87.

Hoffman, L. E. (1984). Psychoanalytic interpretations of political movements, 1900–1950. *Psychohistory Review, 13*(11), 16–29.

Hook, S. (1943). *The hero in history*. Boston: Beacon Press.

Huizinga, J. (1972). The idea of history. In F. Stern, (Ed.), *The varieties of history* (2nd ed.). New York: Vintage Books. (Original work published 1934.)

Janis, I. L. (1982). *Groupthink* (2nd ed.). Boston: Houghton Mifflin.

Jervis, R. (1976). *Perception and misperception in international politics*. Princeton, N.J.: Princeton University Press.

Johnson, R. A. et al. (Eds.). (1977). *Psychohistory and religion: The case of "Young man Luther."* Philadelphia: Fortress Press.

Jones, E. (1910). The Oedipus complex as an explanation of Hamlet's mystery: A study in motive. *American Journal of Psychology, 21*, 72–113.

Kammen, M. (Ed.). (1980). *The past before us: Contemporary historical writing in the United States*. Ithaca, N.Y.: Cornell University Press.

Keniston, K. (1965). *The uncommitted: Alienated youth in American society*. New York: Harcourt, Brace & World.

Keniston, K. (1968). *Young radicals: Notes on committed youth*. New York: Harcourt, Brace & World.

Kiell, N. (1982). *Psychoanalysis, psychology, and literature: A bibliography* (2nd ed.). Metuchen, N.J.: Scarecrow Press.

Knutson, J. (Ed.). (1973). *Handbook of political psychology*. San Francisco: Jossey-Bass.

Kousser, J. M. (1980). Quantitative social-scientific history. In M. Kammen (Ed.), *The past before us*. Ithaca, N.Y.: Cornell University Press.

Kren, G. (1977). Psychohistory in the university. *Journal of Psychohistory, 4*(3), 337–350.

Kren, G., and Rappoport, L. (Eds.). (1976). *Varieties of psychohistory*. New York: Springer.

Kren, G., and Rappoport, L. H. (1980). *The Holocaust and the crisis of human behavior*. New York: Holmes and Meier.

Lane, R. (1972). *Political man*. New York: Free Press.

Langer, W. C. (1972). *The mind of Adolf Hitler: The secret wartime report*. New York: Basic Books.

Langness, L. L., and Frank, G. (1981). *Lives: An anthropological approach to biography*. Novato, Calif.: Chandler & Sharp.

Lasswell, H. (1930). *Psychopathology and politics*. Chicago: University of Chicago Press.

Lasswell, H. (1948). *Power and personality*. New York: Norton.

Latané, B., and Darley, J. (1970). *The unresponsive bystander: Why doesn't he help?* New York: Appleton-Century-Crofts.

Lawton, H. W. (1978). Psychohistory today and tomorrow. *Journal of Psychohistory, 5*, 325–356.

Lefebvre, G. (1982). *The great fear of 1789*. Princeton, N.J.: Princeton University Press. (Original work published 1932.)

Levinson, D. J. (1981). Exploration in biography: Evolution of the individual life structure in adulthood. In A. Rabin et al. (Eds.), *Further explorations in personality*. New York: Wiley.

Levy, L. (1970). *Conceptions of personality*. New York: Random House.

Lifton, R. J. (1967). *Death in life: Survivors of Hiroshima*. New York: Random House.

Lifton, R. J. (1973), *Home from the war: Vietnam veterans—neither victims nor executioners*. New York: Simon and Schuster.

Lifton, R. J. (1986). *The Nazi doctors: Medical killing and the psychology of genocide*. New York: Basic Books.

Lifton, R. J., with Olson, E. (Eds.). (1974). *Explorations in psychohistory*. New York: Simon and Schuster.

Lifton, R. J., with Strozier, C. B. (1984). Psychology and history. In M. Bornstein (Ed.), *Psychology and its allied disciplines: Vol 2. The social sciences*. Hillsdale, N.J.: Erlbaum.

Light, R. J., and Pillemer, D. B. (1984). *Summing up: The science of reviewing research*. Cambridge, Mass.: Harvard University Press.

Loewenberg, P. (1971). The psychohistorical origins of the Nazi youth cohort. *American Historical Review, 76*, 1457–1502.

Loewenberg, P. (1975). Psychohistorical perspectives on modern German history. *Journal of Modern History, 47*, 229–279.

Loewenberg, P. (1980). Psychohistory. In M. Kammen (Ed.), *The past before us: Contemporary historical writing in the United States.* Ithaca, N.Y.: Cornell University Press.

Loewenberg, P. (1983). *Decoding the past: The psychohistorical approach.* New York: Knopf.

Mack, J. E. (1971). Psychoanalysis and historical biography. *Journal of the American Psychoanalytic Association, 19,* 143–179.

Mack, J. E. (1976). *A prince of our disorder: The life of T. E. Lawrence.* Boston: Little, Brown.

Manis, M. et al. (1976). Social psychology and history: A symposium. *Personality and Social Psychology Bulletin, 2,* 371–444.

Manuel, F. E. (1972). The use and abuse of psychology in history. In F. Gilbert and S. Graubard (Eds.), *Historical studies today.* New York: Norton.

Marvick, E. W. (1983). *The young Richelieu: A psychoanalytic approach to leadership.* Chicago: University of Chicago Press.

Marvick, E. W. (1985). The "Annales" and the unconscious: Continuity and contrast within an historical school. *Psychohistory Review, 13*(2–3), 42–52.

Marwick, A. (1981). *The nature of history* (2nd ed.). London: Macmillan.

Marx, K. (1978). Theses on Feuerbach. In R. C. Tucker (Ed.), *The Marx–Engels reader* (2nd ed.). New York: Norton. (Original work published 1845.)

Marx, K. (1978). The grundrisse. In R. C. Tucker (Ed.), *The Marx–Engels reader* (2nd ed.). New York: Norton. (Original work published 1857–58.)

Mazlish, B. (Ed.). (1963; revised 1971). *Psychoanalysis and history.* New York: Grosset and Dunlap.

Mazlish, B. (1966, July 28). Inside the whales. *Times Literary Supplement,* pp. 667–669.

Mazlish, B. (1972/1973). *In search of Nixon: A psychohistorical inquiry.* Baltimore: Penguin Books.

Mazlish, B. (1975). *James and John Stuart Mill: Father and son in the nineteenth century.* New York: Basic Books.

Mazlish, B. (1977). Reflections on the state of psychohistory. *Psychohistory Review, 5*(4), 3–11.

McAdams, D. P. (1985). *Power, intimacy, and the life story: Personological inquiries into identity.* Homewood, Ill.: Dorsey Press.

McClelland, D. C. (1961). *The achieving society.* Princeton, N.J.: Van Nostrand.

McClelland, D. C. (1975). *Power: The inner experience.* New York: Irvington.

McCluskey, K. A., and Reese, H. W. (Eds.). (1984). *Life-span developmental psychology: Historical and generational effects.* New York: Academic Press.

Mendelsohn, G. A. (1978–79). Verdi the man and Verdi the dramatist. *19th Century Music, 2,* 110–142, 214–230.

Mendelsohn, G. A. (1985). *La Dame aux Camelias* and *La Traviata:* A study of dramatic transformations in the light of biography. In R. Hogan and W. Jones (Eds.), *Perspectives in personailty* (Vol. 1). Greenwich, Conn.: JAI Press.

Moraitis, G., and Pollock, G. H. (Eds.). (1987). *Psychoanalytic studies of biography.* New York: International Universities Press.

Namier, L. (1957). *The structure of politics at the accession of George III* (2nd ed.). New York: St. Martin's Press.

Nesselroade, J. R., and Baltes, P. B. (1974). Adolescent personality development and historical change: 1970–1972. *Monographs of the Society for Research in Child Development, 39* (1, Serial No. 154).

Pachter, M. (Ed.). (1979). *Telling lives: The biographer's art.* Washington, D.C.: New Republic Books.

Plummer, K. (1983). *Documents of life.* London: Allen & Unwin.

Pomper, P. (1985). *The structure of mind in history: Five major figures in psychohistory.* New York: Columbia University Press.

Post, J. et al. (1983). Woodrow Wilson re-examined: The mind–body controversy redux and other disputations. *Political Psychology, 4*(2), 289–332.

Prince, M. (1912, March 24). [Theodore] Roosevelt as analyzed by the new psychology. *New York Times,* pp. 1–2.

Prince, M. (1915). *The psychology of the Kaiser: A study of his sentiments and his obsession.* Boston: Badger.

Rabb, T. K., and Rotberg, R. I. (Eds.). (1971). *The family in history: Interdisciplinary essays.* New York: Harper.

Ratcliffe, B. M. (1980). The decline of biography in French historiography: The ambivalent legacy of the "Annales" tradition. *Proceedings of the Annual Meeting of the Western Society for French History, 8,* 556–567.

Renshon, S. A. (1974). *Psychological needs and political behavior.* New York: Free Press.

Robinson, J. H. (1912). *The new history.* New York: Macmillan.

Rogow, A. A. (1963). *James Forrestal: A study of personality, politics, and policy.* New York: Macmillan.

Romano, S. (1982). Biographie et historiographie. *Revue d'Histoire Diplomatique, 96,* 43–56.

Röhl, J. C. G., and Sombart, N. (Eds.). (1982). *Kaiser Wilhelm II: New interpretations.* Cambridge: Cambridge University Press.

Ross, D. (1974). The "new history" and the "new psychology": An early attempt at psychohistory. In S. Elkins and E. McKitrick (Eds.), *The Hofstadter aegis: A memorial.* New York: Knopf.

Runyan, W. M. (1981). Why did Van Gogh cut off his ear? The problem of alternative explanations in psychobiography. *Journal of Personality and Social Psychology, 40,* 1070–1077.

Runyan, W. M. (1982a). *Life histories and psychobiography: Explorations in theory and method.* New York: Oxford University Press.

Runyan, W. M. (1982b). The psychobiography debate: An analytical review. In L. Wheeler (Ed.), *Review of personality and social psychology* (Vol. 3). Beverly Hills, Calif.: Sage.

Runyan, W. M. (1983). Idiographic goals and methods in the study of lives. *Journal of Personality, 51,* 413–437.

Runyan, W. M. (1986). Life histories in anthropology: Another view. *American Anthropologist, 88*(1), 181–183.

Runyan, W. M. (1987). The growth of literature in psychohistory: A quantitative analysis. *Psychohistory Review, 15*(3), 121–135.

Runyan, W. M. (1988). Progress in psychobiography. *Journal of Personality, 56*(1), 293–324.

Sanford, N. (1980). *Learning after college.* Orinda, Calif.: Montaigne.

Sarbin, T. R. (Ed.). (1986). *Narrative psychology: The storied nature of human conduct.* New York: Praeger.

Schlenker, B. R. (1974). Social psychology and science. *Journal of Personality and Social Psychology, 29,* 1–15.

Schlesinger, A. M., Jr. (1986). *The cycles of American history.* Boston: Houghton Mifflin.

Sève, L. (1978). *Man in Marxist theory and the psychology of personality.* Atlantic Highlands, N.J.: Humanities Press.

Shils, E. (1972). Tradition, ecology, and institution in the history of sociology. In G. Holton (Ed.), *The twentieth-century sciences.* New York: Norton.

Simonton, D. K. (1984). *Genius, creativity, and leadership: Historiometric inquiries.* Cambridge, Mass.: Harvard University Press.

Sørenson, A., Weinert, F. and Sherrod, L. (Eds.). (1986). *Human development and the life course: Multidisciplinary perspectives.* Hillsdale, N.J.: Erlbaum.

Stannard, D. E. (1980). *Shrinking history: On Freud and the failure of psychohistory.* New York: Oxford University Press.

Stern, F. (Ed.). (1972). *The varieties of history* (2nd ed.). New York: Vintage Books.

Stolorow, R. D., and Atwood, G. E. (1979). *Faces in a cloud: Subjectivity in personality theory.* New York: Aronson.

Stone, L. (1981). *The past and the present.* Boston: Routledge & Kegan Paul.

Strouse, J. (1980). *Alice James: A biography.* New York: Bantam Books.

Strout, C. (1981). *The veracious imagination: Essays on American history, literature and biography.* Middleton, Conn.: Wesleyan University Press.

Strozier, C. B. (1982). *Lincoln's quest for union: Public and private meanings.* New York: Basic Books.

Strozier, C. B. (1986). Autobiographical reflections on *The Psychohistory Review*. *Psychohistory Review, 15*(1), 1–14.

Strozier, C. B., and Offer, D. (Eds.). (1985). *The leader: Psychohistorical essays*. New York: Plenum Press.

Tetlock, P. E., Crosby, F., and Crosby, T. (1981). Political psychobiography. *Micropolitics, 1,* 191–213.

Tilly, C. (1978). *From mobilization to revolution*. Reading, Mass.: Addison-Wesley.

Tomkins, S. S. (1965). The psychology of commitment. Part I. The constructive role of violence and suffering for the individual and for his society. In S. S. Tomkins and C. Izard (Eds.), *Affect, cognition and personality*. New York: Springer.

Tucker, R. (1973). *Stalin as revolutionary, 1879–1929: A study in history and personality*. New York: Norton.

Veroff, J., Douvan, E. and Kulka, R. (1981). *The inner American: A self-portrait from 1957 to 1976*. New York: Basic Books.

Vokan, V. and Itzkowitz, N. (1984). *The immortal Ataturk: A psychobiography*. Chicago: University of Chicago Press.

Waite, R. G. L. (1977). *The psychopathic god: Adolf Hitler*. New York: Basic Books.

Wallerstein, R. S., and Smelser, N. J. (1969). Psychoanalysis and sociology: Articulations and applications. *International Journal of Psycho-Analysis, 50*(4), 693–710.

Weinberg, S. (1984). *The first three minutes: A modern view of the origin of the universe*. New York: Bantam Books.

Weinstein, E., Anderson, J., and Link, A. (1978). Woodrow Wilson's political personality: A reappraisal. *Political Science Quarterly, 93,* 585–598.

Weinstein, F. (1980). *The dynamics of Nazism: Leadership, ideology, and the Holocaust*. New York: Academic Press.

Weinstein, F., and Platt, G. M. (1973). *Psychoanalytic sociology*. Baltimore: Johns Hopkins University Press.

White, R. W. (1972). *The enterprise of living*. New York: Holt, Rinehart and Winston.

White, R. W. (1975). *Lives in progress* (3rd ed.). New York: Holt, Rinehart and Winston.

White, R. W. (1981). Exploring personality the long way: The study of lives. In A. Rabin, J. Aronoff, A. Barclay, and R. Zucker (Eds.), *Further explorations in personality*. New York: Wiley.

Windelband, W. (1904). *Geschichte und Naturwissenschaft* (3rd ed.). Strasbourg: Heitz.

I

Case Studies in Biography and Psychology

2

A Stalin Biographer's Memoir

Robert C. Tucker

The old maxim *cherchez la femme* can do duty in this case, where the question is why someone who never intended to be a biographer became one, although reluctantly and after long delay. The *femme* was the revisionist of psychoanalytic thought, Karen Horney, with whose writings I became acquainted around 1940.

When her last and synthesizing book, *Neurosis and Human Growth,* was published in 1950, I was serving in the American embassy in Moscow.[1] Having procured a copy from Brentano's via the diplomatic pouch, I read it repeatedly. Despite its lucidity of expression, it is not an easy work to comprehend thoroughly and to use, yet it deeply influenced my thinking.

Horney's subject was the "neurotic character structure." To summarize the core of her argument: a person who experiences "basic anxiety" resulting from adverse emotional circumstances in early life may seek and find a rock of inner security by forming an idealized image of himself or herself. The content of the self-image will depend on the direction the child takes in relations with others—moving against, toward, or away from them. One whose tendency is to move against others may idealize himself as a great warrior, while one whose tendency is to move toward others may imagine himself to be saintlike. Gradually and unconsciously, if the anxiety-causing conditions do not change, the child moves from self-idealizing to the adoption of the idealized image as an *idealized self,* the imagined real identity. Then the energies avail-

This paper from the Stanford conference has also been published in slightly different form in S. Baron and C. Pletsch, eds., *Introspection in Biography: The Biographer's Quest for Self-Awareness* (Hillsdale, N.J.: Analytic Press, 1985).

1. Karen Horney, *Neurosis and Human Growth* (New York: Norton, 1950).

able for growth toward self-realization are invested in the quest to prove the idealized self in action. Horney calls this the "search for glory."

Because the idealized self is free of the faults, blemishes, and limitations that go with being human, it cannot be actualized. Hence, the individual begins to feel estranged from and to accuse, hate, and condemn the fallible, merely human, "empirical self" he is in practice. The drive to enact the idealized self, however, is compulsive, with painful anxiety and self-condemnation as the price of failure. Consequently, the inwardly conflicted individual develops a system of unconscious defenses against the experience of failure. These include repression of the disparity between the idealized and empirical selves, various forms of rationalization, the search for affirmation of the idealized self by significant others, and the projection onto still others—who can realistically be condemned and combated—of both the repressed faults and the self-hatred they arouse. Repressed self-hatred is then experienced as hatred of others. The particular others onto whom the self-hatred is projected are likely to be those who have incurred the neurotic person's animosity by failing somehow to affirm him as the idealized self he takes himself to be. A "need for vindictive triumph" is therefore a regular ingredient, according to Horney, of the search for glory, especially in those whose tendency is to move against others in a drive toward mastery.

When I was reading and rereading this book, my work consisted of directing a translation bureau operated cooperatively by the British, American, and Canadian embassies. It produced a daily bulletin of translations into English of articles I selected from eight Soviet daily papers, as well as from periodicals ranging from the Central Committee monthly *Kommunist* to journals on history, law, philosophy, and the arts. Because my Russian wife, whom I had married in 1946, was not given an exit visa to accompany me back to the United States, I was, so to speak, serving an indefinite sentence in Moscow.

The cold war, raging fiercely at the time, received ample domestic as well as foreign coverage in the Soviet press. Thus, a play running in Moscow theaters, called *The Mad Haberdasher,* featured a thinly disguised villain who was a Hitler-like, younger Harry Truman. The highly favorable press reviews of it were vintage cold-war material. But if hatred for enemies was one pervasive press theme, love was another, love of Soviet citizens and all people of good will abroad for the Soviet regime as personified by Joseph Stalin. What would one day be called the "cult of personality," with Stalin as the centerpiece, was at its zenith. Unlike George Orwell's Big Brother, Stalin really existed. But he was a recluse and hardly ever appeared in public, save for the parades in

Red Square on May Day and November 7. Still, a heroic portrait of him, usually in generalissimo's uniform, appeared almost daily on the papers' front pages, and in myriad other ways Stalin symbolically figured in Soviet public life as an object of reverence.

Two years earlier, in 1949, the cult of Stalin had reached a climax when the celebration of his seventieth birthday resulted in what can only be described as his virtual deification. Although the birthday fell on December 21, the press and radio prepared for it long in advance with a mass of material on Stalin's greatness as a revolutionary and as a Russian Soviet statesman of world-historic stature. Plays were staged, for example, about heroic episodes out of his early life as a revolutionary in Georgia. Reports filled the press on presents coming in from all over Russia and distant countries, and afterward a special "Museum of Presents to J. V. Stalin" was created to display these gifts to the public. On the birthday itself the Politburo members and others contributed laudatory articles, and there was an evening meeting in the Bolshoi Theater to mark the occasion. To keep the momentum going, every day for over a year, *Pravda* carried, under the headline "The Stream of Greetings," long lists in fine print of the names of organizations that had sent birthday congratulations to Comrade Stalin.

One Saturday afternoon in 1951 I had been browsing in the Academy of Sciences bookstore and was walking down Gorky Street toward the U.S. embassy on Mokhovaia. In full view below was the Red Square and, off to its right, the Kremlin. It may have crossed my mind that Stalin was at work there. Suddenly I had what struck me as a momentous thought in the form of a question: What if the idealized image of Stalin, appearing day after day in the party-controlled, party-supervised Soviet press, were *an idealized self in Horney's sense?* If so, Stalin must be a neurotic personality along the lines portrayed in her book, except that he possessed a plenitude of political power unprecedented in history. In that case, the Stalin cult must reflect Stalin's own monstrously inflated vision of himself as the greatest genius of Russian and world history. The cult must be an institutionalization of his neurotic character structure. So the Kremlin recluse, this ruler who was publicly so reticent about himself, must be spilling out his innermost thoughts concerning himself in millions of newspapers and journals published throughout Russia. He must be the most self-revealed disturbed person of all time. Finding out what was most important about him would not require getting him onto a couch; one could do it by reading *Pravda,* while rereading Horney! I began to do just that, and in the process grew more and more convinced of my hypothesis.

At that time, the members of the small colony of Westerners living in Moscow attached no serious importance to the adulatory publicity surrounding Stalin. Everyone knew that a Stalin cult existed and accounted for a large share of the material in the Soviet press. Everyone assumed that this press was regime-managed, regime-censored, and regime-controlled, down to the minutiae that were pondered for potential insight into Soviet policy. But these two facts were not seen as meaningfully related, partly because the regime was not understood to be a personal one. Statesmen who negotiated in Moscow, such as General George Marshall in 1947 and others (although they were very few), sensed that Stalin's was the final word on foreign political issues. But that in itself could be and was interpreted as signifying that he was the ultimate spokesman of a Politburo consensus, and not necessarily a controlling figure in creating the consensus. To illustrate: in an autobiographical account of his ambassadorship between 1946 and 1949, *My Three Years in Moscow,* General Walter Bedell Smith expressed the opinion that Stalin should be seen as a chairman of the Politburo board; and in taking this view, he was certainly relying on advice from embassy officers and Russian specialists in the U.S. government.[2] The received view was reflected in, and perhaps influenced by, a small book published in 1949, *The Operational Code of the Politburo.* Its author, Nathan Leites of the RAND Corporation's Social Science Division in Washington, interpreted the decisions then being made in Moscow as decisions of a group, the Politburo, which was guided by an operational code implicit in Bolshevism as a body of thought.[3] The book gave no inkling that Stalin rather than "the Politburo" might be making the key decisions. I heard later that Admiral Joy, the negotiator for the U.N. side in the long, drawn-out talks with the North Koreans in Panmunjom for an armistice in the Korean War—negotiations that were not successfully concluded so long as Stalin lived—used to take *The Operational Code* with him on his helicopter trips to the conference site.

What, you may be asking yourself, did we foreigners in Moscow suppose was Stalin's attitude toward his cult? I believe the general view was that he simply *tolerated* it as a pragmatic political device for providing a father symbol ("father and teacher of the peoples" was a phrase regularly applied to him in cult articles) for a population that historically personalized authoritarian rule in a *tsar-batiushka* (father-tsar). Very likely, one reason why knowledgeable observers understood the matter

2. Walter Bedell Smith, *My Three Years in Moscow* (Philadelphia: Lippincott, 1949).

3. Nathan Leites, *The Operational Code of the Politburo* (New York: McGraw-Hill, 1949).

in this way was that Stalin himself had given the cue for it in an interview with the German writer Lion Feuchtwanger, who duly recorded the comment in his *Moscow 1937*.[4] It appeared from Feuchtwanger's account that an indifferent and even somewhat bemused Stalin felt he had to make a concession to his backward people's persisting need for a ruler cult as a personalization of Russia's present regime. Some foreigners living in Moscow in the 1940s and early 1950s had read *Moscow 1937*. Much later, Edgar Snow, standing beside Mao Zedong on the reviewing stand in Peking when the Mao cult was close to its orgiastic climax, asked the chairman a question like Feuchtwanger's, and received an answer not very different from Stalin's. What do journalists who ask such questions of rulers surrounded by personality cults expect them to answer? If such a man supported the cult because he craved it, as well as for reasons of *realpolitik,* would he—could he—say: Because I like being adored?

Not surprisingly, my novel hypothesis found little favor with the few acquaintances in the Anglo-American colony in Moscow to whom I confided it. They dismissed it as improbable, or they pooh-poohed it with comments like: "Stalin doesn't give a hoot for the cult, he simply countenances it as a useful propaganda tool in Soviet domestic affairs." After a few such exchanges, I gave up propagating my idea—but I didn't give up the idea.

In the summer of 1952 I flew home for a short leave. While in the United States, I was asked by the State Department to consult with Russian specialists at the Voice of America, which then had headquarters in New York. Two episodes stand out in my memory of the two days spent in New York. One was a remark by Bertram D. Wolfe, who was then becoming famous as the author of *Three Who Made a Revolution,*[5] while also serving as a part-time consultant with the Voice of America. After a morning of discussions with the Russian section's staff, he and I stopped in the washroom on the way to a lunch that had been arranged. There he told me the following story. An unknown man had contacted the State Department and suggested that much of Russia's enigmatic behavior in the cold war might become explicable if one took account of the possibility that Stalin was paranoid. "The department didn't know how to get rid of him and sent him to me," Wolfe said with a wry smile, "and I got rid of him." Not knowing much about paranoia but realizing that the unknown man and I were on the same general

4. Lion Feuchtwanger, *Moscow 1937* (New York: Viking, 1937).
5. Bertram D. Wolfe, *Three Who Made a Revolution* (Boston: Beacon, 1948).

intellectual wavelength, I felt leaden inside. From the point of view of people like Wolfe, not to mention the Department of State, the unidentified person and I were both crackpots.

The other memory is of a conversation with an academic who, by arrangement with the State Department, came for an interview in my New York hotel room. He introduced himself as Walt Rostow of the Center of International Studies at the Massachusetts Institute of Technology, and explained that he was in charge of a collaborative project about the Soviet system. On the advice of the State Department Russian specialist Charles Bohlen (whom I knew and much respected), the group was proceeding on the premise that the Soviet system's behavior could be explained in terms of the regime's drive to preserve, consolidate, and increase its power. What did I think of that? I don't recall exactly what I said to Professor Rostow, only that I was unenthusiastic about his approach. The Rostow study was subsquently published as *The Dynamics of Soviet Society*.[6] However widely read it was in its time, today it is one of the forgotten works in the field.

The conversation with Rostow proved useful, nevertheless, in that it set me thinking more in "system" terms than before. I began to see possible ramifications of my hypothesis. Books were being published in those days about totalitarianism—among them, Hannah Arendt's *The Origins of Totalitarianism*.[7] On returning to Moscow, I began to study this literature. Interesting though much of it was, I found it deeply flawed because the dictator and his psychodynamics were missing from the picture of totalitarianism. Arendt, for example, thought that totalitarian regimes were actuated in their total terror by an "ideological supersense," one not located, so far as her reader could tell, in anyone's individual psyche. Perhaps, I thought, the dictatorial ruler of a totalitarian state could politically institutionalize the inner defenses of his ever-threatened idealized self. If all-powerful, he could then mobilize a vast apparatus of repression to visit revenge not only on individuals whom he had come to perceive as enemies but on entire social groups so perceived. Thus the Holocaust might have been Adolf Hitler's enactment of vindictive hostility stemming from neurotically generated self-hatred projected onto the Jews as a group. This would not absolve those who carried out his lethal orders of responsibility for their actions, but it could help explain some "system" behavior that the theoreticians

6. Walt Rostow, *The Dynamics of Soviet Society* (New York: New American Library, 1954).

7. Hannah Arendt, *The Origins of Totalitarianism* (New York: Harcourt Brace, 1951).

failed to explain convincingly to me. In 1965, I finally set forth this reasoning in an article, "The Dictator and Totalitarianism."[8]

To return to Moscow in late 1952 and the fear-filled early months of 1953: the Soviet press was then printing ominous stories about Jewish "doctor-murderers," who allegedly had conspired with the Anglo-American intelligence services and the American-Jewish Joint Distribution Committee to shorten the lives of Soviet leaders. For my part, I was coming to the conclusion that if Stalin, then in his seventies, were to die, major changes might occur rather suddenly in the Soviet regime's conduct. If the regime were acting out a neurotic personality's political needs, it might no longer be compelled to do so once he was dead. Theoretically, another individual of like character could assume dictatorial power and pursue the same sort of politics. But it was unlikely that a highly neurotic Stalin would tolerate the presence of an individual of his own psychological makeup in his entourage; rather, he would surround himself with steady, pliable, nonthreatening types, unafflicted by compulsions like his own. If Stalin were to die, maybe the regime would call off the terroristic new purge apparently in the making, with preparations for the trial of the "doctor-murderers." Then, in other ways, the Soviet government might stop acting against its own interests (Karen Horney had observed that every neurotic tends to act in ways contrary to his own best interests). For example, early in 1953 the Soviet government was pressuring the American and British governments to move their embassies some distance from their longstanding locations on either side of the Kremlin. Why was this happening? Might Stalin, neurotically enraged against the Anglo-Americans, want the embassies moved out of sight of his Kremlin workplace, whence their flags could be seen flying on special occasions like the Fourth of July?

Such deductions from my psychological hypothesis were very relevant to me personally, because of the denial of an exit visa to my wife. It had never been easy for foreign governments to secure permission for Soviet wives of their nationals to leave Russia. Yet, however grudgingly, a handful of visas were usually issued about once a year. The last time that had happened was early in 1946, shortly before our marriage. Then, in 1947, the official legal gazette published a governmental decree announcing laconically: "To prohibit marriages between Soviet citizens and foreigners." Ever since, Soviet citizens already married before the decree's passage were denied exit visas, even though the antimarriage

8. Robert C. Tucker, "The Dictator and Totalitarianism," *World Politics* 17, no. 4 (July 1965): 555–83.

law was not explicitly retroactive. Numerous high-placed foreigners had interceded with the Soviet government on behalf of the few women married to foreign nationals, but to no avail. At that time, there were six Americans in Moscow with Russian wives (two embassy employees and four press correspondents). When a foreign ambassador took up the matter with Foreign Minister Andrei Vyshinsky, the latter would get red in the face and declare that his government considered it a closed question. Clearly, it was contrary to Soviet government's best interests to allow such a trivial matter to fester in relations with our own and other foreign governments. Why was this happening?

A Horneyan explanation occurred to me. If the public cult of Stalin was an institutionalization of a neurotically idealized self, then given that he was ruler of the Soviet Union, the idealizing must extend to his realm as well. Logically, then, any criticism of the Soviet state over which the idealized Stalin presided, would, by implication, demean him, the all-wise, beneficent genius-leader that he took himself to be. The Soviet press daily provided an image of the Soviet realm that fit with this interpretation: it idealized life in Stalin's Russia, except insofar as enemies tried to harm the state and society. What, then, would have been the aging, neurotic Stalin's response to a statement in, say, 1947 that the foreign ministry was prepared to issue exit visas to some Soviet women married to foreigners? He would have reasoned that the women's willingness to leave Soviet Russia to live abroad was an implicit derogation of his, Stalin's, state. This would have made him furiously reject the proposed issuance of visas and add: "There must be a law against these marriages!" If that was how the matter stood, then Stalin's death might open the way for our departure. One night when my wife and I went out for a walk, I explained this line of thought and predicted: "If Stalin dies, I bet they'll let you go." Discouragingly, she replied: "Georgians are long-lived, he'll probably outlive you and me."

On March 3, 1953, I arrived at my office at the normal time. The Soviet newspapers were late that morning—usually a sign of an especially important item of news coming up. I thought it would be an announcement that the trial of the "doctor-murderers" had begun. Just then I met one of our American typists. Ashen-faced, she reported that she and her husband had heard on Moscow radio that something was the matter with Stalin. A few minutes later the papers came. A front-page announcement said, "Comrade Stalin is gravely ill" and gave details about the stroke he had suffered. This meant that Stalin was dead or as good as dead. The thought crossed my mind that some person or persons high in the regime who felt threatened might have acted to shorten Stalin's life to prevent the trial from starting and the purge from taking place.

But what I mainly want to record is that never in my life, before or since, have I experienced such intense elation as I did at that moment. It was compounded of joy that one of history's awful evil-doers was meeting his end, hope that this might mean early release for my wife and me from a stay in Russia that had now lengthened into nearly nine years, and excitement that my hypothesis was going to be tested. Would Russia after Stalin change in the ways that I anticipated? The answer was not long in coming, and it was affirmative.

For about two weeks, Russia's public life focused on the ceremonial send-off. There was a final burst of the Stalin cult in the press tributes. He was praised in three funeral speeches that were broadcast over the radio, but it was notable that only V. M. Molotov sounded broken-hearted. Georgi Malenkov came across calm and collected, and L. P. Beria was briskly upbeat. Once the leave-taking ended, a deep change came over Soviet public life. The terror-tinged atmosphere of the first months of the year evaporated like mist in the morning sun. The threatened purge never took place. The Ministry of Internal Affairs, now again under Beria, issued a sensational public statement in mid-April denouncing the doctors' affair as a frame-up (it did not say by whom). Beria also revealed that "inadmissible methods," meaning torture, were used to extract from the hapless doctor-victims confessions of guilt for nonexistent crimes, and not all of them had survived the ordeal. In conclusion, the statement assured Soviet citizens that now they could live and work in security. This was a thinly veiled reference to the general insecurity of only two months ago, and it took no Kremlinological expertise for politically literate citizens to grasp the implicit indictment of Stalin. By then his name already was hardly to be seen in the Soviet press; the Stalin cult was a thing of the past. Spring 1953 in Moscow reminded me of Spring 1945, when victory, peace, and hope for the future came to Russia all at once. Ilya Ehrenburg captured the spirit of that time in the title of his novel *The Thaw*.[9]

The change was felt no less quickly in foreign relations. The American and British embassies were informed that they would not need to move to new locations. Steps began to be taken toward winding up the cold war, notably by reviving talks that soon led to an armistice in Korea on terms that the Communist side had stubbornly rejected so long as Stalin lived. In May, when Charles Bohlen arrived in Moscow to take

9. Ilya Ehrenburg, *The Thaw* (Moscow, 1954).

up the post of ambassador, he decided to raise the question of the Russian wives of Americans to test the new atmosphere. Molotov now headed the Foreign Ministry. Instead of angrily refusing to consider the question when Bohlen raised it, he calmly said that he would look into it. Three weeks later, visas that had been denied for seven years were granted, and before the end of June my wife and I were on our way west. Later in 1953, the antimarriage law of 1947 was repealed in a governmental decree as laconic as the earlier one.

Back in the United States after an interim assignment to Paris, I held a job with the Social Science Division of the RAND Corporation while working at night to complete an interrupted doctoral dissertation on Karl Marx and German philosophy. RAND wanted me to write interpretive studies of Soviet internal and external policy after Stalin. In order to clarify what was new in Soviet policy after Stalin, I had to go into Stalin's influence on earlier policies, and this inevitably led me into psychological analysis. The Social Sciences Division under Hans Speier was generally supportive as long as I devoted primary attention to developments *after* Stalin, and I wrote a few studies, subsequently published in scholarly journals, which touched on my psychological interpretation in the course of seeking to explain post-Stalin policies. But my thesis that a really profound change had occurred with Stalin's death *because* of the psychological factor at work while he lived met with resistance. I was advised not to focus on history. Besides, what had really changed? Of course, there was the armistice in Korea and, in 1955, the Austrian peace treaty that Stalin had withheld, and some other smaller steps. But might not all this be explained by pressures on the Soviet regime? Or, might it not be simply "tactical," the politics of a younger, more "flexible" Soviet political leadership? Might not the new Soviet politics for that reason be more dangerous to the West than Stalin's implacable cold-war policies?

I was now experiencing the problem of historical evidence, the circumstance that whatever happens in history is subject to differing interpretations depending on one's assumptions. From my psychological point of view, a small political act like the release of the wives was highly significant, apart from the meaning it had for the few persons immediately affected. Like little changes in a person, it manifested change in the character of the actor—in this case the Soviet regime. Minds trained in the political and social sciences didn't seem to see it that way. They were inclined to reason that small changes in the regime's behavior had best be thought of as having small causes, whereas large changes would stem from large causes. I disagreed, but not persuasively, except to a few friends who found my reasoning plausible, albeit undemonstrable. Without knowing it, I was on my way to becoming a historian of the Stalin era. However, the idea of writing a biography was still remote from my mind. I simply wanted to produce a study of a totalitarian dictatorship that would disclose the personality of the dictator as a motor force of the regime's politics.

Another major problem of evidence confronted me: How could I demonstrate that Stalin really was a neurotic personality? We knew so little of him as a person. In his infrequent public appearances, he had seemed modest, unassuming, oblivious of his own personality. To read his psychological makeup through the public Stalin cult was questionable, to say the least, because the evidential value of this material turned on its meaning to him, and that we didn't know. Then came an unexpected windfall in the form of Nikita Khrushchev's secret report about Stalin to the Twentieth Party Congress, a copy of which came into American hands and was published in the *New York Times* on June 5, 1956. In this lengthy document, significantly entitled "On the Cult of Personality and Its Consequences," a one-time admiring protégé, one of the dictator's lieutenants who had observed him at close hand from the later 1930s to his death, offered abundant first-hand testimony of his former boss. He depicted Stalin as a man of colossal grandiosity, along with profound insecurity that caused him to need constant affirmation of his imagined greatness. Khrushchev portrayed a neurotic personality precisely in Horney's sense, an example of the "arrogant-vindictive" type described in *Neurosis and Human Growth*. A self-idealizer, insatiably hungry for the glorification that the public cult provided, Stalin was easily aroused to vindictive hostility by whatever appeared to detract from his inflated vision of himself as a leader and teacher of genius. His aggressions, typically expressed in purges—it followed from Khrushchev's account—were the other side of his self-glorification.

To give the reader a more concrete picture of Khrushchev's testimony, I will cite some examples. Stalin personally edited the adulatory *Short Biography* of himself published in 1947, according to Khrushchev, and in doing so he "marked the very places where he thought that the praise of his services was insufficient." He therefore inserted the following sentence: "Although he performed his task as leader of the party and the people with consummate skill and enjoyed the unreserved support of the entire Soviet people, Stalin never allowed his work to be marred by the slightest hint of vanity, conceit or self-adulation." He also added this testimonial: "Comrade Stalin's genius enabled him to divine the enemy's plans and defeat them. The battles in which Comrade Stalin directed the Soviet armies are brilliant examples of operational military skill." Stalin, Khrushchev testified, doted on a 1951 film about the civil war, *The Unforgettable Year 1919,* "in which he was shown on the steps of an armored train, practically vanquishing the foe with his own saber." He diminished Lenin as he magnified himself. The draft text of the *Short Biography* said at one point: "Stalin is the Lenin of today." That seemed insufficient to the editor, who altered the sentence to read: "Stalin is the worthy continuer of Lenin's work, or, as it is said in our party, Stalin is the Lenin of today." He created Stalin prizes but no Lenin prizes, Khrushchev said, adding that "not even the tsars" created prizes named after themselves. While Stalin kept postponing the decision passed long ago by the party to build a Palace of the Soviets as a monument to Lenin, in 1951 he signed a resolution of the USSR Council of Ministers for the erection of an impressive monument to himself on the newly built Volga-Don Canal.[10]

My surmise about an organic link between the cult of Stalin and the official idealization of Stalin's Russia found confirmation in Khrushchev's report. He noted that Stalin had last visited a village in 1928, when he went to Siberia to speed up grain collections. But in later years he needed to believe that Soviet agriculture was prospering under his beneficent rule, and films were produced to demonstrate the same. "He knew the country and agriculture only from films. And these films had dressed up and beautified the existing situation in agriculture. Many films so pictured *kolkhoz* life that the tables were bending from the weight of turkeys and geese. Evidently, Stalin thought that it was actually so."[11]

More evidence of this kind was to appear in Soviet publications during Khrushchev's tenure in power, and still more in the memoirs that he dictated following his ouster in 1964. But the secret report was the crucial source of evidence. My hypothesis was now confirmed to my own satisfaction, and the task was to get on with the study. In 1958 I finished and defended my dissertation on Marx and became a teacher of Soviet politics and related subjects, first at Indiana University and later at Princeton. Finally, between 1964 and 1965, I had a year of academic leave at the Center for Advanced Study in the Behavioral Sciences at Stanford, and with it the opportunity to work on Stalin. There was only one problem: I didn't know how to carry out the task. My aim was to write a political scientist's tract on dictatorship from a

10. See *New York Times,* June 5, 1956.
11. Ibid.

psychological perspective, not a Stalin biography. There was and is, as far as I know, no example of such a work. G. M. Gilbert, the American court psychologist at Nuremburg, produced an important study, *The Psychology of Dictatorship,* based largely on what he learned about Hitler from that dictator's surviving ex-associates on trial.[12] It was valuable because it showed that the dictator's personality can be immensely influential in the behavior of a dictatorial regime. But, for various reasons, it was not a model for my projected study.

The idea came of constructing the study as a scholarly whodunit, and I wrote a fifty-page first chapter entitled "The Making of a Dictator." Starting with Stalin's rise to supreme leadership in 1929, it showed how he made himself an autocrat by his terroristic purges of the 1930s. To prove that he was not yet a dictator in 1929, I had to clarify the origin of the role of leader (*vozhd'*) in Russian Communism. Despite the existence of a large literature on Lenin and the early years of Soviet power, I found no study of the leader role that Lenin created as the founder of Bolshevism at the start of the century. Chapter 2 addressed that question, arguing that Lenin could lead the Bolshevik party without being a dictator because he had acquired charismatic authority in the Bolsheviks' eyes from the time of their movement's formation and by the crucial part he played in the party's coming to power in 1917. Why the Bolshevik regime underwent transformation into an autocracy under Stalin became the issue. An important factor favoring that outcome, it seemed, was historical: the political culture of prerevolutionary Russia as a system of autocracy. I knew something about that from my reading in old Russian history books that I had found in second-hand bookstores while in Moscow. So I wrote a third long chapter, "The Tsarist Autocratic Tradition," not realizing at the time that much of this material was destined to become a part of the second volume of a study that would turn into a trilogy.[13]

Now, paradoxically, what was to have been a personality study in its fundamental character was shaping up as something else. Save for the introductory chapter, Stalin as a personality hardly entered the picture until the last part of what would become the first volume of the trilogy. There, in discussing the rise of his personality cult in 1929, I went back to his early life as a revolutionary in order to show the ways in which it was touched up and in places falsified in the idealized Stalin

12. G. M. Gilbert, *The Psychology of Dictatorship* (New York: Ronald Press, 1950).

13. Robert C. Tucker, *Stalin as Revolutionary, 1879–1929: A Study in History and Personality.* (New York: Norton, 1973), *Stalin's Revolution from Above* (in progress), and *Stalin and the Cold War* (in progress).

image that formed the cult's centerpiece. So, when the draft of the volume (later published under the title *Stalin as Revolutionary 1879–1929: A Study in History and Personality*) was finished and submitted to the publisher in 1971, my two editors, having read it, returned it to me with a gentle but clear indication that major revisions were needed because something was wrong with the book's structure. The task was unavoidably mine to solve. A trip to Europe in the summer of 1971 afforded some leisure for thinking, and by fall, when it was my good fortune to have a semester of academic leave, a program of revision was becoming clear in my mind. By now I saw that chronology could not be cavalierly disregarded. At the very least, Stalin's early life and early revolutionary career would have to be treated early in the book. I think this was the point in my own life at which biography as a genre grew interesting to me, or at any rate not something from which I instinctively shrank as outside my ken.

The solution to my structural problem proved rather easy, once my mind was open to the possibility and desirability of being biographical. The chapter on Lenin as the founder and leader of the Bolshevik movement led me naturally to ask: how did a young Georgian of lowly origin named Iosif Djugashvili become a follower of Lenin early in the century? There was no way to answer this question with generalities; an interpretation of my subject as an individual young person became unavoidable. Nor would it help to describe Horney's profile of the "arrogant-vindictive" neurotic personality type, and then try to show that Djugashvili was a case in point. True, his wretched early family life, the brutal beatings inflicted on his mother and on him by his drunken father, would easily have produced the basic anxiety from which a neurosis can grow. Biographical interpretation could and should take this into account. Further, what was known of Djugashvili's boyhood showed a definite streak of self-idealizing, which continued during his years in the Tiflis theological seminary when he entered the local revolutionary underground, and subsequently as well. He *was* neurotic, it seemed.

Instead of dealing in such abstract categories from a book of psychology, however, I was now using that book as guidance in a *biographer's* effort to portray his subject as an individual. Further effort brought to light Djugashvili's discovery, in the far-off charismatic figure of the party's leader, Lenin, a heroic identity figure who inspired him to adopt a Lenin-like revolutionary pseudonym, "Stalin," or man of steel, as the symbol of his idealized revolutionary self. Here I was making use of Sigmund Freud's concept of "identification," a process that "endeavors to mold a person's own ego after the fashion of the one that has been taken as a mode."[14] But, again, the concept was being applied in the context of life-writing.

The Lenin identification carried momentous implications for an understanding of Djugashvili's personality, among them the fact that he would feel driven one day to match or outdo his identity figure in revolutionary accomplishment of world-historic importance. Before then, the Lenin identification resulted in the Russification of Djugashvili's national self-consciousness. Since the identity figure was a Russian revolutionist, *he* must be Russian too, and yet the Russian revolutionary *persona* that he thus fashioned for himself as Stalin was inevitably going to conflict all his life with his ineradicably Georgian empirical self as Djugashvili. This was an inner conflict of the sort that Horney had found to be one of the normal accompaniments of neurotic life experience.

Now one could begin to see how Stalin would necessarily come into murderous collision with many others who were aware not simply of his original national identity but, more important, of the spotted actuality of his character and his revolutionary past. One could see how he would be driven to have history rewritten to conform to his idealized Stalin self, for which purpose unchallengeable power was a prerequisite. This is how a work took shape that might be described as *biography-centered history*. It fortunately never became the political science tract that it started out to be, but neither did it become a conventional piece of life-writing about a historically influential person. It became a study in history and personality designed to show how history shaped an individual who, in turn, greatly influenced the history of Soviet Russia and the world. In producing this study, the author became, *malgré lui,* a sort of biographer.

The reader will doubtless be interested in my attitude toward a figure who has absorbed so large a part of my scholarly lifetime that friends have begun calling me Stalin's last victim. I think it proper here to take the advice of Erik Erikson, who has stipulated as "the first rule of a 'psychohistorical' study, that the author should be honest about his own relations to the bit of history he is studying and should indicate his motives without undue mushiness or apology."[15]

14. Sigmund Freud, *Group Psychology and Analysis of the Ego* (New York: Norton, 1960), p. 47. For a full discussion of the identity concept's uses for a Stalin biography, see Robert C. Tucker, "A Case of Mistaken Identity: Djugashvili-Stalin," *Biography* 5, no. 1 (Winter 1982): 17–24.

15. Erik Erikson, "Review of *Thomas Woodrow Wilson: A Psychological Study*," *International Journal of Psycho-Analysis* 38 (1957): 464.

From the start, as I think this memoir shows, it was intellectual fascination with an unusual hypothesis that inspired me. But by 1950 or so I was also clear in my mind that Stalin was an evil-doer. Have I not been impelled to take biographical revenge upon a man who caused me great personal anguish in the seven years that intervened between my marriage to one of his subjects and her release from Russia, who made us live with the constant possibility that she would disappear one day, as many other Soviet citizens had done? Maybe so, but let us consider the happy outcome.

I shall not forget something Hans Speier said when he interviewed me in 1953 for a position with the RAND Corporation. I was about to say, "I realize that my overextended stay in Moscow is a big handicap, but I think it is one I can overcome," when he remarked offhandedly, "That long stay in Russia is a big advantage for you." I kept quiet and took the job. Those seven Stalin-caused years proved a career boon. Not only Speier but Indiana University's Department of Government took them as the equivalent of the graduate school education in political science and Russian studies I never had. My sole relevant study in college was an intensive course in the Russian language. Thus my ability to establish myself in academia in the later 1950s was due in part to Stalin. Not that he deserves gratitude for having been my benefactor in the strange way that he was. But who can avoid being influenced by such pranks of fortune?

This said, the fact is that I consider Stalin a loathsome man, and the better I have come to know him as my biographical subject, the more intense the feeling has become. Especially in working on the second volume of the projected trilogy, dealing with Stalin's transformation of Soviet Russia in the 1930s by a "revolution from above," I have come to consider him detestable as I never did during the Moscow years or the post-Moscow years when the study was getting under way. Then I was above all conscious of the formidable intellectual challenge of the task being undertaken. I never mistook my subject for a decent man, but the bottomless depth of his villainy was not clear to me. Now it is.

I believe with R. G. Collingwood that history is the reenactment of past thought. Its aim is "the discerning of the thought which is the inner side of the event." Historians' proper task is that of "penetrating to the thought of the agents whose acts they are studying."[16] Now that I have been living through the 1930s with Stalin, trying to reconstruct his acts

16. R. G. Collingwood, *The Idea of History* (London, 1974), pp. 222, 228.

as they first took shape in his mind, I believe that I know him well enough to be able to think things out as he did and, in that sense, to *be* Stalin in the process of reaching key decisions and acting to implement them.

This has led me to comprehend, far more clearly than before, the depth of his duplicity, his capacity to deceive both individuals and large groups, and to lull intended victims into a false sense of security. I have likewise come face to face with Stalin's all but unbelievable indifference to the suffering that he caused, and his ability to take delight in inflicting torment upon people he saw as enemies and upon others whose only guilt lay in association with those "enemies." Khrushchev testifies in the secret report—and this is amply documented in other sources—that on January 20, 1939, Stalin dispatched a coded telegram to high party and police officials throughout the country. It ordered that "physical pressure should still be used obligatorily as an exception applicable to known and obstinate enemies of the people, as a method both justifiable and appropriate."[17] "Physical pressure" meant torture. Stalin was determined that those labeled enemies must be tortured. If, as I believe, the worst of human vices is cruelty, this man must have been one of the most vicious individuals ever to wield power.

Stalin's thoughts and actions have become intelligible to me. The real mystery is why some of his old associates failed to lift a hand against him while it was still possible to prevent his murderous assault upon Soviet society in the later 1930s. Alongside such creatures of Stalin as Lazar Kaganovich and Klim Voroshilov, there were in the Politburo of 1934 such men of independent mind and standing as Sergei Kirov, Valerian Kuibyshev, and Sergo Ordzhonikidze. They were tough Bolsheviks but not evil-doers of Stalin's stripe, and they could not have wanted him to succeed in finally wrecking what was left of the Revolution. Kirov may with difficulty be forgiven his own inaction. But when he was assassinated on December 1, 1934, an act that perceptive men of the inner circle could see must have been Stalin's doing, I cannot comprehend the failure of Ordzhonikidze and Kuibyshev to respond. They must have known then that Stalin, like a mad dog, had to be destroyed. They still had access to him; they sat around the table with him at Politburo sessions. Sometimes in the quiet of my study I have found myself bursting out to their ghosts: "For God's sake, stab him with a knife, or pick up a heavy object and bash his brains out, for the lives you save may include your own!" (Kuibyshev died under mys-

---

17. *New York Times*, June 5, 1956.

terious circumstances in early 1935, and Ordzhonikidze was forced by Stalin to commit suicide in early 1937.) Untold hundreds of thousands of lives could have been saved, and untold damage to Soviet Russia averted. Or consider the behavior of Mikhail Tomsky, to whose apartment Stalin went with a bottle of wine in 1936, very probably to solicit help in his contemplated purge trial of Tomsky's ex-rightist associates Nikolai Bukharin and Alexei Rykov. Tomsky showed Stalin to the door with curses, went back to his study, and shot himself to death.[18] Why didn't he shoot Stalin first?

I cannot answer such questions, but I think the fact that I ask them discloses the nature and strength of my feelings. The issue is whether they impair what capacity I otherwise may have to produce a sound biography-centered study of the Soviet 1930s. In *apologia,* let me revert to my original design to write the work as a scholarly whodunit. It suggests that for a long time I had thought that I was on the track of a criminal and his crimes. Pursuing the analogy, what is or should be the detective's attitude toward his quarry? Like a Collingwoodian historian (following Collingwood's view of history-writing in a section of *The Idea of History* entitled "Who Killed John Doe?"), he must, it seems to me, do everything possible to reenact the thought underlying the criminal deed and then project himself into the fugitive's mind to such an extent that he can divide the man's likely pathways of escape and present whereabouts. Will the detective's horror at the crime and hatred of the criminal cripple his capacity to fulfill his professional duty? My own view is that they will not. But is the analogy itself, the idea of Stalin as a criminal and some of his key historical actions of the 1930s as crimes, misleading? Might it not blind one to the constructive accomplishments of that decade under Stalin's leadership? It could, but it need not, for even criminals, the biggest ones in fact, can make positive contributions to the community in their careers of crime.

One final consideration is in order. When one spends a large part of one's scholarly life seeking to puzzle out the behavior of an infinitely evil person, like Stalin, and that of others around him and people in his society, something can develop in the course of the biographical process that might almost be described as the passion of curiosity. One's inquisitiveness, the urge to illuminate what went on inside the man that led him to act as he did, the need to explain to oneself as well as others, to comprehend and communicate things that may have evaded under-

18. Roy A. Medvedev, "New Pages from the Political Biography of Stalin," in *Stalinism: Essays in Historical Interpretation,* ed. Robert C. Tucker (New York: Norton, 1977), p. 213.

standing, can become a dominating drive, and this drive can counteract the simplifying mental tendencies that hatred of the subject may generate. I think that something of this sort has happened in my case. Stalin is a loathsome figure to me. But the complexity of the thought processes which, as a Collingwoodian historian, I am bound to try to reenact, presents so great an intellectual challenge that I may be protected from the effects of my moral condemnation of the man (the work itself will have to show whether I am right or wrong about this).

In conclusion, Stalin was despicable as man and ruler, but he did not see himself as the villain of history that he was—or so I believe. The Stalin biographer must therefore be careful not to attribute to his villain a consciousness of his own villainy. In the effort to reenact the villain's thought, he must attempt to understand, and if possible to show, how the villain managed to reconcile his duplicities and atrocities with his inner picture of himself as a righteous man and a good and noble ruler. This takes a bit of doing, but the whole meaning and worth of the scholarly enterprise rest upon it. Why this postulate is so important to me probably goes back to the strange way in which I first became involved with the Stalin question.

3

Commentary on "A Stalin Biographer's Memoir"

In his revealing and fascinating paper, Robert Tucker reminds us of Karen Horney's remark that every neurotic acts in ways contrary to his or her best interest. By agreeing to comment on his paper, I am validating that point once again, for I am ill-prepared to challenge the insights generated by the intense and searching "life with Stalin" that our author has been engaged in for the better part of the past thirty years. I admire his work, and we have often (not always) found ourselves on the same side of the barricades—most recently over Solzhenitsyn, a different, yet again very Russian, "case"—so that I am sure that Professor Tucker will take my comments in the right spirit. I can scarcely question the autobiographical observations we have read. Let me, therefore, organize my comments in the form of several questions, drawing on his work on Stalin as a whole.

One concerns alternative interpretations. Thus Tucker describes Stalin's Russification as part of his commitment to out-Lenin Lenin. Maybe so. But are there not alternative explanations? If we think comparatively, we are reminded that the French emperor Napoleon Bonaparte was a Corsican and that Adolf Hitler was an Austrian by birth, much as Stalin was a Georgian. Could one not posit some compensatory mechanism, some inordinate longing to embrace the larger, stronger national identity, with a vengeance, given the insecurities with which all three of our heroes (using the term loosely) began? The preference for Tucker's Lenin identification rests, I guess, ultimately on the author's own intuition, does it not?

And that is perhaps the central problem to raise as a methodological question with the Stalin biography. Time and again, Tucker offers the reader plausible and ingenious hypotheses that—in the nature of the case—cannot be tested (and I suspect that in many cases, Stalin himself, had he been willing to help, could not have validated them either). What it all hinges on, then, is our faith in Tucker's having immersed himself in this material, having seen or felt Stalin, as it were, from the inside, and being able to interpret his drives and personality needs. Ultimately, in other words, he asks the reader to trust his "feel." I am sure that he has reflected on such challenges before, and I wonder what his answer is; I suspect that I know part of the answer: that in the last analysis, all good history is part *Sitzfleisch,* part intuition.

A second order of questions concerns the relationship of Stalin's personality to Russian political culture (another subject on which Professor Tucker has had a good many original and interesting things to say). Would it be unkind to say that he sees a fortuitous symbiosis between the two? We are back here to the old debates over the role of the individual. For, if Stalin could have taken or left that strain in the Russian past—if the choice had been up to him—then we cannot credit the wisest Tocqueville with more than coincidental foresight, then someone else in Stalin's position could have turned the wheel of state and Russia's destiny elsewhere. What is not clear to me is what degree of freedom Tucker assigns to any Soviet ruler, given the momentum of the past, the constraints of the present, and the compelling vision of the future.

A third question concerns the relationship of the rational and the irrational. If I read Tucker correctly, he sees Soviet policy under Stalin essentially as the projection of that man's neuroses and personality needs onto the national arena—personality as the motor force of politics and policy, essentially an irrational mode of behavior and motivation. Yet we can explain a good part of Soviet policy in the 1930s and 1940s without resorting to the special idiosyncratic elements of the master—not all, to be sure, but probably most. How, then, are the two realms—the rational, from economic development and planning to foreign-policy behavior, and the irrational, based on Stalin's personality—reconciled? How do they mesh?

One answer, I suspect, is that in Stalin's armor there were only certain "windows of vulnerability" (as the phrase goes these days) that impeded rational policy making, and there were only certain things that opened them wide. I understand that clinically this is entirely sound. I gather it is also sound to argue that the incidence of Stalin's irrational behavior—his faulty judgment, what might be called his G.Q., or "goof quotient"—increased mightily in his final years, with more advanced age—something that Tucker has in other writings related to a characteristic "mid-life transition." Is that what he would argue here too?

And fourth, I have no doubt that Stalin's personality does indeed give us many fundamental insights into what happened during the years of his rule. I am not sure that all can be explained by his neurosis. (Moreover, while there is no doubt that Stalin was neurotic, not every neurotic becomes a Stalin. Not every aggression, mercifully, is expressed in the form of purges. What was it, then, that was unique about that man— I almost said "madman"—?)

Professor Tucker quotes Khrushchev on Stalin as saying he lived in a world of make-believe. I find this very true. The rewriting of history, the false confessions—it all fits this image of Stalin's shaping reality to conform to his fictions, until things happened that were beyond his power to control. For instance, the Nazi invasion of the Soviet Union in June 1941 may explain what several sources refer to as Stalin's state of shock or nervous breakdown during the first two weeks of the war.

I would suggest a related phenomenon that smacks of more than stubbornness: Stalin's repeated refusal to believe news that contradicted his operating assumptions. Interestingly, this went back to Chiang Kai-shek's break with the Chinese Communists in 1927, when Stalin continued to send Chiang autographed photographs of himself (and similar tokens) long after the Kuomintang had begun to exterminate the "Reds." His order in the spring of 1941 not to report to him intelligence on German preparations to attack the Soviet Union was another such case of "don't bother me with facts." One could cite more.

(I suspect that there was also the reverse phenomenon: a withdrawal after some setbacks. Where he had burned his fingers, he would never go back for another round—not in China, as I just mentioned; in Finland, after 1939 to 1940; or in Iran, after 1946.)

There remains a bigger question: what difference a "personality" approach makes for our understanding of the Soviet system (including its evolution after Stalin, without Stalin). But it would be asking too much to deal with this at the present time.

Let me conclude. I agree with Tucker's basic argument that Stalin's death was a fundamental watershed in Soviet history. We tend to forget how oppressive things were prior to 1953; phenomena like dissidents and emigration were entirely out of the question then. Perhaps some day, a further loosening up will give us more evidence to test Tucker's line of thought and argument.

The field of Russian history is full of forgotten (and forgettable) books—boring, nonsensical, or both. Predictably, this will not be the case with Robert Tucker's work. It continues to instruct, to challenge, occasionally to infuriate, always to interest and enlighten the reader. With "A Stalin Biographer's Memoir" before us, we can better understand how Professor Tucker got hung up on Stalin. For the sake of insight and scholarship, I am very glad he did.

4

Alice James: A Family Romance

Jean Strouse

Modern biography finds its best work in the intersections of history and psychology, of public experience and private life. In the past, biographers focused primarily on public experience, paying much less attention than we do to the internal, emotional dynamics of their subjects' lives. Their job was more or less to record what happened, usually to tell the story of a life that was in one way or another exemplary: questions of motivation and glimpses of the mysterious forces at work beneath the surface of everyday life were left to poets and novelists.

I have heard it said recently that modern biography is "mired in motivation." Freud certainly contributed to this shift in biographical perspective from outside to inside by opening up for general use the possibility of looking into the subterrain beneath ordinary daily life: psychoanalytic theory provides extraordinarily useful ways of understanding human experience in the past and present—I will come back to this point in a moment—and in the twentieth century, questions of psychological motivation have loomed large even for writers who have no use for Freudianism. Freud himself, however, does not deserve all the credit or blame for our age's psychological-mindedness. The evolution of thinking more in terms of what makes people tick than in terms of exemplary behavior had to do with large cultural changes that go beyond the scope of one man's influence. We worry much less than the nineteenth century did about sin, for instance, and we do not look to exemplary lives because there is no consensus about what exemplary be-

Another version of this paper presented at the Stanford Conference appeared in G. Moraitis and G. H. Pollock, eds., *Psychoanalytic Studies of Biography* (New York: International Universities Press, 1987), and a few passages appeared in William Zinsser, ed., *Extraordinary Lives* (New York: American Heritage, 1985).

havior might be. If Freud had not existed, I suspect that we would have had to invent him.

Without reference to psychoanalysis, Lytton Strachey prescribed a methodology for twentieth-century biography in the preface to *Eminent Victorians,* written in 1918. The history of the Victorian age would never be written, Strachey declared, because "we know too much about it." He went on to say, tongue planted blithely in cheek, that "ignorance is the first requisite of the historian—ignorance, which simplifies and clarifies, which selects and omits, with a placid perfection unattainable by the highest art." And he continued:

> It is not by the direct method of a scrupulous narration that the explorer of the past can hope to depict that singular epoch. If he is wise, he will adopt a subtler strategy. He will attack his subject in unexpected places; he will fall upon the flank, or the rear; he will shoot a sudden, revealing searchlight into obscure recesses, hitherto undivined. He will row out over that great ocean of material, and lower down into it, here and there, a little bucket, which will bring up to the light of day some characteristic specimen, from those far depths, to be examined with a careful curiosity.[1]

Although Strachey was not recommending psychoanalysis when he spoke of shooting "a sudden, revealing searchlight into obscure recesses" or bringing up "to the light of day some characteristic specimen . . . to be examined with a careful curiosity," his images have uncanny applicability to the ways in which Freud's ideas can be used well to illuminate the past. Strachey *was* talking about art—the art of selection, omission, and suggestive incident—and it is precisely that quality of artfulness that is missing from many twentieth-century writers' eager applications of psychoanalytic theory to history and biography. Instead of using a revealing searchlight with subtlety and skill, too many analytically oriented writers have tried to get at the past with a kind of intellectual hacksaw. There is no need to cite chapter and verse of the jargon and reductionism that afflict much "psychohistory" and "psychobiography": viewing people as theoretical constructs and mechanistic drives loses all sense of the richness, uniqueness, and emotional complexity of the past.

Instead of criticizing bad psychohistory, it would seem more valuable to think about just how psychoanalytic theory can be used successfully in writing good history and biography. Is it simply a heuristic device,

---

1. Lytton Strachey, *Eminent Victorians* (New York: Harcourt, Brace, 1969. Originally published, 1918), p. vii.

among many others, to be used judiciously in explorations of the past? Or does it constitute a privileged methodological standpoint, demonstrably superior to others, for understanding human lives and history? Can we define what makes a particular biography *work* psychologically— or does it come down to something hopelessly ineffable, the artfulness and sagacity of the writer, rather than a methodology or adherence to a particular theory?

There is a great deal to be said for the ineffable. Many psychoanalysts find that what makes their colleagues good therapists has less to do with training and orientation—they might be Freudians, Jungians, Sullivanians, or eclecticians—than with their qualities as thoughtful, empathic, intelligent human beings. The same can probably be said of biographers. And some of the most skillful psychological portraits in biography have in fact been drawn by people who make no reference to psychoanalytic theory; P. N. Furbank's book about E. M. Forster belongs in this category.[2] To turn to an unlikely source for another example, Benny Green's book about P. G. Wodehouse[3] is very specifically a literary biography, dealing with Wodehouse's early childhood in three pages and his marriage in one sentence. Nonetheless, it is quite sharp—and very funny—in its rare psychological probes. Green begins his last chapter with a disquisition on Victorian parenthood:

> The Aunt, The Nanny and the Governess, that unholy trinity of shuffled-off responsibilities, so dominate the nineteenth-century landscape that the social historian, rummaging for an epithet of definition, can only mourn the absence from the language of a feminine equivalent to "avuncular." The callousness in this regard of the Victorian British middle classes, whose sense of imperial mission persuaded parents to suffer the little children to come unto somebody else, remains one of the wonders of the civilized world. Throughout the imperial heyday, but especially in the period between the Great Exhibition and the Great War, the sons of the well-to-do were dumped on any person or institution willing to accept money for the job. English literature is scattered with the bitter fruits of this dereliction of parental duty: from Kipling and Saki, victimized by relations whose stupidity was outdone only by their barbarism, to Kenneth Grahame, who, placed in the custody of a grandmother of whom it was said, "I don't suppose she could be described as a child-lover," retired into a self-preserving quietism

2. P. N. Furbank, *E. M. Forster: A Life* (New York: Oxford University Press, 1978).

3. B. Green, *P. G Wodehouse: A Literary Biography* (New York: Rutledge Press, 1981).

in the face of that indifference which can sometimes be more hurtful than cruelty itself; or to Maugham, thrown by bereavement upon the bleak shores of Victorian Whitstable and the mercies of a reverend gentleman whose years of exposure to the Realpolitik of the Church of England had taught him that its most expendable tenets were Faith, Hope and Charity, and that the smallest of these was Charity.[4]

Wodehouse himself was dumped at about age three with a succession of hired women and aunts in England while his parents carried on the work of empire in Hong Kong. He claimed in all formal accounts to have had an idyllic childhood, yet late in life he told a biographer that he and his brothers felt "almost like orphans" and that they "looked upon mother more like an aunt." Green then quotes Wodehouse's fictional Bertie Wooster on the subject of his Aunt Agatha:

> Aunt Agatha is one of those strong-minded women. She has an eye like a man-eating fish. . . . My experience is that when Aunt Agatha wants you to do a thing you do it, or else you find yourself wondering why those fellows in the olden days made such a fuss when they had trouble with the Spanish Inquisition.[5]

Green goes on:

> In *The Mating Season,* it is suggested by her nephew Wooster that Aunt Agatha eats broken bottles and kills rats with her teeth; in *Joy in the Morning* that she wears barbed wire next to her skin and conducts human sacrifices by the light of the full moon; in *Jeeves and the Feudal Spirit* that she periodically turns into a werewolf, and that the only reason she desists from devouring her young is that the said young are generally acknowledged to be inedible. . . . Wodehouse's world is littered with the bleached bones of aunts who have failed to measure up to the modest requirements of common decency. Wooster is actually convinced that they are the cause of all the trouble in the world, remarking that "it has probably occurred to all thinking men that something drastic ought to be done about aunts," even stating his willingness to enroll in any society dedicated to their suppression. He tells Jeeves that "behind every poor, innocent, harmless blighter who is going down for the third time in the soup, you will find, if you look carefully enough, the aunt who shoved him into it."[6]

4. Ibid, p. 213.
5. Ibid, p. 216.
6. Ibid, p. 216.

Green never uses the word *displacement,* never says "so much for Victorian motherhood and scenes from an idyllic past." His telling literary anecdotes suggest all that and a great deal more.

Granting, then, that such unquantifiable qualities as intuition, empathy, and artfulness play large roles in the writing of good biography, where and how does psychoanalytic theory come in? I am not a philosopher of the social sciences, and instead of offering a concrete answer to that question just now, I am going to compare biography with psychoanalysis and describe some of my work on the James family.

Both biographers and psychoanalysts engage in historical private detective work, trying to figure out other people's lives. Obviously, their procedures and goals diverge widely. The analyst has a live patient before him, who volunteers information, disagrees with interpretations, and has dreams, thoughts, and strong feelings in the present tense that help both him and the analyst see how his mind and feelings work. The aim of the analyst is modestly therapeutic: what can reasonably be expected from the "talking cure," wrote Freud, is the reduction of neurotic misery to ordinary unhappiness.

Biographers, of course, are not out to cure anybody. They rarely have live people to work with. Henry James could not tap me on the shoulder and say, "No, you're wrong about my sister Alice," and Alice herself could not confirm or deny my cautious interpretations. That is not to say, however, that biographical subjects do not take on vivid, often troubling life in the imaginations of their authors. Henry James was not there to tap me on the shoulder, but he did seem constantly to be peering *over* my shoulder, as it were, to inspect both my assessments and my prose (he would have added that "as it were" to this sentence). And I had very strong reactions to Alice, a cranky hysterical neurasthenic who essentially forced the people she cared about to take care of her by having spectacular nervous breakdowns and becoming a professional invalid.

I hesitated for several months before taking on the task of writing her biography, precisely because her life *was* so limited and depressing: I was not sure I could stand to be around her for what I thought would take two years—it took five. Finally, I decided that her spirit, her illness, her family, and her nineteenth-century milieu were interesting enough to offset the depressing factors. I was partly right and partly wrong. All those other dimensions *were* interesting, and it was a great pleasure to turn to Henry's novels or William's philosophy or the ideas of nineteenth-century doctors about nervous disorders or the history of American women after the Civil War, when Alice herself began to wear a bit thin.

But her character had to be at the center of things, like it or not, if her story was going to have any richness, wholeness, and meaning.

One day, about two years into my research, I suddenly realized that she had worked her powerful will on me, too; there I was, after a hundred years, taking care of Alice. I laughed it off at the time, but later on, at a certain point in the writing, I came to a dead stop. It was when she was in her late twenties and early thirties, and one after another, she was closing down all the options in her life. She could not devote her energies to any intellectual or practical work; she was being scathing and horrid to any man who approached her; her very good mind was wasting its resources on trivia; and her profound conviction of worthlessness was gaining sway, as she took more and more frequently to her bed, rendering herself literally in-valid. I had known all along, of course, that that was the way the story was going to turn out. But somehow, preposterously and without even realizing it, I had begun to hope for a happier ending. That was partly the result of reimagining a life in process; if you get involved in it day by day as it was lived, other paths besides the ones ultimately chosen do seem open. It was also a bit of grandiose delusion on my part—thinking I could somehow rescue or "cure" her by understanding. And partly it was a bit of unwilling, but perhaps inevitable, identification. Largely, however, I think it was a response to Alice herself: she did want to be "taken care of," and although she protested to the contrary, she wanted to be seen as somebody whose life *should have* turned out better. She wanted people to know about what she called her "potent capacity"—her remarkable mind, her sense of humor, her interest in history, her undeveloped writing skills.

"When I am gone," she wrote to William as she was dying, "pray don't think of me simply as a creature who might have been something else, had neurotic science been born."[7] She wrote that in 1891, six months before she died and four years before Freud and Breuer published their *Studies on Hysteria*. She used the word *neurotic* in its nineteenth-century sense—to refer to "nervous disorders"—but it amounts to about the same thing we mean by *neurotic*. Her prescient notion that the "neurotic science" of psychoanalysis would soon be born was based on her thirty years' struggle with raging conflicts that took huge tolls on her body and mind. She knew that there was no simple physical explanation or cure, and she knew that once the real nature of her illness was understood, she would be in a sense exonerated. "Pray don't think of

7. Letter from Alice James to William James, July 30, 1891. The James family letters cited here are quoted by permission of Alexander James and the Houghton Library of Harvard College Library.

me simply as a creature who might have been something else, had neu-rotic science been born." That plea acknowledged that her life had been a failure; but just as it stoically said, "Don't make excuses for me, take me for what I am, limitations and all," it also asserted that she might indeed have been "something else," something powerful, worthy, per-haps creative, perhaps heroic—in any case, something *better* than what she was.

And that was what I had to learn, in that period of being "stuck." I put the writing aside for about a month, and came to see what seems obvious in retrospect—that who Alice James was in fact was much more interesting than who she might have been and that the story's unhappy ending contained its real essence. And yet the pressure not to see it that way, to want a different resolution, was also extremely important in understanding the deepest conflicts in Alice's character, for it was her fierce competitiveness—her ambition in that family to be more than "just" a girl, an invalid, a waste, a failure—that measured the degree of her incapacity. And in groping my way toward seeing into those con-flicts, I had in effect a countertransference reaction. There was no daily patient to idealize me, hate me, dream about me, or disagree with me; but I found that if I gave to Alice the kind of free-floating, receptive attention that analysts are supposed to give their patients, I could learn about her from my own emotional responses.

There was virtually no record, in the first-person singular, of Alice's childhood. Her correspondence did not begin in earnest—or begin to be saved—until she was eighteen and thus all the evidence for her early life lay in other people's accounts and in the diary she kept for the last four years of her life. There, at age forty-two, she looked back at what she called the "vast and responsive reservoirs of the past," and it seemed to her "incredible that I should have drunk, as a matter of course, at that ever springing fountain of responsive love and bathed all unconscious in that flood of human tenderness."[8]

All the James children idealized the family past in just this kind of language. Henry, Jr., wrote of his mother after she died:

> She was patience, she was wisdom, she was exquisite maternity. . . . It was a perfect mother's life—the life of a perfect wife. To bring her children into the world—to expend herself, for years, for their happi-ness and welfare—then, when they had reached a full maturity and

8. Alice James, *The Diary of Alice James,* ed. Leon Edel (New York: Dodd, Mead, 1964), p. 79.

were absorbed in the world and in their own interests—to lay herself down in her ebbing strength and yield up her pure soul to the celestial power that had given her this divine commission.[9]

The mothers in Henry's novels bear no resemblance to this holy image of maternity—and neither did Mary James. It took me a long time to see that these florid tributes housed the inverse truths of longing and family myth. Encouraged constantly to express themselves freely, to come back from private experience with interesting perceptions, and also to subscribe to their parents' views of themselves as perfect parents, the James children grew adept at giving eloquently ambiguous voice to the way things were supposed to be: they learned to see and not see, say and not say, reveal and conceal, all at the same time.

In his paper "Family Romances," Freud writes that children at first idealize their parents, and then, in the process of development and liberation, find flaws in the once-perfect parent and slowly move away—often inventing fanciful "romances" that replace the real parent with someone of higher birth or superior achievement.[10] Alice James never moved away from her father in this way: all her life she preserved an idealized view of Henry James, Sr., that coincided precisely with the view he took of himself as a parent. I think her experience shows—and I will return to this point in a moment—that at a level far below conscious thought, she did have a very different sense of her past, a sense of having been emotionally slighted, deprived, not adequately loved. But in a desperate effort to please, to *earn* affection, she subscribed to the family myth of an "ever springing fountain of responsive love" and dutifully sanctified her parents as "the essence of divine maternity"[11] and the "benignant, adoring pater."[12]

Henry James, Sr., wanted to be her generous, adoring papa, but he was in fact so preoccupied with God and his own troubled spirit, so profoundly self-absorbed, that his extravagant proclamations of affection amounted to empty rhetoric. A letter he wrote during Alice's early adolescence is characteristic of the cruel gap between what he promised her and what he actually gave. He had gone shopping in New York, he

9. Henry James, *The Notebooks of Henry James,* ed. F. O. Mathiessen and K. B. Murdock (New York: Oxford University Press), pp. 40–41.

10. Sigmund Freud, Family romances (1909), in *The Standard Edition of the Complete Psychological Works of Sigmund Freud,* ed. and trans. James Strachey (London, Hogarth Press, 1959), vol. 9: pp. 235–44.

11. Alice James, p. 79.

12. Alice James, p. 149.

wrote, and had picked up a "half-hundred" foreign photographs for her brother William,

> But they are too dear to permit me to buy any fancy ones for you. . . . I shall go into Stewart's this morning to enquire for that style of ribbon for you. If I had *only* brought a little more money with me! I went into Arnold's for a scarf for you, but the clerks were so rapid with me, I couldn't buy & bought two pairs of gloves for myself, one of which turns out too small for me but will suit Harry. . . . Goodbye darling daughter, and be sure that never was daughter so beloved. . . . Keep my letters and believe me ever your lovingest Daddy.[13]

In other words, he had plenty of money to buy things for himself, William, and Henry—but somehow there was not enough for Alice. Nonetheless, she was to believe that "never was daughter so beloved" and that he was her "lovingest Daddy." Money and love often get mixed up together in family negotiations, but rarely is the confusion presented quite so baldly.

James, Sr., constantly stirred up and thwarted his daughter in this way. When his children were young, he devoted himself to what he called their "sensuous" education, exposing them to theater, music, art, and books; searching out unusual schools in Europe and the United States for his four boys, and then quickly finding those schools disappointing and dragging the entire family off to a new city or a new continent in search of the perfect education that existed only in his own mind. For all his originality on the subject of education, however, James, Sr., did not believe in the education of women. He thought that his boys would learn to be "good"—to struggle against selfishness and the evils inherent in the universe—through wide intellectual experience and the interesting uses of perception. Girls, however, he thought good by nature: they could dispense with interesting ideas. To be a James and a girl, then, was virtually a contradiction in terms—"in our family group," wrote Henry, Jr., "girls seem scarcely to have had a chance."[14]

In 1853, James, Sr., published an article, "Woman and the 'Woman's Movement,' " in *Putnam's Monthly Magazine*. He wrote:

> The very virtue of woman, her practical sense, which leaves her indifferent to past and future alike, and keeps her the busy blessing of the present hour, disqualifies her for all didactic dignity. Learning and

13. Letter from Henry James to Alice James, no date.

14. Quoted in Leon Edel, *Henry James*, 5 vols. (Philadelphia: Lippincott, 1953–1972) vol. 2, p. 49.

wisdom do not become her. Even the ten commandments seem unami-
able and superfluous on her lips, so much should her own pure pleasure
form the best outward law for man. We say to her, "Do not tell me,
beautiful doctor, I pray you, what one ought or ought not to do; any
musty old professor in the next college is quite competent to that: tell
me only what I shall do to please you, and it shall be done, though the
heavens fall!"[15]

In attempting to enter the masculine worlds of politics and law, medicine and finance, woman would betray nature's sacred laws, wrote
James. According to an "absolute decree of nature," he went on,
"woman is inferior to man. . . . She is his inferior in passion, his inferior in intellect, and his inferior in physical strength." It was precisely
this inequality that made, in his eyes, for her exalted function. She came
to embody everything man was not; James called her "nature's revelation to man of his own God-given and indefeasible self. . . . Her aim
in life is . . . simply to love and bless man."[16]

For all his opposition to female intellect, however, James, Sr., de-
lighted in the quickness of his daughter's mind. He addressed her as
"heiress of the paternal wit and of the maternal worth."[17] He encouraged
her to read, and they spent long hours together in his study, talking,
joking, and trading opinions and insults. Her early education, then, was
a haphazard mix of encouragement and slight: her father enjoyed sharing knowledge with her piecemeal, but more as a pleasant way to pass
time than as a serious effort to train her mind. Ambiguity characterized
Alice's lifelong estimates of the female sex and her own mental prowess;
toward the end of her life, she wondered wryly whether "if I had had
any education, I should be more, or less, of a fool than I am."[18] She then
went on to contradict by example that assertion of foolishness, for the
modesty and irony of her remarks present a clear contrast to her father's
solemn, inflated rhetoric on the subject of female "didactic dignity":
education, she wrote, "would have deprived me surely of those exquisite
moments of mental flatulence which every now and then inflate the
cerebral vacuum with a delicious sense of latent possibilities—of stretch-
ing oneself to cosmic limits, and who would ever give up the reality of
dreams for relative knowledge?"[19]

15. Henry James, Sr., "Woman and the 'Woman's Movement,' " *Putnam's Monthly Magazine,* vol. 1, March 1853, pp. 279–88.

16. Ibid.

17. Letter from Henry James, Sr., to Alice James, no date.

18. Alice James, p. 66.

19. Ibid., p. 66

William James, like his father, constantly announced his extravagant adoration of Alice, but a close reading of his letters to her shows *his* profound preoccupation with himself, as well as the distinctly sexual nature of his teasing. Just after Alice's first severe nervous breakdown, in 1868, when she was nineteen, William, age twenty-five, wrote a letter to her from Dresden that began as commiseration and ended—character-istically—in self-centered seductiveness: "I am excessively sorry to hear all the time from home that you are still delicate. I would give anything if I could help you my dearest Alice, but you will probably soon grow out of it. . . ." He himself had recently been ill, and now described

> crying all the time for to have you sitting by me stroking my brow and asking me if there was nothing, *nothing* you could do to alleviate my sufferings. And me casting up my eyes to heaven & solemnly shaking my head, like Harry, to command sympathy, and saying in a feeble voice, "no! dear, nothing," and then you saying how beautiful and patient I was. Whole dialogues did I frame of how I wd. work on your feelings if you were there, and longed to cleave the Ocean once more to press you in my arms.[20]

Ten years earlier, when he was sixteen and she ten, William had be-gun writing to Alice in this vein; he referred constantly to her physical attributes and drew portraits of her sensual, untutored, indulged feminine nature. He imagined her in Paris as "Alice the widow, with her eyes fixed on her novel, eating some rich fruit which Father has just brought in for her from the Palais Royal." Then "thousand thanks to the cherry lipped apricot nosed double chinned little [Alice] for her strongly dashed off letter, which inflamed the hearts of her lonely brother with an in-tense longing to kiss and slap her celestial cheeks."[21] One night in 1859, he composed a "sonnate" in her honor and invited the family into the parlor to hear him sing it:

> The moon was mildly beaming
> Upon the summer sea,
> I lay entranced and dreaming
> My Alice sweet, of thee.
> Upon the sea-shore lying
> Upon the yellow sand
> The foaming waves replying
> I vowed to ask thy hand.

20. Letter from William James to Alice James, March 16, 1868.
21. Letter from William James to parents, [August 19, 1860?].

I swore to ask thy hand, my love
I vowed to ask thy hand.
I wished to join myself to thee
By matrimonial band.

So very proud, but yet so fair
The look you on me threw
You told me I must never dare
To hope for love from you.

Your childlike form, your golden hair
I never more may see
But goaded on by dire despair
I'll drown within the sea.

Adieu to love! adieu to life!
Since I may not have thee,
My Alice sweet, to be my wife,
I'll drown me in the sea!
I'll drown me in the sea, my love,
I'll drown—me in—the sea![22]

"Alice took it very cooly [*sic*],"[23] William reported the next day to his father, who was away in London, and another brother, Wilky, wrote that the song had "excited a good deal of laughter among the audience assembled."[24]

It is very easy to misread language from other centuries, and in order to "hear" the messages in the William–Alice correspondence accurately, I read through a number of brother–sister letters from other families, to find out whether this sort of sexy talk was conventional 100 years ago. It was not. Just how Alice did "take" William's gallant rhetorical flourishes emerges only later, and indirectly. What can be seen at the time is the way William, for reasons of his own, kept putting her on display before the family audience like a bright ornament, calling attention to her femaleness, her difference from the others, with playful, mocking praise.

Sex was not a topic of discussion in the James family letters. William disliked the word all his life. He rarely mentioned sex in all his work on psychology and religious experience, but in the chapter "Instincts" in *The Principles of Psychology,* he posited under the heading "Love" an

22. Letter from William James to Henry James, Sr., December 1859.
23. Ibid.
24. Letter from Garth Wilkinson James to Henry James, Sr., December 1859.

antisexual instinct, "the instinct of personal isolation, the actual repulsiveness to us of the idea of intimate contact with most of the persons we meet, especially those of our own sex." ("To most of us," he added in a footnote, "it is even unpleasant to sit down in a chair still warm from occupancy by another person's body. . . .") He suspected that the sexual impulse, "this strongest passion of all, so far from being the most 'irresistible,' may, on the contrary, be the hardest one to give rein to. . . ."[25]

In Henry's novels, sex, although unnamed, often occupies a central place in the characters' preoccupations and actions. It becomes more explicit in his later work (*The Wings of the Dove, The Golden Bowl, The Ambassadors*), but early and late, it is nearly always associated with destruction, cruelty, and corruption. Sex as a metaphor for knowledge and experience (and knowledge and experience as metaphors for sex) is what James's innocent (usually American) characters have to come to terms with (usually abroad). His plots turn on the consequences of this kind of knowledge: in *The Wings of the Dove,* Milly Theale dies; Maggie Verver, in *The Golden Bowl,* orchestrates her own elaborate triumph; in *The Ambassadors,* Lambert Strether renounces.

As the only girl in the James family, Alice grew up like a fragile tropical plant in the close quarters of brothers, parents, governesses, and aunt, fed on special preparations of solicitude, curiosity, and indifference. The overstimulation of this heated atmosphere had no natural means of release, and Alice kept her reactions inside. She shared in the family amusement at William's carryings-on, watching herself as object and learning to detach from the flushed confusions involved in also being the subject of the diversion.

Shortly after William wrote his "sonnate on Alice," Henry, Sr., began to feel "home pulling at his heart," and soon his family found itself settled at Newport, Rhode Island. Years later, in her diary, Alice looked back at her childhood and adolescence, recalling the lessons she had tried to teach herself under "the low, grey, Newport sky . . . as I used to wander about over the cliffs, my young soul struggling out of its swaddling clothes as the knowledge crystallized within me of what Life meant for me. . . ." What it meant for her, as for so many of the people in her brother's novels, was a willed renunciation of active, passionate life. She described, in effect, her own attempt to silence or strangle that young soul as it struggled out of its swaddling clothes, as she wandered alone in Newport, "absorbing into the bone that the better part is to clothe

25. William James, *The Principles of Psychology.* (Boston: Henry Holt, 1907/1890). Vol. 2, pp. 437–39.

oneself in neutral tints, walk by still waters, and possess one's soul in silence."[26]

Condensed in that passage, I think, are some of Alice's responses to her father's simultaneous stimulation and thwarting of her mind and to William's incestuous teasing. She needed both these men too much to acknowledge the complexities behind their extravagant proclamations of love. (I do not mean to paint Alice as simply a victim, or Henry, Sr., and William as malicious. Alice certainly participated in her own eventual fate, and seen in the context of their own preoccupations and troubles, her father and eldest brother seem a great deal more sympathetic than they do in relation to Alice. However, a close look at Alice's childhood shows these two large characters as consistently giving her rather short emotional shrift. Her mother, whom I have mentioned only in passing because hers is another very complicated story, gave even less, and Alice extolled her as the perfect "essence of divine maternity." I have also left out Henry, Jr., with whom Alice did share a deep, generous, sympathetic, and mutually responsive love. But that developed later, and was more reparative than formative.) For Alice to have acknowledged the absence of real love in her early life would have meant giving up hope of receiving it, and that was impossible. Instead, she praised the "responsive reservoirs" of family affection and turned on herself, through illness, depression, and a sense of her profound inherent "badness," to account for the sense of lack she could not help experiencing. This way, she kept alive the hope of finally getting what she wanted. And by punishing herself, in effect, with physical suffering, she exacted a measure of revenge—making her family suffer in sympathy and forcing them to care for her in at least the literal sense of the phrase.

Alice described her first breakdown years later, in her diary. It took place early in 1868, when she was nineteen, and it was the culmination of several years of fainting spells, mysterious pains, attacks, and nervous prostrations. When she dared, finally, in England in 1890, to look beneath these physical symptoms, momentarily putting aside the stoical posture of endurance and self-mockery that she had adopted, she gave a vivid account of the forces that were at war within her.

She had been reading in 1890 an essay by William called "The Hidden Self," in which he discussed hysteria, hypnosis, and the splitting of human consciousness into discrete parts, or "personages." William described Pierre Janet's work with hysterical patients in France, and the "contractions of the field of consciousness" that the French philosopher

26. Alice James, p. 95.

had observed in the hysterical mind. One part of the body or mind splits off from normal consciousness, reported William, and is virtually abandoned; an entire leg, for instance, becomes anaesthetized and loses not only all sensation, but also all memory of past sensation. In her diary on October 26, 1890, Alice endorsed William's description of this process; he had used, she wrote, an "excellent expression" in saying that the nervous victim " 'abandons' certain portions of his consciousness."[27]

Her imagination captured by this formulation, Alice turned to survey her own psychological history. The passage from her diary echoes back to her experiences with her father and William, with their arousals and frustrations of her body and mind. She divided her "good," conscious, moral self from her "bad" body, with its "impossible sensations" and murderous impulses. She thinly disguised her wish to kill her father, calling him the "benignant pater" as she described wanting to knock his head off. And both of the acute episodes she described had occurred when she was trying to do intellectual work—to participate or compete in the realm clearly occupied by her father and her two eldest brothers.

I have passed thro' an infinite succession of conscious abandonments and in looking back now I see how it began in my childhood, altho' I wasn't conscious of the necessity until '67 or '68 when I broke down first, acutely, and had violent turns of hysteria. As I lay prostrate after the storm with my mind luminous and active and susceptible of the clearest, strongest impressions, I saw so distinctly that it was a fight simply between my body and my will, a battle in which the former was to be triumphant to the end. Owing to some physical weakness, excess of nervous susceptibility, the moral power pauses, as it were for a moment, and refuses to maintain muscular sanity, worn out with the strain of its constabulary functions. As I used to sit immovable reading in the library with waves of violent inclination suddenly invading my muscles taking some one of their myriad forms such as throwing myself out of the window, or knocking off the head of the benignant pater as he sat with his silver locks, writing at his table, it used to seem to me that the only difference between me and the insane was that I had not only all the horrors and suffering of insanity but the duties of doctor, nurse, and strait-jacket imposed upon me, too. Conceive of never being without the sense that if you let yourself go for a moment your mechanism will fall into pie and that at some given moment you must abandon it all, let the dykes break and the flood sweep in, acknowledging yourself abjectly impotent before the immutable laws. When all one's moral and natural stock in trade is a temperament forbidding the aban-

27. Alice James, p. 148.

donment of an inch or the relaxation of a muscle, 'tis a never-ending fight. When the fancy took me of a morning at school to study my lessons by way of variety instead of shirking or wiggling thro' the most impossible sensations of upheaval, violent revolt in my head overtook me so that I had to "abandon" my brain, as it were. So it has always been, anything that sticks of itself is free to do so, but conscious and continuous cerebration is an impossible exercise and from just behind the eyes my head feels like a dense jungle into which no ray of light has ever penetrated.[28]

Freud and Breuer might have used that passage in *Studies on Hysteria*. Social historians might see in Alice a vivid example of an obscure life responding in private ways to large social forces—the changing shape of nineteenth-century American life, particularly the changing roles and functions of women. Students of the family might see a "Rashomon" story in this extraordinary collection of individuals—each life experience unique, each reflecting back in its own way to the central emotional dynamics of the group as a whole, each seeing a different constellation from the others, each describing it in words that tell only part of the story. Holography comes to mind as the best metaphor for the biographical process of seeing historical, psychological, and interpersonal dynamics that are ordinarily invisible to the naked eye—the technique of producing images by reconstruction and diffraction patterns until a three-dimensional picture finally emerges.

The state of receptive attention I found useful in learning about Alice James hardly amounts to a biographical methodology, but it does suggest a general way in which the insights and even the techniques of psychoanalysis can be applied to the past. The "voices" that biographers listen to constitute a very special kind of record: it is not always complete, and it does not present a life *as it was lived;* instead, it presents what people (the subject, friends, relatives, other historians) had to *say* about that life. Language expresses a great deal, of course; it also conceals, misdirects, inverts, teases, gives away secrets inadvertently, and steadfastly refuses to give away any secrets at all. Biographers do have to get at the secrets, of course, and words are their main clues. Sometimes, the clues point to deep, unconscious conflicts; sometimes, to thematic obsessions (such as Wodehouse's aunts—but how much less interesting it is to call that a thematic obsession than to look at its various manifestations). At other times, words reveal a state of mind, such

28. Ibid., pp. 149–50.

as depression or anxiety, and a tone of voice tells more than content does about what is going on in relations between two people. A familiarity with psychoanalysis helps a biographer "listen" for these kinds of clues, and slowly to gather a deep sense of who this other person was.

If he were a practicing doctor, he would begin to share these "clues" with his patient, who could learn to see and gain some measure of control over aspects of his life that were not visible before. However, the biographer has a very different task: he or she has to *use* these subtle clues to introduce an audience of strangers to the hidden dynamics at work between and inside other people, to show that audience not only how the subject's mind worked, but also how the biographer's mind does, in making its evaluations and interpretations. Toward that end, psychoanalytic insights can make up what reporters call the "deep background" of the case; they may guide and inform the author's "reading" of the subject, without necessarily ever showing up in the text.

What works best as admissible evidence, by contrast, is *social* experience. Using language as evidence, a biographer can present the interplay of history and psychology—how this particular life fit into the patterns and expectations of its time, how family dynamics worked, how people actually behaved toward one another (which may not be the same as what they *said* about it), how public experience affected private life. The social and personal dimensions of a life are not separate entities; there is constant exchange between, for instance, how people behave toward us and how we feel about ourselves, between a man's economic position and his perception of his career options, or between a father's ideas and feelings about women and his daughter's sense of herself. Keeping the focus on what is visible and able to be documented seems to lead in more fruitful biographical directions than trying to make fancy intrapsychic diagnoses. To call Alice James a narcissistic character, for instance, would not have told anybody except psychoanalysts very much; knowing about narcissistic disorders, however, informed my sense of her essence and troubles, and guided me in sketching for others a picture of her personality. Showing, in biographical narrative, the social and emotional contexts of individual experience does, I think, bring deep private conflicts to the surface in meaningful ways; and it is in such contexts that they have the most to tell, both about history and about private life.

I asked before whether psychoanalysis can be said to constitute a privileged methodological standpoint from which to approach biography. I think the answer is a qualified yes, but not in any scientific or prescribable way. It serves best as a tacit guide to the deepest questions common to human experience—questions about sexuality, hostility, love, productivity, self-esteem. Those questions may be universal, but the interesting story always lies in the specificity of the answers. Every unhappy family, after all, is unhappy in its own way. Before Freud, messages from the unconscious were called madness, or genius. Since Freud, we can still believe in madness and genius, but the concept of an unconscious has opened up new ways of listening to other people's lives. A vigilant, receptive attention to the evidence of language can provide a symptomatic reading of conscious exchange: ellipses, contradictions, repeating themes, tones of voice, denials, slips, verbal style, undertones, jokes, and dreams give demonstrable access to the deeper messages contained in the overt texts of daily experience. Used well, that kind of attention to the covert can reward us with a rich, vivid, fully dimensional sense of "what happened" in the past.

"Perhaps the greatest breach in nature," wrote William James in 1890 in *The Principles of Psychology,* "is the breach from one mind to another."[29] He went on to describe two brothers waking up in the same bed, each reaching back into the stream of his last thoughts before falling asleep, each unable to enter the other's consciousness except by being told. Peter cannot *feel* Paul's last drowsy state of mind; he can only imagine or hear about it. Only through words—carefully chosen for precise meanings—could the brothers cross that greatest breach in nature, and then only fleetingly. And only through words, in all their shades of conscious and unconscious meaning, can biographers, historians, and psychoanalysts cross that breach.

29. William James, vol. 1, p. 237.

II

The Uses of Psychoanalysis and
Psychology in Historical Interpretation

5

Psychoanalysis in History

Peter Gay

Psychoanalysis and history are brothers under the skin, although neither discipline has been willing to acknowledge the fraternity. Both are students of the past; both are deterministic in their search for causes; both are intent on getting to the real meaning of things and to dig beneath the surface; both are sciences of memory, intent on collecting and correcting memories. If the first would seem to be interested principally in private memories and the second principally in the public memory, this is chiefly a matter of emphasis, and one that is wiped out in the field of biography, which partakes, it seems to me, equally of both psychoanalysis and history. Psychoanalysis and history then appear to be dividing the field of the human past by a practical division of labor rather than by some fundamental principle.

In putting it this emphatically, I do not intend to deny, or even to slight, the very real differences between the two disciplines. Their histories differ considerably; their techniques differ greatly. And while it can only lead to confusion to minimize both tactical and strategic differences between psychoanalysis and history, it is my intention to call attention to their affinities, which are closer than practitioners of either field have been willing to concede. My reason for doing so is to underscore the possibilities of employing psychoanalytic concepts as well as, indeed, at least some psychoanalytic techniques in the writing of history.

Both psychoanalysis and history, then, are sciences of the past; both testify to the power of the past over the present, yet both, at the same

Since this paper was first delivered, some material in it has been published in different form in *The Bourgeois Experience: Victoria to Freud*, vol. 1, *Education of the Senses* (New York: Oxford University Press, 1984), and *Freud for Historians* (New York: Oxford University Press, 1985).

time, attempt to establish, for their own reasons, the freedom of the present from the past. In order to permit us to visualize the affinities of which I have spoken, I want to analyze for some space a category that I believe to be fundamental both to psychoanalysis and to history— experience. Since experience is so inexhaustible, it is far easier to demonstrate than to define. I want, therefore, to take as my example one of Sigmund Freud's most highly charged memories and most instructive associations. On October 3, 1897, Freud wrote one in his series of long letters to his best friend, then his only intimate, Dr. Wilhelm Fliess of Berlin, to whom he was transmitting all his startling discoveries without reserve. These were not pleasant days for Freud. His seduction theory of neuroses, which, he had hoped, would make his reputation as an innovative healer of nervous disorders, had to Freud's mind collapsed from lack of credible evidence. The victory he would snatch from this defeat— the recognition of the privileged part that fantasy plays in mental life— was still struggling for formulation. His self-analysis was at its most intense; Freud was dredging up deeply repressed memories and attempting the most far-reaching dream interpretations he had yet ventured to offer. In this atmosphere of tense inquiry and unsparing self-confrontation, he recalled, he told Fliess, that when he had been between two and two and a half years old, his "libido toward matrem had awakened" on the occasion of a railroad trip from Leipzig to Vienna, an overnight journey that had given him the opportunity to see her "nudam."[1] Then, having unburdened himself of this long-repressed recall, Freud immediately added, in a telling association of which he seemed quite unaware, that he had welcomed the death of his infant brother, born a year after him, with "wicked wishes and genuine infantile jealousy."[2] Love and hate proved constant companions, intimate enemies.

This rich and resonant experience condenses with exemplary economy the pressures and the continuous entanglements of sexuality and aggression, those two fundamental drives that make history. It suggests the workings of civilization, the control of wishes, and the delay of gratification in the human mind. And it exhibits the persistence, the sheer vitality, of early encounters, the hold of psychological defenses over the shaping of perception and memory. It exhibits, in other words, what I have called the power of the past over the present. After the passing of half

1. Freud to Fliess, October 8, 1897, *Sigmund Freud analyse: Briefe au Wilhelm Fliess, 1887–1904*, ed. Jeffrey Mussaief Musson (1986), 288.

2. Ibid.

a lifetime, and in a letter to his closest friend, like him a physician, Freud found it necessary to clothe his incestuous desires in the decent obscurity of a learned tongue; the Latin established a space of safety between himself and his forbidden arousal. And it is significant that Freud should have misplaced the date of his seductive glimpse: he had actually been four years old at the time. By making himself younger and smaller than he had really been, he denied the powerful eroticism of the oedipal stage he had reached and portrayed himself as scarcely able to imagine, let alone carry out, his aggressive and sexual intentions. When he told Fliess about his erotic wishes for his mother and his deadly wishes against his brother, he was forty-one years old. The reverberating echoes of his memory, its long, almost unimpaired reach from Freud's troubling current situation to his infantile passions, invite the historian to explore beyond the immediate occasion, to move outward to Freud's cultural environment and back to his early personal history. In a word, with its far-reaching implications for the study of man's most potent, yet secretive springs of action, this vignette is an immensely suggestive exemplar of an experience.

An experience is more than a naked wish or a casual perception. It is an organization of inner urges, ways of seeing, and realities that will not be denied. It is an encounter of the individual with his or her society; its visible surface is the tip of an iceberg. But it offers intimations of its many-layered and interlocked foundations, of the uninterrupted traffic between what the world imposes and the self receives and reshapes. Freud, far from slighting these complexities, recognized—indeed, celebrated—them.

Freud, of course, was not alone in valuing these riches. William James, who observed Freud with a mixture of generosity and skepticism, praised them with his characteristic energy. *"The order of experience,"* he wrote in 1890, "is our educator, our sovereign helper and friend."[3] The order of which he speaks is a cumulative compound of mental events sustaining and confirming, yet also confusing and contradicting one another. Each fresh experience is endowed with a double charm of strangeness and familiarity, and this duality enables it to be suffered or enjoyed, to be understood and assimilated, which is to say, used. Yet experience proved itself, in the nineteenth century, as before and after, often far from charming. It appeared as the nemesis of innocence. "Alas, experience!" Charlotte Brontë exclaims in her novel *Shirley*. "No other

3. *The Principles of Psychology*, 2 vols. (1890), vol. 2, p. 620.

mentor has so wasted and frozen a face as yours: none wears a robe so black, none bears a rod so heavy, none with hand so inexorable draws the novice so sternly to his task, and forces him with authority so resistless to its acquirement." Although sobering, experience was indispensable: "It is by your instructions alone that man or woman can ever find a safe track through life's wilds: without it, how they stumble, how they stray! On what forbidden grounds do they intrude, down what dread declivities are they hurled!"[4] The insight that Freud would add to Brontë's is that this forbidden ground, these dread declivities, confront the innocent as much as the worldly. Children, too, are bombarded by life, whether by concealed passions or by public imperatives; they, too, construct their order of experience.

Experiences, then, have their history and, looking to an unknown although not wholly unpredictable future, leave their deposits. Freud's experience, at forty-one, of seeing his mother naked once again in his mind was, like practically all others, something of a reexperience. Freud would have called it a second edition: it was a revised revival, a mixture of the old and the new, of commands and prohibitions, of wishes and fears, an unfolding of verifiable events that had occurred around 1860 but reshaped into the useful memory emerging in 1897. Freud's boyish desires recalled in adult anxiety were profoundly personal, but they had general implications; they erupted as he was struggling to formulate a psychology in which all little boys' desire for their mothers would be a conspicuous element.

It is hard to say anything fresh about experience, hard not to sound portentous or appear to be straining for the obvious. But what Freud's particular experience discloses, and his work expansively confirms, is anything but banal. I have already alluded to it: experience has its unconscious dimensions, as intricate as they are influential. The invisible iceberg is as important in the making of the mind as its ostentatious tip, normally more important. That historians should generally have shunned these dimensions is perfectly comprehensible. The unconscious is very intractable. At best, however tantalizing the traces it may leave behind, it is almost illegible to the untrained observer. But while the assignment of rendering it legible and accessible to historical inquiry is admittedly difficult, it remains a decisive truth of history, a truth that historians have ignored at their peril and to their loss, that much of the past took place underground, silently, eloquently.

4. *Shirley* (1849; Penguin edition, 1974), 122.

For all the subtle and pervasive activity of the unconscious, a comprehensive interpretation of an experience must be alert to its conscious no less than to its unconscious dimensions, to the work of culture on mind—the world, in short, in which the historian is most at home. The human mind hungers for reality; except for the largely encapsulated id, which is the depository of the raw drives and of deeply repressed material, the other institutions of the mind, the ego and the superego, draw continuously on the culture in which they subsist, develop, and mature. That is why I have defined an experience as an encounter between mind and world. While the mind presents the world with its needs and seeks most of its gratifications there, the world gives the mind its grammar, desires their vocabulary, anxieties their object. The superego is an accumulation of parental and other didactic injunctions; the ego—endowed with capacities for thinking, calculating, comparing, and anticipating—encounters and tests realities. The mind levies on the world for its fantasies, its very dreams. And if these shadowy activities of the mind borrow so heavily from sights and sounds and smells, then the daytime experience of normal neurotics—the principal stuff of history—must cling still more tightly to the social, religious, economic, and technological imperatives that, together, define the possibilities and prescribe the limits of individuals alike.

This is why the reductionism that bedevils much psychohistory is indefensible; it is indefensible not merely because it slights the complexities of the historical process, but also, perhaps even more seriously, because it slights the complexity of the psychoanalytic view of humans in the world. Not all reduction, to be sure, is reductionistic. In an essay of 1913, in which he speculated on the uses of psychoanalysis in historical studies, Freud adumbrated this distinction and hinted at a way in which his individualistic psychology could make itself relevant to the study of collective experience, in which biography could become history. "Psychoanalysis," he wrote, "establishes an intimate connection" between the

physical achievements of individuals and of society by postulating the same dynamic source for both. It starts with a fundamental idea that it is the principal function of the mental mechanism to relieve the person from the tension which his needs create in him. Part of this task can be fulfilled by extracting satisfaction from the external world. For this purpose it is essential to have mastery over the real world. But reality regularly frustrates the satisfaction of another part of these needs, among them, significantly, certain affective impulses. This produces the second task, that of finding some other way of disposing of the unsatisfied impulses.[5]

Persuaded that psychoanalysis has already thrown dazzling light on the origins of religion, morality, justice, and philosophy, Freud now concluded that "the whole history of culture only demonstrates which methods mankind has adopted to bind its unsatisfied wishes under changing conditions, further modified by technological problems, wishes sometimes granted and sometimes frustrated by reality."[6] This little-known passage is nothing less than an ambitious agenda for historians, an invitation whose implications neither psychoanalysts nor historians have even begun to explore. Freud is clearly alert to the way in which mental operations, translated into inventions, institutions, and solutions to problems, emancipate themselves to lead an autonomous public existence. Even technology is, if traced back far enough, a rational method of gratifying unsatisfied wishes. But it is also an external and objective reality that, having freed itself from mind, now faces mind. This is the main reason why Freud saw no essential difference between individual and social psychology.

Mind and world, in short, engage with each other everywhere, at all times. It is a far from casual matter that people should use metaphors drawn from family life when they speak of religion, politics, or the factory. They invest their public environment with their intimate experience, and that environment at once mirrors and, in turn, acts on that experience. Class consciousness, national loyalties, economic decisions—all are species of mental work shaping, and shaped by, realities. Secret feelings and manifest philosophies, unconscious demands and conscious ideas are inextricably interwoven, almost defying analysis. Cults of youth or age or nature, hopes for advancement or despair of mobility, commitments to parliamentary institutions or to charismatic leadership, the choice of business strategies and myriad other sentiments and activities are partly rational, partly nonrational, the fruit of calculation and of ungratified wishes that the individual, and groups, barely know and can hardly acknowledge. Psychoanalytic categories explaining these richly layered experiences are not prescribed channels in which historical interpretations must run; they are descriptions of available, and unavailable human options. They enormously enlarge the historian's opportunity to grasp all the dimensions of the past and their relative share in their pre-

5. "Das Interesse an der Psychoanalyse" (1913), [not in St. A.], G.W., vol. 8, p. 415.

6. "The Claims of Psycho-Analysis to Scientific Interest" (1913), Standard Edition, vol. 13, pp. 185–86.

cipitate—experience. That is why the historian must closely analyze the pressures of reality, whether it is the introduction of the railroad, the vulcanization of rubber, the conquest of childbed fever, the persistence of social hierarchies. All are invested with and, in turn, form mind.

Strictly speaking, of course, there is no such thing as a collective mind. The experience of any individual, as the psychoanalytically oriented historian has particular reason to know, differs, however slightly, from that of all the others. Only the individual loves and hates, develops tastes in painting and furniture, and feels content in moments of consummation, anxious in times of peril, and furious at agents of deprivation; only the individual glories in success or takes revenge on the world. The rest is metaphor.

But it is a necessary metaphor, for all humans share at least their humanity—their passions, their paths of maturation, their irrepressible needs. And all develop social ties, belong to part-cultures that expose them to predictable clusters of experiences, each bearing family resemblances close enough to seduce the historian into collective judgments. Religious denominations, urban or rural neighborhoods, linguistic communities, and classes mold the individual into a recognizable member of several societies. By the time children are ready for school, they are little living anthologies of their culture. The individual, then, is, in a special way, culture writ small; culture is, in its own way, the individual writ large.

My definition of experience is, as you have doubtless noticed, a critique both of historians employing and of historians detesting psychoanalysis. I am not about to join in the easy blood sport of bashing psychohistorians or of gloating over their highly visible disasters. Some pungent and irritated responses to psychohistory have been only too richly deserved. The syllabus of errors rehearsing its offenses includes some disturbing counts, and familiar charges of reductionism and of crimes against good sense, scientific procedure, the rules of evidence, and the English language are not wholly without foundation. However sincere the disclaimers of psychohistorians that they are not turning their subjects into patients, their failure to come to grips with commanding external influences on mental functioning has vitiated, or at least compromised, a good deal of their work. And heavy speculations made on the basis of tenuous evidence, or strained interpretations, have not improved their performance or their reputation. It will therefore not do to diagnose objections to psychohistory as resistance to a risky, inquisitive, and positively indecent auxiliary discipline; the times are long gone when admirers of Freud could paralyze reasoned criticisms by psycho-analyzing the critic.

Conceding all this, it seems to me that the vehemence, the sheer de-fensiveness, that the angriest partisans of common-sense history display is a tribute, far less to their acuity than to the dents that the ablest of the psychohistorians have made in their armor. Their charges resemble the fortifications surrounding medieval cities, concentric rings of moats and walls. If the first must surrender to the aggressor, the second will continue to offer formidable resistance; once the second falls, the third remains as the next, if rather more desperate, bulwark against the in-vader. What the psychoanalytically informed historian wants to recover is, after all, real people in history, with real passions and real conflicts. That is why the most responsible of psychoanalytically oriented work conveys an intense feeling for actuality, far more intense than that avail-able to current popular social historians, really sociologists in historians' clothing, in whose pages the human subject has become almost wholly attenuated and peeks, a restless and forlorn ghost, from behind his tomb-stone engraved with graphs and charts.

To hear common-sense historians talk, and to read some of their anxious and angry reviews, it would appear that psychohistory has taken over the profession. But for all the noise that psychohistorians have been making since 1958, for all the energetic refutations that have confronted them, it is my impression that the Freudian invasion of the historian's terrain has been pretty thoroughly contained. The year 1958 was indeed an exciting one for psychohistory: it was, of course, the year in which William L. Langer's celebrated presidential address, "The Next Assign-ment," and Erik H. Erikson's no less celebrated *Young Man Luther* were published. And it is true that psychohistorians have gained access to historical periodicals and to professional conventions; they have even acquired the supreme stigmata of an established discipline, two journals of their own. But psychohistorians work, on the whole, as an embattled, often isolated minority; specialists normally review their books with un-disguised scorn and warmly recommend that their irresponsible specula-tive experiments be abandoned. Some of this, as I have noted, must be the psychohistorians' and, indeed, the psychoanalysts' fault. Neither has sufficiently appreciated the pressure of realities on the psyche, the activ-ity of the ego in working over the messages of the outside world, or the pressure of the internal drives to translate them into guides for belief and conduct.

I want to distinguish, therefore, very carefully, between psychohistory and psychoanalytically informed history. But even the latter, which I advocate, cannot count on the immediate approval, let alone applause, of the common-sense historian. The plausible assertion, which has reached the status of a truism, that we cannot psychoanalyze the dead stands in the way of any kind of alliance between psychoanalysis and history. My own attitude toward this influential cliché is a rather contradictory one. I should say, first, that it is not necessary for the historian to perform a psychoanalysis on the past before he can gather the benefits of psychoanalytic thinking about human nature and conduct. Certainly, the historian can never duplicate, in an armchair or in the archives, the psychoanalytic situation—hermetic, regressive, facilitating the communication of unconscious with unconscious, and depending on the analyst's feeling for the patient's mental state, the patient's capacity to produce associations for his dreams and his slips, and the patient's response to the analyst's spare interventions. But the historian can at least in some measure approximate the psychoanalytic situation: he can pursue dreams, especially if the dreamer has provided a texture of associations, beyond their manifest content recounted in a diary or a letter; he can read the sequence of sentences in a diary as though it were a chain of associations; he can tease out pervasive unconscious fantasies of individuals and of groups, from their dominance in popular novels or widely admired works of art. And so I would insist that for the historian alert to the work of Freud, psychoanalysis is not a clinical specialty or a rigid recipe but a way of seeing the past.

There are, it seems, two ways in which the historian can profitably employ psychoanalysis in his work. The first is to ask questions that psychoanalysis itself has made prominent. I am referring, in particular, to the study of sexuality and aggression, and of childhood, and to an alertness to dreams and slips of the tongue. Second, and this is more difficult on all accounts, the historian may tentatively and cautiously apply some of the techniques of psychoanalysis to his material. It is true enough, as I have already said, that the historian cannot psychoanalyze the past. He cannot do so even with a fully documented set of letters, diaries, journals, external descriptions, and surviving artifacts of some individual in history. The psychoanalytic process requires an interchange, an interaction, an interplay of two unconsciouses—the unconscious of the psychoanalyst and that of the analysand. There are times when dreamers of the past have recorded not merely their dreams, but also their associations, and then one may proceed at least to play with those dreams as though they were being presented in an analytic hour. But in general, of course, the psychoanalytic situation is unique and should not be transferred to a field in which it does not belong. At the same time, though, if one knows what one is doing, there is no reason why one may not wish to approximate at least these techniques while studying the past.

But I can see that it is necessary now to offer a few vignettes, as the psychoanalysts would call it. I want to move, therefore, from the general to the specific, from the abstract to the concrete. Before I do so, let me offer one particular and heartfelt caution: the interpretation that the psychoanalytically oriented historian may wish to offer of his material may be correct, but it is not likely to be complete. It is awareness of this fact that will contain and, if we are fortunate, wholly eliminate reductionism.

Here is one instance: recently, I have been writing a chapter on the kind of fantasy about love that nineteenth-century fiction enshrines. In reading a number of novels that I had not read before and, more informatively, in rereading some novels that I knew very well, as I thought, I came on family constellations that I simply had never noticed before. The instance of *David Copperfield* is particularly instructive. As we all know, this largely autobiographical novel tells the story of a young Englishman, a writer, from birth to happy middle age, when he settles down cheerfully with his second wife, Agnes, into respectable and prosperous middle-class existence, complete with happy children. The adventures that this successful writer undergoes are only too familiar: born to a loving mother whose husband has died before David's birth, he briefly enjoys a paradise for two, which is disrupted and destroyed by Clara Copperfield's dreadful second husband, Mr. Murdstone, and his even more dreadful sister. He is sent off callously to a school of ruffians and brutal ignoramuses; he is apprenticed even more brutally to a factory in London and runs away in despair, only to find a welcome in the home of his eccentric and formidable aunt, Betsey Trotwood. There are many adventures he undergoes and many people he meets. He marries briefly and happily, although not without troubles, Dora Spenlow and, after her timely, untimely death, finally gets his Agnes. *David Copperfield* is a novel full of adventure, comedy, pathos, and wrong turnings that turn right in the end. But once we analyze the novel from a psychoanalytic point of view, we discover some things that are so obvious that one does not have to be an analyst to notice them. I might add that they have become so obvious because Freud wrote when and as he did. Thus David's first wife, Dora, who appears to be his child in her perpetual and persistent infantilism, is really a replica of David Copperfield's mother. Both women are pretty, frail, and utterly ignorant of the world, refuse to grow up, and die young. Thus the first marriage of David Copperfield is really a revival of unfinished oedipal business. The suspicion that this is in fact

a novel about oedipal relationships is much strengthened once we in-
quire into the family constellations of all the other characters in the
book. We discover that practically none of the families in Dickens's
greatest novel are complete. Dora Spenlow, for example, lives with her
father, her mother having died earlier. Agnes Wickfield lives as house-
keeper and almost incestuous lover with her widowed father; indeed,
Agnes's mother died in childbirth. David Copperfield himself, of course,
has two fathers: the dead father whose absence permits him his Eden
with his mother, and the hated second father, Mr. Murdstone, who is
split off from the pure loving representation of the first father. Dr.
Strong, that aging, benign, and innocent scientist whose lovely wife is
about half his age or less, is really the father—and explicitly called that—
of his beloved Annie. Even the detestable Uriah Heep lives in close
proximity with his widowed mother, and their mutual love, although in
many respects appalling, is a kind of dark shadowy counterpart of the
incomplete families that populate the rest of the novel. And then there
are the Steerforths! Steerforth, David's closest friend, loves his mother
and is passionately loved in return; no Mr. Steerforth appears or is ever
even adverted to. And indeed the Peggottys, who live in that romantic
Noah's Ark on the shore at Yarmouth, are a strange incomplete family.
Little Em'ly loves her nonbiological father above all the others—above
Steerforth, above Ham, above the world.

We might, therefore, say that the novel is essentially an account of the
way in which a young man traverses his unfinished oedipal path to arrive
after the death of his first wife, who is, as I have said, a replica of his
mother, at a new love object, Agnes, with whom he can be truly adult.
But there is more to the novel than this, far more than I have time to
mention here. These oedipal battles are very convenient; most of them
have been won before they were even begun. It follows, therefore, that
they are in their own strange way a mask for earlier, even more primitive
sexual encounters and feelings than the oedipal stage itself. We see this
above all in the Steerforths, who quite openly retain the kind of sym-
biotic relationship that, according to Margaret Mahler, prevails with the
young child and its mother. And there are other incestuous as well as
homoerotic loves concealed, and sometimes half-opened, in that novel
to give the psychoanalytically informed historian pause. Nor is this simply an aberration. We find similar constellations in Dickens's other
novels. And, indeed, this set of constellations and problems arising from
them was really part of contemporary English society as well. Dickens
himself had passionate feelings for two of his sisters-in-law—both
younger sisters of his wife. And this at a time when in England it was

illegal to marry your deceased wife's sister; your wife's sister was your sister, and to contemplate such unions was to approach incest.

What this kind of analysis—of which, of course, I am giving here only the crudest of summaries—does is to combine in its way both the interest that psychoanalytic categories arouse in documents such as the novel and the psychoanalytic categories of the oedipal relationships that lead one directly to the psychoanalytic technique of going beyond the manifest to the latent. Thus the oedipal relationships are manifest enough to the careful reader of *David Copperfield*. The pre-oedipal relationships are only implicit and must be teased out.

Or consider the subject of prostitution. Recent historians have shed a great deal of light on prostitution in nineteenth-century Europe. They have done so in the main as social historians, being much interested in the labor market, in migration patterns, in the kind of sexual habits that prostitution appears to reveal about its customers. But there has been, to the best of my knowledge, no inquiry into what attitudes toward prostitution on the part of respectable people would reveal. It is notorious that William Gladstone picked up prostitutes at night after a long evening in the House of Commons and brought many of them home to remonstrate with them, to pray with them, and to urge their conversion to a better way of life. We also know that Dickens took a great deal of interest in the same unfortunate class and persuaded his friend, the millionairess Baroness Coutts, to establish a disciplined half-way house that would wean young prostitutes away from their calling and fit them for emigration and respectful marriage overseas. We know furthermore that city after city, in the United States as well as in Europe, occupied itself, particularly in the late nineteenth century and the early twentieth, with what came to be called almost universally "the social evil." In reading through this literature, I discovered that there was in the social scientists, as well as in those, like Gladstone, committed to doing good, a powerful underlying fantasy, so powerful that it was conscious in many respects. Here were the tips of a large iceberg: I knew about the function of the rescue fantasy in psychoanalysis, and it occurred to me that what we had here, in this widespread and intense and earnest concentration on the prostitute and her rehabilitation, was a kind of cultural rescue fantasy. I think that the way to understand this occupation is to search the minds of those who attempted to rescue these fallen women and to ask what these rescue attempts meant in their own emotional life, particularly as it related to their own sexual fantasies about their mothers. Here, as with *David Copperfield,* we see the combination of psychoanalytic curiosity and psychoanalytic techniques being employed.

Here is another instance: for all the prudishness that historians have attributed to respectable men and women of the nineteenth century, it is perfectly obvious that the nude—mainly the female, but also occasionally the male nude—was accessible to nearly everyone. Nudes appeared on the friezes of public libraries, loomed over public fountains, and decorated, often in larger than life size, public parks; there were nudes in reclining or heroic postures to be found, often very provocatively, in public exhibitions. One could learn a great deal about the human body by staring at these nudes, and if one allowed them to work on one, one might even find a measure of sexual arousal in oneself. Yet when looked at closely, one notices that most, although by no means all, of these nudes appear in what I can only call distance-making dress. They represent figures from antiquity, mythology, fairy tales, or oriental travel. A painter was free to paint a girl dressed in only a transparent shift and leaning suggestively against a doorway, once that doorway was identified as being, let us say, in North Africa. The same girl, in the same posture, against the same doorway, identified as lounging in Paris, would have been not merely cold but indecent. It will not do and would be in the highest degree unhistorical to be cynical about this kind of half-denial. It was the way in which the prosperous and the proper came to terms with the body in the nineteenth century; this informal doctrine of distance represented the kind of compromise that civilized people always adopt—each culture in its own way. What it did to and for the viewers of Eves and Primaveras and Odalisques is a question that the psychoanalytic historian may feel free to ask and is, in my judgment, best equipped to answer.

The uses of psychoanalysis in detecting the nonrational elements in politics and diplomacy, the share of unconscious passion in such historical issues as the spread of and resistance to birth control, the part that aggression plays in humor, the oedipal admixtures in attitudes toward authority in the law or the factory—these and much more cry out for the discoveries of Sigmund Freud, which should not merely assist the historian's understanding, but also complicate his perceptions. They should help him recognize what he *cannot* say quite as much as what he *can* say.

I could easily offer other instances from my own work or from that of others, but my point should be plain, and I want to return in conclusion to two problematic issues of method that have occupied me in recent years. The first concerns the relation of the individual to the collectivity in psychoanalytically informed history. I said that Sigmund Freud found no distinction between social and individual psychology, and I said also that the individual, drenched in his worlds, is a microcosm of his culture. I have no intention of withdrawing, or even weakening, these claims. I do want to embellish them. It would be an intellectual disaster if psychoanalytic history became a kind of Marxism in reverse, burdened with deadening predictability. The relation of individual and society is a dialectical one: the individual takes from society only what his biological endowment, his early experience, and his training have equipped him to take. Each person, as Sigmund Freud knew better than anyone, is just that: an individual—unique in at least some respects, and in many respects opaque. As Wolfgang Hildesheimer, Mozart's most recent and most rewarding biographer, a biographer deeply indebted to psychoanalysis, has rightly argued, we cannot guess Mozart's state of mind from his compositions and cannot infer Mozart's compositions from his state of mind.[7] The psychoanalytic historian must remember this and remember, too, that there are always more causes for historical events, more subtle interactions than he can comfortably accommodate by means of any rigid causal scheme. To introduce the instrument of psychoanalysis into history may be immensely helpful, but it is also dangerous, an invitation to prudence as well as to daring.

But who among historians is equipped to accept this invitation? This is my final question. H. Stuart Hughes some years ago proposed that younger historians might well undergo analysis for the sake not of alleviating their neurotic symptoms, but of improving their historical works. It is an engaging suggestion, but one that has, for understandable reasons, found little echo in the historical profession. To be psychoanalyzed is expensive, painful, time consuming, and supremely inconvenient. And, of course, some historians would prove to be unanalyzable. But if only a tiny handful of historians can be trained as psychoanalysts, if only a limited number of historians can be psychoanalyzed, the bulk of the profession could at least thoroughly acquaint itself with the ideas of psychoanalysis through some intensive courses in a local institute and some clinical experience. This is not much perhaps. I should wish for more. But at the very least, the historian should think of psychoanalysis as an indispensable foreign language that must be mastered. It is my firm conviction that it is a language worth learning.

7. Wolfgang Hildesheimer, *Mozart* (1977; tr. Marion Farber, New York: Random House, 1982).

6

Commentary on "Psychoanalysis in History"

Peter Paret

When I first read a draft of Peter Gay's paper, I felt that someone else should have been asked to comment on it. Now that I have heard him deliver it, that feeling has been reinforced. I find myself so much in agreement with his general outlook that this really is a case of preaching to the converted. That affinities exist between history and psychoanalysis seems to me undeniable, although I also believe that they are more ambiguous than Professor Gay could indicate in a brief essay. I share his confidence in the promise of analytically oriented studies of the past, as well as his belief that the vehement partisans of common-sense history protest too much—in the debate over psychobiographical interpretations of Woodrow Wilson between Alexander and Juliette George, on the one hand, and Arthur Link, on the other, I am squarely on the side of the Georges—just as I agree that many psychohistorians deserve bashing. The examples from his own work of ways in which historians can apply psychoanalytic ideas I find particularly interesting, and wish there had been time for him to expand on his interpretations of oedipal and pre-oedipal feelings in Dickens's novels, of the Victorians' fascination with prostitutes, and of the striking eroticism of much nineteenth-century art. In this last area, I would, however, place the accents somewhat differently. The distance-enhancing effect of Oriental or historical costume was probably not the decisive factor in allowing artists to depict the nude, but merely an attribute that heightened their appeal to a segment of the public. Certainly in France from the 1860s on, with Manet's *Déjeuner sur l'herbe* and *Olympia,* and with the public showing of some—if not all—of Courbet's more provocative canvases, the representation of the female nude in such nonexotic surroundings as European parks and dressing- or bedrooms became an accepted, if still pleasingly shocking genre.

The three examples from Professor Gay's research suggest what can be done by a historian who believes in psychoanalysis and who is trained in psychoanalytic procedure. Although I do not share his training, I share his belief, and thus am better suited to echo his ideas than to critique them. And yet it would be surprising if there were no skeptics, and for their sake and in order to move the debate forward, let me try to transform myself for the moment from true believer, not to devil's advocate, but to benevolent neutral, and pursue a few of the issues that Professor Gay has raised.

Psychoanalysis is, on the one hand, a theory concerning personality function and development and, on the other, a therapy for personality disorders. Both psychoanalytic therapy and history address the past, but necessarily do so in very different ways. The interaction of the analyst's unconscious and the patient's unconscious becomes in history a one-way process. The informed unconscious of the scholar can still achieve much, but it cannot stimulate the emergence of additional material. Perhaps equally important, the purposes of history and analysis differ. After all, analytic therapy is not concerned primarily with intellectual understanding, but rather with bringing about certain changes in feeling and attitude, which in large measure derive from a gradually coalescing unconscious comprehension. For an analyst to inform his patient that he suffers from a particular type of neurotic reaction is not going to be of much help to the patient. True, a significant element of the patient's personal history has been identified and laid bare, and it can now be read like a book; but the patient continues to suffer. That kind of intellectual recognition is not the ultimate analytic goal; it merely serves the analyst as a guide for further work. Perhaps those analysts who are prone to early and frequent interpretations can be compared with those psychohistorians who construct vast deterministic edifices on supposition and selected evidence. The further we penetrate the structure of the two disciplines—the temple of history, hallowed, somewhat ramshackle, and the snail house (if I may call it that) of psychoanalysis—the more evident the dissimilarities of the disciplines become. Mr. Gay himself acknowledged their very real differences before calling our attention to their affinities. Would it perhaps be preferable to speak of affinities not between the two disciplines—which would encompass scholar or therapist, subject or patient, and their interactions—but merely between their practitioners: historians and analysts? Such a communality would, of course, be shared by other scholars as well—for instance, archaeologists or some literary critics.

Professor Gay realistically limits his hope that more historians undergo analysis to a few individuals, who for their own unique reasons set out on this difficult path. Many more, he suggests, might acquaint themselves with the ideas of psychoanalysis through intensive courses. But here we must distinguish between two different goals, differences that Professor Gay is certainly aware of, but that do not consistently emerge from his paper. One goal is for historians to become acquainted with the basic concepts and ways of thinking of a discipline other than their own. That can only be beneficial. The other goal is to place psychoanalysis at or near the center of history. It seems equally obvious that this can hold true for only a few scholars. Professor Gay suggests that historians consider psychoanalysis as an indispensable foreign language that must be mastered. Freud, in the 1913 essay that Mr. Gay quotes, refers to the "psychoanalytic mode of thought" as "a new instrument of research." And perhaps by claiming less, this is more accurate. Without this instrument, it would be difficult, perhaps impossible, to raise certain questions. But we would not find ourselves uncomprehending and mute, as we would if we lacked an indispensable language. Methodology is important, but in history something else is even more important, and I hope that I will not seem too romantic if I say that what matters above all is intelligence and sensitivity. Marc Bloch and Otto Hintze did not become great historians because they used the comparative method; their development of comparative analysis extended the reach of their talent and led them into areas they otherwise might not have explored.

Historians, who as a group are as subject to trends as other academics, are sometimes too ready to welcome a new method as though it would make all the difference. Some decades ago, that occurred with the development of the new social history, which not only resulted in much valuable work, but also turned some historians into zealots who dismissed other approaches—especially such traditional varieties as diplomatic or military history—as antiquated, naïve, and likely to corrupt the young. This attitude is now fading, and we can all be pleased that there is no prospect that it will be replaced by a new fashion, that of history done by the analyzed or even the psychoanalytically trained historian. Surely, such scholars will always remain a small group—let us hope an elite—that will inspire a larger number of colleagues not necessarily to enter analytic training, but to become sensitive to the psychoanalytic mode of thought.

History has been far too slow to learn from psychoanalysis; but psychoanalysis, too, has shown insufficient inclination to learn from history. I would not dare suggest that analysts enter graduate study in history, although the coming together of such diverse ways of thinking and of such different economic conditions and expectations makes for a not-uninteresting fantasy. But if analysts would read more serious history, it might not reverse, but at least stem the trend that has moved their discipline in the aggregate a considerable distance from the humanistic outlook of its founder.

To conclude, I want to return briefly to the concept of psychoanalysis as one research instrument among many, invaluable in some areas of study, and to the historian's intelligence and sensitivity, which are decisive in all areas. To give these abstractions more meaning, let me mention two well-known, even famous books by historians, neither of whom, as far as I know, was influenced by psychoanalysis. We can only speculate about how these books would have differed had their authors been analyzed; but it seems safe to say that one of the books would not have been significantly improved by its author's comprehension of psychoanalysis, while such comprehension might very much have improved the other.

The first book is *The Great Fear of 1789* by Georges Lefebvre.[1] In this work, Lefebvre interprets certain waves of panic that ran through parts of the French countryside in the second half of July 1789, as a phenomenon separate from other incidents of fear and violence at the time, and one that had a deep impact on the French Revolution. Rumors that criminals in the pay of the aristocracy were entering the neighborhood triggered these panics, which were followed by peasants taking up arms to defend themselves, after which, since no brigands appeared, the peasants destroyed the manorial archives that contained the documents that set out their work and tax obligations. The brigands were, of course, a delusion, but a delusion that caused the peasants to act in ways that realistically were very much in their own interest.

Lefebvre had studied LeBon's crude theories of mass psychology, and in the same year that *The Great Fear* appeared, 1932, published an article on the psychology of revolutionary crowds. But in the book, apart from a few references to autosuggestion, he applies no psychological concepts to the behavior of the peasants, nor are these concepts—although unexpressed—reflected in his interpretation. And yet the feelings and behavior of the peasants, the elements that made their delusion possible, and the practical exploitation of the delusion are traced with

1. Georges Lefebvre, *The Great Fear of 1789* (Princeton, N.J., Princeton University Press: 1932/1982).

such precision and insight that the psychological process becomes clear. It was, of course, not only intelligent and imaginative research that made this possible, but also Lefebvre's attitude to his subject. He neither judges nor glorifies the peasants; he sympathizes with their condition, and tries to understand their feelings and the external and internal causes that generated those feelings.

The second book is *The Sans-Culottes* by Albert Soboul.[2] This work draws a social and political portrait of those Parisian activists during the French Revolution whose politics centered on the city government and the district organizations. By identifying the various social and economic conditions of the people who called themselves sans-culottes and by studying their daily life, their organizations, and their social and political goals, Soboul gave new substance to a vague generalization. But his book suffers from a conflict between the differentiated approach of his research and his ideological, deterministic outlook. He fits the sans-culottes into a dialectical process of history that will eventually bring about the dictatorship of the proletariat. Because of this ultimate rigidity, the book is full of contradictions and missed opportunities. For example, Soboul briefly discusses the question of violence, but he cannot explain the psychological forces that compelled or allowed the sans-culotte to break out of his daily routine of work, time with his family, and attendance at his political club and to become a supporter of—or even participant in—terror. The psychoanalytic mode of thinking would surely have advanced Soboul's interpretation; but his ideological need to see and present the sans-culottes as flawed but nevertheless admirable precursors of world revolution made deeper insights impossible.

Finally, to return to the specifics of Professor Gay's paper. His central argument—that psychoanalysis might be immensely useful to history—can only be endorsed. Beyond that, the paper seems to me a compound of general propositions, very suggestive examples drawn from his research, and personal statements. These three elements are not always smoothly integrated, as perhaps they hardly can be. But it is their conjunction, and the sometimes unresolved tension among them, that help make the paper so interesting and stimulating.

---

2. Albert Soboul, *Les Sans-Culottes Parisiens en L'An II* (La Roche-sur-Yon: Potier, 1958).

7

Psychoanalytic Models of History: Freud and After

Peter Loewenberg

Freud initiated the enterprise we now call psychohistory, not merely because he was a curious commentator, critic, and analyst of civilization who wished to present a "general psychology" that would be valid for all of humankind. He was a deeply cultured man who would have preferred to be a philosopher rather than a clinician. He also committed his psychodynamic ideas to the problems of history, culture, art, and literary criticism as a strategy of presentation to circumvent the evidential problem of case histories. No one fully knows what goes on in any clinical psychoanalytic setting. Even in the "Rat Man" case, for which we have Freud's case notes, there is much that we must infer and will never know. Freud chose to demonstrate his insights and formulae of mental functioning by reference to the works of Leonardo and Michelangelo, Shakespeare and Ibsen, because these data and artifacts belong to the culture at large. Any person may obtain, study, scrutinize, and question Freud's interpretations from the same data base, to see if they make sense or convey conviction. In their persistent quest for a more accurate model of the mind, Freud and his successor psychoanalysts created models that reflected shifts in the culture at large, thus the current interest in narcissism.

What I propose to do in this paper is trace what I perceive was a crucial move from libidinal-drive models of psychology applied to history to a more recent use of ego psychological and object relations paradigms. The libido psychological model has given us neat explana-

This essay is dedicated to Helen Eisenstein: sister, counselor, friend.

tions of great force in biography. This model operates using the principles of repetition-compulsion and the reenactment of trauma. It also has serious limitations that must be recognized and may be improved on in historical writing, just as the libido model has been updated in clinical psychoanalysis.

I also wish to draw attention to the uses of a new and conscious emphasis on what the clinician terms countertransference—the researcher's subjective response to the material as an important datum meriting scrutiny and interpretation. Whereas older models of history would purge such subjective sensations and build rigid barriers to the admission of feeling in the name of an ephemeral "objectivity" in history, today's historian realizes that his or her feelings, sensations, and responses, both to the data and to the manner in which other historians have responded, are preciously significant. As George Devereux, the doyen of psychoanalytic anthropologists, has stressed, "The scientific study of man . . . must use the subjectivity inherent in all observation as the royal road to an authentic, rather than fictitious, objectivity. . . . When treated as basic and characteristic data of behavioral science [this subjectivity is] more valid and more productive than any other type of datum."[1] I will discuss contemporary American historical research and writing on Richard Nixon, Adolf Hitler, Léon Blum, Leon Trotsky, Gustav Landauer, Victor and Friedrich Adler, and the American Civil War in these contexts of drive psychology, psychoanalytic ego psychology, object relations, and countertransference by historians.

II

My late excellent and deeply mourned colleague, Fawn Brodie, wrote a posthumously published biography of Richard Nixon that shows all the strengths and the flaws of an instinctual-drive model of psychohistory. The model is one of great power and persuasiveness as one reads her account of the shaping of the character of the president whose tenure in office ended so ignobly with the exposure of his lies. One of Brodie's major themes is Nixon as a liar in matters large and small throughout his life. She contends that "Nixon lied to gain love, to store up his grandiose fantasies, to bolster his ever-wavering sense of identity. He lied in attacks, hoping to win. . . . And always he lied, and this most

1. George Devereux, *From Anxiety to Method in the Behavioral Sciences* (The Hague, Paris, 1967), p. xvii.

aggressively, to deny that he lied. . . . Finally, he enjoyed lying."[2] She shows Nixon lying about trivia, such as his college major and his wife's first name and birth date, as well as in his first campaign for the Congress against incumbent Jerry Voorhis, about his secret slush fund in the 1952 presidential campaign, and, of course, in the Watergate cover-up.[3] Brodie structures an argument that Nixon learned to lie in boyhood from a "myth making mother," who denied what was uncomfortable and stretched the truth, and from a brutal, hot-tempered father, who punished his boys with the strap and rod when he failed to get instant obedience, and that Nixon learned to be, in his words, "pretty convincing to avoid punishment."[4] She builds a case that "almost every one of Nixon's victories and political achievements save the elections to the vice-presidency had been won as a result of lying attack or the unexpected and fortuitous death of others."[5] Her emphasis on the theme of Nixon the liar from boyhood to maturity, from parental home to the White House, is essentially static and, while powerful, is unsatisfactory in its neglect of Nixon's many ego strengths and adaptations in a long political career.

My suggestion is that the historian must look carefully at the vicissitudes of Nixon's ego functioning in the dimensions of time and circumstance. By "ego functions," I mean the part of Nixon's mind that dealt with reality, coped with stress and defeat, found modes of adapting to new and unforeseen situations, made assessments concerning the future, evaluated in-puts of information, and distinguished or failed to discern facts from his own wishes. The use of ego psychology in history suggests that we look carefully and time specifically at where Nixon effectively reality tested and when and where he did not, when he adapted successfully to stresses and setbacks and when he did not. In short, those areas and times when his personality broke down or functioned most effectively will tell us much about the make-up and patterning of his defense mechanisms and of his character. This model and method are supremely historical because they are preeminently time specific, always posing the question: Why now?

An ego psychological view would look at how skillfully and cleverly during all of his career—until the end, when he had reached the pinnacle of political power—Nixon knew and supplied exactly what the American

2. Fawn M. Brodie, *Richard Nixon: The Shaping of His Character* (New York, 1981), p. 25.

3. Ibid., pp. 27, 179–80, 280.

4. Ibid., pp. 40–41.

5. Ibid., p. 507.

public wished to hear. He was a vicious anti-Communist "gut fighter" in his campaigns against Jerry Voorhis in 1946 and Helen Gahagan Douglas in 1950 and in his investigation of the Alger Hiss case. I emphasize this not to endorse his witch hunting, but merely to say that he knew what the public wanted to hear. He sensed the mood of the electorate and ruthlessly exploited it. Years later, when Americans were prepared to tolerate the recognition of Communist China and détente with the Soviet Union, Nixon was eager to lead the way. I also think that a president deserves credit for discernment and talent in his appointments and that Nixon's choice of Henry Kissinger to steer American foreign policy was of that high order.

In the 1952 presidential campaign, Nixon saved his political career and the Republican ticket with his maudlin "Checkers" speech. General Eisenhower was ready to drop him from the GOP slate. His career appeared to be finished, done for. We may listen to the speech today and find the emotional tone unctuous and revolting, but in that crunch he knew what would sell and he produced it. He was always within the boundaries of the law. He had, as Brodie puts it, "the skill of a man who can profit successfully on the fringes of political graft."[6]

I suggest further that a man who could repeatedly take major defeats and turn them around to mere setbacks, as Nixon did, gives evidence of great ego strength. He lost the race for the presidency to John F. Kennedy in 1960. Two years later, he could not win even the governorship of California, his home state. By any expectable evaluation of political prospects in America, his career was again finally over and done for. Yet he traveled the country and rebuilt a Republican party riven by vituperative conflict between Rockefeller and Goldwater factions; he mended political fences and emerged as the leader of choice to win the presidency he had so long sought.

The psychohistorical problem of Nixon and Watergate, then, is not why he was a liar; rather, it is a question of timing—that most critical historical and psychological question: Why now? He had achieved his life aim. He was an experienced lawyer, a veteran of both the House and the Senate, an accomplished congressional investigator. One has to be highly provocative to bring the Congress to draft a resolution of impeachment, truly the gravest of political rejections that our constitutional system allows. It happened only once before in American history. One must give the congressional committee two pieces of evidence, such as a tape and a transcript, that do not match. To have brought events to

6. Ibid., p. 280. On this and the following section see Peter Loewenberg, "Nixon, Hitler, and Power: An Ego Psychological Study," *Psychoanalytic Inquiry* 6, no. 1 (1986): 27–48.

the pass of political isolation and national demoralization that Nixon achieved requires great unconscious effort and poor reality testing. It demanded that he be profligate with all his natural political advantages and largely alienate the political and opinion-making structures of the society, including those of his own party, which desire to respond positively to the awe and the power that the office of president of the United States confers. The psychohistorical question for research is why did this most cunning of politicians show such poor judgment and reality testing, which was generally uncharacteristic of him, *at that time,* but not all of his prevaricating life.

III

Psychological interpretations have appropriately taken a leading place in the continuing attempts to understand the Nazi movement, the Third Reich, and the person of Adolf Hitler. The current literature provides an excellent forum in which to survey the state of applications of psychology to history.[7] I will discuss the central issues of the new Hitler historiography and use these issues to focus on some of the difficulties and inadequacies of contemporary historical practice in the study of biography and leadership. I will also look at possible areas of future work and point to directions where psychological insight can contribute to Hitler research. The three conceptual areas where a knowledge and use of psychodynamics will make a substantial difference in historical formulation and conclusions are in applying ego psychology, in taking most seriously and interpreting psychoanalytically Hitler's fantasies, and in utilizing the varieties of psychoanalytic object relations theory. In examining these problems, we not only can arrive at an assessment of the present state of Hitler scholarship, but also may come to some conclusions regarding the state and method of psychohistorical writing today and venture some answers as to what psychoanalytic psychology can and cannot do for history.

An early strand of Hitler scholarship puts the spotlight on his destructiveness and self-destructiveness, but without the time-specific developmental dimension that is the essence of both historical and clinical work. James McRandle, in a suggestive essay, lifts out the many depressed and suicidal aspects of Hitler's career, including such early data as the failures at school, in Vienna, and with the 1923 Munich *Putsch*. McRandle

---

7. See the excellent review essay by Geoffrey Cocks, "The Hitler Controversy," *Political Psychology* 1, no. 2 (Autumn 1979): 67–81.

finds in Hitler "a tendency to fail in everything he attempted. He failed at school, he failed as an artist, and he failed in his relationships with other human beings. Furthermore, there is at least some reason to believe that these failures were self-induced."[8] McRandle points to Hitler's youthful suicide threats as one example of a self-destructive tendency, demonstrating that "between 1900 and 1914 Hitler acted in such a manner as to insure his continued failure."[9]

McRandle cogently poses the psychological problem of explanation: "It is amazing that a person who had failed so consistently in the endeavors of the first half of his life should be so astoundingly successful in the following years."[10] The relevant issue is not the presence of failures, for all persons and all parties have failed at some junctures. What must be assessed is how Hitler coped with defeats and twists of fortune, when and where he came back from them and was able to handle them to his own and his movement's benefit.

Erich Fromm, in his work on human destructiveness, finds Hitler to be the prime example of a "necrophilous character," by which he means a person who is dedicated to the destruction of life. Fromm believes this was caused by Hitler's malignant incestuous early relationship with his mother.[11] Certainly, Hitler was one of the most destructive, morbid, deadly, and death-oriented figures in history. The proof that he was so is there in his actions in the historical record. But what is gained by taking this proof and tautologically giving it the labels "necrophilous" and "malignant aggression"? Fromm's circular hypothesis tells us nothing about Hitler that we do not already know. What we now need to know is precisely when Hitler was politically competent and when he was disaster prone in terms of political functioning.

Rudolph Binion proposes an absolute psychic determination of the repetition of a presumed youthful trauma suffered at age eighteen when, according to his reconstruction, Hitler's mother was overdosed with iodoform gauze and prematurely killed by a Jewish doctor, Eduard Bloch, who treated her for breast cancer. From here, Binion moves to Hitler's trauma from mustard-gas poisoning in World War I, and then on to the gassing of the Jews in the Final Solution (1942–45). Thus Binion writes of Hitler's exposure to mustard gas on the Western Front

8. James H. McRandle, "The Suicide," in *The Track of the Wolf: Essays on National Socialism and Its Leader, Adolf Hitler* (Evanston, Ill., 1965), p. 156.

9. Ibid., pp. 163–64, 169.

10. Ibid., p. 170.

11. Erich Fromm, *The Anatomy of Human Destructiveness* (New York, 1973), pp. 330, 332, 365, 377.

in 1919: "When it condensed on his skin Hitler associated it with Bloch's iodoform. But then he expanded it to associate it with asphyxiating gas as well. The gas chambers resulted."[12] This kind of reductionism does poor service to the enterprise of psychology applied to history.

Robert G. L. Waite's study of Hitler is in a broader historical context, yet takes account of the power of fantasy and treats evidence with psychoanalytic perceptiveness. For example, his inference that Hitler had a primal-scene trauma is based on the careful reconstruction of Hitler's self-reference from his fantasied reports of brutal assault by a father and rape of the mother observed by a hypothetical three-year-old boy. The case is convincing because of an overwhelming convergence of fantasied events with the data of Hitler's childhood. Waite is most pertinently psychoanalytic when he says, "We shall never know with finality whether the infant Adolf actually saw the scene of sexual assault. But in his fantasy he did, and it was for him a 'primal scene trauma.' "[13]

The German psychoanalyst Helm Stierlin takes an approach to Hitler based on his clinical work with families, postulating a generational dynamic in which Hitler served as the "delegated" of his mother to remain psychologically deeply dependent on her, to be living evidence of her good mothering, to give glory, excitement, and importance to her life, and to be her avenger and ally against a husband who had neglected and oppressed her.[14] Stierlin draws out the psychological implications of Hitler's "Petronella" story, which describes how his Steyr landlady humiliated her husband by locking him out of the house overnight and not admitting him, cowed and pitiful, until the morning. Hitler tells of his own refusal to unbolt the door to the pleading man and of his disdain for the husband as a "wet rag." Stierlin asks why did Hitler take the part of the wife and not the man? He suggests that the answer lies in Hitler's relation to his mother, who comforted him when his father beat him and to whom he felt as a loyal ally. Thus he avenged her in fantasy and let her triumph over the husband, whom he pictures as a ridiculous

12. Rudolph Binion, *Hitler Among the Germans* (New York, 1976), p. 131. See the critique of Binion's assumptions and method in Peter Loewenberg, *Journal of Modern History* 47, no. 2 (June 1975): 241–44.

13. Robert G. L. Waite, *The Psychopathic God: Adolf Hitler* (New York, 1977), p. 162. Waite's interpretation of these beating fantasies draws on the strongest part of the psychoanalytic study of Hitler prepared for the United States Office of Strategic Services in 1943 and published as Walter C. Langer, *The Mind of Adolf Hitler: The Secret Wartime Report* (New York, 1972), pp. 141–45. See the review essay by Peter Loewenberg in *Central European History* 7, no. 3 (September 1974): 262–75, and "Hitler's Psychodynamics Examined," *Contemporary Psychology* 19, no. 2 (February 1974): 89–91.

14. Helm Stierlin, *Adolf Hitler: Familien perspektiven* (Frankfurt am Main, 1975), pp. 73–74.

weakling.[15] Stierlin lacks historical evidence for his general thesis of maternal "delegation," but when he deals with Hitler's own fantasies as a raconteur and his identifications in sadistic humor, we have evidence of true internalization deriving from his relations with his mother. We can see his mother as he saw her—a powerful object who had a strong reality that was introjected to become a part of him.

When all these identifications are demonstrated, it is still a historically static picture of Hitler. I concur with the thrust of George Mosse's critique of psychological treatments of Hitler:

> I remain puzzled why psychohistory persists in concentrating on one side of Hitler's character, namely his youth and adolescence and his supposed abnormalities and neuroses. It is difficult to see from this approach how his political genius was formed as well as the source of his superb sense of timing and his ability to learn from past mistakes. . . . Why not call a moratorium on analyses of this side of his character (which certainly may have existed) and instead study the personality factor behind his actions which in fact made him one of the most successful statesmen of our century.[16]

That is why we as historians need ego psychology in our research armamentarium.

In order to demonstrate the congruence of psychoanalytic ego psychology with historical method, I will examine closely a few crucial episodes drawn from the political, military, and diplomatic history of the two critical decades 1923 to 1942. Let us examine Hitler in action to determine precisely when his ego functions of reality testing and adaptation in specific foreign and domestic areas worked well, and when they broke down. I propose to examine Hitler's functioning in three particular moments in history: (1) the crisis in the party after the failure of the Munich *Putsch* (1923–25); (2) the period of electoral decline in the party's fortunes in the fall and winter of 1932; and (3) the series of diplomatic and military errors and miscalculations beginning with Dunkirk in 1940, coming to focus in the declaration of war against the United States in December 1941, and including the decision making on the Eastern Front at the battles of Kiev and Stalingrad.

We are immediately struck by Hitler's skill at holding the reins of

15. Ibid., pp. 85–86. The "Petronella" story as told by Hitler is Conversation 100, night of January 8–9, 1942, in *Hitler's Secret Conversations, 1941–44*, ed. Henry Picker, (New York, 1961), p. 201.

16. George L. Mosse, "Comment," *History of Childhood Quarterly* 3, no. 4 (Spring 1976): 506.

leadership even after the debacle of the 1923 Munich *Putsch*. Hitler was in prison, and contending leaders were fighting for the succession. He categorically refused to intervene in their quarrels. His silence encouraged their divisive feuding. Dietrich Orlow writes, "When Hitler emerged from his prison cell in December, he returned as a saint, eagerly awaited and welcomed by all of the volkisch groups." His first speech after his release was "a masterful effort."[17] Harold Gordon evaluates Hitler's ego functioning in the period after the *Putsch:*

> It was here, in the months after the Putsch, that one finds the real Triumph des Willens. By sheer determination and sense of mission Hitler transformed himself from the frenetic revolutionary who had been shattered and silenced by the Putsch into a political leader ready to accept years of careful building and constant struggle as a prelude to power.[18]

Hitler had an extraordinary ability to understand and make use of the weakness of his opponents. Within the party, he knew how to divide them and strike them one by one. In Orlow's estimation, he met the left-wing challenge of Gregor Strasser in 1925 "brilliantly." He coped with a major challenge by the northern leaders of the party by staging a meeting in his stronghold of Bamberg in February 1926. He seduced Joseph Paul Goebbels, the only major northern figure he had not won over. He invited Goebbels to Munich in early April to address a mass rally, lent him his car, and gave him a personal tour of party headquarters. After this treatment, Goebbels was "putty in Hitler's hands." Goebbels wrote in his diary on April 13, 1926, "Hitler is a great man. He forgives us and shakes our hand. Let us forget the past."

The greatest test of the sureness of Hitler's leadership came in the fall of 1932. The Nazis had done sensationally well in the July 31, 1932, Reichstag elections, more than doubling their vote of 1930, from 6.4 million to 13.7 million. Their Reichstag seats went up from 107 to 230, making the NSDAP by far the largest party. There was, however, a feeling of exhaustion, a sense that time was the party's enemy. Subscriptions to party newspapers began to drop off in the fall of 1932. In some *Gaus* (or districts), the number of resignations exceeded applications for membership. The debts from the July election had not been paid. The party's finances were severely strained. It was difficult to raise the new

17. Dietrich Orlow, *The History of the Nazi Party: 1919–1933* (Pittsburgh, 1969), pp. 51, 54.

18. Harold J. Gordon, Jr., *Hitler and the Beer Hall Putsch* (Princeton, N.J., 1972), p. 618.

campaign contributions for the fourth national campaign in a year. Local elections were going against the NSDAP. In a local election held in East Prussia on October 9, 1932, the Nazi vote, which had been 1,074 in Konigsberg in July, dropped to 483; in Gerdauen, it dropped from 1,074 to 126.[19]

The November 6, 1932, Reichstag elections gave the Nazis severe setbacks in all areas of Germany. No *Gau* was able to maintain its July strength. Nationally, the vote dropped from 13.7 million in July to 11.7 million in November, and the number of seats in the Reichstag fell from 230 to 196. It appeared that the strategy of massive electoral victories had come to a dead end and that the Nazi drive for power had peaked in July 1932. Strasser put Hitler under pressure to join a coalition, with the argument that the National Socialist wave had crested. Hitler stood firm, refusing to join any government not headed by himself and having extensive decree powers. He refused to settle for partial power or a partial victory. The pressure on him was intense. Membership increases declined sharply. *Gau* Brandenburg suffered a net membership decline in November. The financial picture was regarded as "hopeless." Local elections in Saxony on November 14 and in Thuringia on December 3 showed disastrous losses in both areas. "In this circumstance," writes Alan Bullock, "it was only Hitler's determination and leadership that kept the Party going. His confidence in himself never wavered. When the Gauleiters assembled at Munich in early October he used all his arts to put new life and energy into them."[20]

Reichschancellor Kurt von Schleicher sought to use the crisis in the party and the pressure on Hitler by offering him a vice chancellorship and the posts of prime minister of Prussia and minister of the interior for other Nazis. Hitler remained adamant. Despite his own and his associates' "hunger for power" and the severe setbacks that he received in election after election toward the end of 1932, Hitler categorically refused all compromises or offers of coalition. In the words of Dietrich Orlow, "The NSDAP at the end of 1932 was well on its way to the rubbish pile of history."[21] Yet, as we know, history turned out otherwise. And in this case, at this particular time, it was the adaptation of Hitler to the political realities of Germany and his capacity to deal with great inner and outer stress that took him to power on his own terms on January 30, 1933. If, as Alan Bullock so memorably notes, "Hitler did not

19. Orlow, *History of the Nazi Party,* pp. 68–69, 72 (Gobbels quote), 284, 288–89.

20. Alan Bullock, *Hitler: A Study in Tyranny,* rev. ed. (New York, 1961), p. 191.

21. Orlow, *History of the Nazi Party,* pp. 290, 308.

seize power; he was jobbed into office by a backstairs intrigue,"[22] we must acknowledge his skill and effectiveness at dealing with such masters of intrigue as Franz von Papen and General Kurt von Schleicher. He understood the unscrupulous political game of the end of Weimar better than did his counterplayers.

One of the earliest and most original interpretations of Adolf Hitler and his relation to the German people is that of Erik H. Erikson. In a formulation that has become a classic, he interprets Hitler's *Mein Kampf* as a myth made by the man himself, a legend of a hard and bitter youth, a harsh tyrannical civil-servant father, and a devoted loving mother. Hitler pictures himself as a talented, sensitive son who wanted to be an artist and who refused to submit to his father's desire to make him a Habsburg civil servant, a good orderly bourgeois. He refused to identify with his father. Erikson said:

> Psychologists overdo the father attributes in Hitler's historical image; Hitler the adolescent who refused to become a father by any connotation, or, for that matter, a kaiser or a president. He did not repeat Napoleon's error. He was the Führer: a glorified older brother, . . . he reserved for himself the new position of the one who remains young in possession of supreme power. He was the unbroken adolescent . . . a gang leader who kept the boys together by demanding their admiration, by creating terror, and by shrewdly involving them in crimes from which there was no way back.

What, we may ask, is the meaning of Erikson's famous interpretation of Hitler: "This combination of personal revelation and shrewd propaganda (together with loud and determined action) at last carried with it that universal conviction for which the smoldering rebellion in German youth had been waiting. . . . Both fathers and sons could now identify with the Führer, and adolescent who never gave in."[23] What is implied is what I wish to explicitly delineate here—to have unconsciously constructed a myth with such a wide appeal to German youth and adults was a major feat of synthesis, creativity, and adaptation. Most of us do not even know what is going on with contemporary youth, let alone be able to appeal to them in a political movement. Here two points I wish to make come together. Erikson is writing of Hitler's ability to use his fantasies and to adapt them to the political purpose of building a movement with a mass following. We must also consider how Hitler's fantasies led to his own and the Third Reich's destruction.

22. Bullock, *Hitler*, p. 213.
23. Erik Erikson, *Childhood and Society*, 2d ed. (New York, 1963), pp. 336–37.

A recent school, represented by J. P. Stern and Friedrich Heer, sees Nazism as a secularized religion, particularly an aberrant form of Roman Catholicism, and Hitler as its psychologically sensitive prophet. By contrast, Ernst Nolte, who defines fascism at its "most fundamental" level as a "resistance to transcendence," dissents from this view. To him, fascism does not qualify as a "process which disengages the individual from traditional ties and increases the power of the group until it finally assails even the primordial forces of nature and history."[24] J. P. Stern disputes both the category of "transcendence" and Nolte's exclusion of Hitler from those who utilized religious expectations and rituals. Hitler's program was successful, says Stern, because it was "conducted under the image and in the language of transcendence, as the answer to a religious longing and demand."[25] Hitler's communion, according to Heer's interpretation, was *Volksgemeinschaft;* his ritual, mass meetings; his Mass, the celebration of the sacred Great War.[26] There is more than a little truth here. Religion expresses the mystical and unconscious needs of its communicants. Repressed by the rationalist science of the nineteenth century, which reached its high point in Germany, the unconscious revenged itself in varieties of pseudorcligions, among them *Volkisch* sects and National Socialism. The founders of religions are often under the sway of delusions, megalomania, and psychotic ideation, as Fawn Brodie has shown in the case of Joseph Smith.[27] To present to the world a set of fantasies that induces others to share them and to become followers is by no means a sign of sanity, but it is the sign of a good salesman. Certain kinds of sociopaths are notorious for their ability to sell with conviction, to lie, and to feel no guilt.

Hitler was flexible on all political issues to the point of being totally unprincipled. He succeeded in accommodating to the churches, including the Vatican in the Concordat of July 20, 1933, which recognized the right of the Roman Catholic Church in Germany to manage its own affairs. On the issue of socialization, he succeeded in neutralizing the party's left wing and appealed to Germany's industrialists for support. He manipulated Reichswehr generals, whom he at first needed, into sup-

24. Ernst Nolte, *Three Faces of Fascism: Action Française, Italian Fascism, National Socialism,* trans. Leila Vennewitz (New York, 1966), pp. 420–21, 429, 433.

25. J. P. Stern, *Hitler: The Fuhrer and the People* (Berkeley and Los Angeles, 1975), p. 97.

26. Friedrich Heer, *Der Glaube des Adolf Hitler: Anatomie einer Politischen Religiosität* (Munich, 1968), p. 184.

27. Fawn M. Brodie, *No Man Knows My History: The Life of Joseph Smith, the Mormon Prophet* (New York, 1945, 1960).

porting him in 1934, and then managed to control them and force them into subservience in 1938.[28]

When we come to the war itself and the spring of 1940, we begin to find the commission of a series of failures, miscalculations, and, finally, self-destructive acts by Hitler that constitute a startling contrast to his prior acute judgement, flexibility, and sense of the possible. In the Norwegian campaign, Hitler was prepared to withdraw after the British made a decisive naval strike in Narvik Fjord, on April 14, 1940.[29] Hitler, notes chief of the General Staff, Franz Halder, "was completely at a loss at the appearance of the first major crisis at Narvik, and but for the energetic intervention of his senior military adviser in Supreme Headquarters would have called off the whole operation."[30]

Hitler's subsequent failure to follow up the Ardennes breakthrough in May 1940 was a major puzzle to military contemporaries and is still a point of controversy among historians. On May 24, Heinz Guderian's tanks, which were part of von Kleist's army group, were at Gravelines on the River Aa, twelve miles west of Dunkirk and in position to capture the last Channel port of escape open to the British Expeditionary Force. The British headquarters was forty-two miles to the southeast, at Lille; thus the German panzers were thirty miles closer to Dunkirk than were most of the British armies. At noon on May 24, Hitler, agreeing with Rundstedt's advice, issued a "Tank Halt" order, which stopped his panzers for three days.[31] Rundstedt's motives were his concern that the western wing of the German advance was too weak to withstand a possible Anglo-French thrust from the south, and he wished to conserve armored strength for an anticipated main battle in France.

Hitler allowed Göring to persuade him that the "National Socialist Luftwaffe" rather than the "conservative-traditional" army could alone destroy the surrounded Allied armies. To the German army would re-

28. Harold C. Deutsch, *Hitler and His Generals: The Hidden Crisis, January–June 1938* (Minneapolis, 1974).

29. Franz Halder, *Kriegstagebuch*, vol. 1, *Vom Polenfeldzug bis zum Ende der West-offensive* (Stuttgart, 1962), p. 259.

30. Franz Halder, *Hitler as War Lord*, trans. Paul Findlay (London, 1950), p. 32.

31. Der "Halt-Befehl," 12:31 hours, May 24, 1940, Heeresgruppenkommando to Armeeoberkommando by telephone, in *Dokumente zum Westfeldzug 1940*, ed. Hans-Adolf Jacobsen (Göttingen, 1960), p. 120. The order was confirmed in Army Order No. 5, 21:00 hours, May 25, 1940, in ibid., No. 12, p. 128, and lifted in Army Order No. 6 21:00 hours, May 26, 1940, in ibid., No. 16, pp. 138–41, which, however, authorized Army Group von Kleist to move only to artillery range of Dunkirk: "The breaking of the resistance in the city itself is to be left to the artillery and the Luftwaffe for the time being" ["Das Brechen des Wilderstandes in der Stadt selbst ist dann zunächst der Art. und der Luftwaffe zu überlassen"] (p. 139).

main the task of merely occupying the territory.[32] On the evening of May 24, the *Luftwaffe* was given the assignment of "breaking all enemy resistance in the encircled area, and to prevent the escape of English forces across the Channel."[33] The army leadership in the field was distressed and protested the "Tank Halt" order, but to no avail.[34] In his postwar memoirs, Guderian writes, "We were stopped within sight of Dunkirk! We saw the German air attacks. But we also saw the small and large ships of every kind with which the English left the fortress."[35] The British Expeditionary Force and its French allies were able, due to this series of miscalculations, to stage the dramatic retreat by sea that has made "Dunkirk" synonymous with seizing moral victory from the specter of annihilation. In the scales of history, notes Walter Ansel,

> Hitler relinquished physical contact with his most dangerous foe on the field of battle at the crucial moment, and thereby he loosened his grip on the operational initiative and likewise the political. This became the eventual result of the Tank Halt Order . . . [a] flagrant blunder in war making [that] gambled that priceless military advantage, the operational initiative on the ground, for dubious psychopolitical effect, and . . . lost.[36]

Hitler also did not follow through with an invasion of England in the summer and fall of 1940. The reason is that Hitler was ambivalent in the extreme. He was indecisive; he obsessed; he kept pushing the date of invasion back; he placed the *Luftwaffe*'s securing of air superiority as a condition precedent to "Operation Sea Lion." Hitler hoped, all evidence to the contrary, that England would sue for peace. The extent of his ambivalence is evident when we look at the wording of the first two sentences of his Directive No. 16 of July 16, 1940, "On Preparations for a Landing Operation Against England":

> Since England, in spite of her hopeless military situation, shows no signs of being ready to come to an understanding, I have decided to prepare a landing operation against England and, *if necessary,* to carry it out.

32. Hans-Adolf Jacobsen, *Dunkirchen: Ein Beitrag zur Geschichte des Westfeldzuges 1940* (Neckargemund, 1958), pp. 94–95, 219–20 nn. 60, 60a, 61a, 62, 90.

33. "Weisung Nr. 13," May 24, 1940, Der Führer und Oberste Befehlshaber der Wehrmacht, in Jacobsen, *Dokumente zum Westfeldzug,* No. 8, p. 121.

34. Jacobsen, *Dunkirchen,* pp. 96–98.

35. Heinz Guderian, *Erinnerungen eines Soldaten* (Heidelberg, 1951), pp. 104–06.

36. Walter Ansel, *Hitler Confronts England* (Durham, N.C., 1960), pp. 89–90.

> The aim of this operation will be to eliminate the English homeland as a base for the prosecution of the war against Germany and, *if necessary,* to occupy it completely. [emphasis added][37]

Twice in these two sentences, Hitler used the phrase "if necessary," indicating his hope that it would not be necessary.[38] Says Ansel, "Invasion England failed to happen, not because Hitler willed against it, but because he could not will at all where she was concerned!" He concludes, "More than any other single factor, Adolf Hitler rendered invasion impossible."[39]

In a 1981 paper, Robert Waite focuses on Hitler's decision making in 1941 and 1942 and analyzes three decisions that he believes "cry out for psychological assistance": (1) the decision to invade the Soviet Union in June 1941; (2) his declaration of war on the United States in December 1941; and (3) his orders to kill all of Europe's Jews from 1942 to 1945.[40] Waite has located the general turning point of Hitler's failure to perceive and adapt to reality in the period after June 1941. Although I think that the events of 1940, at the height of Hitler's success, already presaged the coming series of failures in reality testing and in decision making, Waite's ego psychological approach is congruent with good historical method that should also be applied to the earlier period of the 1920s and 1930s.

When we look at the disasters of the Russian campaign, there are a number of points when, notwithstanding the pervasive postwar efforts of his generals to place all blame on Hitler's doorstep, the judgment of the *Führer* may be considered to have been calamitous for the German armies. Among these disastrous junctures was certainly Hitler's insistence on an early victory at Kiev rather than pushing toward Moscow, the central point of Soviet power, until autumn mud slowed the advance into Russia.[41]

The catastrophe of military catastrophes for the German armies in World War II, the *ne plus ultra* of German advance and disaster, was, of course, the battle of Stalingrad. It is here that Hitler on November 24,

37. The *Führer* and Supreme Commander of the Armed Forces, Führer Headquarters, July 16, 1940, "Directive No. 16, 'On Preparations for a Landing Operation Against England,'" in *Blitzkrieg to Defeat: Hitler's War Directives, 1939–1945,* ed. H. R. Trevor-Roper (New York, 1964), p. 34.

38. I am indebted to Professor Geoffrey C. Cocks for this interpretation.

39. Ansel, *Hitler Confronts England,* pp. 321, 316.

40. Robert G. L. Waite, "Hitler in World War II: Irrationality, Conjecture, Chance, Choice, and Imagination" Phi Alpha Theta Lecture on History (SUNY, Albany, 1981).

41. Halder, *Hitler as War Lord,* pp. 46–47.

1942, forbade the surrounded Sixth Army to break out of its encircle-ment.[42] General von Paulus faithfully obeyed his *Führer*'s orders not to withdraw, and he did not attempt to meet from within the encircle-ment the rescue attempts of Field Marshal von Manstein's Army Group Don from the southwest.[43] We can concur with Hans-Adolf Jacobsen's finding that: "there is no doubt . . . that Hitler, as Commander-in-Chief of the Wehrmacht and Supreme Commander of the Army, bears the greatest share of responsibility for this severe political and military catastrophe in the winter of 1942–1943."[44]

Once again, Hitler chose to trust Göring's promises that he could supply the beleaguered army at Stalingrad by air, although a few min-utes' calculation would have indicated that this was an empty boast.[45] By contrast, according to Percy Ernst Schramm, in the summer of 1944, Hitler was able to set up complex calculations "on a moment's notice" of how far inland Allied ships off the coast would be able to reach with their fire, including variables of the different drafts of various ships, the different depths of offshore waters, and the differences in the caliber of naval guns.[46] We may ask why this virtuosity with technical details had been unavailable to him one and one half years earlier at Stalingrad, and why he had chosen to believe Göring's grandiose claims for the second time.

Hitler's sense of timing in foreign policy was excellent in the 1930s. He knew exactly how to handle to his advantage the likes of Edouard Daladier, Neville Chamberlain, and the Polish colonels. However, when we turn to the diplomatic history of World War II, we find that Hitler's fine sensibility of the 1930s was no longer there. To take only one ex-ample, Hitler's policy toward the United States was a demonstration of impulsive, self-defeating behavior. I here follow Norman Rich, who carefully considers the motivations for Hitler's precipitous declaration of war on the United States on December 11, 1941. Rich asks why Hitler did not procrastinate, maneuver for all the time he could get, before enlisting another enemy at the very time he was hard pressed in the

---

42. December 12, 1942, *Hitlers Lagebesprechungen: Die Protokollfragmente seiner mili-tarischen Konferenzen 1942–1945,* ed. Helmut Heiber (Stuttgart, 1962), pp. 76 n. 2, 84, 102 n. 1.

43. Halder, *Hitler as War Lord,* pp. 58–59.

44. Hans-Adolf Jacobsen, "Zur Schlacht von Stalingrad," in *Probleme des Zweiten Weltkrieges,* ed. Andreas Hillgruber (Cologne, 1967), pp. 147–49.

45. Halder, *Hitler as War Lord,* p. 60.

46. Percy Ernst Schramm, *Hitler: The Man and the Military Leader,* trans. and ed. Donald S. Detwiler (Chicago, 1971), p. 105.

Battle of Moscow. Rich points out that Hitler did not even exact the price of Japanese support against the Soviet Union. His logic is so forceful and by its rationality so well points up the irrationality of Hitler's strategy, that I quote it at length:

> Hitler's declaration of war on the United States [was] an act which brought Germany no appreciable military or economic advantages and one which cancelled out the greatest benefit to Germany of the Japanese attack, namely its diversion of American attention from Europe to the Pacific. Once Japan had committed itself to war with the United States and all danger of a Japanese-American rapproachment had been removed, Hitler might surely have found excuses to procrastinate about fulfilling his pledge to join Japan in that war. At the very least he might have demanded Japanese support against Russia in return for German support against America, if only a promise to stop American shipments to Russia via Vladivostok.
>
> Hitler certainly seemed to have every reason to procrastinate. For, after Japan's dramatic act of aggression, the American government, however much it might regard Germany as the more dangerous enemy, would have had difficulty in convincing the American public that an attack by Japan should be answered by an American attack on Germany. By delaying his own declaration of war on the United States, therefore, Hitler might have gained several months of grace before the Roosevelt government could find cause to direct any large proportion of American power against Germany. Those months might have given him time to defeat Russia or at least stabilize the Russian front, in which case he would have been in a far more favorable position to face the Anglo-American challenge. As it was, by throwing down his own gauntlet to the United States he gratuitously placed Germany on an equal footing with Japan in the ranks of America's enemies. In doing so he put an end once and for all to every possibility of a quick German military victory and thereby created a situation which virtually guaranteed Germany's ultimate defeat.

Well may we subscribe to Rich's finding that Hitler's declaration of war against the United States was an unnecessarily self-destructive act: "By declaring war on America while the greater part of his army was still bogged down in Russia Hitler sealed his fate, and for that reason alone this action must be considered the greatest single mistake of his career."[47]

47. Norman Rich, *Hitler's War Aims, vol. 1, Ideology, the Nazi State, and the Course of Expansion* (New York, 1973), pp. 237–38, 245. The feelings of irritation conveyed in these citations should itself be a clue to subsequent historians that we are on the

I now turn to an object relational interpretation of Hitler's fantasies and actions. When we probe the words and writings of Hitler for the fantasy that dominates his unconscious, we invariably come to the immutable presence of the Jew. There is a letter of Hitler's from as early as September 1919 calling for "the removal of the Jews" ["die Entfernung der Juden"].[48] This is the earliest written document of Hitler's political engagement. The Jew remained his primary fantasied enemy in his fight for German, European, and, eventually, world power: "The struggle for world domination will be fought out only between us two, between Germans and Jews. All else is a false facade. Behind England stands Israel, behind France, and behind the USA. Even when we have driven the Jew out of Germany, he will still remain our world enemy."[49]

If the Jew did not exist, said Hitler, "then we would have to invent him. We need a visible enemy, not just an intangible one" ["Dann mussten wir ihn erfinden. Man braucht einen Sichtbaren Feind, nicht bloss einen unsichtbaren"]. But Hitler realized that placing the enemy outside himself was a defense, that the real enemy lay within: "Der Jude sitzt immer in uns."[50] This is a statement so insightful that, as Friedrich Herr says, one could believe it was made by a Freudian psychoanalyst rather than by Adolf Hitler.[51] "But," Hitler goes on, "it is easier to fight

---

ground of irrationality in action. See Peter Loewenberg "Historical Method, the Subjectivity of the Researcher, and Psychohistory," *Rapports: XVIᵉ Congress International des Sciences Historiques* (Stuttgart 1985), 634–40.

48. Quoted in Ernst Deuerlein, *Hitler: Eine politische Biographie* (Munich, 1969), p. 47. See also Eberhard Jäckel, *Hitlers Weltanschauung: Entwurf einer Herrschaft* (Tübingen, 1969), p. 60. Translated as *Hitler's World View: A Blueprint for Power* (Cambridge, Mass., 1981).

49. Quoted in Hermann Rauschning, *Gespräche mit Hitler* (New York, 1940), p. 223. The reliability of Rauschning's reported conversations with Hitler has been in question. They have been accepted as authentic by H. R. Trevor-Roper, A. Bullock, G. Weinberg, C. J. Burckhardt, K. D. Bracher, W. Sauer, G. Schulz, and D. Shoenbaum. Rauschning's accuracy has been challenged on specific points by H.-A. Jacobsen, G. Moltmann, H. Mommsen, F. Tobias, and E. Jäckel. The evidence is carefully assessed and weighed with a decisively positive conclusion regarding the value of the Rauschning reports as, for the period 1932 to 1934, a unique and irreplaceable documentary, but not a literal source, by Theodor Schieder, "Hermann Rauschnings 'Gesprache mit Hitler' als Geschichtsquelle," *Rheinisch-Westfalische Akademie der Wissenschaften,* Vorträge G 178 (Opladen, 1972), especially pp. 30–34, 51, 54–55, 62. "Sie sind . . . ein Dokument von unbezweifelbarem Quellenwert insofern, als sie Deutungen enthalten, die aus unmittelbarer Einsicht erwachsen sind. . . . Die in ihm enthaltene Gesamtdeutung Hitlers ist fur den Zeitraum von 1932–1934 durch keine andere Quelle ersetzt, so vieles seither über Hitler und von Hitler erschienen ist" (p. 62).

50. Quoted in Rauschning, *Gespräche mit Hitler,* p. 223.

51. Heer, *Der Glaube des Adolf Hitler,* p. 301.

him embodied as a person than as an invisible demon" ["Aber es ist leichter ihn in leiblicher Gestalt zu bekämpfen, als den unsichtbaren Dämon"].[52]

For Hitler, the Jew was omnipresent and omnipotent. Anti-Semitism was central to his ideology and an inflexible part of his political program and rhetoric. This distinguishes it from all other tenets of the Hitlerian faith, such as anticapitalism, anti-Bolshevism, anti-Junkerism, anti-Slavism, or anti-Anglicism. Hitler's anti-Semitism was of a psychotic quality. All lustful, evil, and sadistic parts of himself were projected onto the Jews. He remained pure, good, and righteous. The Jews were a projection of split-off bad feelings about himself. He had to get these feelings away from himself and out to where they could be destroyed. Thus the paranoid defense—the badness is someplace else; therefore, the extreme character of both his sadistic and his constructive fantasies. His persecutors were awesomely frightful, and his idealized "good" parts were perfect.

After 1940, the Jews, having been neutralized and then destroyed, could no longer serve as an external source of danger. Hitler was unable to use them as an effective internal defense. He now megalomaniacally turned his paranoia to foreign targets: the Soviet Union and the United States. He used an omnipotent mania to control and master his inner badness. From June to December 1941, he "suffered from an agonizing heart condition, attacks of dizziness, constant stomach ache and debilitating bouts of shivering."[53] Hitler feared stomach cancer and felt that he was in a race with death. After 1936, he was under treatment by a medical quack, Dr. Theodor Morell, and received daily injections of dextrose, hormones, and vitamins. He also received increasing dosages of stimulants such as amphetamines and barbituates, and of "Dr. Koster's Antigas-Pillen," which included strychnine and belladonna.[54]

What is of great importance is that in a state of physical deterioration, a person's fantasies will still be a unique expression of his personality and inner psychodynamics. Hitler's thoughts in December 1941 turned to inner decay and death, which he associated with the Jews:

> Many Jews were not aware of the destructive character of their existence. But, he who destroy's life chooses death for himself, and they do

52. Quoted in Rauschning, *Gresprache mit Hitler*, p. 223.

53. Werner Maser, *Hitler: Legend, Myth and Reality*, trans. Peter Ross and Betty Ross (New York, 1973), p. 160.

54. Hans-Dietrich Rohrs, *Hitlers Krankheit: Tatsachen und Legenden: Medizinische und psychische Grundlagen seines Zuzsammenbruchs* (Neckargemund, 1966), pp. 73–74, 79–80, 118.

not deserve any better. . . . Their deeds produce the reaction. This follows action, as the bacillus succeeds the body it has killed!

One can be shocked by the way creatures devour each other in nature. The fly is killed by the dragon-fly, which is killed by a bird, which in turn is killed by a larger one. The largest creature, when it grows old, falls prey to bacteria. And finally, in another manner these also find their fate.[55]

The badness and decay was close to home—in his stomach. His defense was megalomania: he could do anything; he could take on the whole world. On December 19, 1941, he dismissed General Brauchitsch and announced that he would take over as commander-in-chief of the German army in the field. On January 30, 1942, Hitler spoke of his "unbounded confidence in myself, so that nothing, whatever it may be, can throw me out of the saddle, so that nothing can shake me." Alan Bullock comments that "supremely confident in his own powers, Hitler did not stop to reflect that, in his new position, it would be less easy to find scapegoats in the future."[56] His judgment was now impaired by grandiosity and defensive manic omnipotence in order to combat the fears of deterioration and disintegration from within.

IV

The acceptance and utilization of countertransference as a tool of insight in clinical practice and research is the most important post-Freudian development in the theory of technique in the past three decades. Whereas countertransference was formerly viewed as an intrusion in the analysis to be guarded against and overcome, it is now welcomed, listened to, analyzed, and utilized in treatment and research. Today, the countertransference is an appropriate part of any case report.

In Sigmund Freud's corpus, there are but five references to the subject of countertransference, and they are in the sense of a problem that interferes with the analysis and, if not resolved, constitutes an indication for the analyst himself to resume his personal psychoanalysis. In 1910, Freud wrote, "We have become aware of the 'counter-transference' which arises in [the analyst] as a result of the patient's influence on his unconscious feelings, and we are almost inclined to insist that he shall recognize this

55. Henry Picker, ed., *Hitlers Tischgespräche im Führerhauptquartier, 1941–1942,* 2d ed. (Stuttgart, 1965), pp. 152–53.

56. Bullock, *Hitler,* pp. 60, 602.

counter-transference in himself and overcome it."[57] He regarded the analyst as needing "a useful warning against any tendency to a counter-transference which may be present in his own mind."[58]

By 1950, Frieda Fromm-Reichmann could champion the use of countertransference as a guide to therapy:

> The psychiatrist who is trained in the observation and inner realization of his reaction to patients' manifestations can frequently utilize these reactions as a helpful instrument in understanding otherwise hidden implications in patients' communications. Thus the therapist's share in the reciprocal transference reactions of doctor and patient in the wider sense of the term may furnish an important guide in conducting the psychotherapeutic process.[59]

More recently psychoanalyst Leo Stone drew attention to the "growing appreciation of the counter-transference as an affirmative instrument facilitating perception, whereby a sensitive awareness of one's incipient reactions to the patient . . . leads to a richer and more subtle understanding of the patient's transference striving." Stone holds that "a view of the relationship which gives great weight to the counter-transference is productively important."[60] The contemporary psychoanalyst Harold Searles, in contrast to Freud, has three columns of references to counter-transference in the index to his *Collected Papers,* as well as a book of papers on the subject. Searles defines countertransference as "all feeling-states in the therapist."[61] He uses those feeling-states in himself as a cardinal principle of cognition in his clinical work and research.

The significance that historians see in their material, the criteria they apply, the feeling of conviction they impart, and the intellectual models they build and find congenial are functions of personal psychodynamics.

57. Sigmund Freud, "The Future Prospects of Psycho-Analytic Therapy" (1910), in *The Standard Edition of the Complete Psychological Works of Sigmund Freud,* ed. and trans. James Strachey (London, 1957), vol. 11, pp. 144–45.

58. Sigmund Freud, "Observations on Transference-Love (Further Recommendations on the Technique of Psycho-Analysis III)" (1915), in *The Standard Edition of the Complete Psychological Works of Sigmund Freud,* ed. and trans. James Strachey (London, 1958), vol. 12, p. 160.

59. Frieda Fromm-Reichmann, *Principles of Intensive Psychotherapy* (New York, 1950), pp. 5–6.

60. Leo Stone, *The Psychoanalytic Situation* (New York, 1961), pp. 79, 81. See also Peter Loewenberg, "Subjectivity and Empathy as Guides to Progress in Counseling," *Counsellor* (Peshawar N.W.F.P., Pakistan), 2–84 (July–Dec. 1984): 31–42.

61. Harold F. Searles, *Collected Papers on Schizophrenia and Related Subjects* (New York, 1965). The definition is on p. 771 n. See also *Counter-transference and Related Subjects* (New York, 1979).

We can research and write rigorously and truthfully about the past only if we remain aware that this is always a transaction between the historian and his or her data. Thus a historian's communication of his unanalyzed countertransference to his subject can be our most valuable clue that we are upon unconscious conflictive material in a historical problem. I will examine four examples, one each from Russian, French, German, and American history, of contemporary historians' countertransferences as communicated in their writings. These reactions are of the historians' irritation, anger, anxiety, and hostility to their subjects; thus they not only communicate the historians' emotional state and theoretical preconceptions about human nature, but also are of value to us as pinpointing conflictive material in the historical subject of research itself.

The late Isaac Deutscher wrote a great three-volume biography that is politically identified and emotionally empathic with the tragic life of Leon Trotsky. When we come to Deutscher's narrative, in Volume 2, of Trotsky's struggle with Stalin for the succession to Lenin's mantle of leadership, there is a pattern of ineffectiveness, delay, inappropriateness, absenteeism, and a refusal to take assertive measures in his own defense. We can palpably feel Deutscher's growing irritation, mounting to anger, at his hero's "self-defeating tactics":

> He missed the opportunity of confounding the triumvirs and discrediting Stalin. He let down his allies. He failed to act as Lenin's mouthpiece with the resolution Lenin had expected of him. He failed to support before the entire party the Georgians and the Ukrainians for whom he had stood up in the Politbureau. He kept silent when the cry for inner-party democracy rose from the floor. He expounded economic ideas the historic portent of which escaped his audience but which his adversaries could easily twist so as to impress presently upon workers, peasants, and bureaucrats alike that Trotsky was not their well-wisher, and that every social class and group ought to tremble at the mere thought that he might become Lenin's successor.[62]

Deutscher's frustration should be a signal to us that something significant is here not being understood by the historian. Trotsky's passivity and ineptness invite psychological examination, analysis, and explanation.

Consider now Joel Colton's sympathetic treatment of the Republican leader Léon Blum when discussing Blum's decision to remain in France during the German occupation, a decision that was to result in five long years in French prisons and German concentration camps. Colton ex

62. Isaac Deutscher, *The Prophet Unarmed: Trotsky, 1921–1929* (Oxford, 1959, 1970 pp. 103–04.

plores the options and is clearly dissatisfied with Blum's rationalizations for not joining Colonel de Gaulle and the Free French government-in-exile in London:

> What can one say of his decision? Would a "true revolutionary" have let himself be hindered by thoughts of what his enemies would say about him? Would a Lenin or a Trotsky have hesitated to flee in such a situation? Only a few months earlier Thorez had fled to Moscow. . . .
>
> From a practical point of view, Blum, if he could have accepted the taunt of "desertion," might have joined the Gaullist cause and perhaps made an important contribution in some capacity. One of its weaknesses in the eyes of British and American official circles—especially American—was its lack of leading political figures. In some cases, those who served the Free French group lacked the diplomatic skill that Blum might have brought. That Vichy would have had an additional weapon with which to belabor the Gaullists is hardly significant, as its diatribes could scarcely have been more violent.[63]

The historian Colton is visibly arguing impatiently with his subject. It is as if he is saying: "Can you not see how you are guiltily playing into the hands of your enemies who will destroy you!" And it is a cue to his successor historians to look very closely at the conflictual motives, especially the irrational and unconscious ones, in the conduct of Léon Blum, not only after the Armistice, but also on issues of action and passivity, guilt and aggression, initiative and reality testing, in hs political decision making.

The defense against anxiety by denial, which leads to not seeing relationships, may be illustrated in a biography by Eugene Lunn of the idealistic German anarchist and socialist Gustav Landauer (1870–1919). Landauer's father forbade him to marry a woman whom he loved. He also opposed Gustav's study of literature and his withdrawal from the university, and refused to support his son financially. Lunn backs away from the fiery intensity of this particular father–son conflict by generalizing it to the culture: "Such a generational conflict was commonplace, of course, in numerous middle-class German homes in this period preceding the youth movement and the expressionist literary revolt." It is not that the generalization is wrong; on the contrary, the description is apposite. But it vitiates the personal psychodynamics of conflict, revolt, guilt, and self-immolation that the historian brushes against but will not see or deal with. Lunn puts it together by telling of Landauer "writing to an aunt that he could think of his father only 'with

63. Joel Colton, *Léon Blum: Humanist in Politics* (New York, 1966), pp. 366–67.

bitterness.' The time of strongest animosity between them was precisely the time when Landauer was exposed to anarchist theories." The connection that the politically liberating antiauthoritarian ideology the son embraced was conditioned by his struggle with the first political authority a child experiences, the authority of the father, is finessed by declaring that "it was independence from his father's authority which he sought, not revenge brought on by hatred."[64]

The historian Lunn fails to relate this conflict with a tryrannical father to the conflict that puzzles him at the conclusion of Landauer's life and of his biography. After the defeat of the Bavarian Revolution and its Soviet Republic and the murder of its leader, Kurt Eisner, in the spring of 1919, Landauer refused to go to Switzerland, as his friends urged. He not only stayed in Germany, but went to the precise place where the Reichswehr and Free Corps troops would be sure to find and kill him; he was arrested in Kurt Eisner's study in a suburb of Munich. Lunn poses the appropriate questions: "Why did Landauer remain in the Munich area and leave himself open to such brutality? When escape was still possible why did he choose not to flee and thus endanger his own life?" His answer is that Landauer committed suicide because he was depressed:

> It is difficult to avoid the impression that Landauer saw little reason to go on living at the end of April 1919. Although he vacillated, and at one point agreed to follow his friends' plans for escape to Switzerland, Landauer had reached a point where personal and political tragedy could no longer be endured.[65]

This too is true, as far as it goes. Landauer did not commit suicide as a personal act of liberation under his own will and control; he delivered himself to the forces of tyrannical authority to be cruelly beaten and trampled to death.

That this puzzling end to Landauer's life, a tragic finale on the scale of the self-mutilation of Sophocle's Oedipus, might be related to the anarchist's feelings about an earlier struggle and rebellion against a personal tyrant is a connection not drawn to Lunn. To be sure, such a relationship is a reconstruction and an inference of unconscious motive. So, of course, is Lunn's attribution of despondency due to personal and political losses. The latter is less intellectually and emotionally satisfying

---

64. Eugene Lunn, *Prophet of Community: The Romantic Socialism of Gustav Landauer* (Berkeley and Los Angeles, 1973), pp. 64–66.

65. Ibid., p. 340.

because the explanation of cause is merely descriptive: Landauer was depressed. The presumed "cause" does not match the gravity of the result, while an explanation that connects Landauer's youthful rage and guilt before his father with his adult self-immolation before authority carries emotional and aesthetic conviction because it explains why he was so depressed and impotent then. It is evident from the material cited that Lunn came very close to making these connections but avoided them.

Kenneth Stampp has presented a remarkably wide-scale psychological interpretation of the major crisis in American history, the Civil War. This interpretation is noteworthy because its author has studied the Civil War and Reconstruction all his scholarly life and because his earlier theses were virtually exclusively material in their analytic paradigm. Now Stampp argues:

> Physical factors, such as manpower, railroads, and resources, can be argued more easily with empirical evidence than behavioral factors; but it does not follow that the former are therefore more readily proved as historical causes than the latter. In neither case does the evidence establish a cause–effect relationship outside the historian's mind, and in both cases it is easy for the historian to fall into the logical fallacy of *post hoc, ergo propter hoc*. *Both* physical and behavioral explanations can be only reasonable hypotheses, and it is as valid to explore one as the other.[66]

Stampp does indeed carefully consider various material, political, and intellectual factors contributory to the Confederate defeat, including the economy, political leadership, states'-rights ideology, and poor morale. However, the critical factor he focuses on is that many Southerners "had inward doubts about [the] validity" of the Confederate cause and that

> in all probability some, perhaps unconsciously, welcomed its defeat. . . . Many seemingly loyal Confederates lacked a deep commitment to the Southern cause and . . . the behavior of some suggested that a Union victory was quite an acceptable result. Students of human behavior frequently encounter cases of persons involved in conflicts which outwardly they seem to be striving to win, when, for reasons of which they are hardly conscious, they are in fact inviting defeat.[67]

66. Kenneth M. Stampp, "The Southern Road to Appomattox," in *The Imperiled Union: Essays on the Background of the Civil War* (New York, 1980), p. 306 n. 5. For an example of Stampp's earlier strategies of historical explanation, see *The Peculiar Institution: Slavery in the Antebellum South* (New York, 1956).

67. Stampp, "Southern Road to Appomattox," pp. 247, 255.

We have from Stampp the application of an ego psychological model that offers an explanation to the problems of why there was no partisan warfare or civil resistance in the South, and why the former Confederate states speedily rejoined the Union and their citizens quickly accepted the abolition of slavery and took oaths of allegiance to the United States. He compares this pattern with that of other modern civil wars in which national fanaticism triumphed over an army of occupation with superior physical force and technology, such as in Yugoslavia in World War II and in Algeria, and he could well have mentioned Vietnam.

In the realm of historical technique, Stampp's interpretation of defensiveness in southerners' rhetoric is particularly convincing. "No people," he writes, "secure in their conviction that slavery was indeed a positive good and unaware of any contradictions between theory and practice would have quarreled with the outside world so aggressively and reassured themselves so often as the slaveholders did."[68] What is elegant in this insight is that the historian is using his countertransference and his informed empathic listening to the discourse of history in order to supply the data of interpretation. He is interpreting a visible defense. In his general interpretation, Stampp is, of course, applying without citation the dynamics of unconscious ambivalence and guilt that Freud first elaborated in the historically and clinically so useful discussion of "Those Wrecked by Success" in his 1916 paper "Some Character-Types Met with in Psychoanalytic Work."[69] This paper is in many ways the first of Freud's formulations of ego psychology, prior to structural theory and before ego psychology was formalized.

V

Although classical psychoanalytic theory still has proven value in historical analysis, among contemporary historians whose researches are informed by psychoanalysis, there is a turn to object relations theory as a model of choice. Just as psychoanalytic theory responds to the governing conflicts in the culture, historical model building in any epoch will refract ascendent theories in the social and behavioral sciences, and for the same reason: because the unconscious preconcerns of a culture are

---

68. Ibid., p. 262.

69. Sigmund Freud, "Some Character-Types Met with in Psychoanalytic Work" (1916), in *The Standard Edition of the Complete Psychological Works of Sigmund Freud*, ed. and trans. James Strachey (London, 1957), vol. 14, pp. 316–31.

inseparable from its creative activities.[70] Perhaps the most daring application of pre-oedipal psychoanalytic insights has been by the colonial historian John Demos, who illuminated Puritan social patterns, including litigation, territory, and persecution of witches, with Kleinian, Kohutian, and other pregenital psychoanalytic theory.[71] The culture-interpretive works of Christopher Lasch and Ann Douglas not only are informed by, but rely on the clinical theories of Heinz Kohut and Otto Kernberg.[72]

Although we do not always have the kind of definitive data from infancy and childhood that the historian might wish, such as the mother's post-partum depressions or the childhood symptoms of our subjects, it is important to note that we rarely get this kind of data clinically. Usually we have only the presenting symptoms. While early data are always welcome, their absence does not preclude an object relations or a pre-oedipal interpretation because we have the residuals in the present, much as Marc Bloch stressed that we live with the vestiges of the past or as a geologist extrapolates and reconstructs from the imprint of a fossil in the present.[73]

The difference between an oedipal and a pre-oedipal object relations perspective and their use with historical data may be illustrated by looking at a historical case. I have described in oedipal terms the conflict between Victor Adler, the pacifist founder of Austria's Social Democratic party, and his son Friedrich (Fritz), who, like an earlier Crown Prince Friedrich, had violent conflicts with his father.[74] The historical material

70. For rich use of classical theory, see Peter Gay, *The Bourgeois Experience: Victoria to Freud*, vol. I, *Education of the Senses* (New York, 1984); vol. 2, *The Tender Passion* (New York, 1986). For an analysis the origin of psychoanalysis itself, see Fred Weinstein and Gerald M. Platt, *The Wish to Be Free: Society, Psyche, and Value Change* (Berkeley and Los Angeles, 1969), pp. 137–96.

71. John Demos, "Underlying Themes in the Witchcraft of Seventeenth-Century New England, *American Historical Review* 75 (1970): 1311–26, and *A Little Commonwealth: Family Life in Plymouth Colony* (New York, 1970); *Entertaining Satan: Witchcraft and the Culture of Early New England* (New York, 1982).

72. Christopher Lasch, *The Culture of Narcissism: American Life in an Age of Diminishing Expectations* (New York, 1978); Ann Douglas, *The Feminization of American Culture* (New York, 1977). For the work of Heinz Kohut, see "Thoughts on Narcissism and Narcissistic Rage," *Psychoanalytic Study of the Child* 27 (New Haven, Conn., 1972), pp. 360–400; "Forms and Transformations of Narcissism," *Journal of the American Psychoanalytic Association* 14 (1966): 243–62; *The Analysis of the Self: A Systematic Approach to the Psychoanalytic Treatment of Narcissistic Personality Disorders* (New York, 1971); *The Restoration of the Self* (New York, 1977). See also Otto F. Kernberg, *Borderline Conditions and Pathological Narcissism* (New York, 1975).

73. Marc Bloch, *The Historian's Craft*, trans. Peter Putnam (New York, 1953), p. 46.

74. Peter Loewenberg, *Decoding the Past: The Psychohistorical Approach* (New York, 1983), pp. 136–160.

seems to suggest such an interpretation: the father drove the terrorists and anarchists out of the party; the son, a militant Socialist pacifist, murdered the Austrian prime minister in 1916 in order, he claimed, to bring the war to an early end. All the elements of Oedipus were there, including father conflict and father identification. There were explicit references to both by Fritz at his murder trial, where he noted that Vienna's last political trial in front of a special tribunal had been his father's trial in 1889 when he was thirty-seven years old—the age Fritz was as he stood his trial. The manifest oedipal content continues as Fritz associates: "I came to know this building very well at that time and *now exercise in the same jail yard where my father walked*" [emphasis in the original].[75] The rivalry and intense competitiveness that one anticipates in Oedipus are in evidence. The son had outdone his father in the realm of attacking the state and its symbols of authority. He was also identifying with his father in living out a specific anniversary of martyrdom and now he had Victor's support in his legal defense.

If we approach these facts with a pre-oedipal object relations perspective, we must look at a mother who was morbidly depressed for long periods, who at times was delusional and spent years in sanitariums. Emma Adler was in a melancholic depression in the summer of 1890, when Fritz was eleven years old. In December 1891, Victor wrote to his friend and party colleague Engelbert Pernerstorfer: "She sleeps a bit more, that is all, on the other hand she and I are tortured by her delusional ideas [*Wahnvorstellungen*] of the most terrible kind, so that I sometimes do not know how I can stand it." Some weeks later, he again wrote his friend: "I am at the end. Emma's condition has not improved despite the change of scene. She suffers from the most frightening anxieties [*Furchtbarsten Angstvorstellungen*]." This illness lasted for almost three years. After Emma took the waters in a sanitarium for over a year, Victor reported: "The anxieties are still there as before, but the inhibition, the numbed staring, the apathy, is beginning to lift, the picture is still very sad, but at least the beginning of hope is there."[76]

Now, we may assume that Emma had problems being a "good enough" mother for Fritz, in which case he would have used his father as a surrogate mother. If this was so, then his ambivalence toward Victor was a pre-oedipal ambivalence to a severely disturbed, unavailable, border-

75. Friedrich Adler, *Vor dem Ausnahmegericht, 18 und 19 Mai 1917,* ed. J. W. Brügel (Vienna, 1967), p. 163.

76. Quoted in Julius Braunthal, *Victor und Friedrich Adler: Zwei Generationen Arbeiterbewegung* (Vienna, 1965), p. 90.

line, or psychotic mother. For example, Fritz complained that his father was distant:

> You never wanted to educate and did not devote time to me. . . . You knew not the least consideration for the individual and its adjunct, the family. . . . You were a personality and not a father. . . . You would have deprived me of the *highest* that I have known in life if you had ever been considerate of us.[77]

This charge must be directed primarily at his sick, depressed, often absent mother. At a critical point after the beginning of World War I, Fritz was offered two opportunities to leave Austria—for Switzerland and for Germany. He said, "I could not tear myself loose from Austria, by this I mean *my* Austria. . . ."[78] This must refer to his love for both his mother and his father. When he was preparing to murder the prime minister, he coped with his anxiety "by ordering a large meal" to "calm his nerves."[79] He delayed his attack an hour and a quarter for fear he would hit a woman sitting at a table behind the prime minister. She was in fact a mother and later thanked him for having spared her life. Fritz, the acting-out radical, tormented his father, just as his mother, Emma, tormented Victor. Much could be said about Fritz's identification with Victor, the imprisoned martyr and socialist. Fritz did not study chemistry, as his father wanted him to; however, he did marry a student of chemistry. After Victor's death, Fritz became like his father, a moderate Socialist statesman. His father's death, Fritz's time spent in prison, and his death sentence was the punishment that made possible an integrated life after the war.

Nancy Chodorow finds the object relations theories of Ronald Fairbairn and the Balints congenial because they view the child's relations to others from earliest infancy as determining personality formation. From this theoretical base, Chodorow rejects biology and libido theory altogether to argue that women are made, not born; that they are sexed and gendered by society; and that there is no innate masculinity or femininity.[80]

77. Quoted in ibid., p. 187.

78. Adler, *Vor dem Ausnahmegericht*, pp. 268–69.

79. Ibid., pp. 182, 214. The pre-Oedipal atachment to the father is stressed in Peter Blos, "The Genealogy of the Ego Ideal," in *Psychoanalytic Study of the Child* 29 (New Haven, Conn., 1974), pp. 43–88.

80. Nancy Chodorow, *The Reproduction of Mothering: Psychoanalysis and the Sociology of Gender* (Berkeley and Los Angeles, 1978), pp. 47–48; W. R. D. Fairbairn, *An Object-Relations Theory of the Personality* (New York, 1952); Alice Balint, *The Early*

If there is any topic in diplomatic history that is overworked and over-written, it is the origins of World War I, especially the relations between England and Germany at the end of the nineteenth century. Therefore, it is all the more noteworthy when Judith Hughes, using an object rela-tional analysis, can say something fresh and historically novel concern-ing the political rivalry between the great powers. Her analysis is of the inner lives of the respective national leaders, assessing their levels of inner trust, social norms, and child raising to draw synthetic inferences about the two national social and psychological cultures.[81] The Swiss historian Kurt Spillmann sees an American "ideology of peace," consist-ing of a "mission" to create a free, prosperous, and peaceful world, as a continuous theme in the American identity throughout American history from Jonathan Edwards to the present. He bases his explanatory model of continuity on the work of James Masterson on borderline adults and of Margaret S. Mahler on early childhood separation and individua-tion.[82]

The derivatives of Wilhelm Reich's character analysis have had great value for historians. The complementarity of the Reichian approach and historical method is their common inception from the phenomenological exterior, from the readily observable and explicitly reported externals of appearance, bearing, manner, conduct, behavior, and personal style. The psychogenetics may be inferred from these, but the essential data are in the *Panzerung,* the character "armor," which is the unconscious and involuntary total presentation of the person. This is what Siegfried Bern-feld in another context called a psychoanalytic "physiognomic judg-ment."[83] A most valuable and thus far scarcely utilized aspect of Reich's characterology is that a person's *styles are of thought* also indicative of character structure. The very mode of presentation, as well as the con-

---

Years of Life: A Psychoanalytic Study (New York, 1954); Michael Balint, ed., *Primary Love and Psychoanalytic Technique* (London, 1965).

81. Judith Hughes, *Emotion and High Politics: Personal Relations at the Summit in Late-Nineteenth-Century Britain and Germany* (Berkeley and Los Angeles, 1983).

82. Kurt R. Spillmann, *Amerikas Ideologie des Friedens* (Bern, 1984); and "Amerikas Ideologie des Friedens—eine kollektive Phantasie?" in *Geschichte in der Gegenwart: Fest-gabe fur Max Silberschmidt,* ed. Jan S. Krulis-Randa, Robert Schneebeli, and Hansjorg Siegenthaler (Zurich, 1981), pp. 37–53; James F. Masterson, *Psychotherapy of the Bor-derline Adult* (New York, 1976); Margaret S. Mahler, *On Human Symbiosis and the Vicissitudes of Individuation* (New York, 1968); Margaret S. Mahler, Fred Pine, and Anni Bergman, *The Psychological Birth of the Human Infant* (New York, 1975).

83. Wilhelm Reich, *Character Analysis* (New York, 1949); Siegfried Bernfeld, "On Psy-choanalytic Training," *Psychoanalytic Quarterly* 31, no. 4 (1962): 471; an excellent ex-ample of character analysis applied to history is Otto Pflanze, "Toward a Psychoana-lytic Interpretation of Bismarck," *American Historical Review* 77 (1972): 419–44.

tent of literature, memoirs, art, and written history convey significant clues to character because they are a product of and syntonic with the governing ego defenses of their creator.[84]

We have seen the value and shortcomings of the trauma and drive models of psychoanalysis as applied to history. We have also seen the current refinements of object relations and ego psychology as they are used by historians. The incorporation of countertransference feelings as a clue to conflictive material in self and research is an established canon of psychoanalytic theory and clinical practice. A new awareness of the subjectivity of the researcher and the value of the use of this subjectivity both in the researcher and as conveyed by other historians on whom he or she relies is now in the forefront of attention as a canon of historical research method. Just as psychoanalytic theory and clinical practice reflect and incorporate the leading concerns of the culture at a given time, so history will respond to the discoveries and permutations of psychological-theory building and advances in clinical technique in the years ahead, as it has in the past three decades.

84. The inference of "deep structures" of plot, topos, metaphysics, and ideology from the text of historical writing is, of course, not new (see Hayden White, *Metahistory: The Historical Imagination in Nineteenth-Century Europe* [Baltimore, 1973]). Yet the emotional content and latent psychological structure of texts in terms of syntax, imagery, cadence, and metaphor have scarcely been probed by historians.

8

Commentary on "Psychoanalytic Models of History: Freud and After"

Robert S. Wallerstein

Freud tried over his lifetime of psychoanalytic work and development to create a general psychology and a general theory of the mind, useful not just as a therapy, but also to illuminate the far reaches of our social institutions and cultural creations. Nonetheless, applied psychoanalysis, and especially that aspect of it that deals with the interface of individual psychology and history, or psychohistory, seems always to have enjoyed an ambivalently checkered career within both of its parent disciplines. According to Robert Jay Lifton (1974, p. 17), we owe the word *psychohistory* to the science-fiction writer Isaac Asimov, and it is that kind of aura that seems to have clung to the field. However, Lifton proudly appropriated it, and the concept it proclaims, as the special arena of the group of psychoanalytic clinicians and behavioral scientists who have attended the annual summer meetings at Wellfleet, on Cape Cod, where the relationship of individual psychology to the sociocultural–historical surround has been so systematically explored. It was in that setting that Erikson presumably first used the term *psychohistorical* to refer to that kind of integrative scholarly endeavor (Lifton, 1974, p. 17).

In its origins, the enterprise rests squarely in Freud's own writings. That it never had quite a central role there reflected a number of influences. Most critically, psychoanalysis, born out of the curative experiences with neurotic sufferers in the consulting room, was centrally a powerful therapy and drew its first generations of adherents, whatever their disciplinary background, medical or nonmedical, to be its practitioners. Freud's theoretical excursions into history and anthropology, as well as religion and mythology, although regarded as boldly interesting forays extending the psychoanalytic vision to the illumination of the culture at large over historic (and prehistoric) time, were never taken quite so seriously as scholarship, either within psychoanalysis or by the other fields of behavioral science that psychoanalysis essayed to touch. Perhaps it was also in part, as Peter Loewenberg suggests, because there was something incidental or parenthetical about the applied psychoanalytic enterprise, that Freud chose to demonstrate his insights into mental functioning through the lives and works of Leonardo and Michelangelo, of Moses and Sophocles, because their creations are part of our culture at large, and Freud could therefore by-pass the evidential problem of living case histories, which were too often constrained by requirements of discretion and privacy.

Out of all these reasons, what Lifton (1974) has called "the logic of a marriage between psychology and history" (p. 21) has not seemed that self-evident to many over the almost century that psychoanalysis has been with us as a general psychology. William Langer's famous call to the American Historical Association for history's "next assignment," the opening of historical scholarship to the insights of depth psychology, goes back to only 1958, and Peter Loewenberg is one of that small group of historians—Peter Gay is another—who have sought out psychoanalytic training and experience in order to be able to bring psychoanalytic perspectives to bear on problems of historical study. Perhaps I can best discuss Loewenberg's present contribution to this area within the context of some more general reflections about why the field has had so slow, so difficult, and, at times, so dubious a development to this point, despite the presumed "logic" of this marriage.

The logic stems from the fact that, as so many have pointed out, the psychoanalytic mode of explanation is itself historical. It deals, of course, in case history, which at its best, in the hands of an Erikson, can fuse into a life history. Stuart Hampshire (1974) calls it historical in two major senses. The first, more methodological sense is in its narrative form; Freud at times half-apologized for the seeming "unscientific" or novel-like character of his case presentations, which are built around the unique configurations of a particular individual history. The other, more conceptual sense is that psychoanalysis is above all a developmental psychology; it explains the present and points to the future in terms of the past. Hampshire said of this that "the arrow of explanation points to the past" (p. 232).

Given the logic of these compatibilities, why have the people involved in the Wellfleet enterprise, Lifton, Keniston, and others, also talked of the skepticism that is in order about such logical marriages—and their offspring—and the undesirability, even, of too easy a union (Lifton, 1974, p. 21). First, such a union is clearly hard to achieve in a way that maintains the integrity of the phenomena in both realms that are being conjoined. It is too easy to fall into the kind of old-fashioned psychoanalytic reductionism that Loewenberg in his paper specifically warns against, but that is really an underlying caution he addresses throughout to all workers in the field, to take full cognizance of *advances* in psychoanalytic conceptualization as providing ever more comprehensive but also more complex models of human mental functioning and malfunctioning. The tracing out of the oedipal dynamics and the infantile trauma of the historical actor who happens to be in a seat of power should no longer be proposed as sufficient explanation for those historical conjunctions when the private sufferings or horrors of powerful individuals get enacted on the world stage with the acquiescence of vast aggregates of people and, at times, to the unspeakable hurt of humankind as a whole.

Besides the difficulty of avoiding the pitfalls of reductionism when bringing together the phenomena and the perspectives of two cognate fields, there is the difficulty that Lifton (1974) called the two fields' "working at cross purposes" or, even worse, that "each has something of an impulse to eliminate the other. And this is so even if we limit our observations to depth psychology and to man-centered history" (p. 23). In a paper I wrote with a psychoanalytically trained sociologist colleague, Neil Smelser (Wallerstein and Smelser, 1969), on the articulations of psychoanalysis and sociology, we argued that the scholarly effort to delineate all the separate specialized disciplines for the study of humanity rested on the selection by each discipline of but a limited range of phenomena, of variables, for study. By thus narrowing its focus, each discipline sets up boundaries that mark off more or less distinctly its separate domain of understanding and makes that chosen sector of human behavior more nearly manageable to our intelligence. To quote from that article, however, "What is concomitantly often not appreciated, because it is a silent additional 'given,' is that this sharpened focus and (relative) isolation for study has been achieved in each discipline by making a variety of simplifying assumptions about the *other* aspects of the world it has not chosen to study" (p. 695), which other aspects are actually the main content areas of the other behavioral sciences. An example of such a gross simplifying assumption about the social environment is Hartmann's psychoanalytic conception of the "average expectable environment," useful perhaps in individual therapeutic work with the patient in the consulting room, with whom the analyst shares a specific culture and place in historic time, but grossly deficient if we are trying to relate psychoanalytic insights across the boundaries of cultures and the unfolding of historic time and event.

Such simplifying assumptions at the boundaries of any discipline are indeed theoretical conveniences. They are, however, also arbitrary artifacts that not only sharply limit the adequacy of the knowledge that can accrue in each discipline of study, but also pose major conceptual barriers to the advance of such interface disciplines as psychohistory. One can readily see the temptation of an easy reductionism that would solve such problems by eliminating them and would reduce all the problems of scholarship in one discipline to but form variants of the problems of scholarship in the other. The opposed tack, the process of modifying the simplifying assumptions that each behavioral discipline makes about the others, of treating those parameters, "average expectable environments," not as givens, but as systematic variables, a process of *mutual* informing and interactive modification that Smelser and I (1969) referred to as the principle of "complementary articulation" (p. 696) between disciplines, is the heart of what psychohistory is all about and what makes it so difficult.

As a last statement of context before turning to my view of Loewenberg's contribution in relation to what I see as the pressing unresolved theoretical issues in the psychohistorical enterprise, let me list and briefly describe the four successive models that in Lifton's (1974, pp. 24–33) view have characterized the development of psychohistory.

The first model is Freud's prehistoric, or mythic, model—for example, the description in *Totem and Taboo* of the origins of society in the primeval encounter between a father and his sons (the primal horde), with the original patricide, guilt and remorse, and the consequent creation of all culture, history, and religion.

The second model, in historic time, is that of individual pathobiography, the lives of great people or at least people of interest to historical scholarship in terms of their individual development, their conflicts, and their psychic turmoil. The collaboration of Freud and Ambassador William Bullitt in the biography of Woodrow Wilson is often held up as a bad example of this genre, just as Loewenberg points to Fawn Brodie's biography of Nixon and Rudolph Binion's of Hitler in the same way. At their best, such endeavors can provide some major illuminations from a psychoanalytic perspective. But the risk of a massive reductionism to infantile trauma and unresolved childhood oedipal issues as the totality of the psychological insights offered in the particular person *in history* is a grave one. Put differently, the play of individual psychopathology is forced to make do for the whole of the psychohistorical interface, and what is not explained is the relation of the individual psychopathology to the movement of history.

The third model, which takes us beyond the effort to explain history as no more than the intrapsychic struggles of the individual writ large, is that given its great thrust by the contributions of Erik Erikson, what Lifton calls the model of the great man in history. In his book *Childhood and Society* and in a more clearly focused way in *Young Man Luther* and *Gandhi's Truth,* Erikson sought out a more specifically *historical* ground, the *intersect* of individual and collective histories. For Luther, for example, to have emerged from the turmoil of his identity crisis, forged in the crucible of an intensely conflicted family situation, he had to bring about a shift in the historical identity of his epoch, and enough people in his epoch had to be willing and able—indeed, ready and yearning—to make that shift. In Erikson's words, he had to engage in a successful effort "to lift his individual patienthood to the level of the universal one, and to try to solve for all what he could not solve for himself alone." In this encounter, we have the real possibility for what Lifton (1974) called "the idea of a transcendent combination of the two ultimate domains of human experience—psychology and history" (p. 17). The conceptual problem that is still here, however, and I will come back to this later, is that pointed out by Hampshire (1974) about the great-man-in-history model: "You don't need to introduce a general theory of social change, because you don't attempt to indicate how Luther differed from all the little Luthers of his time [who could not move the world as Luther did]. This very largely avoids the methodological problem" (p. 237).

And the fourth psychohistorical model propounded by Lifton is the one in which Lifton pursues his own work, whether on the victims of the atomic bomb dropped on Hiroshima or of Chinese Communist thought reform and brainwashing, on the brutalized American soldiers in Vietnam, or on the doctors in the Nazi death camps. The model is that of shared psychohistorical themes. Here the focus is on men and women exposed to particular kinds of individual and collective experience—the themes, forms, and images that are in significant ways shared as the experience and heritage of a specific place in historic time—rather than on the lives or the specific psychological development or maldevelopment of any single person.

Loewenberg, in *his* contribution to this volume, has offered us a differently constructed but equally panoramic sweep of the development of classically psychoanalytic or Freudian historical models. He relates them to the successive developments in the psychoanalytic theories of the mind and of human conflict. The sequence he traces starts with Freud's original conceptualization of psychoanalysis as a psychology of drives, the elaboration of all the vicissitudes of human sexuality in their ramifying complexity. I think that, unhappily, Loewenberg is right that too much of the psychohistorical enterprise as engaged in by the historian has rested at this level of understanding of the developmental history of psychoanalysis and, to put it dramatically, at the cost of shading unjustly the value of those contributions, has constantly risked converting history into just individual psychopathology sometimes writ very large indeed. Loewenberg gives us several unhappy examples of this genre, unhappy because limited and incomplete and therefore misleading, despite whatever worthwhile knowledge has accrued from them. I would like to add and to make explicit a point that is perhaps only implicit in Loewenberg's presentation. Far too often, scholars who may be quite *au courant* in their own discipline, when they bring to it the relevant learned insights from another discipline, even an immediate adjacent one, can be a generation behind in their grasp of the state of the borrowed field.

Although Freud's focal thrust in his first period was properly on the dynamic unconscious and how its exploration illuminated our understanding of psychic phenomena as diverse as neurotic symptoms, dreams, jokes, and myths, so-called ego interests were never entirely neglected, even at the beginning. Once the domain of the instinctual drives and their vicissitudes was adequately marked out and the great scope of the theretofore irrational or incomprehensible finally rendered "rational," or at least understandable, psychoanalysis could properly turn to the more differentiated study of the mediating or adaptive mechanisms. Hence the development, begun with Freud and continued with Anna Freud, Hartmann, Rapaport, and many others of modern-day ego psychology. Loewenberg very properly points to the now far greater explanatory power of ego psychology, not only in regard to Nixon as an inveterate liar and to Hitler's ghastly destruction of millions, but also in regard to ego attributes and capacities in Nixon and in Hitler that could move them so successfully in resonant accord with the moods and yearnings they played on in their compatriots. Clinical psychoanalysis has by now long incorporated the insights of ego psychology into its armamentarium in the analytic focus on character, resistance, and working through, and Loewenberg clearly demonstrates how much more mileage psychohistorians get when they do the same with their subject and, correspondingly, how much less susceptible they are to the pitfalls of reductionism.

The third psychoanalytic model that Loewenberg adduces is that of the object relations perspective, and again the case is appropriate. Incidentally, the object relations perspective is not really new although its emphasis by Kernberg and others on the American scene is. It was prefigured in Freud and carried to a substantial development in England, not only in their idiosyncratic way by Melanie Klein and her followers, but also in far more recognizable and acceptable garb by the English middle school of Fairbairn, Guntrip, Winnicott, and many after them. It should be added incrementally to the available psychoanalytic perspectives, but as an addition to, not a replacement for, what has gone before. Here I should mention what is to me one of the unintended pitfalls in the way that Loewenberg has built his presentation. It is as though each newer perspective can be taken to supersede the previous one, to be more advanced, and therefore to have a wider explanatory power. I do not think that this is what Loewenberg intends, but that he would want, as would I, to incorporate the object relations viewpoint as an incremental avenue of additional insight, supplementary to and complementary to the drive and ego perspectives. The quotation from Hitler that the Jew, the personification of badness, is always *within* us and must therefore be relentlessly hunted down, torn out, and projected outward, becomes an *additional* key to the intensity of the psychotic projection and then extirpation of all evil that Hitler could get a whole nation to act out with such savage and devastating consequences.

Loewenberg's fourth perspective, that of attention to the play of evoked countertransferences, is to me conceptually the poorest integrated and the least developed of the four that he presents. It is not really coordinate with the others as a paradigmatic expression of a major current in psychoanalytic explanation; it is not a next step, but an ancillary step alongside each of the theoretical developmental stages, each of which has had its technical implementation, its typical transferences, and its evoked corresponding countertransferences. Clearly, countertransference *should* always be taken into account, whether one is looking at transferences from the point of view of the drives or the defenses, the ego or reality, the interpersonal or the internalized self and object representations. Once this is said, however, Loewenberg's exposition of this portion of his thesis I find the least satisfactorily developed. But that I hardly regard as a serious flaw, since countertransference phenomena are by their nature private and readily hidden from oneself as well as from others and therefore the hardest to capture and to scrutinize for public discourse and clarification.

The more major problems from my point of view are twofold—one a problem of emphasis that I see in Loewenberg's presentation in relation to my understanding of the state of the field; the other, less a problem of Loewenberg's or of any individual, but certainly of the field as a whole. The first, the problem of emphasis, is perhaps discipline-linked; that is, it is perhaps the problem of emphasis of the historian-scholar who comes to psychoanalysis and to psychohistory from the background of primarily historical disciplinary roots and training. The canvas of history and its requirements are so much a part of the context, the background, and the source of interests and problems that the solutions, whether in regards to the fates of Nixon or Hitler or the American Civil War, are presented in an overemphasized way around the psychological unfoldings of the prime actors. The focus is on the progressively more comprehensive understanding that can derive from the use of the progressively more complex and comprehensive theoretical understandings of psychoanalysis, each employed to enlarge on, and not to replace, historically earlier theoretical models. Loewenberg would have the psychohistorian follow the advances of psychoanalysis as theory and use them knowledgeably. No one would properly question this. He seems correspondingly less concerned with the issues that so occupy the psychoanalytic clinicians turned to psychohistory—for example, Erikson, Lifton, and Coles—whose disciplinary knowledge base has been individual psychology and its malfunctions and who have tried to put their emphasis not on the how of the *individual,* how did he come to be as he was and to play the role that he did, but rather on the *intersect with the societal matrix,* how a wider sociohistorical context was moved to resonate responsively to the moving figure, whatever his individual psychology or psychopathology.

In Hampshire's (1974) words, this is a matter of psychohistory being *more than* "merely adding a complexity and a sensitiveness to ordinary accounts of individual motives in ordinary historical writing" (p. 236). This, of course, may be just a matter of one's disciplinary roots helping to determine the direction in which enrichment is being sought, and, clearly, historian and clinician come to this shared field of psychohistory from different directions. From my own—clinical—direction, a central problem (which might not look exactly the same to the psychoanalytically informed historian-investigator) is put well by Hampshire. It is the question of whether we treat group behaviors or social movements, and we can think of many cases in point as just "a collection of individuals with converging psychic histories which, taken together, hope to explain group behavior" (p. 235). Or does one have to add "some general social theory which has some independent warrant" (p. 235)? Clearly of great interest to me would be the perspective of a psychoanalytic historian like Loewenberg in relation to *this* question.

This brings me to my final point, which to me is *the* central challenging question in the field at this time, for both analytically interested historians and historically concerned analysts. It is in the last question taken up in Hampshire's (1974) essay, that of some adequate bridging concept between the individual and his or her sociohistorical context. Hampshire proposes the family as such a bridging unit, not just because of the natural role of the family as the mediator between individual and society and as the vehicle for the socialization of the individual to society's norms and expectations, but also because the theory of the family and family roles presumably provides the necessary and sufficient framework to effect such bridges. I would submit in disagreement with this view that wherever we think we are in relation to theory in psychoanalysis around issues of individual development, and in history around issues of sociohistorical structure and change, our theory of change in the family, either as it evolves as an institution or as it changes as a result of family therapy, is far too underdeveloped to bear such a bridging burden. It is the theory of the proper bridging unit or conceptual frame that to me is far too little developed and where the important next tasks for this new conjoint field still lie. Clearly, Peter Loewenberg is one of those we will all count on to help make the needed progress.

References

Hampshire, S. (1974). Struggles over theory. In R. J. Lifton, with E. Olson (Eds.), *Explorations in psychohistory: The Wellfleet papers.* New York: Simon and Schuster.

Lifton, R. J. (1974). Preface, and "On psychohistory." In R. J. Lifton, with E. Olson (Eds.), *Explorations in psychohistory: The Wellfleet papers.* New York: Simon and Schuster.

Wallerstein, R. S., and Smelser, N. J. (1969). Psychoanalysis and sociology: Articulations and applications. *International Journal of Psychoanalysis, 5,* 693–710.

9

The Problem of
Subjectivity in History

Fred Weinstein

In his presidential address to the American Historical Association in December 1931, Carl Becker explained that the history "Mr. Everyman" imaginatively re-creates for the sake of orienting himself "in his little world of endeavor" is inevitably "an engaging blend of fact and fancy, a mythical adaptation of that which actually happened. In part it will be true, in part false; as a whole perhaps neither true nor false, but only the most convenient form of error."[1] Becker then went on to declare that the history imaginatively re-created by historians is similar in character, itself "a convenient blend of truth and fancy."[2]

Historians are familiar with Becker's relativism, of course, but they have ignored this other argument of his, and they have failed to appreciate just how great a disciplinary subversive he was. The fact is, nevertheless, that Becker was deeply skeptical about the possibility of verifying interpretive historical statements about why people did the things they did, about the reasons for or the purposes and intentions of their actions.

Thus in his preface to *The Eve of the Revolution,* Becker wrote that he had resorted frequently to the literary device of telling the story by means of

1. Carl Becker, "Everyman His Own Historian," in *Everyman His Own Historian* (Chicago, 1966), pp. 252, 245.

2. Becker distinguished here between fact and interpretation, according to the conventions of the discipline. The results of archival work may be accurately reported, but interpretations are fanciful, or fictional (Ibid., p. 248).

a rather free paraphrase of what some imagined spectator or participant might have thought or said about the matter in hand. If the critic says that the product of such methods is not history, I am willing to call it by any name that is better; the point of greatest relevance being the truth and effectiveness of the illusion aimed at—the extent to which it reproduces the quality of thought and feeling of those days, the extent to which it enables the reader to enter into such states of mind and feeling. The truth of such history (or whatever the critic wishes to call it) cannot of course be determined by a mere verification of references.[3]

Or again, when Becker was asked in 1926 to give a talk on "the Spirit of '76," by way of commemorating the 150th anniversary of the American Revolution, he said that he did not have any clear notion—and he did not think that the people who asked him had any clear notion—of what was meant by the phrase. The paper that Becker presented, entitled "The Spirit of '76," was a fictional account of how people thought and felt about the American Revolution.[4]

Of course, Becker also wrote proper history despite his skepticism, *The Heavenly City of the Eighteenth Century Philosophers* being a notable example. In that work, Becker argued that French Enlightenment philosophers and revolutionaries were sustained by an emotional impulse, that their visions of progress and perfectibility were a compensation for the limitations and frustrations of their everyday lives, and their quest was religious in nature, based on a mystical faith in humanity and not at all, as the philosophers, revolutionaries, and successive generations of historians had supposed, on reason. But Becker must have realized that if he was challenged to verify his claims, to document his construction of the subjective intentions of those Enlightenment and revolutionary actors, he might not be able to do so.[5]

Carl Becker had argued—and thought enough about the argument to present it in his presidential address—that insofar as historians organize their data without any larger interpretive purpose, their work might be factually accurate and interesting as narrative, but it could not be cul-

3. Carl Becker, *The Eve of the Revolution: A Chronicle of the Breech with England* (New Haven, Conn., 1921), pp. vii–viii.

4. Carl Becker, "The Spirit of '76," in *Everyman His Own Historian,* p. 47. Becker obviously knew a great deal about the Revolutionary period and could easily have written a proper history as well. But he wanted to emphasize that making statements about the subjective intentions of people, or guessing at the thought processes of the members of a social or political movement, is far more problematic than laymen imagine.

5. Carl Becker, *The Heavenly City of the Eighteenth Century Philosophers* (New Haven, Conn., 1961).

turally relevant;[6] and insofar as historians express a larger interpretive purpose, which they do by clarifying the subjective intentions and purposes of people, their work becomes culturally relevant but also problematic, since all interpretations of subjectivity seem to involve inferential leaps not warranted by evidence.

The issue of subjectivity in history is an old one,[7] but it is worth recalling this argument of Becker's to point out, first, that historians who have been critical of the inferential leaps characteristic of psychoanalysis and psychohistory have failed to observe how vulnerable to this kind of criticism any history is that acquires depth and force by the interpretation of subjectivity, and, second, that while Becker predicated his argument on the insufficiency of narrative accounts generally (because the facts would never speak for themselves)[8] and on the insufficiency of common sense and intuition to explain complex events, such as the American and French revolutions, the kinds of events Becker was interested in,[9] it must also be emphasized that positivist or "objective" accounts have in turn constantly proved insufficient because neither the most precise description of objective events nor the most systematic accumulation and statistical analysis of objective (for example, census) data can allow for the interpretation of events independent of the perceptions and feelings of the people who gave them their unique shape.[10] Becker sensed

6. Culturally relevant history serves social interests and provides emotional consolations for people by helping to establish the significance of life, and it does so, according to Becker, whether or not it is true (See Becker, "Everyman His Own Historian," pp. 252–53).

7. The issue of subjectivity in history has been reviewed by J. Michael Lennon and Charles Strozier, "Empathy and Detachment in the Narratives of Erikson and Mailer," *Psychohistory Review* 10, no. 1 (1981): 18–32. See also Michael A. Simon, *Understanding Human Action* (Albany, N.Y., 1982), pp. 178–82.

8. There may well continue to be an audience for narrative histories, but once the original expectation of such histories—that the steady accumulation of data would finally reveal some truth—was frustrated, the function of the historical discipline became interpretive: professional historians are expected to help provide the conceptual or interpretive language people need in order to make sense of their world, a task that cannot be fulfilled by the reproduction of narrative accounts based on archival work.

9. Common sense or intuition can prove adequate to an explanation of subjective intentions in certain instances—for example, when interests are crudely affected by tariff regulations. But that kind of simple and evident relationship, in which it can be assumed without much further reflection that the investigator and those being investigated share a common-sense understanding of the significance of profit and loss, is by no means typical of social relationships in general.

10. There are different kinds of objective accounts based on different assumptions. It might be argued, for example, that objective (institutional or social) relationships compel people to act in given ways independent of their subjective perceptions of or feelings about those relationships. Sociologists have been trying to identify and describe such

in these terms that the historical discipline might not be able to play any cultural role other than an ideological one, although he was loathe to draw any final conclusions. However, such conclusions may be forced on us if we cannot solve the problem Becker had already identified— specifically, the insufficiency of objective accounts of whatever pro- venience and the absence of any basis on which to render verifiable sub- jective accounts as a way of making good that insufficiency.

It is interesting, in the context of the sociology of knowledge, that a significant number of contemporary novelists have expressed, in pursuit of their own literary projects, a wish or need specifically to expand his- torical consciousness, or to affect moral consciousness in terms of his- torical events, or to change our way of looking at life, character, or lan- guage in terms of historical events, forcing attention to the same theme that Becker adumbrated a half-century ago.[11] Experimenting with true- life novels, nonfictional novels, or faction, these writers, from different

---

objective relationships since the nineteenth century, and they continue to try (see Theda Skocpol, *States and Social Revolutions: A Comparative Analysis of France, Russia, China* [New York, 1979]). Or it might be argued that perceptions and feelings can be in- ferred from objective location in society, an argument that Marxists routinely and mis- takenly employ in terms of class. Few scholars these days will fall into the trap of hy- postatizing any "laws of history," but clearly there is still in these other kinds of objec- tive accounts a conception of "the cunning of history," which works its will behind the backs of the people involved.

11. So many novels rooted in historical events have been published recently that John Lukacs, in a review of William Gerhardie's *God's Fifth Column,* stated that "history has moved to the foreground—not, alas, in the academic world but in the imagination, specu- lation and writing of novelists, all kinds of novelists . . ." (*New York Times Book Re- view,* November 29, 1981, p. 9). My sense that this phenomenon is related to an epistemo- logical crisis in history is confirmed by Gordon S. Wood's scathing attack on narrative history as fiction and by his reference to various critics and novelists who have made this argument. Yet Wood does not himself see how deep the crisis is or how focused it is, as Becker had suspected, on the issue of subjectivity and the verification of interpreta- tions of subjective intentions (Gordon S. Wood, "Star-Spangled History," *New York Review of Books,* August 12, 1982, pp. 4–9). Of course, not every novelist who has writ- ten on a historical theme is consciously addressing an epistemological crisis in history; but if artists are conceived of as sensitive barometers of cultural change, then the impli- cations of this recurrent emphasis in fiction cannot be ignored. Further, this emphasis, and the critique of history from within, comes at a time when the social and behavioral sciences are also under attack for having failed to live up to expectations (note 41, p. 185). In short, there is a growing apprehension that the kind of knowledge that schol- ars (and laymen) thought possible may not be forthcoming and that it is perhaps time to think about the world in another way. Finally, I could not possibly refer here to all the works of fiction that systematically involve history, but for an idea of what is entailed, see Mary Lee Settle, *The Scapegoat* (New York, 1980) and E. L. Doctorow's review of Settle's novel and Roger Shattuck's interview with Settle in *New York Times Book Re- view,* October 26, 1980, pp. 1, 40–42, 43–45.

perspectives and for different reasons,[12] are breaking down the distinction between the real and the imagined, between literature and history as art forms.[13] They are reconstructing events, in many instances as accurately and carefully as any historian;[14] putting real people in imaginary situations, imaginary people in real situations, and imaginary situations in documentary narratives; and augmenting the significance of historical events by plausible, internally consistent, but unverifiable depictions of the subjective intentions of people.[15] And in doing so, they are implicitly

12. Norman Mailer has discussed his intentions in writing *The Executioner's Song* in an objective style in Michiko Kakutani, "Mailer Talking," *New York Times Book Review,* June 5, 1982, pp. 39–40.

13. Wilfred Sheed points out that Norman Mailer's *Executioner's Song* is called fiction, although it is about real people, whereas Bob Woodward and Scott Armstrong's *Brethren* is called nonfiction, even though it is based partly on conjecture. Kate Millet wrote in her book *The Basement,* based on a true incident, that she had "invented" her character, although the publisher described the book as nonfiction (Michiko Kakutani, "Do Facts and Fiction Mix?" *New York Times Book Review,* January 27, 1980, pp. 3, 28–29). Kakutani notes that "In *Hustling,* her study of prostitution, Gail Sheehy constructed composite characters from various individuals she had interviewed. In her 'interpretive biography,' *Closing Time: The True Story of the 'Goodbar' Murder,* Lacey Fosburgh allowed that she had 'created scenes or dialogue I think it is reasonable and fair to assume could have taken place, perhaps even did.' Mr. Woodward and Mr. Armstrong note in the preface [to *The Brethren*] that they 'attributed thoughts, feelings, conclusions, predispositions and motivations to each of the justices' " (Ibid.). In the same vein, Jean-Paul Sartre referred to his study of Flaubert, *The Family Idiot: Gustave Flaubert, 1821–1856* as a "true novel" (Frederic Jameson, review of *The Family Idiot,* by Jean-Paul Sartre, *New York Times Book Review,* December 27, 1981, p. 5). It should be noted that journalists, too, are augmenting their work in this way. Tom Wolfe, who invented the phrase "new journalism," claims that journalism not only can examine behavior, as it has always done, but also can explain motivation, by "giving the reader the feeling of being inside the character's mind and experiencing the emotional reality of the scene as he experienced it" (Kakutani, "Do Facts and Fiction Mix?" p. 29). In his review of Howard Kohn's *Who Killed Karen Silkwood?* Pete Hamill, himself a journalist, referred to those "accursed 'non-fiction novels,' unbelievable as history, unacceptable as fiction." Hamill objected to Kohn's reconstruction of Karen Silkwood's inner thoughts, about which he could not have known and which he certainly could not verify (*New York Times Book Review,* December 13, 1981, p. 34). See also Pete Hamill, review of *Cold Storage,* by Wendall Rawls, Jr., *New York Times Book Review,* February 24, 1980, p. 13.

14. Norman Mailer claims that he did his best to make *The Executioner's Song* a factually accurate account, while Truman Capote states that *In Cold Blood* is based on all the techniques of fictional art, although the book is also "immaculately factual" (Kakutani, "Do Facts and Fiction Mix?" p. 28).

15. Michiko Kakutani notes that Gore Vidal's *Burr* and Rhoda Lerman's *Eleanor* adhere closely to established fact, but both authors enlarge their characterizations of historical figures by ascribing to them made-up thoughts and feelings. "Presumably, the motive here is to enlarge or ennoble the individual by exploring an undocumented inner life" (Ibid.). Lerman stated elsewhere that she had done three years of research on Eleanor Roosevelt at Hyde Park but felt that she could not use what she knew except in a novel

(and sometimes even explicitly) challenging the primacy of those empirical disciplines presumably devoted to the interpretation of subjectivity—history, psychoanalysis, and psychohistory.[16]

True, novelists have been using historical events and real characters in their work, and have been writing historical fictions and romances, for a long time. They have thought, too, that because historical work must be rooted in fact and verifiable, the historian's search for truth begins on too restricted a plane. What is happening now, however, is something different: novelists are writing—from their different perspectives—as if fiction could replace history as a form of literature.[17] If we consider that the archival work historians do is not special or distinctive and that it can be done by anyone, and if we consider also the implicit contention that historians' judgments about subjectivity are fictional by their own standards and are weak by fictional standards, then we can see how this

---

(Herbert Mitgang, "Fiction Factions," *New York Times Book Review,* April 29, 1979, p. 54).

16. Saul Bellow recently stated that the novelist is "an imaginative historian who is able to get closer to contemporary facts than social scientists possibly can." He did not say why this was so, although he did say that he intends to deal more centrally with historical and social subjects. (Michiko Kakutani, interview with Saul Bellow, *New York Times Book Review,* December 13, 1981, pp. 1, 28–30). Rhoda Lerman has said that "history is just perception that gets concretized. The intuitive is just as valid in a [novel] . . . (Mitgang, "Fiction Factions," p. 54). Norman Mailer has said that history has become more novelistic than the novel ("How Is Fiction Doing? A Symposium," *New York Times Book Review,* December 14, 1980, p. 3). In a review of Robert K. Massie's popular *Peter the Great: His Life and Work,* James Cracraft noted that Massie's kind of history is what Mailer must have had in mind by his statement, surely a naïve view (*American Historical Review* 86, no. 4 [1981]: 886–87). More to the point is Rebecca West's statement that "historians are notorious liars" who peddle their own special readings of the facts (quoted in John J. O'Connor, "TV: Moyers and a Provocative Dame Rebecca West," *New York Times,* July 8, 1981, sec. C, p. 27).

17. This has become so evident that Irving Howe was prompted to note that nonfictional novels are themselves problematic because they "evade the responsibilities of both genres . . . the responsibility of fiction—to create an imaginary world with its own traits, and the responsibility of history—to be verifiable" (quoted in Kakutani, "Do Facts and Fiction Mix?" pp. 28–29). Joseph Lash has also noted that books like Rhoda Lerman's *Eleanor* evade the issue of accountability (Mitgang, "Fiction Factions," p. 54). The process works the other way, too, it should be noted, as historians begin to write fiction as a way of coping with problems of subjectivity. Walter Z. Laqueur, the author of at least a dozen works of nonfiction, wrote a novel, *The Missing Years,* a "memoir" of a Jew who remained in Germany during World War II. Christopher Lehmann-Haupt noted in his review that Laqueur turned to fiction because fiction "seemed to him the best possible way of capturing intimately the history of the era . . ." (*New York Times,* April 11, 1980, sec. C, p. 25). See also Russell McCormmach, *Night Thoughts of a Classical Physicist* (Cambridge, Mass., 1981), and the novel by the historical sociologist Richard Sennett, *The Frog Who Dared to Croak* (New York, 1982).

might be the case, or how a novelist like E. L. Doctorow might conclude that

> there is no longer any such thing as fiction or non-fiction; there's only narrative.
>
> What's real and what isn't—I used to know, but I've forgotten. The book [*Ragtime*] gives the reader all sorts of facts—made-up facts, distorted facts—but I happen to think that my representation of historical characters is true to the soul of them.[18]

The vigor with which novelists are pursuing historical themes stems, of course, from their high estimation of the power of literature to enhance our perceptions of the world.[19] But it seems as well to stem from a shared, if unspoken, sense that the main issues of history are issues of subjectivity and that those disciplines devoted to the systematic interpretation of subjectivity have failed to explain to people why things have worked out the way they have, or to provide people with language and concepts they need to make sense of the world and to locate themselves in it.

Perhaps the most interesting work of fiction in these terms is D. M. Thomas's *White Hotel,* in which Freud, psychoanalysis, and European culture in the period of the two world wars are treated as centrally as they have been in countless contemporary histories. Thomas undoubtedly has his own belletristic purposes in dealing with history and psychoanalysis, but it is not hard to see how his uses of fantasy and his depiction of a particular therapeutic encounter and of the Holocaust can form the basis of a real critique of history, psychoanalysis, and psychohistory.[20] That is, Thomas's construction of a fictional case study, his ability

18. Quoted in Kakutani, "Do Facts and Fiction Mix?" pp. 28–29. Doctorow's is one of the standpoints from which historical events are being addressed. That is, whatever Doctorow's literary intentions are, there is a clear desire to write on historical themes or to expand historical consciousness, and to take the themes about American culture and history out of Doctorow's *Ragtime* would fundamentally alter the work in a way that taking the historical references out of works by Zola or Stendahl would not.

19. Norman Mailer has characteristically observed that "only great fiction can save the world. So believe all good novelists! For fiction still believes that one mind can see it whole" (quoted in "How Is Fiction Doing? A Symposium," p. 3).

20. Thomas does have a critical sense of what psychoanalysis or psychoanalytic therapy might actually be about, which informs his intentions as a novelist (see his review of *A Secret Symmetry: Sabina Spielrein Between Jung and Freud,* by Aldo Carotenuto, *New York Review of Books,* May 13, 1982, pp. 3, 6). The novelists' awareness of psychoanalysis and their treatment of it as a failed cultural enterprise is another old story, of course. See, for example, Erica Jong's portrayal of a fleeting homosexual encounter between two psychoanalysts (*Fear of Flying* [New York, 1974], pp. 143–44, 121–144).

to re-create Freud's language and imagination and to mingle it with his own, blurring the boundary between the real and the imagined, allows him to examine the ways in which Freud's language and personality could have served a healing and integrative purpose in therapy, and even in the larger culture, without ever becoming objective or scientific or acquiring the explanatory power that Freud had envisioned, allowing Thomas to state as well that the life people experienced at the time, the history they were a part of, were far beyond even Freud's awesome powers to anticipate, understand, or explain.[21]

Thomas's fictional account of Freud's analysis of "Anna G" and of their subsequent correspondence reveals that Freud's interpretations of Anna's conflicts were based on incomplete, distorted, and deliberately falsified reporting. Freud's patient lied and otherwise withheld important information, and in subsequently filling in crucial details that she really could have provided all along, she ended up reversing and contradicting herself, suggesting to Freud, who had written for permission to publish the case study, that perhaps the project ought to be abandoned.[22] Freud replied that he would go ahead because it served his purposes to do so, despite the lies, the evasions, and the retrospective recollections.[23] At

---

Jong's portrayal suggests that unanticipated situations, the unexpected encounters of everyday life, serve to undermine not only personal discipline, but theoretical categories as well. No systematic or theoretical scheme can come close to describing life as people must live it. This is a common theme, whether psychoanalysis is treated in a scornful way, as it was by Jong and by William Styron (*Sophie's Choice* [New York, 1980]), or whether it is treated as a gallant but doomed effort, as it was by Thomas Pynchon (*The Crying of Lot 49* [New York, 1967], pp. 98–103), by John Irving (*The Hotel New Hampshire* [New York, 1981], pp. 286, 338–39), and, of course, by D. M. Thomas (*The White Hotel* [New York, 1980]).

21. The figure of Freud appeared once in E. L. Doctorow's *Ragtime,* a fictionalized account of early-twentieth-century America ([New York, 1976], pp. 39–44). Doctorow offered a version of Freud's trip to the United States to deliver the Clark lectures. D. M. Thomas began his fictionalized account of Central European history, *The White Hotel,* by offering a version of Freud's trip to the United States to deliver the Clark lectures. It is hard to believe that the use of this same theme in two fictional works of "history" is merely coincidental. The figure of Freud and the various uses of psychoanalysis have had an extraordinary impact on this culture, and this is an interesting problem, too, from the standpoint of the sociology of knowledge, regardless of whether one is "for" or "against" psychoanalysis.

22. Thomas, *The White Hotel,* pp. 89–144 (the case history), 181–200 (the correspondence).

23. The reconstruction by a psychoanalyst of events in a patient's past, a patient's guess, or a psychoanalyst's suggestion about something that "must have happened," are sometimes verified by independent observers who happen to recall the events in question. But verification is not the only psychoanalytic standard for correct interrpetation. Quite often, as Freud wrote, "We do not succeed in bringing the patient to recollect what has been

the same time, Anna G. rejected many more of Freud's interpretations than she accepted, although the "cure" was effective and she was relieved of her symptoms. The cure, in other words, was a result of the transference relationship and not a result of Freud's interpretations.[24] Finally, although she was relieved of the burdens of life, and she went on to become the witness and the victim of the Nazi slaughter of the Jews at Babi Yar, part of an extermination process whose significance, Thomas claims, is really beyond either psychoanalysts or historians to fathom. For what the Holocaust demonstrates to us at the least is that individual lives and cultures are never as unified and continuous as psychoanalysts and historians must make them out to be, and if that is the case, then there is no way for people to connect to the incredible texture of life except through fiction.

Thomas's treatment of psychoanalysis is familiar and unobjectionable. He observes that psychoanalysts have available to them the language of patients, including the body language, and that they are able to observe constantly the formation of associative links, the expression of various kinds of idiosyncratic symptoms, and the fleeting but indicative mood swings that people experience. They also have an excellent facilitating environment, which allows them to suspend the sense of time and of the

---

repressed. Instead of that, if the analysis is carried out correctly, we produce in him an assured conviction of the truth of the construction which achieves the same therapeutic result as a recaptured memory" (Sigmund Freud, "Constructions in Analysis," in *The Standard Edition of the Complete Works of Sigmund Freud,* ed. and trans. James Strachey [London, 1964], vol. 23, pp. 265–66). Freud assumed that if an interpretation or construction of his evoked a visible sense of conviction in a patient, then likely it was true whether or not it was verifiable. But Freud had no right to make such an assumption, as integrative and healing thoughts are not necessarily true ones, and the sense of conviction could just as easily have arisen from the transference as from the correctness of the interpretation. Freud often made such inferential leaps, and this is what Thomas is commenting on. See also Michael Franz Basch, "Theory Formation in Chapter VII: A Critique," *Journal of the American Psychoanalytic Association* 24, no. 1 (1976): 88.

24. Didier Anzieu discussed this problem at length in 1970, so that it was available in the literature, as are all the other elements of the critique (see Stanley A. Leavey, *The Psychoanalytic Dialogue* [New Haven, Conn., 1980], p. 14, and Heinz Kohut, "The Two Analyses of Mr. Z.," *International Journal of Psychoanalysis* 60, no. 3 [1979]: 7–8). Psychoanalysts are aware of these criticisms, although obviously they are loath to discuss them in public. Even so, Donald Spence has stated, for example, that links between ideas in clinical practice may well be imposed, that psychoanalysts impose more structure on material than they like to admit, that consensus among psychoanalysts is not a criterion of validation, that a patient's agreement with one or another interpretation is more often a mark of passivity than a confirmation, and that psychoanalytic reconstructions are usually but poor approximations of what might have been (Donald Spence, "Clinical Interpretation: Some Comments on the Nature of Evidence," in *Psychoanalysis and Contemporary Science,* ed. Theodore Shapiro [New York, 1978], vol. 5, pp. 367–88).

social world, and they have the advantage of the transference relationship, since it is stimulated particularly by this kind of environment. Still, every analysis is incomplete; patients evade the fundamental rule, they always know more than they say about important things, and what is important to them changes over time anyway, as they face different tasks in life. In addition, favorable and unfavorable things happen in the transference and countertransference that psychoanalysts are not aware of or in control of, and as must be the case with the best-intentioned of professionals, psychoanalysts also make mistakes.

Thomas's portrayal of a case history, of psychoanalysis, and of European history is framed by his sense of the preordained failure of the basic therapeutic relationship. And however pertinent this may be to his literary purposes, it is also pertinent to the issue of subjectivity raised here and to the issue of psychohistory, particularly as it has been grounded in psychoanalysis,[25] in that the basic element of investigation in psychoanalysis is the individual, that the chances of the availability of data sufficient by psychoanalytic standards to support an interpretation are remote, and that even when such data are available, they are so only for elite individuals, a situation that harbors dilemmas of its own, not only for ideological reasons, but also for the reason that if all others in a population are excluded from consideration in the same terms, we never can tell how or whether any particular character described is typical.[26]

25. Psychohistory has been too exclusively linked to psychoanalysis in these terms, for even if psychoanalysis could be demonstrated to have failed, the problem of subjectivity in history would remain, and hence psychohistory, the systematic exploration of subjectivity, would also remain. It should be noted, too, that the function of the best work, regardless of provenience, is polemical—to raise issues, focus attention on unresolved problems, and provoke or expose contradictions. The history of the historical discipline illustrates the value of clearly defined, explicit hypotheses, independent of whether they are right or wrong. Stanley Elkins's *Slavery* (Chicago, 1963) is a prominent example from the psychohistorical literature. Before Elkins's book, the major question about the slave South was whether or not slavery had been profitable. After Elkins's book, the major question was how such a social organization had been sustained, how people had perceived one another in terms of that organization, how the priorities of the culture had been imposed on individuals and families, and so forth. Elkins's work is undoubtedly "wrong," but he affected the work of any number of other writers and fundamentally changed the basic direction of the study of the slave South.

26. There are many other arguments that have been raised against the various psychoanalytic orientations, including drive and object relations theories, self-psychology, and the notion of shared traumatic experience. Because these arguments are already available in the literature and are familiar to many, I will note them here in only a brief and summary way. Freud's propositions with respect to drives, psychic energy, and affect lead away from history and sociology because drives, energy, and affect achieve behavioral expression in idiosyncratic ways. The idea of a shared, universal mental content underlying human behavior was the result of an unwarranted inference. The concept of famil-

These arguments, which constitute a real critique of history, psychoanalysis, and psychohistory, as I have suggested, are familiar and true as
far as they go. However, there are still two further arguments to consider that underscore the seriousness of the critique, raising the question
not only of what historians and psychoanalysts think they are doing, but
also of what any writer thinks he or she is doing, or why any writer, regardless of viewpoint, should think that he or she has special access to
subjectivity and can succeed (that is, in analytic rather than in normative terms) where others have failed.[27] The first is that any population
is socially and dynamically heterogeneous, so that even if certain relationships and tendencies can be systematically described, the basis of
peoples' perceptions and feelings is idiosyncratic.[28] The second is that

ial socialization, also suggested by Freud in *The Ego and the Id,* is useful perhaps for
explaining social stability, since it indicates how people are integrated into social life; but
it is not useful for explaining social change—that is, rapid and violent social change—
and certainly not in the drive terms that Freud otherwise preferred. Moreover, it is not
as though there were a unity of familial experience in a culture either; on the contrary,
clinical practice suggests that different types of familial constellations give rise to different forms of pathological expression. It is not known how many such constellations
there are, and especially not in historical terms. At the same time, age-graded stage
theories, useful in their way for biography, are problematic for any larger sociological
purpose, because all societies (or social movements) integrate and unify heterogeneous
populations (in terms of age, but also in terms of class, occupation, region, religion, educational attainment, and the like), and it is hard to say how people are related to and
remain loyal to one another in terms of an age-graded theory. Finally, the proposition of
unity or identity of unconscious perception can neither be confirmed nor disconfirmed
and must therefore be considered theoretically negligible. None of these psychoanalytic
positions can deal with the heterogeneous reality, and all of them tend to contradict the
data by collapsing heterogeneous tendencies and strivings into "underlying," "deep,"
shared tendencies and strivings by inferring shared wishes from shared behavior or by
inferring the motives of the group from the motives of single, prominent individuals.
Writers do this because there seems otherwise not to be a common cause for a common
effect and hence no possibility of thinking systematically about social and historical
problems.

27. Tracy Kidder, author of *The Soul of a New Machine,* noted that his earlier book,
The Road to Yuba City, a study of the victims of the California mass murderer Juan
Corona, did not sell because "he was unable to penetrate Corona's psyche the way that
Truman Capote and Norman Mailer penetrated the psyches of the murderers they wrote
about." (Edwin McDowell, "Behind the Best Sellers," *New York Times Book Review,*
November 29, 1981, p. 46). Kidder did not indicate why he thought Capote and Mailer
had done that correctly, presumably an important consideration.

28. This point is confirmed by both clinical and historical practice (see Charles Brenner,
An Elementary Textbook of Psychoanalysis [New York, 1974], pp. 26, 77, and Fred
Weinstein, *The Dynamics of Nazism: Leadership, Ideology, and the Holocaust* [New
York, 1980], pp. 3–60). In "Freud and the Soul," Bruno Bettelheim states that psychoanalysis utilizes "unique historical occurrences to provide a view of man's development
and behavior" and that as an idiographic science, psychoanalysis deals with events that
can never recur in the same form, "that can neither be replicated nor predicted." Bettel-

the people who respond contemporaneously to events do not themselves have an adequate conception of the significance of events or of the reasons for their response. This means, taken together, that any writer, armed with psychoanalytic or with any other sociopsychological theory (Piagetian theory or a theory of cognitive dissonance), or with common sense or intuition, must interpret other peoples' interpretations of events by supplying from outside the conscious experience—and for the most part from outside the recorded experience—of the people themselves the links that permitted or fostered concerted action among members of a heterogeneous population, accounting as well for the discrepancies between the recorded interpretations of events and his or her own. Any writer must choose a basis for inferring reasons and intentions from incomplete or empirically deficient information. Any writer must therefore approach the problem as a social theorist approaches the problem, in an

heim states further that Freud concluded that to different people, the same symbol (or event) could have entirely different implications, that "only a study of the individual's unique associations with a symbol permitted understanding of what it signified" (*New Yorker*, March 1, 1982, pp. 52–93, especially pp. 70, 72). Bettelheim's emphasis, which radically distorts the situation by ignoring Freud's fierce Lamarckianism and the contradictions that followed from it, is so strange, so far off the mark, that I can only imagine it to be a belated attempt to clean up Freud's act and make psychoanalysis respectable for the 1980s. Of course, Freud would never have agreed with Bettelheim's assessment if it meant abandoning his conception of the universality of the Oedipal project, as he explained it in *Totem and Taboo,* for example. However, in strictly clinical terms, or in terms of psychoanalytic practice as such, Bettelheim is certainly right, regardless of what Freud thought, which means that Freud had no right to make the inferential leaps he made in locating the origins of religion, morality, and social order in a real historical event, or in assuming the universal (phylogenetic) consequences of that event, and that Freud and successive generations of psychoanalysts have had to ignore or contradict the results of their own practice just to be able to continue to think systematically about society and social processes. Bettelheim's assessment means, too, that there are no solutions to historical problems (other than biographical ones, perhaps) or to sociological problems in psychoanalytic terms. That is, the basic concepts of interest may well continue to be internalization; loss; affect; realistic, moral, and wishful thinking; the vicissitudes of self-esteem and of affection; and hostility, as these routinely appear in the psychoanalytic literature. But the concepts must be structured in sociological terms, particularly in terms of language and ideology, as these have been discussed, for example, by Benjamin Nelson, "Cultural Cues and Directive Systems" and "Sociology and Civilizational Analysis," in *On the Roads to Modernity: Selected Writings of Benjamin Nelson,* ed. Toby Huff (Totowa, N.J., 1981), pp. 17–33, 230–43; Clifford Geertz, "Ideology as a Cultural System," in *The Interpretation of Cultures* (New York, 1973), pp. 193–233; Gerald M. Platt, "Thoughts on a Theory of Collective Action: Language, Affect, and Ideology in Revolution," in *New Directions in Psychohistory,* ed. Mel Albin (Lexington, Mass., 1980), pp. 69–94; and Weinstein, *The Dynamics of Nazism,* pp. 101–08, 117–22. See also Natalie Z. Davis, *Society and Culture in Early Modern France* (Stanford, Calif., 1975), and Peter Shaw, *American Patriots and the Rituals of Revolution* (Cambridge, Mass., 1981). Shaw noted the problems raised by the idiosyncratic resolution of personal conflicts and tried to develop a strategy to solve them.

abstract and general way; and any writer is faced with the possibility of constructing a fictional argument rather than reconstructing a true one in the absence of abstract criteria that would allow us to determine the difference.

Thus the problematic of psychoanalysis and psychohistory, that which is unknown or uncertain, the verification of interpretations of subjectivity, is the problematic of historical interpretation in general, whether it appears in fiction or nonfiction, or whether it is based on theory, intuition, or common sense. However, it would be possible to address this problematic if we could establish criteria for determining the verifiability of interpretive statements or for distinguishing reconstructions of the past from constructed or fictional versions of the past, regardless of the standpoint from which they were derived. I intend to suggest certain criteria that I think are applicable, but before I do that, it would be useful to review some examples of interpretation so that we may see more clearly what the problems are.

We may recall that Karl Marx argued in *The Eighteenth Brumaire of Louis Bonaparte* that the French revolutionaries of the eighteenth century found in the "classically austere traditions of the Roman Republic . . . the ideals and the art forms, the self-deceptions that they needed in order to conceal from themselves the bourgeois limitations of the content of their struggles and to keep their enthusiasm on the high plane of the great historical tragedy."[29] This extraordinary interpretation of the subjective intentions of French revolutionaries—involving concepts of cognitive lack, lapse, or failure; the moral rationalization of interest; and the power of moral strivings to determine appropriate latitudes of behavior—is deficient in only one important respect: Marx cited no documents, he offered no proof, he provided no basis for the independent verification of his argument. The interpretation followed logically from his own theory of history, but it was not based on evidence.

In the same vein, Sartre has argued, in his work on Flaubert, that the French bourgeoisie, which had invented the idea of a universal human nature as a weapon against the particularistic and ascriptive aristocracy, was faced, in turn, in 1848, with a proletarian underclass that it could not recognize unless it also conceded to that class a share of power. The bourgeoisie solved this problem by becoming Victorian, repressing the animal and physical nature it seemed to share with proletarians, and by transforming its earlier humanism into a misanthropic positivism. Once again, however, no data are offered in confirmation of the interpretation,

29. Karl Marx, *The Eighteenth Brumaire of Louis Bonaparte* (New York, 1968), pp. 16, 47.

which is, in fact, a fictional construction, normative rather than analytic in import.[30]

Or again, Andrzej Walicki, discussing the fate of the Russian nobility in the eighteenth century, has argued that after the Pugachev rebellion, the more enlightened younger members of the nobility were faced with a disturbing dilemma:

> [T]he peasant uprising represented a terrible warning and an induce-ment to abandon their enlightened liberal ideas; but at the same time they could not contemplate a return to the previous matter-of-course acceptance of the exploitation of the peasantry by the upper classes. What remained was flight into the realm of individualistic self-perfec-tion, the "inner life of the soul," or . . . the Masonic lodge.[31]

Walicki's interpretation of the subjective intentions of Russian nobles is a plausible one, but he, too, could not offer any confirming documenta-tion.

Lest anyone think that this is a problem peculiar to Marxism or to theory, we should view it from another, strictly nontheoretical perspec-tive. Michael Haines, in a study of fertility and occupation, has stated that mine workers tended to marry younger and to have higher marital fertility rates than workers in other occupations, and that they were well paid but their incomes tended to stabilize at a relatively early age. Haines concluded on the basis of these data that mine workers married at a younger age and had more children because the earnings of teen-age children could supplement family income when the head of the family grew older. Haines acknowledged that people have children for many reasons and that there is a great deal of personal, individual variation in such decisions. Still, he could not come to any conclusions about the group on the basis of idiosyncratic or personal strivings, and thus he in-ferred the subjective intentions of mine workers from objective, demo-graphic data. There is no way to justify such an inference, however, and his interpretation is again unsupported by any relevant documentation.[32]

30. Jean-Paul Sartre, *The Family Idiot: Gustave Flaubert, 1821–1856,* vol. 1, trans. Carol Cosman (Chicago, 1981). It should be pointed out that in Marx's own terms, this kind of interpretation can be confirmed only "in the final analysis," which, as Louis Althusser pointed out, never comes. But then, Sartre did refer to his work as a "true novel" (see note 13, p. 170.

31. Andrzej Walicki, *A History of Russian Thought from the Enlightenment to Marxism,* trans. Hilda Andrews-Rusiecka (Stanford, Calif., 1979), p. 20.

32. Michael Haines, *Fertility and Occupation: Population Patterns in Industrialization* (New York, 1979), pp. 244–49. Lawrence Stone wrote, in his review of David Stannard's *Puritan Way of Death: A Study in Religion, Culture and Social Change,* that Stannard

Finally, the most strident critics of psychohistory, Jacques Barzun and David Stannard, have both argued that psychohistorians do the kind of work they do in theory and history because they do not have the nerve to tolerate a complex reality, preferring to simplify reality for the sake of achieving a sense of certainty through closure. Of course, this is not what psychohistorians say, either in personal or in abstract, academic terms, which means that the interpretation cannot be confirmed by appropriate forms of evidence.[33]

These interpretations of subjectivity fail, then, because they cannot be verified, and I do not mean this in any lofty sense, as might occupy the attention of a philosopher of science, but in the plain and simple historian's sense that no documentation can be provided in defense of them. Indeed, by inferring the reasons, purposes, and intentions of people inappropriately from objective data, or by supplying reasons, purposes, and intentions from outside the conscious, reported experience of people, the authors have precluded the possibility of appropriate documentation and hence of verification.[34]

---

was tempted "to associate a revival of funerary pomp in eighteenth century New England with the growing instability of colonial society as it was threatened by the Franco-Indian wars, and as the population pushed toward the natural frontiers of growth. This is an intriguing but historically almost wholly unsubstantiated hypothesis, and I believe he might have been better advised to leave it alone" (*New York Review of Books,* October 12, 1978, p. 44). It is worth emphasizing, however, that this is not an extreme example of historical argument, but rather a common example. I might note additionally, in biographical terms, that according to Carl Becker, Condorcet, proscribed and in hiding, his revolutionary hopes fallen around him, offered his sketch of man's progress because never more than at that moment, with death staring him in the face, did he need to express a consoling belief in the perfectibility of man (Becker, *The Heavenly City,* p. 150). And James Billington has much more recently written that Karl Marx was seeking in his revolutionary ambitions "cosmic compensation for political frustration" (James Billington, *Fire in the Minds of Men* [New York, 1980], p. 265). Neither author could establish a basis in documents for his judgment.

33. Jacques Barzun, *Clio and the Doctors: Psycho-History, Quanto-History and History* (Chicago, 1974), pp. 60, 69, 146; David Stannard, *Shrinking History: On Freud and the Failure of Psychohistory* (New York, 1980), p. 121.

34. One cannot be deceived by the fact that numbers of professional historians agree on the utility of a particular mode of interpretation or of a particular interpretive language, or that a culture may come to see the world in shared terms provided by historians or historical thinkers. The shared use of terms, or the common acceptance of a particular point of view, does not necessarily speak to the accuracy of these terms and views; it may speak only to their cultural utility, constituting thereby a problem in the sociology of knowledge. Given the kinds of interpretation I have described, it is not hard to see that historians have been involved constantly in an ideological process—that is, not so much appraising reality as characterizing it in a normative sense, confirming the validity of some language that people need or want, and reassuring them about the world by suggesting that social processes are knowable, comprehensible, ordered, and even predictable.

Not only that, but historians typically have no strategy for coping with the problem of subjectivity, having systematically divorced themselves from the kinds of sources that could provide or constitute evidence: individual reporting, which is idiosyncratic and presents problems for the accumulation of aggregate data; and ideology, which is codified in high- and low-level language that, conventionalized by a community of speakers, is used to explain reality to themselves and to others, linking personal, idiosyncratic strivings to concerted social action. That is, ideology could in these terms be treated as expressive of the subjective intentions of groups of people, although it is typically treated as Marx and Freud proposed, as masking or rationalizing intentions rather than revealing anything significant about them.[35]

Thus in the overwhelming number of instances, historical interpretations of subjectivity (or of the subjective intentions of people) are based on empirically unwarranted leaps of imagination.[36] Moreover, in all these

35. Of course, there are authors who have developed useful strategies for coping with the problem of subjectivity or have integrated the subjective reasons, purposes, and intentions of historical actors successfully in their work. In addition to Davis, *Society and Culture in Early Modern France,* and Shaw, *American Patriots and the Rituals of Revolution,* I would include William R. Taylor, *Cavalier and Yankee,* 2d ed. (Cambridge, Mass., 1979), and Paul Fussell, *The Great War and Modern Memory* (New York, 1975). Fussell, for example, showed how language was used to bring a potentially overwhelming reality under control, how "in the prevailing atmosphere of anxiety," certain routine forms of expression or procedure took on "a quality of the mythical or prophetic," or how battles were named in a conventional way in "an attempt to suggest that these events [of World War I] parallel Blenheim and Waterloo not only in glory but in structure and meaning." That is, "unprecedented meaning thus had to find precedent motifs and images" (pp. 9, 127, 139). One could refer to this use of language in Erikson's terms of identity and continuity, in Kohut's terms of narcissism (as a means of defending against narcissistic injury), or in still other rather routine psychoanalytic terms of denial and repression. Or one could forget the technical language and just concentrate on the capacity of people to repair a discontinuous and threatening reality in order to be able to continue to act. In any event, it is more important to be able to offer documented empirical instances of particular phenomena such as denial or repression than it is to worry about whether or not Freud's specific definitions of them remain useful. Given the evidence, and given also the constant resort to such phenomena by dramatists and novelists, it is clear that some definition would be useful. In these terms, I consider the books by Fussell and Taylor to be important examples of psychohistory, whether or not they were based explicitly on psychoanalytic assumptions.

36. The most important problem in theory that can be characterized in these terms is the cultural regulation of sexuality through rules about incest and exogamy, which are conventionally held to distinguish humans from other related species and to be constitutive of social order. There are many general types of explanation of incest taboos, the most familiar ones being those of Freud, Lévi-Strauss, and Talcott Parsons. All these explanations appear to be arbitrarily constructed attempts to bring order to vast quantities of data without themselves really being rooted in data (David F. Aberle et al., "The Incest Taboo and the Mating Patterns of Animals," *American Anthropologist* 65, no. 2

instances, historical interpretations share crucial features with psychoanalytic interpretations, regardless of any author's intentions: they must in some measure be based on conceptions of unconscious mental activity and repression, the only realistic criteria for defining what all the varieties of psychoanalysis still have in common.[37] And interpretations must also share the arbitrary and constructed quality of fiction, a result of

---

[1963]: 253–65). The most interesting (if not the most important) problem in history that can be characterized in these terms is the social history of scientific ideas. In fact, a defensible social history of scientific ideas has not yet been written, despite Merton's effort, which foundered on the issue of heterogeneity described earlier, and despite what Marxists like to think; the paramount reason for this is the inability to link up subjective processes to any social condition or situation. Of course, Thomas Kuhn (*The Structure of Scientific Revolutions* [New York, 1962]) discusses the subjective bases of change in scientific ideas or theories, including fantasy, although this involves individual responses to perceived anomalies, without reference to social conditions (as distinct from Paul Fussell's discussion, for example, which involves collective responses emerging precisely from particular social conditions). Ironically, one of the reasons for the popularity of Kuhn's book was that scholars mistakenly imagined it to provide the basis for a social history of scientific ideas, which it was not meant to do. The history of scientific ideas is typically treated as intellectual history, but that is clearly not a matter of choice (Elizabeth Garber and Fred Weinstein, "History of Science as Social History," in J. Rabow, et al., eds., *Advances in Psychoanalytic Sociology* [Malabar, Fl., 1987]).

37. With respect to the varieties of psychoanalysis, the following obtains: there are different and even competing object relations theories, some of which have challenged very fundamental propositions of classical psychoanalysis while attempting to remain within the boundaries of the group that traces itself back to Freud. For example, Joseph Sandler, the editor of the *International Journal of Psychoanalysis,* has written that "wishes to establish and reestablish certain types of relationship with others need not be motivated by sexual or aggressive drives alone, but may primarily represent attempts to restore or maintain feelings of well-being and security. The need to maintain or sustain such feelings is an overriding one in mental functioning. . . . A psychoanalytic psychology of motivation related to the control of feeling states should, I believe, replace a psychology based on the idea of instinctual drive discharge" (Joseph Sandler, "Unconscious Wishes and Human Relationships," *Contemporary Psychoanalysis* 17, no. 2 [1981]: 188). In addition, a number of authors have pointed out that Heinz Kohut's self psychology, although intended to be complementary, "is well on its way to becoming a general psychoanalytic theory that requires no complementarity at all" (Roy Schafer, "Action Language and the Psychology of the Self," *Annual of Psychoanalysis* 8 [1981]: 86). It should also be noted that there are other versions of unconscious mental activity than the psychoanalytic one, in Claude Lévi-Straus and Michel Foucault, for example. And Foucault has objected to such a conception as repression (and to censorship) because it appears to have exclusively defensive implications. His point is well taken; in fact, it is the same point Max Weber made in regard to Protestantism: the enormous creative and world-constituting power released by such convictions cannot be encompassed or understood in the kind of defensive terms that Freud was inclined to use. But absorbing this kind of criticism has not been a problem for psychoanalysis since the 1950s, and the psychoanalytic versions of unconscious mental activity and repression are still the most useful, since they suggest also active rather than passive responses to real problems, while encompassing affective responses to problems that can sometimes be quite extravagant.

working at the level of theory without attending to the problems that follow from it.

The notion that historical interpretations of subjectivity share crucial features with psychoanalytic interpretations and with fiction, regardless of any author's intentions, should not be surprising. For if we take seriously such concepts as ideology (a network of ideas that serves the moral rationalization of interest or the repair of a threatened sense of continuity, fostering in either case some kind of cognitive lapse) or relativism (the idea that interpretations of historical events change as generational needs change), then there will always be a discrepancy between any writer's interpretation of the reasons and intentions that people had for doing the things they did and the reasons and intentions given and believed by people at the time. And there is no better way to account for this discrepancy than by assuming, as writers routinely do whether or not they say so explicitly, the existence of unconscious mental activity and repression. At the same time, however, without some kind of dynamic sociology or psychohistory, there is no theoretical basis and hence no justification for the assumption.[38]

The problem is that writers—historians, psychoanalysts, social scientists, novelists—cannot make complex statements about the subjective intentions of people in the past without some such organizing preconception of how the mind works. Thus the notion that every writer willing to make such statements functions as a theorist in any event should also not be surprising: such a preconception shares the characteristics of theory even if it is not derived from any particular one or appears to be derived

38. Most historians do not want their work to be merely narrative; they want it to have some "deeper" cultural significance, to have interpretive force, to be sociological or psychological in effect, although derived from common sense or intuition rather than from theory, which presumably makes the work "humanistic" rather than "mechanistic." But trying to establish a particular interpretation by discussing contents (for example, cultural ideals or modes of production) without discussing the process by which such contents became primary or effective is empirically irrelevant and even misleading. And it is the discussion of process that compels attention to and knowledge of theory. It is also the discussion of process that makes psychohistory, or social-scientific history, ring false to many historians. But in this matter, historians cannot have it as they would like it. They can try to elucidate the process that gave rise to particular contents in terms of some theory; or they can write descriptive accounts (a history of ideas, a constitutional history, an institutional history), which the profession has not considered fundamental or primary since at least World War II (there is little more professional interest now in the *Journal of the History of Ideas,* for example, than there is in *American Imago*); or they can do what is evident from the interpretations of subjectivity discussed earlier, that is, write fiction—or ideology, if one prefers. Of course, there may continue to be an audience for all these different approaches, but the question of audiences is different from the question of getting it right.

from common sense or intuition. Such a preconception serves to transform the character of the empirical world; it facilitates abstraction from the myriad events, allowing the events to be presented in a unified and ordered way in terms unavailable to the people who lived through them.

Historians complain that theorists distort the character of the empirical world when they transform it for their different purposes. But any writer distorts the world whenever he or she offers any interpretive statement, given the need to explain the reasons, purposes, and intentions of people on the basis of empirically deficient reporting and given the fact that there are no immaculate perceptions of reality, no perceptions unmediated by memory and experience and by the need to demonstrate loyalty to some group or principle.

Some distortion of the world is as unavoidable, in short, as the use of some theory to order it. The question is not who can better avoid distortion—historian, psychoanalyst, novelist, or social scientist—or which theory provides the best chance of avoiding distortion, but whether distortion—for the sake of theoretical fit or ideological commitment—can be avoided at all, or at least sufficiently controlled to permit statements about the subjective intentions of people that can in principle be verified. Such a degree of control is possible, providing that statements about subjectivity are made in terms of the following criteria:

1. That events be described or written about in two languages, the language of the actors (because that is the only access we have to their subjectivity) and the language of theory (because people are not aware of different, significant reasons for action, which may be retrospectively identified, and because their world is being ordered in a way that they did not experience). Choosing only one of the two languages violates the experience of one of the two groups of people involved, a situation that can lead only to ideologically contaminated conclusions.[39]

2. That a description of the action people engaged in be formulated in a manner consistent with what actually occurred. It will not do to argue, to take a prominent example, that Protestant reformers were really fulfilling capitalist ambitions or requirements, a conclusion that people

39. This criterion has been available in the literature at least since Wilhelm Dilthey's organization of hermeneutic theory. But it has not been much honored because historians and social scientists have treated people as objects to be described, or their activities as events to be explained, in the manner of the empirical sciences; that is, even if historians and social scientists took seriously the issue of subjectivity, the idiosyncratic quality of subjective perceptions and feelings made it appear as if there were no common cause for a common effect, hampering the ability to think systematically about the world. They typically solved the problem by imposing a conception of subjective intentions from the outside, divorced from the reporting of the involved people themselves. Needless to say, this could never work except as ideology.

were not then aware of and that cannot yet be confirmed, but that may be confirmed "in the final analysis." Such an argument denies the authenticity of the religious experience of the people involved, falsifying the world in which they lived by denying the reality of the problems of the world as they perceived them. Put another way, the writer's interpretive stance must include the actors' perspective, so that the writer's abstract, ordered, unifying version of events could arguably or conceivably have made sense to the people who lived through them.

3. That data be analyzed as they exist, meaning particularly that statements about the subjective intentions of people must take into account the dynamically and socially heterogeneous composition of groups, addressing the question of how heterogeneous groups are mobilized to pursue a common goal. The heterogeneous composition of groups is an invariable characteristic of socially significant events and cannot be ignored without an unjustifiable degree of distortion.

These criteria constitute a challenge to psychohistorians, obviously, but they also constitute a challenge to historians generally. The criteria provide a necessary basis for controlling the degree of distortion that may exist for the sake of theoretical fit or ideological commitment, in the sense that they are useful for allowing us to distinguish potentially verifiable from unverifiable interpretations of subjectivity.[40] In addition, however, the criteria underscore the necessity for continuing to theorize about subjectivity. There is no way to by-pass such theorizing because the nature of evidence compels a process of abstraction and inference that common sense and intuition do not obviate. It may well be argued that the current theories of subjectivity are weak,[41] but the solution to

40. Of course, these criteria are not meant to guarantee that the problem of subjectivity can actually be solved; they are meant to serve only as a standard for, or a guide to, discussions about the problem.

41. Psychoanalytic theory is usually singled out as particularly weak because of its prominent cultural role. But there is really not much one can say about psychoanalytic theory that is not true of all other theories in the social and behavioral sciences. In fact, it is more likely that some kind of theory consistent with psychoanalytic theory, and perhaps even informed by it, will be developed in academic psychology than it is that psychoanalytic theory will disappear because of its deficiencies. On this, see John W. Atkinson, "Studying Personality in the Context of an Advanced Motivational Psychology," *American Psychologist* 36, no. 2 (1981): 126–27. The reason is that the positivist theories characteristic of academic psychology have consistently led either to trivial conclusions or to conclusions already suggested by common sense, while the concerns of the more recently emphasized cognitive psychology are not all that remote from the concerns of psychoanalysis. From a humanistic point of view, the problem of memory is particularly interesting in terms of the weaknesses of contemporary psychology (and psychiatry). "The plain fact is, no one really knows what memory is, how distinct it is from other intellectual functions, how it works, or precisely what's happening . . . when you remember

that problem is the development of stronger theories, for to give up on the systematic study of subjectivity, or on theories of subjectivity, relying exclusively on intuition and common sense, only leaves us at the point at which Carl Becker often found himself long ago—that is, consciously inventing plausible arguments because the documentation necessary for making verifiable arguments seem not to exist.

---

something" (Robert Kanigel, "Storing Yesterday," *Johns Hopkins Magazine,* June 1981, p. 31). With respect to the social sciences, Charles E. Lindblom and David K. Cohen have stated that social-scientific knowledge is not usable for the formulation of policy, that what social scientists actually know is quite meager, that the results of all social-scientific investigations have yielded but a small trickle of findings, so small that the authors did not give examples of any in their book (Charles E. Lindblom and David K. Cohen, *Social Science and Social Problem Solving* [New Haven, Conn., 1980]). It is important to note, given the class structure of the academic world, that the authors teach at Harvard and Yale. Finally, Leonard Silk was so impressed with the theoretical dilemmas of economists these days that he stated that at least some economists "are ready to begin again, aware that economics is failing. . . ." Silk reported that economists aware of the ideological traps of their discipline would like to base their work on "fresh and relevant observations and on concepts closely modeled upon the actual behavior of human beings and institutions . . ." (Leonard Silk, "How Did We Go Wrong?" *New York Times,* January 1, 1982, p. 36). But where, in light of the above, are they going to find such concepts?

10

Commentary on "The Problem of Subjectivity in History"

Frederick Crews

I am afraid that Professor Weinstein's paper is less interesting as a consecutive argument than as a reflection of divided allegiance. The real issue he appears to be wrestling with is nothing so vast as "the problem of subjectivity in history"; it is, rather, the intellectual standing of psychoanalysis. Is Freudian theory coherent and empirically warranted, and are its concepts well adapted to a historian's purposes? Weinstein evidently believes that the answer in both cases is *no,* but he seems reluctant to face the consequences of that answer. The result is a paper so evasive and inconsistent that it might almost be read as a dialogue. Speaker A does all he can to admit deficiencies that psychoanalysts "are aware of . . . although obviously they are loath to discuss them in public." Speaker B tries to minimize those very deficiencies; he appears to be motivated not by intellectual scruples but by "the need to demonstrate loyalty to some group or principle."

Readers familiar with Weinstein's three books will know that his relation to psychoanalysis and psychohistory has been eroding for some time. In *The Wish to Be Free* (1969), he and Gerald M. Platt psychoanalyzed whole epochs with small regard for methodological uncertainties. They scoured the historical record for signs of the pre-oedipal mother and "the instinct of aggression as an original, motivating force" (p. 189); they purported to show how "wishes that are codified and directed toward value change have become conscious as a result of lapsed repressions . . ." (p. 9); and they displayed their ideological affinity by treating all revolutionaries as exemplars of a regressive type, lacking adequate ego control and hence prey to raw pregenital needs and paranoid reactions.

Similar articles of Freudian faith appear in the same authors' *Psychoanalytic Sociology* (1973). For example,

> Persistent threats from the external world . . . will force the regression of drives to pregenital stages and the regression of ego and superego functions as well. Submission to a leader (or to authority generally) abates anxiety both in terms of the social world and in terms of the dominance of pregenital wishes (from whence comes the capacity for violence). . . . (p. 108)

But by then, Weinstein and Platt had repented of their "nurturance-submission model" of historical explanation; they were beginning to think that identifications and internalizations are less noteworthy than the external events that trigger them. In the wake of the campus politics of the 1960s, they no longer wanted to maintain that whole movements of protest are psychically regressive. And they showed a good deal of skepticism toward orthodox Freudian theory, even expressing a doubt that the early years of life are necessarily the most formative ones.

In *The Dynamics of Nazism* (1980), finally, Weinstein made a decisive-looking break with both psychoanalysis and psychohistory. If a mass leader like Hitler was authoritarian or even paranoid, he argued, that fact tells us nothing about the psyches of his followers, who could have played along with the regime for any number of ordinary self-interested reasons. Although Weinstein half-heartedly invoked some terms from his previous Freudian lexicon, he confessed that psychoanalysis has "failed to meet the standards of empirical adequacy, especially the standard of verifiability, which serves as an obligated check against unwarranted conclusions" (pp. x–xi). And he added that even if by good fortune the mind does happen to be constructed along Freudian lines, psychoanalytic inquiry is powerless to find the roots of any given historical event. For how can particular causes be located in factors that are alleged to be ubiquitous in psychic life? By 1980, in short, Weinstein stood closer to Barzun and Stannard—the gadflies who come in for ritual swatting at every psychohistory conference—than to his own position of a decade earlier.

If one attended only to Speaker A in the present paper, one would conclude that Weinstein's disengagement from applied Freudianism is now complete. How much remains of psychoanalysis and psychohistory after the following criticisms, all cheerfully embraced by Weinstein, have been granted?

- That Freud deceived himself in thinking that his patients' agreement and improvement amounted to confirmation of his interpretations.
- That Freud's propositions regarding drives, psychic energy, and affect impede historical understanding.
- That Freud's concept of familial socialization is useless for explaining social change.
- That Freud foolishly adhered to a "fierce Lamarckianism and the contradictions that followed from it."
- That "links between ideas in clinical practice may well be imposed" and that "psychoanalysts impose more structure on material than they like to admit."
- That "consensus among psychoanalysts is not a criterion of validation."
- That "psychoanalytic reconstructions are usually but poor approximations of what might have been."
- That psychoanalytic patients are too atypical of whole populations for their case histories to yield trustworthy general findings.
- That "[t]he idea of a shared, universal mental content underlying human behavior was the result of an unwarranted inference."
- That "age-graded stage theories . . . are problematic for any larger sociological purpose."
- That the idea of "unity or identity of unconscious perception" must be considered "theoretically negligible."
- That rival schools of thought have deprived psychoanalysis of any agreed-on core of theory.
- That psychoanalysis has failed of "ever becoming objective or scientific or acquiring the explanatory power that Freud had envisioned."
- That psychoanalytic positions, when applied to history, "tend to contradict the data by collapsing heterogeneous tendencies and strivings into 'underlying,' 'deep,' shared tendencies and strivings by inferring shared wishes from shared behavior or by inferring the motives of the group from the motives of single, prominent individuals."
- That "Freud and successive generations of psychoanalysts have had to ignore or contradict the results of their own practice just to be able to continue to think systematically about society and social processes."
- That "there are no solutions to historical problems . . . or to sociological problems in psychoanalytic terms."

No wonder that Peter Gay, responding to my summary of these points, remarked indignantly that with a friend like Weinstein, psychohistory has no need of enemies. Weinstein had spoken—or more accurately, I had tactlessly disinterred from his footnotes—more than enough hard truths to warn the unwary against the fallacies and gratuitous assumptions that pervade psychohistorical practice. Had he built his whole paper around those insights, I could have reduced my critique to a single sentence of praise.

But then there is Speaker B, who wants to put the best face on psychohistory after all. To do so, he adopts four rhetorical strategies, which I will examine in turn:

1. *Saving Graces.* Here and there, Weinstein attempts to rehabilitate psychoanalytic doctrine by saying something flattering about it or by claiming that it is no worse than other systems of thought. For example:

A. Since the 1950s, he says, psychoanalysis has not had a problem absorbing criticism of its arbitrarily passive-defensive orientation.

Of course not; no adaptation to the shifting *Zeitgeist* will cause problems for a theory in which all concepts are continually up for grabs.

B. "[T]here is really not much one can say about psychoanalytic theory that is not true of all other theories in the social and behavioral sciences."

On the contrary, Weinstein himself makes many damaging observations that pertain uniquely to psychoanalytic theory.

C. "[T]he concerns of the more recently emphasized cognitive psychology are not all that remote from the concerns of psychoanalysis."

Possibly so, but "concerns" have nothing to do with theoretical rigor, which is present in cognitive psychology but wholly missing from psychoanalysis.

D. "[I]t is more likely that some kind of theory consistent with psychoanalytic theory, and perhaps even informed by it, will be developed in academic psychology than it is that psychoanalytic theory will disappear because of its deficiencies."

But Weinstein offers no evidence to support this wishful prediction—and he supplies many indications of its unlikelihood.

2. *Broad Horizons.* If psychohistorical method does not bear close scrutiny, perhaps we should widen our gaze and consider the ineffability of all historical knowledge. Hence Weinstein's sweeping title; hence, too, his discussion of novelists whom he strains to regard as "addressing an epistemological crisis in history"; and hence his claim that "the problematic of psychoanalysis and psychohistory . . . is the problematic of historical interpretation in general." It seems that "historians who have been critical of the inferential leaps characteristic of psychoanalysis and psychohistory have failed to observe how vulnerable to this kind of crit-

icism any history is that acquires depth and force by the interpretation of subjectivity." Weinstein repeatedly brackets "history, psychoanalysis, and psychohistory," as if a justification of the first would somehow include the other two as well.

In other words, if you've seen one "inferential leap," you've seen them all. "The question is not who can better avoid distortion . . . but whether distortion . . . can be avoided at all. . . ." But in whose mind is this lofty issue "the question"? A better question might be why apologists for applied psychoanalysis so often make a show of all-around epistemological fastidiousness, casting modish doubt on knowledge in general instead of dealing with the much-denounced liabilities of their own method.

3. *Theory to the Rescue.* Through a complex chain of reasoning, Weinstein argues that certain Freudian concepts are ideally suited to the reform of historical practice. Historians, he claims, "have no strategy for coping with the problem of subjectivity, having systematically divorced themselves from the kinds of sources that could provide or constitute evidence. . . ." "They typically solved the problem [of subjectivity] by imposing a conception of subjective intentions from the outside, divorced from the reporting of the involved people themselves." If historians are to improve on this sorry record, says Weinstein, they must begin attending to participants' utterances. But the more reliance they place on such evidence, the more they will need to maintain their own analytic stance through recourse to an explicit theory of motivation— one that passes beyond mere "common sense and intuition." Here is where Freud can be admitted into the historical academy after all. Psychoanalysis, according to Weinstein, prominently features the two concepts already assumed by any writer who wants to distinguish between his own analytic perspective and the subjectivity of long-dead figures, namely, "unconscious mental activity and repression."

This argument strains credulity in at least three ways. In the first place, Weinstein's claim that historians typically ignore "subjectivity" verges on the unintelligible. One can guess *why he wants* to make such an assertion, but without any cited instances, one cannot tell what complaint is being lodged against an entire profession. Second, it is possible and indeed usual for historians to maintain analytic independence without recourse to ideas of "unconscious mental activity and repression," especially as those ideas are conceived in a Freudian framework. There they entail a host of dubious postulates about intrapsychic agencies, castration fears, incestuous and parricidal wishes, and symptom formation—assumptions that most historians consider too speculative and culturally dated to be serviceable. And finally, Weinstein himself tells us—although for some reason, he cannot keep the point in mind—that psychoanalytic concepts, having been illegitimately inferred from epistemologically contaminated settings, are not to be trusted. It is hard to see why we should make exceptions for "unconscious mental activity and repression" merely because they propel us beyond "common sense and intuition."

Indeed, the whole trouble with applied psychoanalysis is that it predisposes us to scorn common sense, preferring a dogmatically "deep" psychobiographical interpretation before more proximate alternatives have been given a hearing. The notoriously pliable notion of repression, which allows the analyst to take an apparent absence of his cherished themes as a sure sign of their hidden presence, is probably the worst joker in the Freudian deck. Yet repression is one of the two concepts Weinstein specifically prescribes for adding *rigor* to the historical study of subjectivity.

4. *Up from Freud.* Weinstein's revised paper contains a fourth line of argument which may startle those who remember the original version. *Perhaps psychohistory is not really psychoanalytic at all!* Thus where his conference paper resignedly alluded to the difficulties arising "if we must consider a psychohistory grounded in psychoanalytic insight," Weinstein now makes a break for freedom: "Psychohistory has been too exclusively linked to psychoanalysis . . . , for even if psychoanalysis could be demonstrated to have failed, the problem of subjectivity in history would remain, and hence psychohistory, the systematic exploration of subjectivity, would also remain."

In later paragraphs, Weinstein continues this work of easing Freud offstage, referring inclusively to "some kind of dynamic sociology or psychohistory" and to "psychohistory, or social-scientific history." And now that psychohistory has been at least prospectively shorn of its methodological bias, it can be seen to include many honored practitioners who did not even suspect that they were closet adherents to the movement. Stanley Elkins's *Slavery,* for instance, turns out to be "a prominent example from the psychohistorical literature," as are William R. Taylor's *Cavalier and Yankee* and Paul Fussell's *Great War and Modern Memory,* "whether or not they were based explicitly on psychoanalytic assumptions." (They were not.) The goal, I gather, is to conscript so many excellent non-Freudian authors into the psychohistorical ranks that an attack on psychohistory would look like a threat to the very idea of investigating dead people's minds.

There is no refuting a redefinition, however arbitrary and questionably motivated it may be. If Weinstein wants to gerrymander the borders of psychohistory until it is no longer a Freudian district, no one can stop him. It is worth remarking, however, that this dissociative tactic under-scores the ineffectuality of his other, pro-Freudian, arguments. All Weinstein can salvage at the end is a banality—a concluding exhortation that, however muddled our favorite theories may be, we not "give up on the systematic study of subjectivity." At this moment he is rather like a doubt-stricken astrologer bravely asserting that his science must march ahead because, all present failures notwithstanding, the stars will remain in the sky, begging for interpretation.

But my arrival at Weinstein's last page is premature, for I have yet to discuss the positive heart of his paper, the three "criteria for determining the verifiability of interpretive statements" about historical intentions. Even though he has inserted a new footnote assuring us that he is "of course" only trying to help us *discuss the problem* of subjectivity, his criteria are prescriptive and universal:

1. *Events should be described in two languages, that of the actors and that of the theorist.* Thus, presumably, we will be fair to "the two groups of people involved"—as if the theory-bound historian and his subjects somehow constituted a polity—and we will avoid "ideologically contaminated conclusions." But will we? Suppose the theory in question is itself ideologically contaminated or simply wacky. Criterion 1 offers no control against the grinding out of foregone conclusions—the besetting vice, need I add, of psychohistory.

2. *The historian's "interpretive stance must include the actors' perspective, so that the writer's abstract, ordered, unifying version of events could arguably or conceivably have made sense to the people who lived through them."* In illustration, Weinstein forbids us to argue that "Protestant reformers were really fulfilling capitalist ambitions or require-ments," since those subjects "were not then aware" of playing such a role. This criterion does supply a constraint on interpretation, but it is an unreasonable one. Is there no such thing as a tendency that works without being conceivable by the affected parties? Explanations of, say, witchcraft delusions and faith healing would not get far if criterion 2 were in force, nor would arguments about the effects of background radiation or lead poisoning in ancient times. Nor, in fact, would the typical hypotheses of psychohistorians, which, Weinstein insists, "must all in some degree be based on conceptions of unconscious mental activ-ity and repression." Under his second rule, historical subjects must have been "then aware" of what they had allegedly repressed—a plain con-tradiction.

3. *Data should be "analyzed as they exist, meaning particularly that statements about the subjective intentions of people must take into account the dynamically and socially heterogeneous composition of groups. . . ."* The point is unexceptionable. As Weinstein knows, it constitutes a judgment against virtually the entire tradition of psycho-historical writing, including even such relatively circumspect examples as the contributions of Erik H. Erikson.

Something can be salvaged, then, from Weinstein's criteria: the truism that historians ought to show a due regard for social differences. Even so, his whole discussion of "verification" is radically misleading. For him, verification resides in what he variously calls "relevant documentation," "appropriate documentation," and "confirming documentation." He apparently believes that one interpretation must be preferred to a rival one if more data can be mustered in its support. But this shows a lapse of epistemological sophistication, for, as subjectivists are forever telling us, the very same data can be cited in support of two incompatible interpretations. Nothing is easier than to scoop up particulars that *look congruent with* one's idea—even if the idea is something as perverse as a denial that the Holocaust ever occurred.

Besides, it is simply not the case that we trust historians according to their marshaling of facts. Fogel and Engerman, in *Time on the Cross* (1974), supplied mounds of documentation for conclusions that are now widely rejected; Gibbon supplied scant documentation for conclusions that still bear authority after 200 years. Reliability, it would appear, is not primarily a matter of citing appropriate facts, but one of offering propositions that make sense in themselves and fit well with the rest of what we believe.

Why, then, should we care in advance about any historian's methodology? Why not simply attend to the results? Yet sectarian assumptions on the historian's part do raise legitimate doubts about his ability to serve the larger cause of truth. If, for example, we see that he is compelled by his method to explain past events as intrapsychic dynamics writ large, we will be neither surprised nor impressed by his findings to that effect. And if he puts causal emphasis on psychological folklore without being deterred by its lack of empirical support, we may reasonably wonder whether he has been credulous about other matters as well.[1]

---

1. Some readers may suspect an inconsistency between this reference to "empirical support" and my earlier denigration of "citing appropriate facts" as a benchmark of reliability. But two very different conceptions of evidence are involved. Any writer can gather corroborative-looking information to adorn a theory or interpretation; thus no amount of such information has probative force. By contrast, the "empirical support" that lends

In short, a cabalistic school of thought such as psychohistory inspires distrust precisely to the degree that it plays by private rules.

Such rules, however, confer a parochial solidarity that is hard to renounce on merely intellectual grounds. Otherwise, for example, one could have expected that at least a few of the Freudians participating in the Stanford conference would show concern that their subdiscipline remains the laughingstock of most well-trained historians. No one came closer to doing so than Professor Weinstein, but no one, as a consequence, felt required to produce so many reassuring non sequiturs and fuzzy assertions.

I can draw encouragement only from Weinstein's afterthought that psychohistory may eventually disembarrass itself of psychoanalysis—or, in plainer terms, that psychohistory as we know it may cease to exist. Let us keep on studying "subjectivity," by all means, but preferably without the help of a hermeneutics whose pre-oedipal mothers, toilet traumas, and repressed aggressions supply us with ready-made answers to any question we might pose.

References

Crews, F. (1980, July). "Analysis terminable," *Commentary,* pp. 25–34.

Fogel, W., and Engerman, S. (1974). *Time on the cross: The economics of American Negro slavery* (2 vols.). Boston: Little, Brown.

Weinstein, F. (1980). *The dynamics of Nazism: Leadership, ideology, and the Holocaust.* New York: Academic Press.

Weinstein, F. and Platt, G. M. (1969). *The wish to be free: Society, psyche, and value change.* Berkeley: University of California Press.

Weinstein, F., and Platt, G. M. (1973). *Psychoanalytic sociology: An essay on the interpretation of historical data and the phenomena of collective behavior.* Baltimore: Johns Hopkins University Press.

---

weight to a scientific theory or hypothesis derives from *tests* (1) of its predicted factual consequences, and (2) of its cogency relative to rival theories or hypotheses. The Freudian tradition is overstuffed with the former, anecdotal, kind of support and is totally devoid of the latter (Crews, 1980).

11

Assessing the Personalities of Historical Figures

Kenneth H. Craik

The contemporary field of psychology is a tremendously diverse enterprise, steadily expanding across many domains of life and constantly developing new lines of inquiry and areas of specialization. Historians moving bravely away from the popular sociological perspective and seeking a fuller and richer understanding of the historical actors they must analyze and interpret can only be daunted by the complexities of modern psychology as a scientific endeavor (see, for example, the *Annual Review of Psychology,* 1950–88).

Despite the breadth of historical scholarship and the scope of psychological investigations, points of contact and mutual relevance are not necessarily assured. History has its own trajectory, perhaps now shifting from a brief fascination with the social sciences to a revival of narrative (Stone, 1981). If psychology is usefully viewed as an array of distinct scientific paradigms (Craik, 1977), then its several internally driven research agendas may speed off in directions that make, at best, only tangential contact with current historical concerns. Certainly, the yield of interdisciplinary ties between history and psychology since William Langer's (1958) call for them thirty years ago must be appraised as meager in quantity and, more notably, as narrow in range.

It is reasonable for historians in search of conceptual tools for better understanding the actions and experiences of individuals in history to look to the field of personality as the obvious port of entry to psychology's domain. It is true that since Gordon W. Allport's founding textbook (1937) for this field, the study of personality has been that branch of psychology that takes the person as the unit of analysis, rather than selected processes (such as cognition, perception, learning, or interpersonal relations, etc.), and attempts to pull together the scientific achievements of these other branches of psychology, plus those from the biological and social sciences, to understand individuals and their fates.

Thus the field of personality is not established on a single theoretical orientation, but is the abiding intellectual clearing house for examining the psychological nature of persons. Psychoanalysis, which has continued as a separate intellectual tradition and guild, stands to the field of personality as does, say, cognitive psychology or anthropology—one approach among many that may contribute to our knowledge of individual functioning (Liebert and Spiegler, 1982; Pervin, 1984). To ask how historical inquiry and the contemporary field of personality might forge collaborative interactions is to put quite a different question than to ask whether psychoanalysis is valid or invalid, developing or stagnant, useful or not useful to historians.

Nothing can be more humbling to a personality psychologist than to stand at this port of entry to psychological studies, ready to welcome warmly the curious visitor from the province of history while desperately scanning his limited range of goods and wondering anxiously what he can possibly offer up for trade that the historian might find to be useful or attractive. Modesty is clearly the order of the day. At the outset, I will eschew explanation entirely. Instead of *explaining* persons, I will deal with the general problems involved in simply *describing* persons and the specific challenge of systematically describing historical personages.

In reviewing the potential relevance of certain concepts and methods of personality assessment for historical inquiry, I have selected an intriguing and, I think, feasible task to draw on for illustrations: the systematic personality assessment of the individual members of the Continental Congress from 1774 through 1789. To support the notion that individual variations in personality do have a bearing on the functioning of such a historically important political body, I will bring to my defense John Adams, a successful politician himself and a shrewd observer of the human scene. In an exchange with John Taylor, Adams contrasts his own conception of a natural aristocrat with Jefferson's image of the noble yeoman. Adams sets up a hypothetical legislature in which the 100 members initially control their own votes. Soon, certain members will control the votes of others; then over time, a handful will control the votes of the rest. Adams asserts:

Once for all I give you notice that whenever I use the word *aristocrat* I mean a citizen who can command or govern two votes or more in society, whether by his virtues, his talents, his learning, his loquacity, his taciturnity, his frankness, his reserve, his face, figure, eloquence, grace, air, attitude, movements, wealth, birth, art, address, intrigue, good fellowship, drunkenness, debauchery, fraud, perjury, violence, treachery, pyrrhonism, deism, or atheism; for by every one of these instruments have votes been obtained and will be obtained. You seem to think aristocracy consists altogether in artificial titles, tinsel decorations of stars, garters, ribbons, golden eagles and golden fleeces, crosses and roses and lilies, exclusive privileges, hereditary descents, established by kings or by positive laws of society. No such thing! (Peek, 1954, p. 202).

While we may lack methods in personality assessment appropriate for testing certain of those characteristics, this wide range and variety of personal attributes called forth by Adams captures the nature and spirit of the task that faces personality assessors.

Before turning to the Continental Congress, let me comment briefly on the nature of personality assessment generally and then more specifically on the problem of assessing persons at a distance.

Describing Persons

Personality assessment addresses systematically the age-old problem of how best to describe a person. But, of course, the rendering of descriptions of persons is not confined to personality assessors; it is practiced ubiquitously in everyday social life and within many scholarly fields, including history and biography. The more formal efforts of personality description vary in their occasions, intentions, formats, and audiences (Craik, 1976), as Table 11.1 indicates.

Perhaps the oldest kind of formal personality descriptions were commemorative in intent, to celebrate the dead, in the form of eulogies to friends and acquaintances or in the briefer but more lasting epitaphs addressed to strangers of subsequent generations. Personality descriptions can also accomplish didactic aims, in offering models and exemplars for the young, the aspiring, and the nonelite. Here we have the well-known "lives" of Caesars and the saints, the biographical portraits of heroes and other estimable persons, and, more recently for the edification and admiration of the voters, the campaign biographies of political candidates. In contrast, the formulations of case studies in psychiatry and clinical psychology are used to acquaint novices with infrequently

TABLE 11.1.   Occasions, Intentions, and Audiences of
Personality Assessments

Occasion and intention	Type of assessment	Audience
Commemorative		
To celebrate the dead	Eulogies Epitaphs	Friends Strangers
Didactic		
To provide models and exemplars	"Lives" of the saints and of the Caesars Early biographies "Campaign" biographies Case studies	The young The nonelite (for example, voters) The aspiring
Intrinsic or instrumental		
To portray accurately	"Pure" or objective biographies Reports of Renaissance diplomats	Ideal standards of truth and objectivity The government
Scientific		
To specify standards and create methods for portraying others accurately in order to understand them	Personality assessment techniques	Scientists
Communicative		
To convey an impression of one person to another	Letters of introduction Letters of recommendation	Common acquaintances Decision makers
Applied		
To employ accurate assessments of persons in order to select and assign them to societal positions and to predict their performances	Personality assessment techniques	Institutional managers and decision makers

Adapted from Craik (1976).

encountered sorts of persons who exemplify psychodiagnostic categories. In didactic personality descriptions, the goal of detached portrayal is put aside, while virtues, vices, and psychological impairments are highlighted, depending on the didactic service to which the assessment is put.

Harold Nicholson (1928) has traced the trend within biographical studies to adopt the goal of balancing empathy and esteem with realism in achieving more detached descriptions of persons. This intention of accurate portrayal is shared by the modern field of personality assessment. In both cases, the audience is difficult to specify; perhaps it entails the ideal standards of truth and objectivity monitored by a community of practitioners who endorse them in common.

Of course, striving for accuracy is enhanced if the uses to which the personality description is put are consequential. Thus diplomats posted in rival Italian states during the Renaissance were expected to gain an audience with the prince and to size him up in reports back to their own governments. This combination of applied and communicative functions of personality descriptions in decision making has grown at a steady pace, of course. Such personality descriptions are cultural products influenced by trends toward increasing individual mobility, urbanization, occupational specialization, and complex social structures. The earlier letter of introduction, the much-too-familiar letter of recommendation, and the application of modern personality assessment techniques for selection and placement all offer surrogates to direct acquaintance and are geared to accurate and predictive forms of personality description (Sundberg, 1977; Wiggins, 1973).

Personality Assessment Programs

The contemporary approach to personality description within psychology begins with the recognition expressed so well by John Adams that persons are extraordinarily complex and multidimensional entities. Personality assessors, by professional commitment, take delight in the diversity of persons and are connoisseurs of individuality. They are also, importantly, comparative in their approach to the description of persons, without necessarily losing their appreciation of the specific qualities of the individual.

The optimal methods for the assessment of persons remain a matter of discussion and analysis within the field, but perhaps the most comprehensive approach is the assessment program pioneered in this country at the Harvard Psychological Clinic by Henry A. Murray and his associates in the 1930s (Murray, 1938). Earlier known as the "country house" method or the "living-in" assessment because staff and assessees would be quartered together for several days in country reteats, as in the selection of agents for the Office of Strategic Services in World War

II (Office of Strategic Services Assessment Staff, 1948), variants of the basic program continue to be used at the Institute of Personality Assessment and Research at the University of California, Berkeley, and elsewhere.

During three-day personality assessment programs, for example, a team of psychologists interacts with and observes ten or twelve persons as they engage in situational procedures (for example, role improvisations, charades, leaderless group discussions) as well as in interviews and during informal encounters at social hours and mealtimes. Subsequently, the staff observers independently record their impressions and formulations of each individual by means of adjective checklists, trait ratings, and Q-sort descriptions—techniques that permit systematic quantitative comparisons and statistical analysis. Thus the degree of consensus, or reliability, among staff descriptions can be appraised, and consensual assessments can be related to important actions, performances, and life outcomes (for example, relative creativity among architects; comparisons of medical school students who later become internists, psychiatrists, and surgeons). These procedures can be augmented by pencil-and-paper inventories assessing personality dispositions, interest patterns, and value orientations as well as by various projective techniques. By means of these procedures, our institute has conducted studies that have assessed highly effective persons in the fields of architecture, law, mathematics, medicine, literature, and management (Barron, 1969; Barron and Egan, 1968; Cartwright, 1977; Craik, 1986; Gough, 1975; Helson and Crutchfield, 1970; LaRussa, 1977; MacKinnon, 1978).

Assessing Personality at a Distance

The modern personality assessment program presumes direct interaction between assessors and assessees. But often, of course, the personalities of interest remain at a distance. The nature of the distance can be geographical, social, or temporal. In the case of geographical distance, the standard personality assessment inventories (which themselves do not require direct interaction with the personality assessor) can be mailed to the individuals, completed, and mailed back to the researcher (for example, Costantini and Craik, 1980). The distance may be social, in cases where the personality assessor does not have direct access to or the cooperation of the assessee (for example, the researcher may be in Washington, D.C., but fail to gain access to the president for these purposes). Or, as in the case of our problem at hand, the distance may be temporal, when personality assessments of historical figures are sought. The combination of social and temporal distance is keenly recognized by researchers seeking to study the interplay of personality and political leadership, and various solutions to the problem have been explored (Hermann and Milburn, 1977).

The key to the solution, in my judgment, is the fact that observers can formulate impressions of personality on the basis of sources other than direct acquaintance. In the observational strategy of personality assessment, observers are presented in some way, whether directly or indirectly, with the assessees. The observers then formulate a personality description, which they record in some more or less comparable form. They may use common-sense notions of personality or special conceptual systems, such as that of psychoanalysis in formulating their descriptions. The facets and issues of observational assessment remain the same, regardless of whether the assessment is, directly, of contemporaries or, at a remove, of historical figures. An informal group of us at the University of California, Berkeley, known as the Historical Figures Assessment Collaborative (HFAC, 1977), has reviewed and illustrated the use of observational-assessment strategies in depicting historical figures.

A Process Model for Observer-Based Personality Assessment

As Table 11.2 indicates, there are three basic procedural issues in observational assessment: (1) How are the persons presented to the observers? (2) What formats are used by the observers in recording their personological impressions? and (3) On what basis are observers selected?

Media of Presentation

As in the case of eulogies, personality descriptions can be based on life-long acquaintance. Another candidate for thoroughness is the personality formulation by an analyst following a full-fledged psychoanalysis. Other forms of face-to-face interaction have been noted already. Some biographers currently have the opportunity to interview contemporary subjects (Blum, 1981), while technology is making filmed and videotaped versions of face-to-face occasions available in the case of historical figures (see, for example, Walter Langer's resources for his analysis of Hitler, published in 1972). Nevertheless, the typical sources available to the assessor of historical personalities are limited to biographies, autobiographies and memoirs, personal productions, and biographical source materials.

TABLE 11.2.   A Process Model for the Assessment of Historical Figures

Presentation of assessees	Nature and format of judgments	Observers

Face-to-face interactions
   Interviews
   Projective tests
   Situational tests
   Living-in assessments
   Field observations
	Free descriptions
	   Character sketches
	   Case studies
	
	Rating scales
		Contemporaries
		   Acquaintances
		   Oral-history informants
		
		Experts
		   Biographers

Motion pictures, videotapes, and tape recordings	Adjective checklists Q-sort descriptions	Historians Psychologists Sociologists
Portraits and photographs		Political scientists
Biographies		General public
Autobiographies and memoirs		

Personal productions
   Drawings and paintings
   Poems and stories
   Speeches
   Legislation		

Biographical source materials		

Adapted from Craik (1971) and HFAC (1977).

Response Formats

By whatever means, the individual has been presented to the observers. Now they must record their impressions, descriptions, and formulations. Free descriptions, such as character sketches and psychodynamic case studies, have the advantage of allowing each observer to employ his or her favorite concepts and terminology, but carry heavy disadvantages if the goal is comparable descriptions of personality. Apparent disagreements among observers may amount to only differences in phrase making. Genuine disagreement may go undetected because each observer may focus on different aspects of personality. Even gauging the *extent* of consensus among four free descriptions of personality presents formidable difficulties. To supplement free descriptions, the practice of living-in assessment programs has generated an array of techniques that record personality formulations in comparable and quantifiable form.

The oldest version is the rating scale, whereby observers compare an individual's standing on various personal dispositions (for example, drive, dominance, impulsiveness, verbal fluency) with some implicit or explicit referent population.

A more global impression of personality can be recorded on a standard Adjective Check List (ACL) (Gough and Heilbrun, 1983), consisting of 300 terms drawn from everyday usage, each of which the observer checks if descriptive of the individual or skips if inapplicable. An illustration can be given from personological portraits of two historical figures in the field of personality itself: Sigmund Freud and Carl G. Jung (Table 11.3). These portraits were rendered by panels of graduate students in psychology, based on various source materials (Welsh, 1975).

A third useful technique is the Q-sort description. A Q-sort deck typically consists of 100 statements, each on a separate card and each expressing an important characteristic (for example, "Has social poise and presence; appears socially at ease"; "Tends to ruminate and have persistent, preoccupying thoughts"); the observer sorts the cards into piles of specified number along a dimension ranging from "most characteristic" to "least characteristic."

Placement value	1	2	3	4	5	6	7	8	9
Number of statements per category	5	8	12	16	18	16	12	8	5

The method is person-centered, in that it records the relative importance and configuration of attributes for a given individual. A widely used personality Q-sort deck (Block, 1961) is the product of an extensive effort to cover the personality domain comprehensively as conceptualized by a variety of current theories and viewpoints.

To illustrate this technique, Table 11.4 presents the more and less characterizing statements in a personality description of Woodrow Wilson. The depiction is based on the combination of independent judgments made by members of two assessment panels; one panel used as a biographical source the volume by Freud and Bullitt (1967), and the other used the work of George and George (1956). Based on the intercorrelation matrix for the panel of twelve judges, the reliability of the composite description is +.87. This correlation is an estimate of the

TABLE 11.3.   Sigmund Freud and Carl G. Jung: ACL Descriptions

Adjectives checked by at least 70 percent of judges for both:

active	industrious
capable	ingenious
civilized	insightful
complicated	intelligent
conscientious	interests wide
courageous	moody
curious	original
determined	preserving
energetic	reflective
honest	resourceful
imaginative	sensitive
individualistic	serious

Adjectives checked by at least 70 percent in describing Freud but by less than 70 percent in describing Jung:

aggressive	clear-thinking	egotistical	outspoken
alert	clever	fault-finding	pessimistic
ambitious	confident	forceful	rational
anxious	daring	formal	responsible
argumentative	defensive	headstrong	self-confident
arrogant	deliberate	intolerant	stern
assertive	demanding	logical	stubborn
autocratic	dominant	opinionated	thorough
bossy	efficient	organized	wise

Adjectives checked by at least 70 percent in describing Jung but by less than 70 percent in describing Freud:

adventurous	peculiar
artistic	reserved
dreamy	sincere
emotional	spontaneous
gentle	superstitious
idealistic	thoughtful
independent	unconventional
initiative	versatile
inventive	

Adapted from Welsh (1975).

correspondence between the obtained composite description and one that would be rendered by any equivalently selected panel of assessors. It is typical in magnitude of the reliability of Q-sort descriptions made after three-day assessment programs by our institute's staff members (Petersen, 1965).

TABLE 11.4.   Woodrow Wilson: Q-sort Descriptions

Most characteristic (5)

10. Anxiety and tension find outlet in bodily symptoms. (N.B.: If placed high, implies bodily dysfunction; if placed low, implies absence of autonomic arousal.)
41. Is moralistic. (N.B.: Regardless of the particular nature of the moral code.)
71. Has high aspiration level for self.
72. Concerned with own adequacy as a person, either at conscious or unconscious levels. (N.B.: A clinical judgment is required here; number 74 reflects subjective satisfaction with self.)
98. Is verbally fluent; can express ideas well.

Highly characteristic (8)

8. Appears to have a high degree of intellectual capacity. (N.B.: Whether actualized or not. N.B.: Originality is not necessarily assumed.)
19. Seeks reassurance from others.
38. Has hostility toward others. (N.B.: Basic hostility is intended here; mode of expression is to be indicated by other items.)
52. Behaves in an assertive fashion. (N.B.: Item 14 reflects underlying submissiveness; this refers to overt behavior.)
68. Is basically anxious.
86. Handles anxiety and conflicts by, in effect, refusing to recognize their presence; repressive or dissociative tendencies.
90. Is concerned with philosophical problems; e.g., religious values, the meaning of life, etc.
91. Is power oriented; values power in self or others.

Highly uncharacteristic (8)

14. Genuinely submissive; accepts domination comfortably.
18. Initiates humor.
30. Gives up and withdraws where possible in the face of frustration and adversity. (N.B.: If placed high, implies generally defeatist; if placed low, implies counteractive.)
33. Is calm, relaxed in manner.
48. Keeps people at a distance; avoids close interpersonal relationships.
64. Is socially perceptive of a wide range of interpersonal cues.
73. Tends to perceive many different contexts in sexual terms; eroticizes situations.
84. Is cheerful. (N.B.: Extreme placement toward uncharacteristic end of continuum implies unhappiness or depression.)

Least characteristic (5)

22. Feels a lack of personal meaning in life.
31. Regards self as physically attractive.
60. Has insight into own motives and behavior.
74. Is subjectively unaware of self-concern; feels satisfied with self.
85. Emphasizes communication through action and non-verbal behavior.

Adapted from HFAC (1977).

Selection of Observers

The range of potential observers in the assessment of historical figures includes contemporaries, experts, and the general public. Given the increasing tendency to gain a head start in the systematic documentation of recent historical figures through oral history interviews and other procedures, it would be attractive to have acquaintances and informants participating in those sessions complete rating scales, ACL descriptions, and Q-sort descriptions. The second category consists of expert panelists, who are essential in the assessment of remote historical figures and to whom I will return. The third category is the general public and suggests a line of research on popular conceptions of historical personages (see, for example, Gough and Heilbrun, 1983).

Assessment Procedures

These components can be assembled into at least three distinct procedures for assessing historical figures.

Existing Experts

For many historical figures, a remarkable number of biographical experts can be identified at any given time. These assessors can draw on the full range of their understanding of the individual. The use of Q-sort descriptions, for example, would gauge the extent of consensus among experts about the overall personality configuration and would help to identify areas of disagreement. It is quite likely that general consensus could be found, despite isolated issues of strong disagreement. It would be useful to know, for example, the extent of agreement about Wilson's personality entertained by George and George (1981–82), on the one hand, and by Weinstein, Anderson, and Link (1978–79), on the other, even in the light of their dispute concerning the role of cerebrovascular disease in Wilson's political performance. Indeed, this example usefully highlights the distinction between describing persons and explaining their personalities. Consensus can predominate about the former in the context of disagreements about the latter. In any case, the composite personality description rendered by experts is an important procedure in those cases in which a community of experts is available.

Created Experts

For many historical figures, a community of experts may not be available. In that case, special panels of three to five members can be constituted to review materials, independently formulate their personality descriptions, and record them. Two kinds of sources can be made available to such panels.

Standard Biographies. Biographies offer a ready compilation of organized source material on a historical figure. The limitation lies in the fact that the biographer has already, through selection and implicit or explicit commentary, asserted his or her own formulation of the personality (for example, see an analysis of Suetonius's implicit theory of personality in Cochran, 1980). The portrait of Wilson presented in Table 11.4 is based on the judgments of two panels that reviewed different biographical treatments (HFAC, 1977). When the Q-sort descriptions are analyzed separately for the two panels, each demonstrates adequate composite reliability (+.88 for the George and George panel of seven; +.75 for the Freud and Bullitt panel of five), and the two composite descriptions display considerable convergence (+.67). However, certain descriptive statements were placed differently by the two panels as indicated in Table 11.5. They appear to capture evidence of the animosity that Freud and Bullitt are reported to have brought to their

TABLE 11.5.   Comparison of Sources on Wilson:
Freud and Bullitt vs. George and George

Q-sort Items Differing by 3 or More Placements on a 9-Category Scale

Statements placed higher in descriptions based on Freud and Bullitt:
16. Is introspective and concerned with self as an object. (7 vs. 3)
30. Gives up and withdraws where possible in the face of frustration and adversity. (4 vs. 1)
45. Has a brittle ego-defense system; has a small reserve of integration; would be disorganized and maladaptive when under stress. (8 vs. 5)
49. Is basically distrustful of people in general; questions their motivations. (7 vs. 4)
78. Feels cheated and victimized by life; self-pitying. (7 vs. 4)
94. Expresses hostile feelings directly. (6 vs. 1)

Statements placed higher in descriptions based on George and George:
3. Has a wide range of interests. (5 vs. 2)
8. Appears to have a high degree of intellectual capacity. (9 vs. 6)
15. Is skilled in social techniques of imaginative play; pretending and humor. (5 vs. 2)
54. Emphasizes being with others; gregarious. (5 vs. 2)
69. Is sensitive to anything that can be construed as a demand. (8 vs. 4)
81. Is physically attractive; good-looking. (4 vs. 1)
40. Behaves in an ethically consistent manner; is consistent with own personal standards. (6 vs. 3)

---

biographical project (Erikson, 1967). It should be noted that in this exploratory analysis, members of the two panels were not assigned in a strictly random fashion. A study is warranted that would collect Q-sort descriptions based on preconceptions of Wilson, followed by random assignment to the two volumes (or perhaps more) and a second Q-sorting. This design would allow more precise delineation of the differential impact of the various source volumes.

Biographical Source Materials. A better documentary foundation, but one requiring greater effort, consists of organized original source materials. The standards for what should be included in these compilations and for how extensive they should be are still open questions. Within this category, two kinds of material can be identified. First, a complete collection of all third-person descriptions of the target individual, made by peers and preserved in the archives, would provide one mode of presentation of the individual to an assessment panel. Second, some abbreviation of the full range of materials typically employed by a biographer could be presented in a systematic form to the assessment panels.

Comparisons Among the Personality Descriptions of Historical Persons

One of the advantages of comparable formats for recording personality descriptions is the opportunity they afford for systematic comparison. The composite Q-sort descriptions of any two individuals can be correlated, indexing the degree of similarity and dissimilarity obtaining in the overall formulations of their personalities. In one assessment exercise, separate two-member panels independently described the personalities of selected presidents, based on standard biographies (HFAC, 1977).[1] The intercorrelations among Q-sort descriptions displaying composite reliabilities of at least +.60 are given in Table 11.6. Note that Wilson and Harding earn relatively distinctive personality descriptions, while a modest degree of commonality is shared among the descriptions of Eisenhower, Kennedy, and the two Roosevelts.

In summary, personality assessments of historical figures can be conducted in a systematic and comparable fashion. Rather than lament the fact that we cannot psychoanalyze important figures of the past, we should set about to identify what can be done reasonably and reliably.

1. More recently, Simonton (1986, 1987) has employed selected biographical sources as a basis for panel descriptions of the personalities of presidents. The judges recorded their assessments on the Adjective Check List (Gough and Heilbrun, 1983).

TABLE 11.6.   Presidential Q-sort Descriptions: Intercorrelation Matrix[a]

	DDE	WGH	JFK	FDR	TR
D. D. Eisenhower					
W. G. Harding	.49				
J. F. Kennedy	.54	.18			
F. D. Roosevelt	.53	.18	.63		
T. Roosevelt	.49	.07	.66	.58	
T. W. Wilson	.10	.13	.02	.00	.17

[a] Pearson product-moment correlations

Adapted from HFAC (1977).

Assessing the Personalities of the Members of the Continental Congress (1774–1789)

Why focus on the members of the Continental Congress? A number of substantive and methodological reasons can be cited. As a background, I have had experience in studying the relations between personality and political career among contemporary elites within California political parties, primarily delegates to the national presidential nominating conventions, plus members of delegation slates for candidates who lost in the state primaries (Costantini and Craik, 1969, 1980). The limitation of this strategy is the restricted role of the modern convention delegate, although it does reflect status earned through other important activities within the parties. The study of members of a political body offers a much tighter, more circumscribed, and richer arena for examining the part that personality plays in political action and interaction. The option is still available to study a contemporary political body, such as the California legislature, rather than a historical body. Obviously, both paths should be explored, but distinctive advantages rest with the latter course.

The first advantage with the Continental Congress is that the course of events, both political and biographical, has unfolded. Second, the Continental Congress met during the heyday of personal written expression; the documentation is impressive. Available are 34 volumes of journals by the members of the Congress (Ford et al., 1904–37) and 8 volumes of letters (Burnett, 1921–36). A new series of 25 volumes of letters (presenting over 17,000 items) has begun to be published (Smith, 1976). The quantity of material is encouraging, and it is by the hand of the delegates themselves (not that of staff aides or speech writers).

Also, there probably is a significant amount of additional source material written by observers on the scene who were not members of the Congress (Rakove, 1979). Third, with all due respect to contemporary political bodies, the Continental Congress *is* a certified historically important entity, whose impact has received extensive analysis. Fourth, given the commitment of the Institute of Personality Assessment and Research, with which I am associated, to the study of highly effective individuals, the large number of remarkable and distinctive persons in the Congress is widely acknowledged. Fifth, the quantity of source materials available provides a good and fair test of approaches to assessing personality at a historical distance and offers the opportunity to grapple with and perhaps resolve various methodological issues. Finally, if the endeavor were successful, the product of the undertaking—that is, systematic personality descriptions of the members of the Congress in comparable and quantified form—would serve as an enduring resource to historians of that era.

As an outsider to historical studies, I see a project of this kind as falling within the development of prosopography (Stone, 1971) and in the spirit of Namierism (Brooke, 1964). The link to prosopography, or collective biography, is through common purpose and extension. The aim is to understand "a group of actors in history by means of a collective study of their lives" and to use biographical information to search "for internal correlations and for correlations with other forms of behavior or action" (Stone, 1971, p. 46). Thus far, this tradition has been restricted to sociodemographic variables, such as family origins, place of residence, occupation, education, and religion. Systematic personality descriptions can readily augment this class of variables and afford the opportunity for similar kinds of analysis.

The personological analysis of the members of the Continental Congress would have close parallels with the prosopographical history of Parliament undertaken by Sir Lewis Namier and his colleagues (Namier and Brooke, 1964). They studied a historically important, intact political body—the House of Commons—during a period that overlaps (1754–90) with the Continental Congress. Beyond that, Namier's tremendous dedication to learning as much as possible about each and every member of the House of Commons is well known and would certainly encompass systematic personality characterizations. Brooke (1964) reports that when asked what the phrase "Namierizing history" really meant, Namier would laugh and reply, "It means finding out who the guys were" (p. 333).

During the 14 sessions of the Continental Congress, a total of 343 men served, many for brief periods. The management of the assessment program would require certain strategic decisions. For example, priority in selecting individual members for assessment might be based on (1) length of service, (2) amount of source material available, (3) estimated influence on the Congress, and (4) frequency of attendance. Or the sessions could be ordered in priority, and all members of each session assessed in turn.

Four assessment procedures could be employed. Each has its merits and limitations, and, of course, convergence in findings yielded by them would be reassuring.

Personality Description by Existing Experts

Present-day editors of the members' correspondence (such as Paul H. Smith and his colleagues), close analysts of the Congress (such as Jack N. Rakove and H. James Henderson), and biographers of principal actors in that body (such as James Thomas Flexner) already have working knowledge of the personalities of the members, as manifested and as described by others of the time. This knowledge would form one basis for systematic personality descriptions (via trait ratings, adjective checklist descriptions, and Q-sort descriptions).

Summary Interpretations of Extant Personality Descriptions by Peers

Among the letters and journals of the members as well as the writings of other contemporaries can be found many thumbnail portraits of the individual members of the Continental Congress. These materials vary in length and are scattered throughout the total body of source materials on the members of the Congress. The first task would be to search out, identify, and assemble these contemporary personological impressions of each member of the Congress. Thus each member would eventually have a file containing the impressions that his personality made on others and their depiction of it. A panel of assessors would then be constituted for each member. The assessors would individually and independently review the material and then record a summary description of personality based on it. Various niceties in analysis could also be pursued (for example, having separate panels review the portraits left by allies and enemies), but the basic goal is to make use of these peer descriptions as a basis for rendering systematic and comparable personality descriptions (via trait ratings, adjective-checklist descriptions, and Q-sort descriptions). In addition, at a qualitative level, analysis of these distinctive sets of source materials would be rewarding both for historians and for personality psychologists.

Personality Descriptions by Created Experts

Roger Sherman of Connecticut served in the Continental Congress for eight years, during the 1774 to 1781 and the 1784 sessions, but existing experts on this historical figure might be hard to find. The solution is to *create* experts for each member of the Congress, by establishing three-person teams that would independently review all the available source material on their target individual. The task is more demanding in time and effort than that presented to the panels that would review the peers' impressions of the members of the Congress, but the yield would be a richer formulation of the personality. Systematic personality descriptions would be recorded by each panel member (via trait ratings, adjective checklist descriptions, and Q-sort descriptions), and a character sketch would be formulated by each panelist.

Assessment of Specific Dispositions, Styles, and Attitude Orientations.

This approach would make use of an array of techniques that have been developed to assess specific personality characteristics at a distance, primarily through analysis of written documents. These techniques have been applied, often singly, to various samples of political leaders. The proposal here is that the array of techniques be surveyed and evaluated for their promise and then a subset be selected for application to the same set of members of the Continental Congress. Possible attributes include achievement and power motivation (Donley and Winter, 1970), conceptual complexity (Suedfeld and Rank, 1976; Tetlock, 1981), and authoritarian orientation (Hoffer, 1978, 1983; Hull, Hoffer, and Allen, 1978). These variables are readily combined with the more comprehensive systematic personality descriptions for analytic purposes.

In my judgment, the broad comparative assessment of personality resulting from the combined use of these four strategies would rival in reliability and validity that gained from the most intensive personality assessment programs that we now employ to study contemporary individuals.

Neither the time available for this presentation nor my knowledge of the historical context of the Continental Congress permits me to spell out in full detail the array of substantive analyses to which these personality descriptions could be put. One question is the influence of personality on the kinds of roles that members either adopted or were urged into (for example, on Franklin's perennial role of negotiator–conciliator, see Bushman, 1966). Another question is the relation of personality characteristics to the legislative style displayed by each member; here the work of Barber (1965) would provide guidance. Yet another question is the relation of personality characteristics to membership in cliques and factions within the Congress and to alignment around certain issues. Through an analysis of roll-call votes, Henderson (1974) has identified clusters of delegates who showed a high level of agreement among themselves and who opposed other blocs of delegates. The relation, if any, of personality to these issue-based alliances would warrant investigation, as would the bearing of personality on choice among major options facing the delegates (for example, Federalist vs. anti-Federalist) (Chambers, 1963). Finally, from the point of view of the personality psychologist, there remain interesting questions regarding the ability of the personality assessments made at the time of the Congress to forecast the personal and political careers and fates of its members in the years after 1789.

Conclusion

In closing, I wish to come back to the methodological theme of my presentation. The methods available for assessing personality systematically and comparatively at a historical distance can be applied to many other situations than the Continental Congress. I do hope that this example has served its purpose in stimulating the interest of historians in the usefulness of the approach and in conveying the possibility of an undertaking that is at least imaginable and perhaps even feasible. A project of this kind is attractive because it would require an interdisciplinary team whose members would work together to solve a host of technical, procedural, and interpretative problems. Indeed, I believe that intellectual ties between history and psychology will continue to languish until settings that require actual collaborative efforts are created.

A clear agenda of mutual tasks can be envisioned, with progress in learning more about how best to assess the personalities of historical figures almost ensured. I cannot speak for the value of the potential substantive analyses and findings for history and political science, but I do consider a project of this kind as pure, fundamental research in personality—*not* simply the export of a bag of tricks and techniques to another discipline for applied use.

I am sure that a host of specific technical questions have occurred to you. If so, we are practically rolling up our sleeves and getting down to work on a task that is intrinsically interesting; that would enlist the skills of historians, personality psychologists, archivists, and political scientists; and that would have solid intellectual payoffs for each of the disciplines. We have historians who know thoroughly the time and place and events; we have personality psychologists who understand the technical problems in assessment; we have archivists who can marshal the documents and order them usefully; and we have political scientists who are devoted to analyzing political bodies and their functioning. With a relatively small and congenial set of collaborators and a substantial amount of funds, we could begin to address these issues in assessing the personalities of historical figures and in understanding their historical consequences.

References

Allport, G. W. (1937). *Personality: A psychological interpretation.* New York: Holt.

Annual Review of Psychology. (1950–88). Palo Alto, Calif.: Annual Review.

Barber, J. D. (1965). *The lawmakers.* New Haven, Conn.: Yale University Press.

Barron, F. (1969). *Creative person and creative process.* New York: Holt, Rinehart and Winston.

Barron, F., and Egan, D. (1968). Leaders and innovators in Irish management. *Journal of Management Studies, 3,* 41–61.

Block, J. (1961). *The Q-sort method in personality assessment and psychiatric research.* Springfield, Ill.: Thomas.

Blum, R. H. (1981). Psychological processes in preparing contemporary biography. *Biography, 4,* 293–311.

Brooke, J. (1964). Namier and Namierism. *History and Theory, 3,* 331–347.

Burnett, E. C. (Ed.). (1921–36). *Letters of members of the Continental Congress* (8 vols.). Washington, D.C.: Carnegie Institution of Washington.

Bushman, R. L. (1966). On the uses of psychology: Conflict and conciliation in Benjamin Franklin. *History and Theory, 5,* 225–240.

Cartwright, L. K. (1977). Personality changes in a sample of women physicians. *Journal of Medical Education, 52,* 467–474.

Chambers, W. N. (1963). Party development and party action: The American origins. *History and Theory, 3,* 91–120.

Cochran, L. R. (1980). Suetonius' conception of imperial character. *Biography, 3,* 189–201.

Costantini, E., and Craik, K. H. (1969). Competing elites within a political party: A study of Republican leadership. *Western Political Quarterly, 22,* 879–903.

Costantini, E., and Craik, K. H. (1980). Personality and politicians: California party leaders, 1960–1976. *Journal of Personality and Social Psychology, 38,* 641–661.

Craik, K. H. (1971). The assessment of places. In P. McReynolds (Ed.), *Advances in psychological assessment* (Vol. 2, pp. 40–62). Palo Alto, Calif.: Science and Behavior Books.

Craik, K. H. (1976). The personality research paradigm in environmental psychology. In S. Wapner, S. B. Cohen, and B. Kaplan (Eds.), *Experiencing the environment* (pp. 55–79). New York: Plenum Press.

Craik, K. H. (1977). Multiple scientific paradigms in environmental psychology. *International Journal of Psychology, 12,* 147–157.

Craik, K. H. (1986, August). *Combining personality and managerial assessment.* Paper presented at the Symposium on Recent Trends in Personality and Industrial-Organizational Psychology, ninety-fourth annual meeting of the American Psychological Association, Washington, D.C.

Donley, R. E., and Winter, D. G. (1970). Measuring the motives of public officials at a distance: An exploratory study of American presidents. *Behavioral Science, 15,* 227–236.

Erikson, E. H. (1967). Review of Freud, S., and Bullitt, W. C., *Thomas Woodrow Wilson: A psychological study. International Journal of Psychoanalysis, 48,* 462–468.

Ford, W. C. et al. (1904–37). (Eds.). *Journals of the Continental Congress 1774–1789* (34 vol.). Washington, D.C.: U.S. Government Printing Office.

Freud, S., and Bullitt, W. C. (1967). *Thomas Woodrow Wilson: A psychological study.* Boston: Houghton Mifflin.

George, A. L., and George, J. L. (1956). *Woodrow Wilson and Colonel House: A personality study.* New York: John Day.

George, J. L., and George, A. L. (1981–82). Woodrow Wilson and Colonel House: A reply to Weinstein, Anderson, and Link. *Political Science Quarterly, 96,* 641–665.

Gough, H. G. (1975). Specialty preferences of physicians and medical students. *Journal of Medical Education, 50,* 581–588.

Gough, H. G., and Heilbrun, A. B., Jr. (1983). *Manual for the Adjective Check List* (2nd ed.). Palo Alto, Calif.: Consulting Psychologists Press.

Helson, R., and Crutchfield, R. S. (1970). Creative types in mathematics. *Journal of Personality, 35,* 48–51.

Henderson, H. J. (1974). *Party politics in the Continental Congress*. New York: McGraw-Hill.

Hermann, M. G. and Milburn, T. W. (Eds.). (1977). *A psychological examination of political leaders*. New York: Free Press.

Historical Figures Assessment Collaborative. (1977). Assessing historical figures: The use of observer-based personality descriptions. *Historical Methods Newsletter, 10*, 66–76.

Hoffer, P. C. (1978). Psychohistory and empirical group affiliation: Extraction of personality traits from historical manuscripts. *Journal of Interdisciplinary History, 9*, 131–145.

Hoffer, P. C. (1983). *Revolution and regeneration: Life cycle and the historical vision of the generation of 1776*. Athens, Ga.: University of Georgia Press.

Hull, N. E. H., Hoffer, P. C., and Allen, S. L. (1978). Choosing sides: A quantitative study of the personality determinants of Loyalist and Revolutionary political affiliation in New York. *Journal of American History, 65*, 344–366.

Langer, W. C. (1972). *The mind of Adolf Hitler: The secret wartime report*. New York: Basic Books.

Langer, W. L. (1958). The next assignment. *American Historical Review, 63*, 283–304.

LaRussa, G. W. (1977). Portia's decision: Women's motives for studying law and their later career satisfaction as attorneys. *Psychology of Women Quarterly, 1*, 350–364.

Liebert, R. M., and Spiegler, M. D. (1982). *Personality: Strategies and issues* (4th ed.). Homewood, Ill.: Dorsey Press.

MacKinnon, D. W. (1978). *In search of human effectiveness: Identifying and developing creativity*. Buffalo, N.Y.: Creative Education Foundation.

Murray, H. A. (1938). *Explorations in personality*. New York: Oxford University Press.

Namier, L., and Brooke, J. (1964). *The history of Parliament: The House of Commons, 1754–1790* (Vol. 1). New York: Oxford University Press.

Nicolson, H. (1928). *The development of English biography*. London: Hogarth Press.

Office of Strategic Services Staff. (1948). *Assessment of men*. New York: Rinehart.

Peek, G. A., Jr. (Ed.). (1954). *The political writings of John Adams: Representative selections*. New York: Liberal Arts Press.

Pervin, L. A. (1984). *Personality: Theory, assessment and research* (4th ed.). New York: Wiley.

Petersen, P. G. (1965). *Reliability of judgments of personality as a function of subjects and traits being judged*. Unpublished doctoral dissertation, University of California.

Rakove, J. N. (1979). *The beginnings of national politics: An interpretive history of the Continental Congress.* New York: Knopf.

Simonton, D. K. (1986). Presidential personality: Biographical use of the Gough Adjective Check List. *Journal of Personality and Social Psychology, 51,* 1–12.

Simonton, D. K. (1987). Presidential inflexibility and veto behavior: Two individual-situational interactions. *Journal of Personality, 55,* 1–18.

Smith, P. H. (Ed.). (1976). *Letters of delegates to Congress, 1774–1789* (Vol. 1). Washington, D.C.: Library of Congress.

Stone, L. (1971). Prosopography. *Daedalus, 100,* 46–79.

Stone, L. (1981). *The past and the present.* London: Routledge & Kegan Paul.

Suedfeld, P., and Rank, A. D. (1976). Revolutionary leaders: Long-term success as a function of changes in conceptual complexity. *Journal of Personality and Social Psychology, 34,* 169–178.

Sundberg, N. D. (1977). *Assessment of persons.* New York: Prentice-Hall.

Tetlock, P. E. (1981). Personality and isolationism: Content analysis of senatorial speeches. *Journal of Personality and Social Psychology, 41,* 737–743.

Weinstein, E. A., Anderson, J. W., and Link, A. S. (1978–79). Woodrow Wilson's political personality: A reappraisal. *Political Science Quarterly, 93,* 586–594.

Welsh, G. S. (1975). Adjective Check List descriptions of Freud and Jung. *Journal of Personality Assessment, 39,* 160–168.

Wiggins, J. S. (1973). *Personality and prediction: Principles of personality assessment.* Reading, Mass.: Addison-Wesley.

12

Alternatives to Psychoanalytic Psychobiography

William McKinley Runyan

The bulk of work in psychobiography has, unquestionably, been done from a psychoanalytic point of view. Originally, this was true by definition, as early workers in the field were psychoanalysts and regarded the interpretation of historical figures as an exercise in "applied psychoanalysis." In recent years, however, many (Anderson, 1981b; Glad, 1973; Tucker, 1977; and others) have argued that the field of psychobiography should be defined by the explicit use of any branch of psychology in biography. Thus psychoanalytic psychobiography could be complemented by phenomenological psychobiography, behavioral psychobiography, cognitive psychobiography, and so on.

The task I have undertaken here is to explore several of the possible alternatives to psychoanalytic psychobiography. The discussion is divided into three parts. The first section examines several common criticisms of psychoanalytic psychobiography, indicating some of the reasons for wanting to consider alternatives to psychoanalytic approaches. The second section outlines the contributions of different areas of personality, social, and developmental psychology to psychobiography, while the concluding section contains some personal speculations about the relative promise of psychoanalytic and nonpsychoanalytic approaches to the field of psychobiography.

Methodological Problems in Psychoanalytic Psychobiography

One extreme point of view is taken by David Stannard in his book *Shrinking History: On Freud and the Failure of Psychohistory* (1980), in which he argues that not only are individual psychohistorical works flawed, but "the best possible psychohistory would still be bad history because of the limitations imposed by the weaknesses of the underlying theoretical structure" (p. 21). He says that psychoanalytic theory provides the strongest foundation for psychohistory, claims that psychoanalytic theory "suffers from problems of illogic, experimental nonconfirmation, and cultural parochialism" (p. 30), and concludes that psychoanalytic theory is so defective that psychohistorical work should be abandoned.

A number of reviewers (Adelson, 1981; Basch, 1980; Crosby, 1980) have pointed out the flaws and limitations in Stannard's argument. For one thing, to say that psychohistory is necessarily psychoanalytic is incorrect. Second, the research evidence supporting psychoanalytic theory (reviewed in Fisher and Greenberg, 1977; Kline, 1972) is both more complex and more positive than indicated by his polemical and one-sided review. Finally, the examples of cultural parochialism and historical naïveté that he identifies do not mean that such problems have not been adequately handled by some practicing psychohistorians, much less that they never could be. In short, Stannard's attack on the psychoanalytic foundations of psychohistory is largely unpersuasive. There are, however, a number of problems in psychoanalysis and in psychoanalytic psychobiography that make it worthwhile to at least explore the potential contributions of other approaches.

The Question of Inadequate Evidence

One of the most frequent criticisms of psychoanalytic psychobiography is that interpretations are based on inadequate evidence. "The historian's most serious objection to psychohistory is that sweeping declarations about actions or personalities are based on sparse evidence" (Anderson, 1978, p. 11). The issue of inadequate evidence is frequently raised in regard to psychoanalytic biography in the form: "You can't put the person on the couch." Kohut (1960) notes that applied psychoanalysis "must proceed without the central instrument for the investigation of the unconscious: free association" (p. 571). Finally, there is the criticism that if early childhood experience is particularly influential, this is just the period about which the psychohistorian is likely to have the least information. "Freudian psychology has not been much use to the historian, who is usually unable to penetrate the bedroom, the bathroom or the nursery. If Freud is right, and if these are the places where the action is, there is not much the historian can do about it" (Stone, 1981, p. 53).

There are, in sum, claims of insufficient evidence, of evidence of the wrong kind (not enough free associations or dream reports), and of not enough evidence from the right period (that is, childhood). These are criticisms which need to be taken more seriously than they have been. Both Freud in his study of Leonardo and Erikson in his analysis of Luther have been severely criticized for having developed psychological interpretations from inadequate data about early experience.

What are the implications of problems of evidence for the psychobiographical enterprise? They do not mean that psychobiography is impossible, as has sometimes been suggested, but that attention is best devoted to historical figures about whom there is sufficient evidence to develop and test psychological explanations. Also, in the absence of evidence about childhood experience, some types of early developmental explanations are best avoided, as psychological theory is often not sufficiently determinate to permit accurate retrodictions or reconstructions (see Runyan, 1982). The problems of evidence mean that some types of questions cannot be answered about some individuals, but this in no way impairs the possibility of developing psychological interpretations of the many aspects of behavior and experience of historical individuals for which there is adequate evidence. On a comparative basis, the problems of evidence are not as severe as they may first appear, since there are also a number of evidential advantages that the psychobiographer has over the psychotherapist.

It seems undeniable that the psychobiographer typically has less access to material such as free associations, dreams, and transference reactions than does the psychoanalyst. On the other hand, the psychobiographer often has the advantage of having information about a person who has lived his or her entire life. The average patient in psychoanalysis is relatively young, and has often not yet lived through such important life experiences as the rearing of children, the peak of his or her career, or the death of parents. Reactions to these experiences, which may be revelatory of personality, are thus not available for interpretation. But the usual subject of psychobiography "has lived his entire life and has met death. Not only the development and mid-stages of his life are available for inspection but also its ultimate unfolding and final resolution. This means that in discovering the dominant psychological themes of his subject's emotional evolution the psychoanalytic biographer has at his disposal a broader spectrum of behavior through more decades of life than has the analyst with a living patient" (Cody, 1971, p. 5).

Second, the psychobiographer is not limited to information coming from the subject alone, but may draw heavily on "outside sources" (Hofling, 1976, p. 229). He or she is able to learn how a variety of other informants perceived the situations the subject was in, and their reactions to the individual's personality (Anderson, 1981a).

Third, if the subject is a literary or creative person, the psychobiographer has a wealth of creative material, perhaps expressing inner psychological states and conflicts, that may, with caution, be drawn on in interpretation of the subject's personality.

Fourth, there are sometimes substitutes for a person's dreams or free associations (Anderson, 1981a). For example, Davis (1975) analyzes drawings and caricatures made by Theodore Roosevelt in adolescence when he portrayed himself and members of his family turning into animals. Equivalents to free associations have been found in the "language exercises" of archaeologist Heinrich Schliemann, in which he revealed dreams and unconscious wishes, and in the conversation books written by Beethoven to cope with his deafness (Bergmann, 1973, p. 842).

A fifth advantage is that the evidence used in psychobiography is available to all, so that original interpretations may be critically examined and alternatives may be proposed and tested. In psychoanalysis, the data are typically not publicly available, which makes it less likely that such a corrective process can take place. In sum, the psychobiographer often has access to information not available to the psychotherapist, such as information about the person's whole life span, from associates of the individual, and from the analysis of expressive or creative activities.

Reconstruction

In response to the paucity of evidence on childhood experience and the importance of such experience within psychoanalytic theory, psychobiographers have sometimes used psychoanalytic theory to reconstruct or postdict what must have happened to their subjects in childhood. Greenacre (1955), for example, argues that childhood wants can be "reconstructed from known characteristics, problems, and repetitive actions supported by memory traces." Indeed, "the experienced psychoanalyst knows just as definitely as the internist observing later sequelae of tuberculosis . . . that the deformity is the result of specific acts upon the growing organism" (p. 107). Such reconstructions have, however, not gone uncriticized, even when executed with considerable sophistication. Erikson, for example, has been criticized for having reconstructed Luther's relationship to his mother on the basis of adult behavior: "In his study of the young Luther, Erikson literally invents little Martin's relation to his mother using as a basis (as a "document") the behavior of Luther the man. . . . Erikson does not interpret a repetitive behavior on young Luther's part in terms of an unconscious dynamic; he jumps from a presumed characteristic of the Reformer to the inferential reconstruction of essential data about the latter's family environment" (Friedländer, 1978, p. 27).

The reconstruction of specific life events is not as extreme as the practice of hagiographers, who sometimes reconstructed entire lives if information was not available. Agnellus, a bishop of Ravenna in the ninth century, while completing a series of lives of his predecessors in that position, confessed that "in order that there might not be a break in the series, I have composed the life myself, with the help of God and the prayers of the brethren" (quoted in Clifford, 1962, p. x). Some historians are outraged at the more limited psychobiographical practice of reconstructing particular events or relationships and feel that it is no more acceptable than the reconstructive techniques of the bishop. The practice of retrodiction is especially troubling when an earlier event is retrodicted, and then later assumed to have been firmly established.

Is retrodiction always to be avoided? Perhaps there are a few cases in which extensive evidence is available and in which a clear and well-supported theoretical structure exists that would justify the tentative reconstruction of the gross features of an unknown event. Even so, biographical reconstruction is extremely risky, and in most cases unjustified. In light of the uncertainties in developmental theory, the lack of empirical support for psychoanalytic genetic theory, and the many possible processes leading to any given outcome, the case for banning reconstruction altogether in psychobiography is a fairly strong one. But if retrodiction is to be practiced at all, it is essential that reconstructions be clearly labeled as such and kept distinct from events for which there is documentary evidence.

Reductionism

Another common charge against psychobiography is that of "reductionism." One form of the reductionist critique is that psychological factors are overemphasized at the expense of external social and historical factors. "In turning to Freud, historians interested in the psychological aspect of their discipline have concentrated upon the internal biographies of individuals to the almost complete exclusion of the society in which the lives of their subjects take place" (Hundert, 1972, pp. 467–468).

A second version of the reductionist criticism is that psychobiography focuses excessively on psychopathological processes and gives insufficient attention to normality and creativity. Particularly in the early history of psychobiography, works were sometimes called pathographies, "thereby emphasizing the basic concern with abnormality and leading to the conclusion that what psychoanalysis had to offer to an understanding of the lives of great men consisted mainly in a documentation and explication of their foibles and follies" (Meyer, 1972, p. 373).

A third type of reductionism is to explain adult character and behavior exclusively in terms of early childhood experience while neglecting later formative processes and influences. "What is chiefly wrong with the conventional psychoanalytic biography is its crude unilateralism. It suggests a one-to-one relationship, arguing that the protagonist did this or that because of some painful experience in early childhood" (Hughes, 1964, p. 58). Erikson (1969) identified this form of reductionism as "originology," or "the habitual effort to find the 'causes' of a man's whole development in his childhood conflicts" (p. 98). Two other reductive fallacies are " 'the critical period fallacy,' which attempts to build a study of a man's life around a certain 'key' period of development, and 'eventism,' the discovery in some important episode in a man's life of not only the prototype of his behavior but *the* turning point in his life from which all subsequent events and work are derived. Both these oversimplifications lend artistic grace to a biographical study, but also impose unnatural order, shape, and direction to the often rather amorphous nature and fitful course of a human life, even that of a great man" (Mack, 1971, p. 156).

In response to these charges of reductionism, it must be acknowledged that too many psychobiographies have suffered from flaws such as overemphasizing the psychological, the pathological, and the influence of childhood conflicts. A number of contemporary psychobiographers (for example, Bate, 1977; Erikson, 1969; Mack, 1976; Tucker, 1973) are, however, aware of such dangers and are avoiding them by integrating the psychological with the social and historical, by analyzing not just pathology but also strengths and adaptive capacities, and by studying formative influences not just in childhood but throughout the life span.

The Relationship of Childhood Experience to Adult Behavior

One of the most complex and difficult issues in the field of psychobiography is that of assessing the influence of childhood experience on adult character and behavior. In psychoanalytically oriented psychobiographies, aspects of adult behavior are often attributed to circumstances and experiences in childhood. In the worst cases, "hypotheses about early developments are speculatively deduced from adult events and then used to explain those events" (Izenberg, 1975, p. 139). In more fortunate cases, available evidence about childhood experience is interpreted as an important causal determinant of adult personality and behavior.

This practice of interpreting the whole life in terms of early childhood experience has, however, come under attack from a number of different directions. Historians have challenged the causal interpretations provided for particular cases: "I just do not think that such things as the extermination of six million Jews can be explained by the alleged fact that Hitler's mother was killed by treatment given her by a Jewish doctor in an attempt to cure her cancer of the breast; or that Luther's defiance of the Roman Church can be explained by the brutal way he was treated by his father or by his chronic constipation" (Stone, 1981, p. 220). Stone's statement exaggerates the issues, though, as there is an important difference between claiming that childhood experience is *the* cause of later events and arguing that it is a partial or contributing cause of individual behavior.

From another direction, empirical tests of Freudian theory, reviewed in Kline (1972) and by Fisher and Greenberg (1977), raise serious questions about aspects of Freud's theories of psychosexual development. Although there is some evidence about clusters of traits consistent with Freud's conception of oral character, and substantial evidence about orderliness, obstinancy, and parsimony clustering together as Freud suggested in the anal or obsessive character, the bulk of quantitative empirical studies do not demonstrate connections between character types and specific childhood experiences associated with feeding or toilet training. Whether more methodologically sophisticated studies done in the future will provide more support for these theories is an open question, but at present, a substantial number of studies do not support them and provide little reason for believing them to be valid.

The study of childhood experience may be of some importance in psychobiography, but perhaps not in the way suggested by classical Freudian theory. There has, in recent years, been a widespread shift in thinking within developmental and personality psychology about the influence of early childhood experience. In contrast to earlier beliefs about the crucial impact of childhood experience on adult behavior (Bloom, 1964; Bowlby, 1952; Kelly, 1955), there is a growing belief that the effects of early deprivation can be substantially modified by later experience and that behavior and personality are shaped and changed throughout the life course (Brim and Kagan, 1980; Clarke and Clarke, 1976; Mischel, 1968; Rutter, 1979). The argument is not that early childhood experiences have no effects, but that the effects of such experiences are mediated by intervening experiences and contingencies, and that personality and behavior are continually shaped throughout the life cycle.

Early experience, of whatever form, rarely has a direct impact on adult personality, but early experience shapes early personality, which influences the kinds of environments one is likely to encounter, which, in turn, influence later experience, which affects personality, and so on in an interactive cycle (Wachtel, 1977). The effects of early experiences are mediated through a chain of behavior-determining, person-determining, and situation-determining processes throughout the life course (Runyan, 1978). Thus any given event or experience can have a variety of possible effects and meanings, depending on initial personality structure, initial environment, and the causal structure of subsequently encountered environments and experiences (Runyan, 1984).

The study of formative influences throughout the life cycle makes analysis more complicated, but it also has certain advantages for psychobiography in that early childhood experience, for which evidence is usually unavailable, is no longer so predominantly important. Attention can then be directed to those formative periods and processes for which adequate evidence is more often available. One of the advantages of Eriksonian theory, in which character and identity are importantly shaped at later ages, is that the psychobiographer is more likely to have usable evidence on these periods of the subject's life (Stone, 1981, p. 53).

Psychology can be used in psychobiography for many purposes other than drawing causal connections between childhood experience and adult behavior. It can be useful for identifying patterns in current behavior, for providing concepts and categories for analyzing experience, for suggesting hypotheses about the meaning of circumstances or events for an individual, for providing normative or comparative data about phenomena of interest, for providing methods to use in analyzing biographical evidence, and so on. It may be that the greatest contributions of psychology to biography lie in just such areas, in the conceptualization and interpretation of biographical evidence, without always attempting to relate adult behavior to childhood experience.

The Problem of Alternative Explanations

One final criticism is that psychoanalytic theory can be used to generate an excessive number of different interpretations of the same events. Consider, for example, the question of why Vincent Van Gogh, then thirty-five years old, cut off the lower half of his left ear and took it to a brothel, where he asked for a prostitute named Rachel and handed the ear to her, asking her to "keep this object carefully." How is this extraordinary event to be explained? Over the years, more than a dozen psychodynamic explanations have been proposed (Runyan, 1981).

One explanation is that Van Gogh was frustrated by two recent events: the engagement of his brother Theo, to whom he was very attached, and the failure of an attempt to establish a working and living relationship with Paul Gauguin. The aggressive impulses aroused by these frustrations first were directed at Gauguin, but then were turned against himself.

A second interpretation is that the self-mutilation resulted from a conflict over homosexual impulses aroused by the presence of Gauguin. According to this account, the ear was a phallic symbol (the Dutch slang for "penis," *lul,* resembles the Dutch word for "ear," *lel*), and the act was a symbolic self-castration.

A third explanation is in terms of Oedipal themes. Van Gogh was sharing a house with Gauguin, who reported that Van Gogh had previously threatened him with a razor. According to this interpretation, Gauguin represented Van Gogh's hated father, and that "in giving the ear to a prostitute, Vincent fulfilled an unconscious wish to possess his mother following the fantasied assault upon a father-substitute, Gauguin" (Lubin, 1972, pp. 157–158).

A fourth interpretation is that Van Gogh was influenced by bullfights he had seen in Arles. In such events, the matador is given the ear of the bull as an award, displays his prize to the crowd, and then gives it to the lady of his choice. The proponent of this interpretation suggests that Van Gogh was deeply impressed by this practice, confused himself in a psychotic state with the bull and the matador, and then presented the ear to a lady of his choice.

Fifth, in the months preceding Van Gogh's self-mutilation, there were fifteen articles in the local paper about Jack the Ripper, who mutilated the bodies of prostitutes he had killed, sometimes cutting off their ears. "These crimes gave rise to emulators, and Vincent may have been one of them. As a masochist instead of a sadist, however, it is conceivable that he would reverse Jack's act by mutilating himself and bringing the ear to a prostitute" (Lubin, 1972, p. 159).

Sixth, Van Gogh was emotionally and financially dependent on his brother Theo, and usually spent the Christmas holidays with him. This year, however, Vincent learned that Theo would spend the holidays with his new fiancée and her family. This interpretation suggests that Van Gogh's self-mutilation was an unconscious strategy for holding on to his brother's attention, and a way of getting Theo to come and care for him rather than spend the holidays with his fiancée.

What is one to make of such a variety of psychodynamic interpretations of the same event? One point of view is that these various explanations constitute a richly woven tapestry, connecting this single event to many themes, conflicts, and unconscious wishes and processes in Van Gogh's life. According to the psychoanalytic principle of "overdetermination," which suggests that actions typically have multiple causes and meanings, this material can be seen as a complex set of interrelated explanations of Van Gogh's behavior (Lubin, 1972).

Another possible response is to think that all this symbolic and psychodynamic interpretation is somewhat arbitrary, perhaps even hopelessly arbitrary. If interpretations can be generated merely by noting psychological similarities between the event in question and earlier events and experiences, then connections are "embarrassingly easy to find," and "the number of possible (and plausible) explanations is infinite" (Spence, 1976, pp. 377, 379). A skeptic could argue that the process of psychodynamic interpretation is so arbitrary, leading to so many different possible interpretations, that the whole enterprise should be viewed with suspicion. A milder version of this criticism would maintain that the process of psychodynamic interpretation is perfectly legitimate, but that it has been used with insufficient constraint in this particular example.

The problem of alternative explanations and how to choose among them must be faced within any theoretical orientation, but seems particularly acute in psychoanalysis. One of the glories of psychoanalysis as a theoretical system is that it can be used to provide several explanations of almost any human behavior, but the corresponding liability is that it is not certain how much faith should be put in any of the particular explanations.

Psychobiographical interpretations need to be critically evaluated (in a way that often does not happen) in terms of such criteria as (1) their comprehensiveness in accounting for a number of puzzling aspects of the events in question, (2) their survival of tests of attempted falsification, (3) their consistency not just with fragments of evidence, but also with the full range of available evidence, and (4) their credibility relative to other explanatory hypotheses. Applying these criteria, perhaps the single most strongly supported explanatory factor in Van Gogh's breakdown was the perceived loss of his brother's care. Specifically, the ear-cutting incident and two later mental breakdowns coincided with learning of Theo's engagement, his marriage, and the birth of his first child. In each case, Van Gogh was threatened by the prospect of losing his main source of emotional and financial support, as it seemed that Theo might redirect his love and money toward his new family (Runyan, 1981).

There are, in short, a variety of problems encountered in psychoanalytic approaches to psychobiography, including issues such as the limitations of available evidence, problems of historical reconstruction and reductionism, and criticisms of the process of psychoanalytic interpretation. These problems, along with a more general interest in the relationships between psychology and biography, led me to the topic of this paper: What are the alternatives to psychoanalytic psychobiography? What has been done, and what could be done, in applying other branches of psychology to the interpretation of historical figures?

Nonpsychoanalytic Approaches to Psychobiography

Psychobiography may be defined as the explicit use of systematic or formal psychology in biography (Runyan, 1982). Three aspects of this definition should be noted. First, the field is defined by the use of psychology, which may or may not be psychoanalytic. Second, the use must be explicit, or visible, in order to distinguish psychobiography from all those biographies that make implicit use of common-sense psychology. Third, the definition refers not solely to the application of personality theory, but also to the use of psychology, which is intended to include within psychobiography those works drawing on the full range of resources of the field of psychology, including psychological concepts, data, and methods, as well as theory, from developmental, abnormal, social, and personality psychology.

It seems that each of these branches of psychology *should* have something to contribute to the psychological understanding of individual historical figures. What though, has actually been done in using non-psychoanalytic contributions from personality, social, and developmental psychology?

Personality Psychology

The field of personality psychology can be conceived as being organized around several major theoretical orientations: the psychodynamic; behavioral, or social learning; trait-factor and psychometric approaches; and phenomenological, or humanistic, psychology. In this survey, I will not discuss the many contributions of psychoanalytic theory and its more recent developments in ego psychology, object relations theory, and self psychology, which have been reviewed elsewhere (Loewenberg, 1982; Strozier, 1980), or the related psychodynamic systems of Jung and Adler, which have also been used in psychobiography (for example, Ansbacher, 1966; Brink, 1975; Progoff, 1966; Ward, 1961).

Since behavioral or learning theory is a general theory of human behavior, it could, in principle, provide a foundation for psychobiographical interpretation. What, in fact, has been done with it?

In the clinical literature, perhaps the best known example of a learning theory interpretation of historical material is Wolpe and Rachman's (1960) reinterpretation of the case of Little Hans. Little Hans was a five-year-old son of one of Freud's followers who was afraid of going out into the street out of fear that a horse would bite him. Freud's (1909/1963) interpretation of Little Hans's horse phobia is that it stemmed from oedipal conflicts, which erupted during a period of intensified sexual attraction toward his mother. "Hans was really a little Oedipus who wanted to have his father 'out of the way,' to get rid of him, so that he might be alone with his handsome mother and sleep with her" (p. 148). Little Hans experienced

> hostile and jealous feelings against his father, and sadistic impulses (premonitions, as it were, of copulation) towards his mother. These early suppressions perhaps have gone to form the predispositions for his subsequent illness. These aggressive propensities of Hans's found no outlet, and as soon as there came a time of privation and of intensified sexual excitement, they tried to break their way out with reinforced strength. It was then that the battle which we call his 'phobia' burst out. (pp. 173–174)

Freud argued that Little Hans transposed his fear of his father onto horses and that he was most afraid of horses with muzzles and blinkers, which may have resembled his father's moustache and eyeglasses. The phobia served to keep Little Hans at home with his beloved mother, and thus was successful in attaining his libidinal aims. This is necessarily an abbreviated account of the psychoanalytic interpretation, and cannot substitute for Freud's compelling presentation of the original case.

Wolpe and Rachman (1960) argue that "there is no scientifically acceptable evidence showing any connection" (p. 135) between Little Hans's sexual life and his phobia for horses. They claim that Freud's interpretation of this case is not supported in whole or in part by the available evidence. More specifically, they argue that there are no adequate grounds for believing that Little Hans had sexual impulses toward his mother, that he hated and feared his father, that his fear of horses was symbolic of his fear of his father, or that his phobia disappeared because he resolved his oedipus complex.

Wolpe and Rachman suggest that the origin and course of Little Hans's phobia can more plausibly be interpreted in terms of learning theory. Phobias are seen as conditioned fear reactions that can arise through the pairing of any neutral stimulus with a fear-producing situation. They argue that such a conditioning process may well have been the source of Little Hans's fear of horses, and that what Freud saw as "merely the exciting cause of Hans's phobia was in fact the cause of the entire disorder. Hans actually says, 'No, I only got it [the phobia] then. When the horse in the bus fell down, it gave me such a fright, really.' That was when I got the nonsense" (Wolpe and Rachman, 1960, p. 146). The fact that the anxiety broke out immediately afterward was confirmed by Hans's mother. Two other incidents may also have sensitized or "partially conditioned" Hans to fear horses. One was a warning from a father of one of his friends to avoid a horse so that he would not get bitten, and in a second incident, one of Hans's friends fell and cut himself while playing horse.

Wolpe and Rachman say that the actual mechanism responsible for Hans's recovery cannot be identified because of the absence of relevant information, but that remission may have been due to repeated exposure to the phobic stimulus in a nonthreatening context, so that the aroused anxiety responses were weak enough to be inhibited by other concurrently aroused emotional responses. They suggest that the gradualness of Little Hans's recovery is consistent with an explanation of this type.

A second example of a behavioral approach to psychobiography is provided by the article "Ben Franklin the Protobehaviorist . . ."

(Mountjoy and Sundberg, 1981). The authors argue that Benjamin Franklin's efforts to arrive at moral perfection can be seen as an early example of behavorial self-management. Franklin made a list of thirteen virtues—including temperance, frugality, industry, chastity, and humility—and attempted to make his practice of each of these virtues habitual. He drew up a chart on which he recorded on a daily basis his failure to practice any of the thirteen virtues. For a week at a time, he would concentrate on practicing one of the virtues, and then, once the practice of that virtue became more habitual, he would move on to concentrate on the next virtue on his list. Described in behavioral terms, Franklin identified response classes that he wanted to change, recorded a baseline of the frequency of different classes of behavior, recorded data on his performance at the end of each day, and was reinforced by seeing the frequency of undesirable behaviors decrease over time as he repeatedly worked his way through the chart.

Probably the most extensively developed behavioral interpretation of a life history is in the three volumes of B. F. Skinner's autobiography: *Particulars of My Life* (1976), *The Shaping of a Behaviorist* (1979), and *A Matter of Consequences* (1983). Skinner (1967) states that "whether from narcissism or scientific curiosity, I have been as much interested in myself as in rats and pigeons. I have applied the same formulation, I have looked for the same kinds of causal relations, and I have manipulated behavior in the same way and sometimes with comparable success" (p. 407). A goal of his autobiography is to provide a case history of human behavior analyzed from an operant point of view. The focus is on changes in the external environment and their effect on his overt behavior, without referring to inner experiences or feelings.

One of the more dramatic examples is Skinner's description of the end of a love relationship. Nedda, the woman he was in love with, told him at dinner that they should break it off, as she was going back to a former fiancée. "It was a reasonable decision, but it hit me very hard. As we walked back to her apartment from the subway, I found myself moving very slowly. It was not a pose; I simply could not move faster. For a week I was in almost physical pain, and one day I bent a wire in the shape of an N, heated it in a Bunsen burner, and branded my left arm" (Skinner, 1979, p. 137). This dramatic description of environmental events and his behavioral response is not accompanied by a description of his thoughts and feelings about the incident. Skinners' work illustrates that a behavioral approach to psychobiography is possible, although there may be disagreement about whether this approach illuminates or obscures our understanding of a life.

The possibilities for applying trait-factor and psychometric approaches to the lives of historical figures are suggested by the work of Kenneth Craik in applying standard personality assessment procedures such as the adjective checklist, trait-rating scales, and Q-sort personality descriptions to figures such as Adolf Hitler, Woodrow Wilson, and other American presidents (Historical Figures Assessment Collaborative, 1977). Techniques of intraindividual correlational analysis developed by Raymond Cattell have been applied to individual clinical cases (Bath, Daly, and Nesselroade, 1976; Cattell, 1966; Luborsky and Mintz, 1972) and might in some instances be applicable to historical figures. It could be argued, however, that such approaches are concerned primarily with describing the personalities of individuals, which is one facet of biography, but do not provide a foundation for interpreting or explaining an entire life history.

Another influential theoretical orientation in personality psychology is phenomenological–existential, or humanistic, psychology, represented by the works of Abraham Maslow, Carl Rogers, Charlotte Bühler, and Rollo May. How extensively has humanistic psychology been used in psychobiography? As one example, Carl Rogers (1980) reinterpreted the case of Ellen West (originally described by Binswanger), a young woman with anorexia nervosa who eventually committed suicide. A second example is a study of Clarence Darrow presented in terms of Charlotte Bühler's theory of stages of goal seeking (Horner, 1968). A third example is a book by Nancy Clinch, *The Kennedy Neurosis* (1973), which claims to rely in part on humanistic psychology, although the book has often been criticized as a psychological hatchet job.

The most extensive use of existential theory in psychobiography is in the work of Sartre, with his biographical studies of Baudelaire, Genêt, and Flaubert. In his magnum opus on Flaubert, Sartre (1981) says that the question he wants to address is, "What at this point in time, can we know about a man? It seemed to me that this question could only be answered by studying a specific case. What do we know, for example, about Gustave Flaubert?" (p. ix). This complex book might best be described, though, as an example of an eclectic work, drawing on psychoanalysis, Marxism, and Sartre's own version of existentialism (Barnes, 1981).

Social Psychology

The field of social psychology tends to be organized around the study of particular kinds of events or processes, such as person perception, interpersonal attraction, persuasion and influence, obedience to authority, prejudice and discrimination, socialization, self-concept and self-esteem, attitude change, and so on. In principle, research and theory on any of these specific processes could be drawn on to interpret related events in a psychobiography. For example, research on obedience to authority (Milgram, 1974) could be used in analyzing the behavior of Lieutenant Calley during the My Lai massacre in Vietnam or the behavior of Adolf Eichman and other Nazis during World War II, or research on group influences on judgment and decision making could be used in studying the decisions of President Kennedy in planning the Bay of Pigs invasion (Janis, 1972).

One increasingly influential part of social psychology is concerned with processes of social cognition, or the cognitive processes by which individuals perceive, interpret, and attribute causes to the behavior of others. Research on social cognition and the common biases in everyday cognitive processes (Nisbett and Ross, 1980) may well be drawn on in studying the attitudes, belief systems, and decision-making processes of individual historical figures, issues of particular importance in the lives of political leaders. An extensive review of the use of theories of social perception and cognition is provided in Jervis's *Perception and Misperception in International Politics* (1976) and Janis and Mann's *Decision Making* (1977).

In sum, social psychology seems to have significant promise in psychobiography, not as a foundation or organizing principle for the study of an entire life, but as a resource to draw on in understanding particular events or processes.

Developmental Psychology

Developmental psychology, which is concerned with the description and explanation of age-related changes in behavior and psychological structures, would seem to have a special relevance to psychobiography. The field of developmental psychology can be seen as being organized around (1) major theoretical orientations, such as the Piagetian–cognitive, psychodynamic, or behavioral; (2) the growth of particular systems, such as motor behavior, sensory processes, linguistic ability, or personality; (3) particular classes or types of behavior, such as aggression, altruism, or creativity; (4) particular periods or stages of the life cycle, such as infancy, childhood, and adolescence; and (5) in adult developmental psychology, particular events or transitions, such as leaving home, becoming a parent, or getting divorced.

Each of these components of the field of developmental psychology could at times be used in psychobiography. Since major theoretical orientations were discussed in the section on personality psychology, I will not repeat this topic, except to note the use of some aspects of Piagetian concepts in Gruber's (1981) study of intellectual growth and change in the career of Charles Darwin. Studies of the development of particular classes of behavior or of particular life transitions (such as choosing a marriage partner, establishing a career, retiring, or grieving at the loss of a spouse) could be drawn on as needed.

Within developmental psychology, some of the most relevant theory may come from work in adult developmental psychology and life-span developmental psychology. One theoretical framework that appears particularly promising for psychobiographical purposes is presented in Daniel Levinson's *The Seasons of a Man's Life* (Levinson, with Darrow, Klein, Levinson, and McKee, 1978; also Levinson, 1981). Levinson argues that the course of adult development can be understood not as the development of personality, but as the development or evolution of the life structure, with life structure defined as the pattern or fit between self and world in areas such as occupation, relationships, and leisure activities. In every period of adulthood, a man must make certain key choices, form a structure around them, and pursue his goals and values within this structure. Adult life alternates between a sequence of stable, or structure-building, periods and one of transitional, or structure-changing, periods, in which individuals assess and reevaluate their existing life structure, and may make new choices in regard to career, marriage, family, or other aspects of life.

Two components of the life structure that Levinson discusses are "The Dream" and mentor relationships. The Dream is an imagined vision of oneself in the world that generates excitement and vitality. The mentor, typically a person of greater experience and seniority, facilitates realization of the life dream by serving as teacher, model, guide, and sponsor. One of Levinson's students has drawn on this framework to examine two important mentoring relationships in the career of Willy Brandt before he became chancellor of West Germany (Kellerman, 1978).

A more comprehensive application of Levinson's theory is in a study of Jung by Staude (1981). Staude looks at Jung's relationship to Freud as an example of a mentor relationship, and analyzes Jung's midlife transition in terms of Levinson's conception of a structure-changing period. After considerable success in the tasks of early adulthood—as indicated by scientific accomplishments, a happy marriage and family life, a successful private practice, and international recognition in the psychoanalytic movement—Jung entered a period of profound questioning of his previous life structure. With the advent of this midlife re-examination, Jung saw "his early adult life structure crumble and fall apart before his eyes" (Staude, 1981, p. 47) and was forced to forge a new life structure that took greater account of his mystical and archetypal inner experience.

Additional Examples

In addition to the studies already mentioned, there are, of course, a substantial number of psychobiographical works that are at least partly nonpsychoanalytic, such as (1) Barber's (1977) fourfold typological analysis of presidential personalities; (2) an application of Tomkins's theory of affect and motivation to the lives of four American abolitionists (Tomkins, 1965); (3) an investigation of medical or biological pathology in political leaders (L'Étang, 1970), and a medicopsychological study of King George III (Macalpine and Hunter, 1969); (4) a study of Winston Churchill that draws on Sheldon's theory of somatotypes, Jungian psychology, and descriptive psychiatry, as well as psychoanalysis (Storr, 1968); and (5) a variety of forms of content analysis applied to biography, such as "value analysis" (White, 1947), "personal structure analysis" (Baldwin, 1942), application of the computerized "General Inquirer" system to personal documents (Paige, 1966), and a content analytic study by Robert Sears et al. (1978) of longitudinal changes in indications of separation anxiety or fear of loss of love in Mark Twain's novels and letters.

Further examples are discussed in the Winter 1979 issue of the *Psychohistory Review,* on "Non-Psychoanalytic Ventures in Psychohistory," with two bibliographies on this topic by Gilmore (1979a, 1979b), although most of the examples are more broadly psychohistorical rather than specifically psychobiographical.[1]

1. Additional examples of nonpsychoanalytic approaches have come to my attention since the Stanford conference, including a notable one by an audience member at the Stanford conference, Elisabeth Griffith (1984), who used Bandura's social learning theory in a psychobiography of Elizabeth Cady Stanton. A recent study of unusual methodological sophistication analyzes Henry Kissinger's implicit personality theory through a quantitative analysis of 3,759 trait descriptions of political leaders that he provided in *White*

The Relative Contributions of Psychoanalytic and Nonpsychoanalytic Approaches

What can one conclude from this attempt to survey nonpsychoanalytic approaches to psychobiography? Work in nonpsychoanalytic psychobiography does exist, but it is scattered and disorganized, appearing in discrete bits and pieces, and has not developed anything like the cumulative tradition of work in psychoanalytic psychobiography. It is, in fact, difficult to identify more than a handful of psychobiographies which rely primarily on nonpsychodynamic theory.

I began this search with an expectation that it would be relatively easy to uncover a substantial number of effective uses of other psychological theories and approaches in psychobiography. After searching the literature, corresponding with individuals I thought might have leads on the topic, and pestering my friends and colleagues to come up with examples, the yield has been frustratingly meager. I have the feeling of a hunter going out looking for bear, but coming back with a few quail.

In short, the field seems clearly dominated by psychoanalytic approaches to psychobiography. In light of the many criticisms of psychoanalytic theory and interpretation, particularly in academic psychology, how is one to account for the preeminence of psychoanalytic approaches to psychobiography and the relative lack of development of other approaches?

A number of possible explanations come to mind. First, perhaps psychoanalytic theory has a special relevance to the kinds of explanatory problems encountered in psychobiography in that it seems effective in explaining just those kinds of odd or irrational patterns of behavior that the psychobiographer feels are most in need of explanation.

Second, perhaps psychoanalytically oriented theorists are able or willing to speculate from the fragments of evidence available about historical figures, while adherents of other theoretical orientations, more accustomed to quantitative or experimental methods, are unable or unwilling to do so.

Third, perhaps the explanation lies in *how* psychoanalytic theory is used. It may be that psychoanalysis provides a set of conceptual tools that can be employed in a flexible and partially idiographic way; they are

---

House Years (Swede and Tetlock, 1986). Further examples are in Gilmore's (1984) bibliographic survey of the field, and in a forthcoming special issue of the *Journal of Personality* (March 1988) edited by Dan McAdams and Richard Ochberg on "Psychobiography and Life Narratives."

flexible enough to be used to construct interpretations of a wide range of patterns of human behavior. This characteristic of the theoretical system may be a liability for theory-testing purposes (Popper, 1962), but a virtue for interpretive purposes. The theory identifies a large number of mechanisms and processes, which can then be used in constructing interpretations of the particular patterns found within an individual case.

Fourth, perhaps historians and biographers are just not familiar with other psychological theories, and have not tried them. Or if they have been tried, they have not been found very useful.

A fifth possibility is that psychobiographers who believe that psychoanalysis has been helpful in their interpretive tasks have been mistaken. While having the subjective experience of gaining insight, they may actually have been led into errors or false interpretations. Perhaps psychoanalytic theory satisfies a human need to find pattern or meaning, but such patterns can be found in biographical material even where none actually exist, or at least not the ones suggested by the theory.

Finally, perhaps psychodynamic theory is profoundly true in some ways, not necessarily all of it, but at least parts of it. Perhaps working intensively with biographical data leads writers to find that psychoanalytic theory repeatedly proves itself more illuminating or more useful than any other body of psychological theory, just as many clinicians find it useful in clinical situations. Personally, this search for alternatives has led me to have increased respect for the utility of psychoanalytic theory in psychobiography. While some aspects of psychoanalytic theory, such as a belief in the primary causal importance of early psychosexual experience, should probably be modified or abandoned, other aspects of the theory, such as the concept of unconscious motives and conflicts, or the operation of defense mechanisms, may prove of fundamental utility for psychobiographers. Psychoanalytic theory also has the heuristic value of leading investigators to explore a range of hypotheses that might not otherwise have occurred to them.

In conclusion, what do nonpsychoantlytic approaches have to contribute to psychobiography? There does not seem to be any serious contender looming on the horizon, threatening to challenge the position of psychoanalysis as the dominant theoretical orientation in the field. My search, though, inevitably missed important examples, and I would greatly appreciate hearing of other examples of nonpsychoanalytic psychobiography.

The *potential* contributions of nonpsychoanalytic personality, social, and developmental psychology to psychobiography seem substantial, even if accomplishments to date are limited. The direction in which I would look for the most progress in nonpsychoanalytic approaches to psychobiography is not as a theoretical framework for the interpretation of an entire life, but rather as a pool of theory and research to be drawn from in an eclectic manner for interpreting particular events, dispositions, processes, or life transitions.

One recent example of such targeted and specific use of nonpsychoanalytic theory is in the controversy over psychological interpretations of Woodrow Wilson. A remarkable feature of Wilson's childhood is that he did not learn his letters until he was nine, and could not read until he was eleven. Alexander and Juliette George originally suggested that Wilson as a boy was filled with rage at his demanding and perfectionist father, which he could not openly acknowledge or express, and perhaps, this "failing—*refusing*—to learn was the one way in which the boy dared to express his resentment against his father" (George and George, 1956/1964, p. 7). In response, Weinstein, Anderson, and Link (1978) argued that Wilson's delay in reading was not due to emotional difficulties, but to developmental dyslexia, caused by a delay in the establishment of the dominance of one cerebral hemisphere (usually the left) for language.

In rebuttal, the Georges (1981) draw on details of the recent professional literature on dyslexia. In particular, they argue that it is not established that the absence of cerebral dominance is responsible for dyslexia, that many specialists continue to believe that emotional factors are responsible for some reading disorders, and that details of Wilson's life—such as the amount of his reading, the neatness of his handwriting, and his excellent spelling—are inconsistent with a diagnosis of developmental dyslexia. In this debate, they draw on a specialized body of psychological theory and research in order to critique an alternative explanation and to argue that the bulk of the evidence is consistent with their original interpretation.[2]

The possibilities for using particular theories and bodies of research from nonpsychoanalytic psychology seem vast, although relatively underdeveloped. One optimistic view of the future of nonpsychoanalytic approaches is that "a likely prospect would see the emergence of academic psychology as the central treasury upon which thoughtful researchers and an intelligent public would draw" (Schoenwald, 1973, p. 17). To date, however, this promise is largely unfulfilled. Academic psychology can be extremely valuable in shedding light on particular

2. The debate over psychological and medical interpretations of Woodrow Wilson has continued in extensive detail (references cited in Link et al., 1986).

processes, classes of behavior, and life transitions, and can provide a useful corrective to excesses and errors in psychodynamic interpretations. It remains to be seen, though, if adherents of nonpsychoanalytic approaches can be equally or more effective in interpreting lives than the best practitioners of psychodynamic psychobiography.

References

Adelson, J. (1981, January). Review of D. Stannard, *Shrinking history: On Freud and the failure of psychohistory. American Spectator,* pp. 31–33.

Anderson, J. W. (1981a). The methodology of psychological biography. *Journal of Interdisciplinary History, 11,* 455–475.

Anderson, J. W. (1981b). Psychobiographical methodology: The case of William James. In L. Wheeler (Ed.), *Review of personality and social psychology* (Vol. 2). Beverly Hills, Calif.: Sage.

Anderson, T. H. (1978). Becoming sane with psychohistory. *Historian, 41,* 1–20.

Ansbacher, H. et al. (1966). Lee Harvey Oswald: An Adlerian interpretation. *Psychoanalytic Review, 53,* 55–68.

Baldwin, A. L. (1942). Personal structure analysis: A statistical method for investigation of the single personality. *Journal of Abnormal and Social Psychology, 37,* 163–183.

Barber, J. D. (1977). *The presidential character: Predicting performance in the White House.* Englewood Cliffs, N.J.: Prentice-Hall.

Barnes, H. (1981). *Sartre and Flaubert.* Chicago: University of Chicago Press.

Basch, M. F. (1980). Comment on Stannard's *Shrinking history. Psychohistory Review, 9,* 136–144.

Bate, W. J. (1977). *Samuel Johnson.* New York: Harcourt Brace Jovanovich.

Bath, K. E., Daly, D. L., and Nesselroade, J. R. (1976). Replicability of factors derived from individual P-technique analyses. *Multivariate Behavioral Research, 11,* 147–156.

Bergmann, M. S. (1973). Limitations of method in psychoanalytic biography: A historical inquiry. *Journal of the American Psychoanalytic Association, 21,* 833–850.

Bloom, B. (1964). *Stability and change in human characteristics.* New York: Wiley.

Bowlby, J. (1952). *Maternal care and mental health.* Geneva: World Health Organization.

Brim, O. G., and Kagan, J. (Eds.). (1980). *Constancy and change in human development.* Cambridge, Mass.: Harvard University Press.

Brink, T. L. (1975). The case of Hitler: An Adlerian perspective on psychohistory. *Journal of Individual Psychology, 31*, 23–31.

Cattell, R. B. (Ed.). (1966). *Handbook of multivariate experimental psychology*. Chicago: Rand McNally.

Clarke, A. M., and Clarke, A. D. B. (Eds.). (1976). *Early experience: Myth and evidence*. New York: Free Press.

Clifford, J. L. (Ed.), (1962). *Biography as an art*. New York: Oxford University Press.

Clinch, N. (1973). *The Kennedy neurosis*. New York: Grosset & Dunlap.

Cody, J. (1971). *After great pain: The inner life of Emily Dickinson*. Cambridge, Mass.: Harvard University Press.

Crosby, T. L. (1980). Comment on Stannard's *Shrinking history*. *Psychohistory Review, 9*, 145–150.

Davis, G. (1975). The early years of Theodore Roosevelt: A study in character formation. *History of Childhood Quarterly, 2*, 461–492.

Erikson, E. H. (1969). *Gandhi's truth*. New York: Norton.

Fisher, S., and Greenberg, R. P. (1977). *The scientific credibility of Freud's theories and therapy*. New York: Basic Books.

Freud, S. (1963). Analysis of a phobia in a five-year-old boy. In S. Freud, *The sexual enlightenment of children*. New York: Collier Books. (Original work published 1909)

Friedländer, S. (1978). *History and psychoanalysis*. New York: Holmes and Meier.

George, A. L., and George, J. L. (1964). *Woodrow Wilson and Colonel House: A personality study*. New York: Dover. (Original work published 1956)

George, A. L., and George, J. L. (1981). *Woodrow Wilson and Colonel House:* A reply to Weinstein, Anderson, and Link. *Political Science Quarterly, 96*, 641–665.

Gilmore, W. (1979a). Paths recently crossed: Alternatives to psychoanalytic psychohistory. *Psychohistory Review, 7*(3), 43–49.

Gilmore, W. (1979b). Paths recently crossed: Alternatives to psychoanalytic psychohistory (continued). *Psychohistory Review, 7*(4), 26–42.

Gilmore, W. (1984). *Psychohistorical inquiry: A comprehensive research bibliography*. New York: Garland.

Glad, B. (1973). Contributions of psychobiography. In J. Knutson (Ed.), *Handbook of political psychology*. San Francisco: Jossey-Bass.

Greenacre, P. (1955). *Swift and Carroll: A psychoanalytic study of two lives*. New York: International Universities Press.

Griffith, E. (1984). *In her own right: The life of Elizabeth Cady Stanton*. New York: Oxford University Press.

Gruber, H. E. (1981). *Darwin on man: A psychological study of scientific creativity* (2nd ed.). Chicago: University of Chicago Press.

Historical Figures Assessment Collaborative. (1977). Assessing historical figures: The use of observer-based personality descriptions. *Historical Methods Newsletter, 10,* (2), 66–76.

Hofling, C. K. (1976). Current problems in psychohistory. *Comprehensive Psychiatry, 17,* 227–239.

Horner, A. (1968). The evolution of goals in the life of Clarence Darrow. In C. Buhler and F. Massarik (Eds.), *The course of human life.* New York: Springer.

Hughes, H. S. (1964). *History as art and as science.* New York: Harper & Row.

Hundert, E. J. (1972). History, psychology and the study of deviant behavior. *Journal of Interdisciplinary History, 2,* 453–472.

Izenberg, G. (1975). Psychohistory and intellectual history. *History and Theory, 14,* 139–155.

Janis, I. L. (1972). *Victims of groupthink.* Boston: Houghton Mifflin.

Janis, I. L., and Mann, L. (1977). *Decision making.* New York: Free Press.

Jervis, R. (1976). *Perception and misperception in international politics.* Princeton, N.J.: Princeton University Press.

Kellerman, B. (1978). Mentoring in political life: The case of Willy Brandt. *American Political Science Review, 72,* 422–433.

Kelly, E. L. (1955). Consistency of the adult personality. *American Psychologist, 10,* 659–681.

Kline, P. (1972). *Fact and fantasy in Freudian theory.* London: Methuen.

Kohut, H. (1960). Beyond the bounds of the basic rule. *Journal of the American Psychoanalytic Association, 8,* 567–586.

L'Étang, H. (1970). *The pathology of leadership.* New York: Hawthorn.

Levinson, D. J. (1981). Exploration in biography: Evolution of the individual life structure in adulthood. In A. Rabin et al. (Eds.), *Further explorations in personality.* New York: Wiley.

Levinson, D. J., with Darrow, C., Klein, E., Levinson, M., and McKee, B. (1978). *The seasons of a man's life.* New York: Knopf.

Link, A. et al. (Eds.). (1986). Introduction. In *The papers of Woodrow Wilson, Vol. 54.* Princeton, N.J.: Princeton University Press.

Loewenberg, P. (1982, May). *Psychoanalytic models of history: Freud and after.* Paper presented at the Conference on History and Psychology, Stanford University. (Chapter 7, this volume)

Lubin, A. J. (1972). *Stranger on the earth: A psychological biography of Vincent Van Gogh.* New York: Holt, Rinehart and Winston.

Luborsky, L., and Mintz, J. (1972). The contribution of P-technique to personality, psychotherapy, and psychosomatic research. In R. M. Dreger (Ed.), *Multivariate personality research: Contributions to the understanding of personality in honor of Raymond B. Cattell.* Baton Rouge, La.: Claitor's.

Macalpine, I., and Hunter, R. (1969). *George III and the mad business.* New York: Pantheon Books.

Mack, J. E. (1971). Psychoanalysis and historical biography. *Journal of the American Psychoanalytic Association, 19,* 143–179.

Mack, J. E. (1976). *A prince of our disorder: The life of T. E. Lawrence.* Boston: Little, Brown.

Meyer, B. C. (1972). Some reflections on the contribution of psychoanalysis to biography. In R. Holt and E. Peterfreund (Eds.), *Psychoanalysis and contemporary science* (Vol. 1). New York: International Universities Press.

Milgram, S. (1974). *Obedience to authority.* New York: Harper & Row.

Mischel, W. (1968). *Personality and assessment.* New York: Wiley.

Mountjoy, P. T., and Sundberg, M. L. (1981). Ben Franklin the protobehaviorist I: Self-management of behavior. *Psychological Record, 31,* 13–24.

Nisbett, R., and Ross, L. (1980). *Human inference: Strategies and shortcomings of social judgment.* Englewood Cliffs, N.J.: Prentice-Hall.

Paige, J. M. (1966). Letters from Jenny: An approach to the clinical analysis of personality structure by computer. In P. Stone (Ed.), *The general inquirer: A computer approach to content analysis.* Cambridge, Mass.: MIT Press.

Popper, K. R. (1962). *Conjectures and refutations: The growth of scientific knowledge.* New York: Basic Books.

Progoff, I. (1966). The psychology of Lee Harvey Oswald: A Jungian approach. *Journal of Individual Psychology, 23,* 37–47.

Rogers, C. R. (1980). Ellen West—and loneliness. In *A way of being.* Boston: Houghton Mifflin.

Runyan, W. M. (1978). The life course as a theoretical orientation: Sequences of person–situation interaction. *Journal of Personality, 46,* 569–593.

Runyan, W. M. (1981). Why did Van Gogh cut off his ear? The problem of alternative explanations in psychobiography. *Journal of Personality and Social Psychology, 40,* 1070–1077.

Runyan, W. M. (1982). *Life histories and psychobiography: Explorations in theory and method.* New York: Oxford University Press.

Runyan, W. M. (1984). Diverging life paths: Their probabilistic and causal structure. In K. Gergen and M. Gergen (Eds.), *Historical social psychology.* Hillsdale, N.J.: Erlbaum.

Rutter, M. (1979). Maternal deprivation, 1972–1978: New findings, new concepts, new approaches. *Child Development, 50,* 282–305.

Sartre, J.-P. (1981). *The family idiot: Gustave Flaubert, 1821–1857* (C. Cosman, trans.). Chicago: University of Chicago Press.

Schoenwald, R. L. (1973). Using psychology in history: A review essay. *Historical Methods Newsletter, 7*(1), 9–24.

Sears, R. R., Lapidus, D., and Cozzens, C. (1978). Content analysis of Mark Twain's novels and letters as a biographical method. *Poetics, 7,* 155–175.

Skinner, B. F. (1953). *Science and human behavior.* New York: Macmillan.

Skinner, B. F. (1967). B. F. Skinner [autobiography]. In E. G. Boring and G. Lindzey (Eds.), *A history of psychology in autobiography* (Vol. 5). New York: Appleton-Century-Crofts.

Skinner, B. F. (1976). *Particulars of my life.* New York: Knopf.

Skinner, B. F. (1979). *The shaping of a behaviorist.* New York: Knopf.

Skinner, B. F. (1983). *A matter of consequences.* New York: Knopf.

Spence, D. P. (1976). Clinical interpretation: Some comments on the nature of evidence. In T. Shapiro (Ed.), *Psychoanalysis and contemporary science* (Vol. 5). New York: International Universities Press.

Stannard, D. E. (1980). *Shrinking history: On Freud and the failure of psychohistory.* New York: Oxford University Press.

Staude, J.-R. (1981). *The adult development of C. G. Jung.* Boston: Routledge & Kegan Paul.

Stone, L. (1981). *The past and the present.* Boston: Routledge & Kegan Paul.

Storr, A. (1968). The man. In A. J. P. Taylor (Ed.), *Churchill revised: A critical assessment.* New York: Dial Press.

Strozier, C. B. (1980). Heinz Kohut and the historical imagination. In A. Goldberg (Ed.), *Advances in self psychology.* New York: International Universities Press.

Swede, S. W., and Tetlock, P. E. (1986). Henry Kissinger's implicit theory of personality: A quantitative case study. *Journal of Personality, 54*(4), 101–130.

Tomkins, S. S. (1965). The psychology of commitment: The constructive role of violence and suffering for the individual and for his society. In M. Duberman (Ed.), *The antislavery vanguard.* Princeton, N.J.: Princeton University Press.

Tucker, R. C. (1973). *Stalin as revolutionary, 1879–1929: A study in history and personality.* New York: Norton.

Tucker, R. C. (1977). The Georges' Wilson reexamined: An essay on psychobiography. *American Political Science Review, 71,* 606–618.

Wachtel, P. (1977). Interaction cycles, unconscious processes, and the person–situation issue. In D. Magnusson and N. Endler (Eds.), *Personality at the crossroads.* Hillsdale, N.J.: Erlbaum.

Ward, T. (1961). *The capsule of the mind: Chapters in the life of Emily Dickinson.* Cambridge, Mass.: Harvard University Press.

Weinstein, E., Anderson, J., and Link, A. (1978). Woodrow Wilson's political personality: A reappraisal. *Political Science Quarterly, 93,* 585–598.

White, R. K. (1947). *Black boy:* A value analysis. *Journal of Abnormal and Social Psychology, 42,* 440–461.

Wolpe, J., and Rachman, S. (1960). Psychoanalytic "evidence": A critique based on Freud's case of Little Hans. *Journal of Nervous and Mental Disease, 131,* 135–148.

III

Conclusion and
Future Directions

13

Reconceptualizing the Relationships Between History and Psychology

William McKinley Runyan

The question of how psychological structures and processes are related to the flow of historical events is a fundamental one, with implications cutting across all of the human sciences. Sociology, anthropology, economics, and political science all wrestle with a common set of problems in understanding relationships between individual psychology and continuity and change in social institutions. This chapter attempts to provide a relatively comprehensive conceptualization of the uses of psychology in historical interpretation, one which reveals the internal structure of psychohistory, as well as indicating its place in a wider intellectual landscape. This conceptualization of psychohistory is intended to direct attention not so much to "an established body of knowledge, but to the potentials of a field of inquiry" (LeVine, 1973, p. vii).

To provide a brief preview, this chapter first discusses a number of common themes emerging in earlier chapters. The second section outlines six system levels from persons through groups, organizations, institutions, social systems, and international relations as a framework for conceptualizing the structure of psychohistory. The third section explores how psychology can be used not only directly in history, but used also in fields such as social structure and personality, psychological anthropology, or political psychology, which in turn are drawn upon by historians. Fourth, the chapter argues that there are important conceptual distinctions between the uses of psychology in historical interpretation ("psychohistory"), the inclusion of psychological phenomena in historical accounts ("history with psychological content"), and the study of transhistorical generality or particularity in psychological phenomena ("historical psychology"). The fifth section outlines work in historical psychology and argues that such research can not only facilitate the use of psychology by historians, but can also make basic contributions to the discipline of psychology. In the sixth section the relationships between history and psychology are placed in a wider evolutionary context, suggesting relationships with other historical sciences such as evolutionary biology, paleoanthropology, or historical sociology. The final section reviews a number of recent examples and exemplars of work in psychohistory as a concrete way of indicating something of the potentials of the field.

Common Themes

As the reader can see from the preceding chapters, there is considerable diversity of opinion about the accomplishments, failures, and promise of psychologically informed history. A number of basic issues emerged repeatedly within different chapters, with various positions on them taken by individual authors. A first controversial issue is the status of psychoanalysis as a foundation for psychohistory, with substantial acceptance of classical Freudian theory by Gay and Wallerstein, with Loewenberg arguing for the greater utility of more recent theoretical developments within psychoanalysis, with Weinstein and Runyan critical of some aspects yet appreciative of other facets of psychoanalytic theory, while Crews was critical of the entire structure of psychoanalytic theory and interpretation.

A second recurrent theme was the *process* of doing psychobiography or psychohistory, including the significance of the emotional relationship of an author to his or her subject, most notably in Robert Tucker's reaction to Stalin, Jean Strouse's impulse to want to rescue Alice James, and Peter Loewenberg's discussion of the importance of understanding countertransference reactions in psychohistorical research.

A third set of questions emerged about the critical evaluation of psychohistorical interpretations, either in the form of questions about particular interpretations, as in the commentaries of Alexander Dallin on Stalin or Peter Paret on the Victorians; or in Kenneth Craik's discussion of methodological issues in systematically describing historical personalities; or in questions about the appropriate criteria and procedures for assessing psychohistorical interpretations, as discussed by Weinstein, Crews, and Runyan.

Much of the debate about the accomplishments and failings of psychohistory has centered around the problems and potentials in applying psychoanalysis to history and biography. Most commentators agree that reductionistic errors are too often made in neglecting the social-institutional environment, in focusing exclusively on individual psychopathology, or in neglecting basic canons of evidence, inference, and interpretation. The literature of psychohistory is strewn with examples of inadequate psychohistorical interpretation, which are embarrassing to serious practitioners, as well as with slipshod critiques of the field, which may be equally embarrassing to responsible critics. Whatever the reasons for its embattled status, psychohistory is often perceived as marginal or disreputable by both historians and psychologists. However, the problem of the relationship of psychological processes to historical events is an enduring one, even if it temporarily falls out of intellectual fashion and no matter how many simplistic or wrong-headed solutions to it are proposed. As expressed by Clifford Geertz (1973), "Legitimate questions . . . are not invalidated by misconceived answers" (p. 61).

Six System Levels and Relationships Between Them

What relevance, if any, does the study of psychological structures, elements, and processes have to understanding the flow of history? How can we conceptualize the relationships between psychological phenomena and the course of historical events? Given the internal diversity of psychology and the multifarious branches of history—divided by time period, area of the world, analytic approach, and substantive focus—these questions are enormously complex, and at times feel overwhelmingly so.

It can be frustratingly elusive to get a grasp on what counts as "history." Everything has a history, in the sense of extension over time, but what is the discipline of history the history of? Historians often state that history is primarily concerned not with the history of individual persons (that is, biography), but rather with the history of aggregates of persons, the history of institutions, and with stability and change in society as a whole.

There is considerable controversy about the role of persons as compared with that of larger impersonal, institutional, demographic, and economic forces in shaping the course of history. Historians often have grave reservations about the study of individuals (see the discussion of antibiographical tendencies in Chapter 1), believing that their importance in the overall historical process is naïvely overemphasized. If individuals are not so significant, then their internal psychological processes are not so important either, and there is no need for historians to be concerned with the details of psychological processes of perception, interpretation, unconscious motivation, belief, decision, and action. For other historians, the solution is not to deny the relevance of psychology to history, but rather to argue that a social psychology, dealing with the psychology of groups, is more relevant than the psychology of individuals (Barraclough, 1978; Marwick, 1981). According to this view, the most significant contributions of psychohistory would not be in individual psychobiography, but in group psychohistory.

What, if anything, does an understanding of psychological structures and processes have to do with the whole range of traditional and contemporary historiographic questions about continuity and change in such large-scale phenomena as international relations? the history of Germany, England, China, or the United States? the French, American, or Russian revolutions? peasants in sixteenth-century France? the Mediterranean basin in the age of Phillip II? intellectual history? the history of women? the history of blacks, Indians or Chicanos? the history of social classes? the history of popular culture? or other major historiographic questions?

I will argue that psychology is relevant to understanding such central historical questions, and not merely in peripheral ways. One way of addressing these questions about the relationship between psychological processes and historical events is outlined in Figure 13.1, which shows six different system levels, from persons up through international relations, and three levels of aggregation within each system level, from one to some to all. This figure is based on the premise that history can usefully be analyzed as the history and interaction of a number of distinguishable system levels. The six system levels used here are persons (including their psychological processes), groups (sets of persons interacting with one another, ranging from two-person relationships, through families, to social groups), organizations (such as formally organized business, church, and political bodies), institutions (such as economic, political, military, and religious institutions, which would include a number of specific organizations within them), nations (or entire sociocul-

	One	Subsets	All
International relations	1	2	3
Sociocultural systems	4	5	6

Institutions
  Economic
  Political
  Military
  Religious
  Educational
  Scientific
  Social welfare
  Mass media
  Other
	7	8	9

Organizations	10	11	12
Groups	13	14	15
Persons	16	17	18

FIGURE 13.1. Six system levels and three levels of aggregation.

tural systems), and, finally, international or intersocietal relationships.[1]

The diagram in Figure 13.1 is intended to provide a framework for exploring three kinds of questions: (1) the relationship of psychological structures and processes to historical events; (2) the issue of studying single individuals or aggregates of persons; and (3) the role of persons in history as compared with that of larger impersonal structures.

The discipline of history unquestionably includes the history of international relations, the history of nations, the history of major social institutions (for example, economic systems, political systems, higher education), the history of particular organizations (Standard Oil, the Democratic party, the *New York Times,* the American Historical Association), the history of particular groups or social movements (e.g., abolitionists, student activists in the 1960s), and the history of aggregates of people (women, blacks, or immigrant groups).

1. The six system levels outlined here bear some similarity to the system levels outlined by James G. Miller in *Living Systems* (1978), although he includes suborganismic system levels of cells and organs, and I include a level of institutions between organizations and social systems.

While historians often focus on the history of a particular system, they may also analyze the history of a period, event, or process cutting across system levels. For example, historical works are often organized around a particular period (such as Victorian England, or Germany from 1933 to 1945), a single event (French Revolution, American Civil War), or a process (industrialization, colonization). For these kinds of studies, it is typically useful to draw on material from a variety of relevant system levels which interact over time. History just *is* the history of different entities within these various system levels and relationships among them, and of the periods, events, and processes that cut across them.

Psychological processes of perception, sensation, learning, memory, motivation and emotion, unconscious dynamics, decision making, planning, and action all occur within persons (in interaction with their environment), in the bottom row of Figure 13.1. The relationships between psychological structures and processes within persons and aggregates of persons and the course of history are outlined by the multiple connections between the bottom row and the top five rows.

If one could demonstrate the relationships between psychological processes within cells 16 to 18 and each of the other system levels, then one would have laid out the relationship of psychological structures and processes to historical events and have established the relationship of psychology to problems and interests that are central to historians.

Conversely, those maintaining that history has no need for psychology would need to contend that the history of groups, organizations, institutions, nations, and international relations is unaffected by the psychological functioning of individuals, sets of persons, and populations within those systems. Formulated in this light, it is difficult to see how an antipsychological position could be seriously maintained or plausibly defended.

To illustrate the application of the framework outlined in Figure 13.1, consider the range of examples in *Our Selves/Our Past: Psychological Approaches to American History* (Brugger, 1981), which suggests the range of psychological approaches that have been taken toward events in American history. This edited book includes chapters on the psychology of witchcraft in colonial New England, the psychology of Revolutionaries and Tories during the American Revolution, the psychology of slavery, the psychology of abolitionists, the psychology of the progressive movement, the psychology of sex roles and female hysteria in the nineteenth century, the psychology of Populists in the 1890s, the psychology of anger and survival guilt among American soldiers who participated in the My Lai massacre, and the psychology of narcissism in contemporary American society, as well as psychological studies of prominent individuals, including Jonathan Edwards, Abraham Lincoln, Theodore Roosevelt, and Richard Nixon.

In each of these examples of group or collective psychohistory, analyses are made of the relationships between psychological structures and processes and an important group, social movement, institution, or event in American history. The point is that psychological structures, elements, and processes within individuals and collectivities of individuals are inextricably related to events and processes at each of the other system levels—are actively involved in producing a Revolutionary War, maintaining slavery or fighting to abolish it, living within or rebelling against women's roles in the nineteenth century, participating in or demonstrating against the Vietnam War, and so on.

To take a second and more detailed historical illustration, the relevance of psychological processes for understanding each of the six system levels in Figure 13.1 will be illustrated with examples from the Nazi era. Psychological analyses may be useful, or probably even necessary, for understanding those Germans who joined the Nazi party and the S.S., those who engaged directly in the killing of Jews, those Germans who actively opposed Hitler or aided the Jews, the behavior of Jews in the ghettos and concentration camps, those who violently resisted the Nazis, the bystanders in other nations who failed to intervene, and finally, the psychological impact of the Nazi era and the Holocaust on survivors of the concentration camps, former Nazis, emigrants, descendants of those directly involved, and all those who study this historical period.

To illustrate the relevance of the relationships between psychological factors and the six system levels of persons, groups, organizations, institutions, sociocultural systems, and international relations within the Nazi era, let us begin with the bottom row of Figure 13.1, the level of persons. The most obvious starting point for studies of individuals is with analyses of Adolf Hitler. In a population with widespread anti-Semitism, what contributed to the unusual intensity of his own anti-Semitic feelings? How did he manage to attain and wield so much power, and then to contribute to his own destruction? The psychobiographical literature on Hitler is enormous, from an early study by Erik Erikson (1942); to Walter C. Langer's study for the United States Office of Strategic Services during World War II (published in 1972 as *The Mind of Adolf Hitler: The Secret Wartime Report*); to an analysis by Rudolf Binion (1976), who argues that Hitler's anti-Semitism had its emotional origins in the trauma caused by his mother's death while being treated by a Jewish physician and also in his linking the traumatic German defeat in World War I to the Jews; to Helm Stierlin's (1976) argument that Hitler's hatred of his authoritarian father was displaced onto the Jews, against whom Hitler protected his German "Motherland"; to perhaps the most comprehensive psychobiographical analysis in Robert Waite's *Psychopathic God: Adolf Hitler* (1977), which critically evaluates a number of earlier interpretations and argues for, among other factors, the importance of Hitler's abnormal sexual development.

There are, of course, also biographical, autobiographical, and psychobiographical analyses of an immense number of other persons within the Nazi era, including Heinrich Himmler, Joseph Goebbels, Herman Göring, Adolf Eichmann, war criminals tried at Nuremberg, concentration-camp directors such as Rudolf Hoess (commandant of Auschwitz from 1941 to 1943), Raoul Wallenberg and others who aided Jews in escaping, autobiographical accounts by concentration-camp survivors, and many others (see Cargas, 1985; Mensch, 1979–80).

Staying at the level of persons, but moving to their aggregation into sets of persons (cell 17 in Figure 13.1), a variety of additional psychological questions come to mind:

1. What psychological processes were involved in supporting, voting for, and joining the Nazi party? What psychological (and other) differences were there between those who joined the party in its early years in the 1920s, those who joined in the early 1930s, and those derogatorily nicknamed "March violets," who joined in March 1933 or later, after Hitler had come to power?

2. What was the psychology of those actively engaged in mass murder?

3. What was the psychology of the Jewish and non-Jewish victims of the Holocaust? What psychological considerations are necessary in order to understand their behavior and experience, such as widespread disbelief in the death camps, processes of adaptation to and survival in the concentration camps, or longer term psychological consequences for survivors and their families (Dimsdale, 1980)?

4. What psychological attributes and processes characterized those who actively fought against Nazism? For example, what was the psychology of those Jews involved in the Warsaw ghetto revolt of 1943? of those in the armed revolts in the Treblinka and Sobibor death camps in 1943? of those in the German "White Rose" student group, whose members distributed anti-Hitler leaflets in 1942 and 1943, for which they were beheaded? or of those involved in various plots to assassinate Hitler (see Hoffman, 1977; Scholl, 1983; Trunk, 1979)?

5. What was the psychology of all the bystanders in Germany, Brit-

ain, the United States and elsewhere who might have helped end the Holocaust, but did not?

6. What about the psychology of the refugees and emigrants from Nazi Germany? Focusing on a subgroup of scholars and intellectuals who emigrated from Nazi-controlled territory, what was the impact of their experiences on their later lives, ideas, motivations, and subsequent intellectual careers (see Bailyn and Fleming, 1969; Coser, 1984)?

In each of these six groups, there is substantial internal heterogeneity, and psychological elements are only one of several kinds of operative factors; yet psychological analyses are still a necessary component of any comprehensive understanding.

Moving to questions about the psychological aspects of populations of persons (cell 18 in Figure 13.1), much earlier research focused on questions about the authoritarian personality and the German "national character," characterized by such features as ethnocentrism, anti-Semitism, anti-intraception (impatience with fantasies, feelings, and inner subjective phenomena), idealization of parents, and a rigid conception of sex roles (Sanford, 1973). Paralleling the wider course of research on national character (Bock, 1980), it became clear that such global psychological characterizations of a population had to be disaggregated, as there is a wide range of personality types within a population. This more differentiated analysis, working downward from population-level data to finer and finer subgroups, has probably progressed farthest in analyses of those who voted for the Nazi party, moving from initial aggregate data about the number of people voting for the Nazis in 1928, 1930, or 1932, down to ever more differentiated analyses of election-by-election voting patterns broken down by town, geographical area, religion, age, income, occupation, and a variety of other factors (see Childers, 1984; Hamilton, 1981).

To be complete, psychohistorical analyses at the level of persons cannot be restricted to individual psychobiography, but must move along the whole continuum of levels of aggregation, from one, to some, to all, and correspondingly, to move along the whole continuum of levels of analytic generality, discovering what true statements can be made about the population as a whole, about various groups within it—such as perpetrators, victims, bystanders, and resisters—and, finally, about particular persons within each of these groups. Such psychohistorical analyses, moving back and forth across the whole continuum of levels of generality, hold promise for reducing both psychological and historical oversimplifications.

Let us now consider the second system level, that of groups, families, and interpersonal relationships (the fifth row in Figure 13.1). The distinguishing feature of this system level is people interacting directly with one another, whether in two-person relationships, families, or informal social groups. In the Nazi era, examples would include the structure of the German family and processes of child rearing; the interpersonal relationships of Nazis, Jews, gypsies, and others; and a variety of informal face-to-face groups, such as the group of Nazis confined with Hitler in Landsberg Prison in 1924 or the group of death-camp inmates planning the escape from Sobibor in 1943. Within this system level, it is also possible to distinguish among three levels of aggregation—the analysis of a single group, a set of groups, or a whole population of groups. Using the example of interpersonal relationships, attention might be focused on psychological aspects of Hitler's relationship with a particular person, such as Joseph Goebbels; on his relationships with a set of people, such as the seven women with whom he presumably had intimate relationships, six of whom attempted or committed suicide (Waite, 1977, p. 239); and, finally, on the entire set or population of his interpersonal relationships. Similarly, attention to German child-rearing processes might focus on characteristics of the population as a whole, on child-rearing patterns in different social classes or religious groups, or, finally, on child-rearing processes in a particular family.

At the next system level, that of formal organizations (the fourth row in Figure 13.1), attention can be directed to psychological structures and processes related to a variety of formal organizations, such as the Storm Troops, the Hitler Youth, the Gestapo, the *Judenrat* (organization of Jewish leaders in the ghettos), or I. G. Farben, the biggest chemical company in Germany, which ran a large synthetic-rubber plant near Auschwitz using Jewish slave labor.

To take an example of just one organization, consider the psychology of and the psychological changes over time in the S.S. (*Schutzstaffeln,* or "protective squads"), which began in 1923 as a group of eight men selected as a personal bodyguard for Hitler. The group, renamed the S.S. in 1925, was taken over by Heinrich Himmler in 1929, and the membership grew from 280 in that year to approximately 30,000 in 1932, 250,000 in 1942, and more than 1 million in 1944, including some 24,000 concentration-camp guards, the infamous "Death's Head" detachments (Höhne, 1969; Kren and Rappoport, 1980, Chapter 3; Steiner, 1980).

After Germany invaded the Soviet Union on June 22, 1941, the troops were followed by four *Einsatzgruppen,* or "special-action groups," whose job was to liquidate Jews, Bolsheviks, gypsies, the deranged, and other "racial enemies." Hundreds of thousands of victims were rounded up, sometimes ordered to dig their own graves, and then shot. A psychological consequence faced by the S.S. was the effects of these murders on the soldiers, a number of whom committed suicide or suffered from nervous breakdowns, nightmares, and alcoholism. After the war, one of their leaders, Paul Blobel, made the not overly sensitive claim that "the nervous strain was far heavier in the case of our men who carried out the executions than in that of their victims. From the psychological point of view they had a terrible time" (Höhne, 1969, p. 364). After watching 200 Jews being shot in Minsk, Himmler was so shaken that he said a new method of killing must be found, which led to the development of gas vans (Höhne, 1969, p. 366). Rudolf Hoess, commandant at Auschwitz, said in his autobiography (1959) that he was relieved at the use of gas, since "I always shuddered at the prospect of carrying out exterminations by shooting, when I thought of the vast numbers concerned, and of the women and children . . . I was therefore relieved to think that we were to be spared all these bloodbaths, and that the victims too would be spared suffering until their last moment came" (p. 165).

A number of psychological questions are relevant to understanding the history and activities of the S.S. For example, what motivated men to join and remain in the S.S.? How could an organization manage to recruit, train, and coerce or encourage its members to engage in such brutal activities? What were the personality characteristics of S.S. members; were they seriously disturbed or relatively normal? What was the psychological impact of participating in mass murder, particularly on that subgroup of S.S. men involved in the killing of Jewish and other civilians and those working in the death camps? What psychological and other processes led a number of S.S. leaders and members to turn against Hitler in the last years of the war? Finally, how did former S.S. members adapt psychologically to their experiences after the war? These are complex questions, which are addressed elsewhere in more detail than will be possible here (see Dimsdale, 1980; Höhne, 1969; Kren and Rappoport, 1980; Steiner, 1980; Sydnor, 1977).

After Himmler became head of the S.S. in 1929, a public-relations campaign for the S.S. was launched, identifying it as the elite National Socialist organization. Beginning in 1935, S.S. members had to produce proof of an "Aryan" ancestry going back to 1800, and for officers and officer candidates, back to 1750. Members of the social and economic elite were given honorary titles in the S.S., and ordinary citizens made financial contributions in order to be identified as a "sponsoring member" of the S.S. A rigorous officer-training program was instituted, and many young men from aristocratic backgrounds were attracted to the organization. These recruitment practices had changed dramatically by the end of the war, when 200,000 dissident ethnics from the Soviet Union and Eastern Europe, previously identified as "subhuman" by the Nazis, were incorporated into auxiliary S.S. military forces. By 1944 and 1945, when information about the death camps was rumored throughout Germany, many German parents would not permit their sons to enlist in the S.S. (Kren and Rappoport, 1980).

By the last years of the war, a number of S.S. officers were involved in unsuccessful attempts to kidnap or assassinate Hitler. Heinrich Himmler attempted to escape from Berlin at the end of the war, but was caught several weeks later and committed suicide by swallowing a cyanide capsule. In 1951, a mutual-aid society of former members of the *Waffen*-S.S. (the military branch of the S.S.) was formed. In a study of 229 former S.S. men (Steiner, 1980), the majority of those in the *Waffen*-S.S. reported no regrets about their wartime activities, while those members of the S.S. who had served in concentration or death camps, the security police, or the mobile killing units would not have wanted to participate again and expressed regrets. According to Steiner, a former concentration-camp inmate himself, there was some anti-Semitism among former S.S. members, but predominantly indifference or mild sympathy toward Jews, and a belief that the S.S. had served a valuable mission fighting "to bring about a United Europe defending itself against communist aggression and world domination" (p. 444).

An understanding of the history and functioning of the S.S. as an organization requires analysis of a substantial number of psychological topics and processes, including the changing motivations and attitudes of those who joined, Himmler's emphasis on forming an elite and quasi-religious cult, the personalities of S.S. members engaged in mass killings, the psychological impact of such activities, the turn against Hitler by a number of S.S. officers, and finally, the psychology of former S.S. members after the war in organizations of S.S. veterans.

Working within the organizational system level, and moving to higher levels of aggregation, the study of a specific organization such as the S.S. may be compared with the study of other organizations within Nazi Germany or of paramilitary police groups in a number of other countries. Or, if one starts by focusing on a smaller organization, such as a particular concentration camp, a particular church, or a specific business firm, then analyses can be made of a specific group or population of comparable organizations within Nazi Germany. For example, one recent study of a set of death camps is Arad's *Belzec, Sobibor, Treblinka: The Operation Reinhard Death Camps* (1987).

The next system level to be concerned with is that of institutions (the third row in Figure 13.1). This would include an analysis of the psychological aspects of each of the major social institutions in Germany from 1933 to 1945. Extensive studies have been made of the functioning of political, military, legal, business, church, educational, scientific, cultural, mass media, and other institutions during the Nazi era (see Cargas, 1985; Szonyi, 1985). Just as a sample of this literature, there is Turners' *German Big Business and the Rise of Hitler* (1985), arguing that big business was less responsible for Hitler's rise to power than commonly believed; Conway's *Nazi Persecution of the Churches, 1933–1945* (1969), detailing Hitler's undermining of the churches; Beyerchen's *Scientists Under Hitler* (1977), analyzing the responses of physicists to National Socialism; and Blackburn's *Education in the Third Reich* (1984), outlining the massive educational propaganda efforts to shape the minds of German youth in line with Nazi racial theories, political beliefs, and anti-Christian and anti-Marxist ideology.

Psychohistorical study would analyze the psychological elements and processes related to the history and functioning of each of these institutions during the Third Reich. In spite of the massive amount of literature on the Nazi era, and even massive amount of psychohistorical literature (Gilmore, 1984; Kren, 1984; Loewenberg, 1975; Mensch, 1979–80), there is still much more that remains to be done with psychologically informed analysis of each of the major institutions in Nazi society.

Questions about the sociocultural system as a whole (the second row in Figure 13.1) have troubled students of the Nazi era and of the Holocaust for decades. As expressed by Lucy Dawidowicz (1975), "(1) How was it possible for a modern state to carry out the systematic murder of a whole people for no reason other than that they were Jews? (2) How was it possible for a whole people to allow itself to be destroyed? (3) How was it possible for the world to stand by without halting this destruction?" (p. xxi). How are we to understand the values and beliefs of a culture; the political, legal, religious, educational, scientific, and other institutions; the variety of specific organizations; and the array of individual persons from Hitler on down that made this possible?

The entire literature on the Nazi era and the Holocaust deals with different aspects of these questions. Questions about the functioning of the sociocultural system as a whole may be pursued by focusing on the specifics of Nazi Germany, or by comparing its history with the histories of such other societies as Spain under Franco, Italy under Mussolini, the Soviet Union under Stalin, or Cambodia under Pol Pot.

At the level of international relations (the first row in Figure 13.1), there are a good many issues that have been examined in detail, including (1) most obviously, the psychology of diplomatic and military relations between Germany and the Soviet Union, Austria, Poland, France, Great Britain, the United States and other nations throughout the Nazi period (for an interesting psychological study of German-British diplomatic relations in the late nineteenth century, see Hughes, 1983); (2) the collaboration of international business with the Third Reich, including officials from firms such as ITT, Ford, Standard Oil of New Jersey, and the Chase Bank (Higham, 1983); and (3) the response or lack of response of other nations to the events of the Holocaust, as discussed in Wyman's *Abandonment of the Jews: America and the Holocaust, 1941–1945* (1984).

This discussion of the psychological aspects of six system levels does *not exhaust* the range of important psychohistorical questions. Within a given historical period and geographical area, such as Nazi Germany from 1933 to 1945, important questions can also be investigated about the psychological aspects of a chain or sequence of *events* occurring throughout the period, interwoven with the six system levels. This would include such events as Hitler's accession to power on January 30, 1933; the Night of the Long Knives, on June 30, 1934, when the S. S. murdered the leaders of the Storm Troops and gained control over their rival organization; *Kristallnacht* (the Night of the Broken Glass), on November 9–10, 1938, when the Nazis attacked Jews in the streets and looted their shops; the psychology of the German invasion of Poland on September 1, 1939; the German defeat at Stalingrad in early 1943; the psychology of the Warsaw ghetto revolt in April 1943; the Allied invasion at Normandy, beginning on June 6, 1944; the psychology of Hitler's suicide on April 30, 1945; and the surrender of Germany on May 8, 1945.

For each event, important psychohistorical questions can be asked about (1) the antecedent psychology of hopes, plans, fears, expectations, and preparations that led up to it; (2) the concurrent and constitutive psychology of beliefs, perceptions, feelings, interpretations, statements, and actions directly involved in the event; and (3) the psychological consequences, subjective meanings, and later memories and interpretations of the event.

To illustrate with a single event, such as the *Kristallnacht* pogrom on

November 9–10, 1938, psychohistorical analysis would include research about the psychological antecedents of the event, such as the anti-Jewish riots following the assassination by a young Jew of a German diplomat in Paris, and the fanning of these flames by Hitler, Goebbels, and Heydrich; the psychology of those participating in the looting, refusing to participate, or actively opposing it; the psychological experience of those Jews associated with the 200 synagogues that were destroyed or some 7,500 shops that were looted, or who were related to the approximately 90 Jews who were killed and the more than 20,000 Jewish men who were sent to concentration camps; and, finally, the subsequent psychological impact of this event as it was perceived and interpreted by Jews, Nazis, Germans, and citizens around the world (see Gordon, 1984).

To discuss just one facet of the psychology of this event, the reactions of the German public and even among the Nazi party members were far less homogeneous than might initially be assumed. There was, it seems, substantial opposition to the *Kristallnacht* pogrom within the German populace and even among members of the Nazi party. The Nazi press directives were to report that the German people had "spontaneously erupted" on *Kristallnacht,* and all other interpretations were prohibited, but the actual reaction seems to have been somewhat more complex. According to Wilson, the United States ambassador to Germany at the time, "A surprising characteristic of the situation here is the intensity and scope among German citizens of a condemnation of the recent happenings against Jews. . . . Such expressions are not confined to members of the intellectual classes but are encountered here throughout all classes" (quoted in Gordon, 1984, p. 176).

Gordon (1984) argues that a large segment of the previously indifferent German population condemned the murder, destruction of property, and violence, and that many Germans aided Jews by forewarning them of Nazi attacks, hiding them in their homes, and providing food and medical supplies. For such help, a large number of Germans were arrested in an effort by the Nazis to stamp out criticism of their racial policies (p. 178). Disapproval of *Kristallnacht* was found not only in the German population, but even within the Nazi party, as some Nazi party leaders "refused to obey orders to destroy Jewish property and issued counterorders to prevent this destruction. . . . Indeed, many Nazis aided Jews in escaping from the SA, SS, and Hitler Youth during Kristallnacht" (p. 266).

The sources of opposition to *Kristallnacht* were varied, partly humanitarian but not solely humanitarian, in that many Germans accepted legally imposed economic and social sanctions against the Jews, but opposed *Kristallnact,* destruction of property, and physical violence that harmed Germany's image abroad. Gordon (1984) argues that public opposition to anti-Semitism peaked at this time, and was followed by widespread arrests of critics of the Nazi regime. This tactic may have been successful, since the subsequent more orderly "Aryanization" programs were never widely condemned by the German public (p. 180).

The discipline of history may focus on (1) the history of a period and geographical area, (2) the history of particular systems within a period, (3) the history of events and processes, or (4) the history of particular topics or themes. Psychohistorical analysis of *topics* in the Nazi era would include different classes of behavior and experience during the period, such as the psychology of mass murder, the psychology of violent resistance or passive accommodation, the psychology of denial and disbelief at what was happening in the death camps, the psychology of terror, the psychology of lying and deceit, the psychology of survivor guilt, the psychology of mourning and denial, and so on.

Perhaps the most studied class of behavior related to the Nazi era is that of "obedience to authority" (Milgram, 1974; Miller, 1986). Most notably, Adolf Eichmann and other war criminals claimed that they had acted only in obedience to authority and had had no choice about their actions. Although obedience to authority can certainly be a powerful force, and may have been the dominant factor in some cases, there are reasons to doubt that it provides an adequate explanation of Eichmann's behavior. Eichmann seems not to have been a man filled with human sympathy who was driven by authority to transport Jews to death camps against inner moral objections. For example, in an interview with a Dutch Nazi journalist in 1957, Eichmann confessed, "To be frank with you, had we killed all of them, the 10.3 million, I would be happy and say, All right; we managed to destroy an enemy" (quoted in Hausner, 1966, p. 11). Eichmann was also selective in his following of orders, and attempted to sabotage or reverse requests for leniency in the treatment of Jews. In 1944, for example, Hitler authorized that 8,700 selected Jewish families and 1,000 children be allowed to emigrate from Hungary so that the Hungarian government would agree to the deportation and execution of the 300,000 Jews remaining in the Budapest ghetto. Eichmann was outraged at this leniency and appealed the matter to Himmler. In accord with Eichmann's objections, Hitler canceled the emigration permits (Hausner, 1966, pp. 142–145). There are extensive literatures on many of the other classes of behavior and experience related to the Nazi era, although few have remained as perennially controversial as the topic of obedience to authority.

One additional topic with particular relevance to the Nazi era is that of "countertransference," or more generally, the psychological relationship of the researcher to his or her subject. Studying the period is gut-wrenching for almost everyone, including myself. The strong emotional reactions that the topic engenders are intensified and complicated by the variety of interests involved, whether on the part of concentration-camp survivors, former Nazis, other Germans, descendants of those involved, or even those encountering it solely through the literature.

The Nazi period is of particular importance to psychohistorians, as it has claimed the attention of so many significant contributors to the field, beginning with Erik Erikson's (1942) study of Hitler's imagery and German youth, and including studies by Peter Loewenberg of the Nazi Youth cohort (1971), Himmler's adolescence (1975), and overviews of psychohistorical work on modern Germany (1983); Saul Friedländer on anti-Semitism (1971, 1978), the Catholic Church's uninvolvement (1966), and contemporary German treatment of the Nazi period (1984); Kren and Rappoport's overview of Nazi psychohistory in *The Holocaust and the Crisis of Human Behavior* (1980); Fred Weinstein's *Dynamics of Nazism* (1980); the many psychobiographies of Hitler, including those by Langer (1972), Binion (1976), Stierlin (1976), and Waite (1977); and, most recently, Geoffrey Cocks's *Psychotherapy in the Third Reich: The Göring Institute* (1985), and Robert Jay Lifton's *Nazi Doctors* (1986). Psychohistorical studies of the Nazi era are so extensive that they are on the cutting edge of helping to define both the possibilities and the limitations of psychohistorical analysis.

To summarize, the study of psychological aspects of each of the six system levels in Figure 13.1—from persons up through international relations—provides a far more differentiated and fine-grained analysis of the structure of the field of psychohistory than does one that makes only the gross distinction between individual psychobiography and group psychohistory.

According to the present analysis, there is a substantial array of different kinds of psychohistorical studies, including psychobiographical studies of single individuals; psychohistorical analyses of different sets of people within a historical period (for example, perpetrators, victims, bystanders, and resisters in the Nazi era); psychohistorical analyses of groups, families, and interpersonal relationships; psychohistorical analyses of organizations; psychohistorical analyses of the major institutions in a society; psychohistorical analyses of aspects of the whole sociocultural system; and psychohistorical analyses of diplomatic, military, economic, and other forms of international relations. In addition, psychohistorical analyses may also be organized around the study of particular events, processes, and topics cutting across the six system levels.

The more one studies the Nazi period—from the cruelty of individual Nazis, to the brutality of certain organizations, to the agony of the victims, to the heroism of resistant Jews and Germans, to the thoughts and emotions of scholars engaged with the period—the more one sees a need for psychologically informed analyses of the issues. To emphasize again, analyses of psychological threads of these events and processes are *not* a substitute for sociological, economic, political, demographic, cultural, and other forms of analysis, but rather their necessary complement.

I have found this diagram helpful in analyzing a wide range of questions about the relationships between psychology, biography, and history, but several comments about its limitations need to be made. First, the particular system levels outlined in Figure 13.1 are for contemporary Western culture, and are not immutable in time and space. For working with the medieval, classical, or prehistoric world, one would need to use a somewhat different set of social-system levels, including systems such as tribes, feudal estates, or city-states. There is, in short, a history both of particular entities and of the system levels themselves. Second, the six system levels in Figure 13.1 need to be seen against a background of, and in continuous interaction with, the physical, biological, and technological world. Geographical, climatic, agricultural, technological, and other aspects of the physical world are continuously interacting with the human and social systems sketched in the figure. This is represented graphically in Figure 13.5. Figure 13.1 does not provide a comprehensive analysis of the historical process, but rather focuses on the interconnections between the psychological processes within individuals and collectivities and the histories of groups, organizations, institutions, nations, and international relations.

The relationships among these six system levels over time are represented in Figure 13.2. What are causal and noncausal relationships between these six system levels over time? In particular, what are the relationships between persons and their psychological processes and the other, more aggregate system levels?

As social theorists and historians frequently point out, persons do not exist in a vacuum and are not entirely free and independent agents, but are shaped, formed, and have their existence and being within particular sociohistorical contexts. Strong determinists even say that indi-

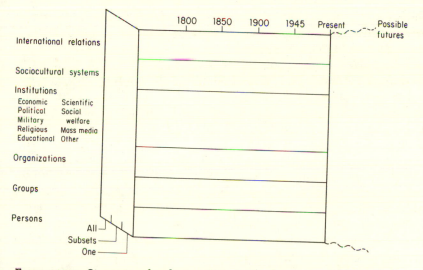

FIGURE 13.2. Six system levels over time in the human-social-historical sciences.

viduals are totally determined by their social, economic, and historical context, or are "nothing but" the intersection of social forces or social relationships.

The causal relationships, however, go in both directions, from social structures to persons, and from persons to social structures. These two-way relationships are analyzed by theorists of personality and social structure within sociology (Smelser and Smelser, 1970, 1981; Yinger, 1965), by theorists of culture and personality within anthropology (Bock, 1980; LeVine, 1982), and by interaction theorists within personality psychology (Magnusson and Endler, 1977; Pervin and Lewis, 1978).

As argued by sociological theorists such as Giddens (1976, 1984), *"the production of society* is a skilled performance, sustained and 'made to happen' by human beings" (1976, p. 15). Social structures "only exist as the reproduced conduct of situated actors with definite intentions and interests" (1976, p. 127). Finally, "the production and reproduction of society thus has to be treated as a skilled performance on the part of its members" (1976, p. 160). To relate these ideas to the system levels described here, each of the five aggregate system levels—groups, organizations, institutions, sociocultural systems, and international relations—are formed, maintained, and changed through the skilled and knowledgeable action of their members. Psychological processes of belief, motivation, and action are necessarily involved in maintaining or changing social groups or institutions.

It is *not* as though social institutions and practices had some inevitable inertia of their own, which would keep them rolling along regardless of how persons thought, felt, or acted in relation to them. Social institutions, systems, and relationships are constructed, kept in motion, and changed by the skilled, knowledgeable, and motivated practice of persons and aggregates of persons.

Without such practice by individuals, the institutions decay or disappear, as happens in cases of social change. If all employees go on strike, the company stops functioning. If everyone refuses to join the military, then there is no army. As the saying from the 1960s goes, "What if they gave a war, and nobody came?" Without the active and skilled participation of persons and aggregates of persons (as mediated by psychological processes of perception, knowledge, belief, motivation, decision, and action), groups, organizations, institutions, and social systems would not endure and would not be reproduced or changed from one generation to the next.

The story of the relationship among these six system levels over time is not confined to the story of their causal relationships over time. We can often describe a phenomenon and "place it in its historical context," or relate it to other structures, events, and processes surrounding it in time and space, without being able to talk with any precision about its causal relationships with other events. Biographers have written a great deal about Napoleon, Martin Luther, or Louis XIV without having been able to analyze very precisely their causal influence or to know in a counterfactual sense how the course of historical events would have been different if they had not lived, or had not acted as they did.

Causal analysis, at least in its rigorous forms, is possible in only a limited set of conditions that enable us to infer how things would have been different without the event in question (von Wright, 1971). For many historical situations, we simply do not know enough and/or the flow of events is too complex and idiosyncratic to permit any rigorous kind of causal analysis. Even under conditions when causal analysis is impossible, there is a great deal to say about a historical person, institution, or event, such as describing it in detail, tracing its changes over time, indicating how it was perceived and interpreted by various individuals and groups, analyzing its "meaning" to contemporaries and subsequent generations, and placing it in time, in space, and in relation to other events.

In short, causal relationships are only a subset of the relationships of system levels over time. Even when the flow of events is too complex and idiosyncratic to permit causal analysis, there is much to be learned about the history, details, meanings, and contexts of particular entities and processes. Ideally, we want forms of inquiry that deal with the historical evolution and interrelationships among these six system levels over time and that include, but are not limited to, analysis of their causal relationships.

This diagram of six system levels and their relationships over time is quite abstract, and due to limitations of space, will have to remain so; but one of its purposes is to construct a conceptual framework that is sufficiently spacious to indicate relationships among many different levels of analysis, so that researchers do not feel forced to suppress other forms of analysis as if their very existence were a threat to the integrity of their own program or level of analysis. The aim is to avoid the perspective of *Annales* historians, who at one time felt it necessary to suppress the biographical in order to survive; of Marxists, who felt it necessary to suppress individual and psychological levels of analysis; or of psychohistorical reductionists, who felt impelled to ignore institutional and structural levels of analysis. In particular, the diagram is addressed to the concerns of historians who feel that acknowledging psychological factors and processes is somehow incompatible with their interests in institutions, nation-states, social structures, aggregates of persons, and long-term continuity and change in social systems. The objective is to avoid structural, economic, or psychological forms of reductionism by constructing a conceptual framework comprehensive enough to encompass these diverse forms of analysis and indicate their relationships to one another.

Inquiry at any one system level is often enriched by or even dependent on analysis of its relationships with other system levels. Many historical questions require analysis of the interplay between continuity and change in social structures and the psychological processes of persons and aggregates of persons. Dare it be said, this is "psychohistory"—a psychological history not reducing history to psychology, but also not reducing history by leaving out the psychology.

Disciplinary-Mediated Relationships

I have argued that the relationships between psychology and history can usefully be conceptualized by disaggregating "history" into the evolution and interaction of six or so system levels. The six system levels outlined in Figures 13.1 and 13.2 are relevant to a wide array of problems and discourses in the social sciences, with sociologists, anthropologists, and historians focusing primarily on the social-system end of the spectrum; political scientists and economists, on political and economic institutions and their contexts; and psychologists, on psychological processes within and between persons and groups of persons. In order to understand the relationships between history and psychology as disciplines and between historical events and psychological processes as phenomena, it is necessary to analyze the relationships between psychological structures and processes and each of these other system levels.

Research on the relationships between psychological phenomena and these other system levels is currently pursued within a variety of disciplines. To indicate briefly the disciplines engaged at each system level, there is research on the interrelationships between psychological structures and processes and (1) the functioning of groups, families, and interpersonal relationships, as studied in sociology and social psychology; (2) the functioning of organizations, as studied in organizational and industrial psychology, and in the sociology of organizations and organizational careers; (3) the functioning and change of major social institutions, as studied in political science, economics, sociology, and anthropology; (4) the functioning and history of cultures and social systems, as studied in sociology and anthropology in such subfields as socialization, deviance, social control, personality and social structure, historical sociology, culture and personality, and cognitive anthropology; and (5) the structure and history of international or intersocietal relations, as studied in international politics, international economics, cultural-diffusion analysis, and world-systems theory.

In short, the relationships between history and psychology can be mediated by the relationships of psychology with each of the other aggregate-level social-science disciplines, as illustrated in Figure 13.3. The figure emphasizes those areas of the social sciences that have explicitly developed their connections with psychology. In sociology, anthropology, and political science, there are formally developed subfields that focus on relationships with psychology, including social structure and personality, psychological anthropology, and political psychology, and others such as socialization theory or life course sociology.

The essential point of Figure 13.3 is that all the connections between history and psychology need not be direct ones. The contributions of psychology to history may come not only directly from the discipline of psychology, but also indirectly through other disciplines that, in

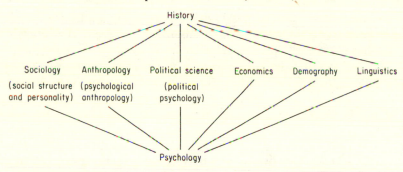

FIGURE 13.3. Disciplinary-mediated relationships between history and psychology.

turn, have made use of psychology. There is a substantial literature in each of these hybrid fields for historians to draw on. The literature is too vast to review in detail, but to mention only a few significant works, with an emphasis on overviews, historically relevant work is discussed in the literature in social structure and personality (Inkeles, 1983; Rosenberg and Turner, 1981; Ryff, 1987; Smelser and Smelser, 1970, 1981; Yinger, 1965), in psychological anthropology (Barnouw, 1985; Bock, 1980; LeVine, 1982; LeVine and Shweder, 1984; LeVine and White, 1986; Rosaldo, 1980; Runyan, 1986; Spindler, 1978; Westen, 1986), and in political psychology (Davies, 1980; Elms, 1976; Greenstein, 1975; Hermann, 1986; Janis, 1982; Jervis, 1976; Jervis, Lebow, and Stein, 1985; Long, 1981; Roazen, 1968; Tetlock and McGuire, 1986; White, 1986). Figure 13.3 is not intended to be complete and could be supplemented by adding fields such as socialization theory, life course sociology, historical sociology, and historical anthropology. To the best of my knowledge, the literatures on relationships between psychology and economics (Katona, 1975; Maital, 1982), and between psychology and demography (Easterlin, 1980; Miller and Godwin, 1977), are not as well developed, although there will be more to draw on over time.

Psychological history is not some bizarre fringe movement that just ought to go away and stop bothering people, but is intimately related to a number of those aggregate-level social sciences with which historians have already established relationships and that they are often more comfortable dealing with. As Lawrence Stone (1981) has noted, there are historical trends in the relationships between history and the social sciences, with history borrowing at first most heavily from economics, then from sociology, and most recently from anthropology. Psychology is sometimes mentioned as a possibility, but the reception of psychology by historians has often been far more ambivalent (see Gay, 1985). Historians may borrow with profit from each of these interdisciplinary social-scientific and psychological hybrids and, in turn, may make significant contributions to each of them by directing attention to issues of continuity and change in relationships between psychological processes and social structures over the course of time.

Conceptual Distinctions Between Psychohistory, Historical Psychology, and History with Psychological Content

There is considerable confusion about the scope and definition of psychohistory. Many define it as the use of psychology (often psychoanalytic psychology) in historical interpretation (Anderson, 1978; Brugger, 1981; Friedländer, 1978), while others define it more broadly as also including the history of psychological phenomena and/or the history of thought about psychological development and the life course (Gilmore, 1984; Manuel, 1972; Schoenwald, 1973).

There are at least three analytically separable issues which need to be distinguished. These three, with proposed terminology, are (1) *psychohistory,* or the explicit use of formal psychological theory in historical interpretation; (2) *historical psychology,* or research on the transhistorical generality or specificity of psychological structures, elements, and relationships; and (3) *history with psychological content,* or the extent to which psychological phenomena such as human motivations, beliefs, emotions, and actions are included as subject matter in a historical study.

These three analytically separable enterprises can be placed on a continuum between their parent disciplines of history and psychology, as shown in Figure 13.4. We can proceed by first attempting to characterize the objectives of the disciplines at each end of this continuum, and then examining how history with psychological content, psychohistory, and historical psychology fit between them.

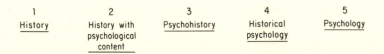

FIGURE 13.4. Conceptual distinctions in the relations between history and psychology.

In the most general terms, history is *phenomena-centered,* in that it is concerned with the description and interpretation of particular phenomena and events in the past. Psychology, on the other hand, and particularly academic psychology, tends to be *theory-centered,* concerned with developing general conceptual and theoretical analyses of various classes of psychological phenomena, as in the areas of developmental, social, personality, abnormal, cognitive, and biological psychology. Another way of putting this distinction is to say that historians typically collect evidence in order to develop more adequate descriptions and interpretations of particular phenomena in the past, while psychologists carry out research in order to collect evidence for the somewhat different purpose of testing the adequacy of general theoretical formulations. These theoretical formulations, in turn, are intended to apply to a whole universe of psychological structures and processes.

In relation to these characterizations of the objectives of history and psychology, history with psychological content (column 2) can be described as historical accounts that include the description and interpretation of particular psychological phenomena in the past. Psychohistory (column 3), draws explicitly on systematic psychology in the description and interpretation of the psychological dimension of historical events. Historical psychology (column 4) is concerned with studying the transhistorical generality or specificity of psychological theories.

The most developed work in terms of these three distinctions would be a historical work including a focus on psychological phenomena, explicitly interpreted with formal psychological theory, and using psychological theory whose transhistorical generality has been explicitly tested.

To provide an example of the relationships among the different kinds of studies noted in Figure 13.4, consider the case of obedience to authority. In column 5, psychological research on obedience to authority would consist of experimental and other forms of research designed to assess those factors that produce, maintain, or minimize obedience to authority (Milgram, 1974). Research on historical psychology (column 4) would investigate questions about the degree to which there is historical stability or change in these theoretical relationships. For example, have there been changes in patterns of authoritarian child rearing (Sanford, 1973) that make obedience to authority less likely? Has the level of obedience to authority or the factors shaping it changed in Germany since the 1930s? Have there been reflexive or enlightenment effects from the study of obedience to authority or from the study of the Nazi era that make uncritical obedience to authority less likely?

In psychohistorical inquiry (column 3), what use of psychological theory and research about obedience to authority could be made in explaining the behavior of specific individuals and groups, such as Adolf Eichmann, other Nazis tried as war criminals, or Lieutenant Calley during the My Lai massacre in Vietnam? History with psychological content (column 2) would include the description (and perhaps interpretation in lay terms) of a number of examples of obedience to authority, such as S.S. men performing atrocities when ordered to, or examples of defiance of authority, such as Jews resisting Nazi authority (Trunk, 1979) or Germans opposing Hitler's authority (Gordon, 1984). History (column 1) would include accounts of the Nazi era that gave varying amounts of attention to psychological phenomena, from almost no attention, to a history with a substantial emphasis on psychological phenomena (as in column 2.)

The degree to which psychological phenomena are included within a historical analysis may range from nonexistent or marginal, to auxiliary interest, as in constituting one strand in a complex bio-psycho-socio-historical analysis, to central or primary interest, as in studies of *mentalités* or the history of intimate relationships. The limiting case of history with psychological content would be a history *of* psychological phenomena, such as a history of psychosocial identity (Baumeister, 1986), the history of American national character (Bellah, Madsen, Sullivan, Swidler, and Tipton, 1985; Lasch, 1979; Riesman et al., 1961), the history of relationships and intimacy within the family (Shorter, 1975; Stone, 1977), the history of anger and the conventions controlling it (Stearns and Stearns, 1986), the history of different forms of psychopathology (Shorter, 1986), or the history of attitudes, values, and subjective well-being (Hamilton and Wright, 1986; Veroff, Douvan, and Kulka, 1981).

A key controversy dividing many historians from psychohistorians is not just the place of psychological phenomena in historical studies, which most would include to varying degrees, but whether such phenomena should be interpreted with formal or informal psychological theory. Critics of psychohistory claim that the use of systematic psychology is unilluminating and ahistorical, while supporters of psychohistory argue that even those vehemently opposed to systematic psychology are forced to rely on an implicit psychology (Erikson, 1958). "The professional historian has always been a psychologist—an amateur psychologist" (Gay, 1985, p. 6). If historians necessarily rely on either a formal or an informal psychology, "are historians, then, like modern versions of Monsieur Jordan, practicing psychohistory without knowing it? I am afraid so. They have to" (Degler, 1987, p. 80).

While psychohistorical interpretation relies importantly on an empathic understanding of the particulars of an individual case (Kohut, 1986), the choice of a conceptual framework to use in interpreting these particulars is not a simple matter, either for psychohistorians making explicit use of formal psychology or for more traditional historians relying on implicit psychological theories. For those drawing on formal psychology, there are a multitude of psychoanalytic, neoanalytic, and nonanalytic frameworks to draw from (see Chapters 7 and 12). Even for those relying on implicit or lay theories, there is more than one relevant framework to draw on. For a biography, this would include the psychological beliefs and interpretations of the subject, of those who interacted with him or her, of the biographer, and of the intended audience of the work. Any biographical or historical work requires some negotiation and reconciliation between the everyday psychological beliefs and interpretations of the historical subjects and those of the author and intended audience.

Is there any reason for the historian to go beyond a purely intuitive or implicit psychology to use formal psychology in interpreting historical events? The issue has been extensively debated (for example, Erikson, 1958; Gay, 1985; Loewenberg, 1983; Runyan, 1982; Waite, 1977), and I do not propose to enter into an extended discussion of it here, but rather to place it in the context of a wider set of issues about the connections between history and psychology. My own view is that although formal psychology has substantial gaps and deficiencies, its accomplishments are not without merit, particularly when compared with lay psychology. A total rejection of formal psychology in the interpretation of history is not much more convincing than the position of a person on the street who rejects historical research on the grounds that we intuitively already know what happened in the past and why, without bothering with formal historical research to test or extend that knowledge. Just as history has contributed something, although flawed and incomplete, to our knowledge of the past, psychology has learned a good deal, although imperfect, about human motivation, unconscious processes, personality, development, social interaction, decision making, and behavior that can be of use to historians. One controversial issue is the transhistorical generality of this psychological research, an issue to be discussed in the next section.

In summary, there are important conceptual distinctions between (1) the extent to which psychological phenomena are or are not included in historical analyses, (2) the degree to which such psychological phenomena are interpreted in terms of formal or informal psychology, and (3) the extent to which the formal psychology available for use has or has not been tested for its transhistorical generality or specificity. I have proposed that these three issues can usefully be designated by the terms of history with psychological content, psychohistory, and historical psychology. Others may prefer different labels, but the important issue is to maintain an awareness of the underlying conceptual distinctions. For those preferring a broader definition of psychohistory, these three kinds of work might be seen as distinctive sub-types of psychohistory.

I hesitate to introduce any additional conceptual categories here, as I fear that readers' eyes may begin to glaze over, but at least two additional distinctions seem necessary in order to delineate the variety of ways in which history and psychology can be related to each other. First, historical evidence can be used to develop nomothetic psychological theories, as in William McGuire's (1976) review and analysis of "the use of historical cross-era data to develop and test psychological theories" (p. 161), Paul Rosenblatt's (1983) use of nineteenth-century diaries to test contemporary theories of grieving, or Dean Simonton's (1984) massive transhistorical analysis of factors affecting creativity and leadership. In the discipline of "historiometry," which is defined as "the method of testing nomothetic hypotheses concerning human behavior by applying quantitative analysis to data abstracted from historical populations" (Simonton, 1984, p. 3), Simonton tests nomothetic theories about creativity and leadership as related to age, education, birth-order effects, role-modelling influences, and the principle of cumulative advantage in careers.

A second possible relationship between historical and scientific analysis is in those studies that use social scientifically collected data to address particular historical questions, as in Glen Elder's (1974) use of longitudinal data from the Institute of Human Development studies at the University of California, Berkeley, to address historical questions about the impact of the Great Depression on the psychological and social development of children who experienced it, or in Hamilton and Wright's (1986) use of survey research data to critically evaluate a number of popular claims about psychological changes in the values, attitudes, and subjective well-being of Americans in recent decades. They find, for example, no evidence in survey data that worker dissatisfaction is rising, that a new and higher "Consciousness III" is developing, or that social concerns are replacing economic ones for most Americans.

These two enterprises of (1) using historical data to develop or test nomothetic psychological theories, and (2) using scientifically collected data to study historical questions are different in focus from psychohistory, but they help to fill out the range of ways in which historical and psychological inquiry can be related to each other. In terms of the categories in Figure 13.4, which are based on the objectives of different types of study rather than on the sources of evidence as in these two distinctions, using historical data to test nomothetic psychological theories would be a branch of psychology and using scientifically collected data to study historical questions would be a branch of history.

Historical Psychology as a Resource for Psychohistory

One of the most common criticisms of psychohistory is that it relies on a parochial psychology that is naïvely presumed to hold across space and historical time. The problem was clearly formulated in 1938 by historian Lucien Febvre: "How can we as historians make use of psychology which is the product of observation carried out on twentieth-century man, in order to interpret the actions of the man of the past?" (quoted in Gilmore, 1979, p. 31). It is claimed that many psychohistorians "begin by postulating that there is a theory of human behavior which transcends history" (Stone, 1981, p. 40). Or, "The psychohistorian employs theoretical models and cognitive assumptions created from the material of the present—and then imposes them on the past. In so doing, he or she must assume that in most fundamental ways all people, at all places, at all times, have viewed themselves and the world about them in substantially the same fashion" (Stannard, 1980, p. 143).

One way of addressing this concern is to develop a historical psychology that explicitly examines the extent to which psychological concepts and theories do or do not apply across historical eras. As Kluckhohn and Murray (1953, p. 53) stated, every person is in certain respects (1) like all other persons, (2) like some other persons, and (3) like no other persons. On the historical dimension, some psychological generalizations can be expected to hold across all historical periods; others, within limited historical periods; and others, perhaps only within specific historical circumstances. Psychohistorical interpretation is a complex, three-tiered intellectual enterprise that has to draw on psychological theories that hold universally, other theories that hold only within limited sociohistorical contexts, and, finally, idiographic relationships that hold only within specific cases. A range of idiographic relationships, such as particular subjective meanings, idiosyncratic patterns and correlations, and causal relationships holding within only a single case, are reviewed elsewhere (Runyan, 1983).

Psychologists often talk about the generality of a theory as an ideal, but only rarely do they explicitly assess the transhistorical generality of theories. There is considerable concern for generalizing across subjects, across situations, and across measurement instruments, but far less research on generalizing over time. To the extent that psychologists intend to develop truly general psychological theories holding across space *and* time, there is a crying need for research on the historical stability and mutability of psychological relationships.

This need has been expressed most vividly within social psychology, with a seminal article by Kenneth Gergen, "Social Psychology as History" (1973); a rebuttal, "Social Psychology and Science," by Schlenker (1974); a symposium on the issue in the *Personality and Social Psychology Bulletin* (Manis et al., 1976); and subsequent publications by Gergen (1982, 1984), Gergen and Gergen (1984), Cronbach (1975, 1986), and others. Gergen's central arguments are first, that since social phenomena and relationships are undergoing rapid historical change, many social-psychological generalizations have only a short half-life, and, second, that social-psychological research can produce reflexive "enlightenment effects" and change the phenomena under investigation.

Fortunately, an increasing concern with the transhistorical generality of theory seems to be emerging across several branches of contemporary psychology (see the comprehensive bibliography in Peeters, Gielis, and Caspers, 1985). For example, within historical social psychology, there is new research on historical changes in attitudes and motives, gender relationships, structure of the family, aesthetic tastes, expressive gestures, and conceptions of the self (see Gergen and Gergen, 1984).

Steps toward a historically sensitive psychology are also being taken within life-span developmental psychology, where there has been an increasing recognition of the importance of historical or cohort effects on the course of human development, with many features of the developmental trajectory, such as intellectual capacity, achievement, gender roles, and parenting, varying widely across generations (see Bronfenbrenner, 1979; Caspi, 1987; Keniston, 1981; McCluskey and Reese, 1984; Nesselroade and Baltes, 1974; Runyan, 1984).

Third, there is a long tradition of inquiry into historical changes in personality and national character, such as the work of Riesman in *The Lonely Crowd* (1961), on changes from traditional, to inner-directed, to outer-directed American social character; the study by Barbu (1960) of the formation of personality in classical Greece and early modern England; analyses of the history of selfhood and identity (Baumeister, 1986; Broughton, 1986); the extensive research on "modernization" of personality in developing countries (Inkeles, 1983; Inkeles and Smith, 1974); the work of Philip Greven (1977) in delineating three types of early American character, the evangelical, the moderate, and the genteel; the analysis by Christopher Lasch (1979) of the narcissistic personality of our time; and the work of many others (Bellah et al., 1985; Direnzo, 1977; Fromm, 1942; Horney, 1937; Marcus, 1984).

Fourth, there is research on the history of cognitive structures and processes, such as Julian Jaynes's speculative and thought-provoking *Origins of Consciousness in the Breakdown of the Bicameral Mind* (1976); Radding's (1985) study of cognitive processes in the Middle Ages, which argues that most people made only very limited progression in terms of the stages of cognitive development outlined by Piaget; a study of the increase in intelligence of the American people from 1750 to 1870 (Calhoun, 1973); studies of the evolution of artistic styles and aesthetic tastes (Blatt, with Blatt, 1984; Martindale, 1984); and a line of work influenced by Vygotsky on historical changes in cognitive development (Luria, 1971, 1976; Scribner and Cole, 1981; Wertsch, 1985).

In short, just as there is a *Historical Social Psychology* (Gergen and Gergen, 1984), there are also possibilities for a historical developmental psychology, historical personality psychology, historical cognitive psychology, and historical abnormal psychology. In every branch of psychology, important questions can be asked about the transhistorical generality or specificity of psychological phenomena that have remained constant over varying periods of time.

The scope of inquiry in historical psychology is suggested by the following question: Starting with any contemporary psychological theory of interest (whether in social, developmental, personality, cognitive, or abnormal psychology), what hypotheses can be formulated about its transhistorical generality or specificity, and what bodies of evidence can be brought to bear on these questions? Some questions cannot be answered because of gaps in the accessible evidence, but there are still intriguing possibilities of research in historical psychology, glimpses of which are provided by the body of work already done.

An Evolutionary Perspective

It is sometimes difficult to imagine the extent to which psychological structures and processes can be different from the way they are at present. An abstract argument for the existence of such differences may seem a little thin in comparison with the weight of everyday experience, which seems to provide palpable evidence of their solidity and fixedness. One way of making vivid the temporal fluidity of the psychological world is to consider it in evolutionary perspective. Not only *could* the psychological world be radically different than it is at present, it *has* been radically different.

Consider stages of psychosocial development. There was a time when the demands and opportunities provided by childhood, adolescence, and old age were substantially different than at present, or when these stages did not even exist. Consider contemporary forms of psychological disturbance, such as narcissistic and borderline disorders or anorexia nervosa. It is unlikely that their prevalence and distribution has been constant across historical periods. Consider processes of sensation and perception. There was a time before organs of sensation and perception even existed. In short, the structures and processes studied in every branch of psychology have all changed over time.

One way of conceptualizing the most comprehensive evolutionary story is shown in Figure 13.5. The universe can be roughly divided into three worlds or levels, the physical, biological, and human-social-historical worlds, which mutually influence one another. Temporally, these three worlds emerged in chronological sequence, with the Big Bang origin of an expanding universe occurring approximately 15 billion years ago; the formation of the earth, about 4.6 billion years ago; the origin of life on earth, about 3.4 billion years ago; the evolution of mammals, about 200 million years ago; the appearance of *Homo habilis,* about 2 million years ago, through *Homo erectus,* about 1.5 million years ago, to *Homo sapiens sapiens,* or "modern man," about 40,000 years before the present; the domestication of plants and animals, about 8000 B.C.; and the rise of "civilization," about 3000 B.C. These dates are necessarily approximate estimates, but there is substantial consensus on their sequence and scale (Delbruck, 1986; Lewin, 1984; Weinberg, 1984).

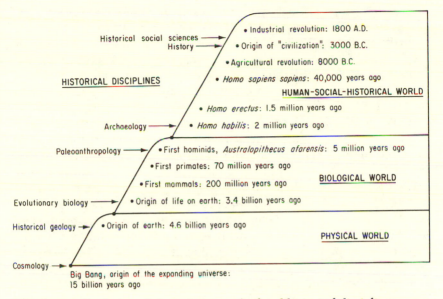

FIGURE 13.5. Evolution of the universe and related historical disciplines.

Earlier phases of the evolutionary process are investigated in a variety of historical disciplines, including cosmology, historical geology, evolutionary biology, paleoanthropology, archaeology, and history. Within this array of historical sciences, the study of historical psychology is at present relatively underdeveloped, particularly when compared with the substantial developments in historical sociology (Abrams, 1982; Skocpol, 1984). If historical psychology is distinguished from evolutionary psychology, then historical psychology would focus on continuity and change in psychological structures and processes in the relatively recent past (perhaps the last 3,000 to 5,000 years, with an emphasis on the past several centuries, for which more evidence is available), with evolutionary psychology studying the evolution of psychological structures and processes in earlier human history and in other species.

An evolutionary perspective directs attention to the interactions among biological evolution, the development of psychological structures and processes, and growth and change in sociocultural systems (see the sociobiology debate; for example, Caplan, 1978; Lumsden and Wilson, 1981, 1983; Kitcher, 1985; Montagu, 1980; Wilson, 1975, 1978). The rationale for introducing an evolutionary perspective into the present discussion is not to address this entire set of issues, but rather to emphasize the temporal fragility of psychological structures, relationships, and processes. Current psychological structures and processes are not eternally fixed, and for most of the history of the universe and most of the history of life on earth, did not even exist. They have developed substantially since their initial emergence, have continued to change during the course of recorded history, and are unlikely to remain fixed in the future.

Some biological and neurological aspects of psychic structure and function may well have remained relatively stable since the emergence of *Homo sapiens sapiens,* but those structures and processes influenced by social, cultural, and historical conditions, including much that is studied in social, developmental, cognitive, personality, and abnormal psychology, are likely to have changed substantially during the course of recorded history. After taking an evolutionary perspective on the history of the universe, one is less likely to rest content with a purely contemporaneous psychology, assuming that it is likely to be "general" across time and space.

The next section moves beyond these relatively abstract considerations, and discusses several recent exemplars of work in psychohistory which more concretely illustrate the field's accomplishments and potentials.

Examples and Exemplars

Advances in psychologically informed history may proceed through at least two processes: (1) through attempting to lay conceptual foundations for the field, which provide an orienting vision and suggest a framework for assessing the current status and future possibilities of the field, with progress coming through filling in the spaces of a relatively programmatic vision, or (2) through building up and out from a small number of paradigmatic studies, which catch the imagination of others and inspire them to imitate, replicate, and extend such approaches in their own work. In the field of psychohistory, works such as Freud's *Leonardo da Vinci and a Memory of His Childhood* (1910/1957) and Erikson's *Young Man Luther* (1958) have served as inspirations for many.

The intent of this section is to identify and briefly describe a number of additional studies that may serve as exemplars in stimulating further growth in the field. This is not to say that these works are flawless, but rather that they are exemplary in a number of aspects and provide much that others can learn from. Beginning with the work of contributors to this volume, I would like to call attention to Robert Tucker's *Stalin as Revolutionary, 1879–1929: A Study in History and Personality* (1973), with its emphasis on interconnections between individual personality and the social, political, and historical context; Jean Strouse's *Alice James* (1980), for its artful and unobtrusive use of psychoanalytic theory in presenting the particulars of an individual life; and Peter Gay's *Education of the Senses* (1984), with its wide-ranging illumination of sexual attitudes and behavior in the Victorian world.

Two of the most important contributors to the field of psychohistory are Peter Loewenberg, beginning with his classic article "The Psychohistorical Origins of the Nazi Youth Cohort" (1971) and continuing with major chapters on psychohistorical methodology, education, and substantive studies of German and Austrian leaders in *Decoding the Past: The Psychohistorical Approach* (1983), as well as the papers "Psychohistorical Perspectives on Modern German History" (1975) and "Why Psychoanalysis Needs the Social Scientist and the Historian" (1977); and Fred Weinstein, whose contributions include *Psychoanalytic Sociology* (with G. Platt, 1973), with its illuminating analysis of linkages between psychological theory and the interpretation of collective behavior, and *The Dynamics of Nazism: Leadership, Ideology, and the Holocaust* (1980), which emphasizes the heterogeneity of the subjective appeals of the Nazi movement to its members. I am also partial to my own *Life Histories and Psychobiography: Explorations in Theory and Method* (1982), which analyzes such issues as psychological reductionism, the reconstruction of earlier events, the influence of childhood experience on adult personality and behavior, the testing of alternative explanations, and ethical problems in the study of living political figures.

I would like to briefly discuss several additional exemplars, indicating both the present accomplishments of the field and suggesting future possibilities. The first work is John Demos's *Entertaining Satan: Witchcraft and the Culture of Early New England* (1982), which is unusually effective in integrating biographical, psychological, sociological, and historical approaches. In analyzing witchcraft in seventeenth-century New England, Demos combines detailed *biographical* studies, asking about the age, gender, social status, and life histories of those who were accused of witchcraft; a *psychological* analysis of the motives, emotions, unconscious processes, and developmental trajectories of those identified as witches; a *sociological* analysis of group and community tensions involved in witchcraft accusations and trials; and a *historical* analysis of conditions associated with the rise and decline of witchcraft trials over the years. All four vantage points usefully complement one another in illuminating the place of witchcraft within the lives, psyches, communities, and changing historical circumstances of early New Englanders. The work also combines scientific quantitative analyses with narrative and aesthetic evocations of the lives and circumstances of witches and their persecutors. As expressed by Demos (1982), "Biography, psychology, sociology, history: four corners of one scholar's compass, four viewpoints overlooking a single field of past experience. Each captures part, but not all, of the whole. . . . To see all this from *different* sides is to move at least some way toward full and final comprehension" (p. 15).

A second example is Robert Jervis's *Perception and Misperception in International Politics* (1976). Two features of this book are particularly relevant for present purposes. First, the book illustrates the application of cognitive psychology to the analysis of historical actors; thus it complements the bulk of literature in psychohistory, which utilizes psychodynamic theories. Jervis draws on literature from cognitive psychology, social psychology, attitude change, and visual perception to analyze the processes used by political decision makers in perceiving, interpreting, predicting, and making inferences about other political actors in international relations. A second feature of the book is its persuasive discussion of the "level of analysis" problem, or the relationships between individual and social-system levels of analysis. Jervis makes a powerful case for the importance in political analysis (and hence in historical analyses that involve politics) of studying not only the international environment of states, their national politics, and the bureaucracies surrounding politicians, but also the perceptions, beliefs, and decisions of individual political actors. All four levels of analysis—personal psychological, bureaucratic, national political, and international—are valuable in analyzing political affairs, with the importance of each level varying from one issue to another and possibly varying at different stages of the decision-making process (Jervis, 1976, pp. 16–17). For the purposes of this book, I have identified six system levels of analysis, ranging from persons through international relations, but the basic point is the same— that for understanding many political events or historical processes, the psychological level of analysis is, in conjunction with other levels, an *indispensable* level of analysis.

This is not the place for a comprehensive review of contributions to psychohistory, but a few additional works can be mentioned. In psychobiography, we are in the fortunate position of having excellent studies of three members of the same family: Leon Edel's (1953–72) pioneering five-volume study of Henry James, recently revised in one volume

(1985); Jean Strouse's (1980) study of Alice James; and, most recently, a study of intergenerational dynamics and processes of career choice and identity formation in the oldest brother, William James (Feinstein, 1984). A sample of other outstanding psychobiographies would include studies of Woodrow Wilson (George and George, 1956/1964; George et al., 1984), T. E. Lawrence (Mack, 1976), Samuel Johnson (Bate, 1977), James and John Stuart Mill (Mazlish, 1975), Beethoven (Solomon, 1977), Hitler (Waite, 1977), Picasso (Gedo, 1980), and Wilhelm Reich (Sharaf, 1983). On the psychological involvement of authors with their subjects, a distinguished recent collection is *Introspection in Biography: The Biographer's Quest for Self-Awareness* (Baron and Pletsch, 1985), which includes reflections by John Mack (1976) on his work with T. E. Lawrence, Richard Westfall (1981) on his massive biography of Isaac Newton, Arnold Rogow (1963) on his study of the first Secretary of Defense, James Forrestal, and Steven Marcus on his biographically related work on Charles Dickens (1965) and Friedrich Engels (1974). On the applications of psychoanalysis to biography, a valuable new collection based on a conference at the Institute for Psychoanalysis, Chicago, has been edited by Moraitis and Pollock (1987). In a recent paper, I have attempted to outline the processes that contribute to "progress" in psychobiography (Runyan, 1988).

In group psychohistory, a stimulating collection of work on American topics is provided in a volume edited by Brugger (1981), which contains selections from psychohistorical analyses of witchcraft (Boyer and Nissenbaum, 1974), the American Revolution (Burrows and Wallace, 1972; Hull, Hoffer, and Allen, 1978), slavery (Elkins, 1959), abolitionists (Walters, 1976), women's "hysteria" and role conflict in the nineteenth century (Smith-Rosenberg, 1972), public responses to Theodore Roosevelt (Dalton, 1979), and Vietnam veterans (Lifton, 1973). Collective psychohistorical analyses have also shed light on and raised important questions about topics as diverse as the rise of Nazism, anti-Semitism, student activists and revolutionaries, intellectual groups, religious movements, achievement motivation and economic growth, effects of the Great Depression, consequences of military experience, and responses to life-threatening disasters (in studies such as those of Elder, 1974, 1986; Feuer, 1963; Friedländer, 1978; Greven, 1977; Keniston, 1968; Lifton, 1967; Manuel and Manuel, 1979; Mazlish, 1976; McClelland, 1961; Scharfstein, 1980). A number of significant methodological papers are collected in a recent volume by Cocks and Crosby (1987).

Within group or institutional psychohistory, a good deal of interesting work has been done in recent years within political psychology (or political psychohistory, as some of it can be called), including analyses of the impact of psychological and group processes on political decision making (George, 1980; Janis, 1982), a survey of processes of perception and misperception in international politics (Jervis, 1976), an analysis of psychological factors in nuclear deterrence (Jervis, Lebow, and Stein, 1985), a recent collection of articles by leading researchers on *Psychology and the Prevention of Nuclear War* (White, 1986), and a variety of other topics covered in surveys of the field (Davies, 1980; Elms, 1976; Etheredge, 1978; Falkowski, 1979; Greenstein, 1975; Hermann, 1986). For further references, extensive bibliographies on psychobiography and psychohistory are provided by Kiell (1982) and Gilmore (1984).

There are, in short, a substantial number of high-quality works to be learned from and built on. Assessments of the state of psychohistory can no longer focus on several well-known errors, such as Freud's mistranslation of the word *nibbio* as "vulture" rather than "kite" in his study of Leonardo, or on one of Lloyd deMause's less plausible inferential leaps, as a basis for critiquing the field as a whole. Margaret Mead has commented that theoretical positions are sometimes known primarily through caricatures by their opponents, and there is a danger of this happening to psychohistory. Critical evaluations of psychohistory cannot responsibly be based on citation of a few widely known errors, but need to consider the full range of work in the field.

Conclusion

This chapter has attempted to provide a sounder conceptual foundation for the use of psychology in historical analysis. The argument is based on an analysis of six system levels, ranging from persons through groups, organizations, and institutions to social systems and international relations; on consideration of the relationships between history and psychology as mediated by developments in the aggregate-level social sciences; on a discussion of historical psychology as a resource for psychohistory; on an evolutionary perspective on the human-social-historical world; and, finally, on a selective review of substantive contributions to psychohistory.

A reconceptualization of psychohistory suggests a "new case" for the use of psychology in history, a case based on the following components: (1) the use not only of classical psychoanalytic theory, but also of recent developments within psychodynamic theory, and of psychoanalytic theory in relationship to the extensive empirical and philosophical literature assessing its strengths and limitations (see Eagle, 1984; Fisher and Greenberg, 1977; Grünbaum et al. 1986); (2) reliance not exclusively on psychoanalytic theory, but also on the full range of resources of personality, social, developmental, cognitive, biological, and abnormal psychology; (3) reliance not solely on a contemporary psychology, but also on a historical psychology that systematically assesses the transhistorical generality and specificity of its claims; and finally (4) the use of psychology not only applied directly to history, but also the use of psychology mediated through the aggregate-level social sciences, particularly such subfields as social structure and personality, historical sociology, psychological anthropology, and political psychology.

This is a demanding set of aspirations, which will be difficult to realize, but we can be encouraged by the amount of high-quality work in these areas already being produced, both within psychohistory and in the adjacent fields of historical sociology, historical anthropology, and political psychology. An appropriate criterion for evaluating work in this domain is not analytic perfection, which can be paralyzingly ambitious, but rather, comparisons with the level of rigor and confusion in the parent disciplines of history and psychology, and comparisons with historical studies that neglect psychological factors and analyses.

I am acutely aware of limitations in this discussion of relationships between history and psychology, limitations that stem from the perspective of one trained primarily in psychology, from difficulties in mastering the range of relevant literatures, and from such a brief treatment of a complex set of issues. The possibilities for working out relationships between history and psychology have only begun to be explored, and with the range of unresolved problems, there is a great need for contributions and alternative analyses by those from a variety of disciplines.

The issues that psychosocial history forces us to address are, I believe, of fundamental importance across the human-social-historical sciences, issues such as the relationships between human agency and institutional determinism, between individual biography and population processes, and between the search for theoretical generality and the understanding of particular sequences of events. Work in psychosocial history has too often been a flawed addition to the intellectual landscape, but at its best, it promises to shed light on problems cutting across each of the human sciences, as well as revealing the deep interconnections between psychological processes, social structures, and historical continuity and change.

References

Abrams, P. (1982). *Historical Sociology*. Ithaca, N.Y.: Cornell University Press.

Anderson, T. H. (1978). Becoming sane with psychohistory. *Historian, 41,* 1–20.

Arad, Y. (1987). *Belzec, Sobibor, Treblinka: The Operation Reinhard death camps*. Bloomington: Indiana University Press.

Bailyn, B., and Fleming, D. (Eds.). (1969). *The intellectual migration*. Cambridge, Mass.: Harvard University Press.

Barbu, Z. (1960). *Problems of historical psychology*. Westport, Conn.: Greenwood Press.

Barnouw, V. (1985). *Culture and personality* (4th ed.). Homewood, Ill.: Dorsey Press.

Baron, S. H., and Pletsch, C. (Eds.). (1985). *Introspection in biography: The biographer's quest for self-awareness*. Hillsdale, N.J.: Analytic Press.

Barraclough, G. (1978). *Main trends in history*. New York: Holmes and Meier.

Bate, W. J. (1977). *Samuel Johnson*. New York: Harcourt Brace Jovanovich.

Baumeister, R. (1986). *Identity: Cultural change and the struggle for self*. New York: Oxford University Press.

Bellah, R. N., Madsen, R., Sullivan, W. M., Swidler, A., and Tipton, S. M. (1985). *Habits of the heart: Individualism and commitment in American life*. Berkeley: University of California Press.

Beyerchen, A. (1977). *Scientists under Hitler*. New Haven, Conn.: Yale University Press.

Binion, R. (1976). *Hitler among the Germans*. New York: Elsevier.

Blackburn, G. (1984). *Education in the Third Reich*. Albany: State University of New York Press.

Blatt, S., with Blatt, E. (1984). *Continuity and change in art: The development of modes of representation*. Hillsdale, N.J.: Erlbaum.

Bock, P. K. (1980). *Continuities in psychological anthropology: A historical introduction*. San Francisco: Freeman.

Boyer, P., and Nissenbaum, S. (1974). *Salem possessed: The social origins of witchcraft*. Cambridge, Mass.: Harvard University Press.

Bronfenbrenner, U. (1979). *The ecology of human development*. Cambridge, Mass.: Harvard University Press.

Broughton, J. M. (1986). The psychology, history, and ideology of the self. In K. Larsen (Ed.), *Dialectics in ideology and psychology*. Norwood, N.J.: Ablex.

Brugger, R. J. (Ed.). (1981). *Our selves/our past: Psychological approaches to American history.* Baltimore: Johns Hopkins University Press.

Burrows, E. G., and Wallace, M. (1972). The American Revolution: The ideology and psychology of national liberation. *Perspectives in American History, 6,* 266–303.

Calhoun, D. (1973). *The intelligence of a people.* Princeton, N.J.: Princeton University Press.

Caplan, A. L. (Ed.). 1978). *The sociobiology debate.* New York: Harper & Row.

Cargas, H. (1985). *The Holocaust: An annotated bibliography* (2nd ed.). Chicago: American Library Association.

Caspi, A. (1987). Personality in the life course. *Journal of Personality and Social Psychology, 53*(6), 1203–1213.

Childers, T. (1984). *The Nazi voter.* Chapel Hill: University of North Carolina Press.

Cocks, G. (1985). *Psychotherapy in the Third Reich: The Göring Institute.* New York: Oxford University Press.

Cocks, G., and Crosby, T. (Eds.). (1987). *Psycho/History.* New Haven, Conn.: Yale University Press.

Conway, J. (1969). *The Nazi persecution of the churches, 1933–1945.* New York: Basic Books.

Coser, L. (1984). *Refugee scholars in America.* New Haven, Conn.: Yale University Press.

Cronbach, L. J. (1975). Beyond the two disciplines of scientific psychology. *American Psychologist, 30,* 116–127.

Cronbach, L. J. (1986). Social inquiry by and for earthlings. In D. Fiske and R. Shweder (Eds.), *Metatheory in social science.* Chicago: University of Chicago Press.

Dalton, K. (1979). Why America loved Teddy Roosevelt: Or, charisma is in the eyes of the beholders. *Psychohistory Review, 8*(3), 16–26.

Davies, A. F. (1980). *Skills, outlooks and passions: A psychoanalytic contribution to the study of politics.* Cambridge: Cambridge University Press.

Dawidowicz, L. (1975). *The war against the Jews, 1933–1945.* New York: Bantam Books.

Degler, C. (1987, May 27). Should historians be skeptical about using psychological methods? *Chronicle of Higher Education,* p. 80.

Delbruck, M. (1986). *Mind from matter?* Palo Alto, Calif.: Blackwell Scientific.

Demos, J. P. (1982). *Entertaining Satan: Witchcraft and the culture of early New England.* New York: Oxford University Press.

Dimsdale, J. (Ed.). (1980). *Survivors, victims, and perpetrators: Essays on the Nazi Holocaust.* Washington: Hemisphere.

Direnzo, G. (Ed.). (1977). *We, the people: American character and social change.* Westport, Conn.: Greenwood Press.

Eagle, M. (1984). *Recent developments in psychoanalysis: A critical evaluation.* New York: McGraw-Hill.

Easterlin, R. A. (1980). *Birth and fortune: The impact of numbers on personal welfare.* New York: Basic Books.

Edel, L. (1953–72). *Henry James* (5 vols.). Philadelphia: Lippincott.

Edel, L. (1985). *Henry James: A life* (rev. ed.). New York: Harper & Row.

Elder, G. H., Jr. (1974). *Children of the Great Depression.* Chicago: University of Chicago Press.

Elder, G. H., Jr. (1986). Military times and turning points in men's lives. *Developmental Psychology, 22*(2), 233–245.

Elkins, S. (1959). *Slavery: A problem in American institutional and intellectual life.* Chicago: University of Chicago Press.

Elms, A. C. (1976). *Personality in politics.* New York: Harcourt Brace Jovanovich.

Erikson, E. (1942). Hitler's imagery and German youth. *Psychiatry, 5,* 475–493.

Erikson, E. H. (1958). *Young man Luther: A study in psychoanalysis and history.* New York: Norton.

Etheredge, L. S. (1978). *A world of men: The private sources of American foreign policy.* Cambridge, Mass.: MIT Press.

Falkowski, L. S. (Ed.). (1979). *Psychological models in international politics.* Boulder, Colo.: Westview Press.

Feinstein, H. M. (1984). *Becoming William James.* Ithaca, N.Y.: Cornell University Press.

Feuer, L. (1963). *The scientific intellectual: The psychological and sociological origins of modern science.* New York: Basic Books.

Fisher, S. and Greenberg, R. D. (1977). *The scientific credibility of Freud's theories and therapy.* New York: Basic Books.

Freud, S. (1957). *Leonardo da Vinci and a memory of his childhood.* In J. Strachey (Ed. and Trans.), *The standard edition of the complete psychological works of Sigmund Freud* (Vol. 2). London: Hogarth Press. (Original work published 1910.)

Friedländer, S. (1966). *Pius XII and the Third Reich.* New York: Knopf.

Friedländer, S. (1971). *L'Antisemitisme nazi: Histoire d'une psychose collective.* Paris: Editions du Seuil.

Friedländer, S. (1978). *History and psychoanalysis.* New York: Holmes and Meier.

Friedländer, S. (1984). *Reflections of nazism.* New York: Harper & Row.

Fromm, E. (1942). *Escape from freedom.* New York: Rinehart.

Gay, P. (1984). *The bourgeois experience: Victoria to Freud: Vol 1. Education of the senses.* New York: Oxford University Press.

Gay, P. (1985). *Freud for historians.* New York: Oxford University Press.

Gedo, M. (1980). *Picasso: Art as autobiography.* Chicago: University of Chicago Press.

Geertz, C. (1973). *The interpretation of cultures.* New York: Basic Books.

George, A. L. (1980). *Presidential decisionmaking in foreign policy: The effective use of information and advice.* Boulder, Colo.: Westview Press.

George, A. L., and George, J. L. (1964). *Woodrow Wilson and Colonel House: A personality study.* New York: Dover. (Original work published 1956.)

George, J. L. et al. (1984a). Research note/issues in Wilson scholarship: References to early "strokes" in the papers of Woodrow Wilson. *Journal of American History, 70,* 845–853.

George, J. L. et al. (1984b). Communication. *Journal of American History, 70,* 945–956.

George, J. L. et al. (1984c). Communication. *Journal of American History, 71,* 198–212.

Gergen, K. J. (1973). Social psychology as history. *Journal of Personality and Social Psychology, 26,* 309–320.

Gergen, K. J. (1982). *Toward transformation in social knowledge.* New York: Springer-Verlag.

Gergen, K. J. (1984). Accounting and recounting. *Contemporary Social Psychology, 10*(5, 6), 6–10.

Gergen, K. J., and Gergen, M. M. (Eds.). (1984). *Historical social psychology.* Hillsdale, N.J.: Erlbaum.

Giddens, A. J. (1976). *New rules of sociological method.* New York: Basic Books.

Giddens, A. J. (1984). *The constitution of society.* Berkeley: University of California Press.

Gilmore, W. (1979). Paths recently crossed: Alternatives to psychoanalytic psychohistory (continued). *Psychohistory Review, 7*(4), 26–42.

Gilmore, W. J. (1984). *Psychohistorical inquiry: A comprehensive research bibliography.* New York: Garland.

Gordon, S. (1984). *Hitler, Germans and the "Jewish question."* Princeton, N.J.: Princeton University Press.

Greenstein, F. (1975). *Personality and politics: Problems of evidence, inference, and conceptualization* (new ed.). New York: Norton.

Greven, P. (1977). *The Protestant temperament: Patterns of child-rearing, religious experience, and the self in early America.* New York: Meridian.

Grünbaum, A. et al. (1986). Précis of *The foundations of psychoanalysis: A philosophical critique.* Plus, open peer commentary. *Behavioral and Brain Sciences, 9*(2), 217–284.

Hamilton, R. (1981). *Who voted for Hitler?* Princeton, N.J.: Princeton University Press.

Hamilton, R., and Wright, J. (1986). *The state of the masses.* New York: Aldine.

Hausner, G. (1966). *Justice in Jerusalem.* New York: Holocaust Library.

Hermann, M. G. (Ed.). (1986). *Political psychology*. San Francisco: Jossey-Bass.

Higham, C. (1983). *Trading with the enemy*. New York: Delacorte Press.

Hoess, R. (1959). *Commandant of Auschwitz*. London: Pan Books.

Hoffman, P. (1977). *The history of the German resistance, 1933–1945*. Boston: MIT Press.

Höhne, H. (1969). *The Order of the Death's Head: The story of Hitler's S.S.* New York: Coward-McCann.

Horney, K. (1937). *The neurotic personality of our time*. New York: Norton.

Hughes, J. (1983). *Emotion and high politics: Personal relations at the summit in late nineteenth-century Britain and Germany*. Berkeley: University of California Press.

Hull, N., Hoffer, P., and Allen, S. (1978). Politics and personality: Loyalists and Revolutionaries in New York. *Journal of American History, 65*, 344–366.

Inkeles, A. (1983). *Exploring individual modernity*. New York: Columbia University Press.

Inkeles, A., and Smith, D. (1974). *Becoming modern: Individual change in six developing countries*. Cambridge, Mass.: Harvard University Press.

Janis, I. L. (1982). *Groupthink* (2nd ed.). Boston: Houghton Mifflin.

Jaynes, J. (1976). *The origin of consciousness in the breakdown of the bicameral mind*. Boston: Houghton Mifflin.

Jervis, R. (1976). *Perception and misperception in international politics*. Princeton, N.J.: Princeton University Press.

Jervis, R., Lebow, R., and Stein, J. (1985). *Psychology and deterrence*. Baltimore: Johns Hopkins University Press.

Katona, G. (1975). *Psychological economics*. New York: Elsevier.

Keniston, K. (1968). *Young radicals*. New York: Harcourt Brace Jovanovich.

Keniston, K. (1971). Psychological development and historical change. *Journal of Interdisciplinary History, 2*, 329–345.

Kiell, N. (1982). *Psychoanalysis, psychology, and literature: A bibliography* (2nd ed.). Metuchen, N.J.: Scarecrow Press.

Kitcher, P. (1985). *Vaulting ambition: Sociobiology and the quest for human nature*. Cambridge, Mass.: MIT Press.

Kluckhohn, C., and Murray, H. A. (1953). Personality formation: The determinants. In C. Kluckhohn, H. Murray, and D. Schneider (Eds.), *Personality in nature, society, and culture* (rev. ed.). New York: Knopf.

Kohut, T. (1986). Psychohistory as history. *American Historical Review, 91*(2), 336–354.

Kren, G. (1984). Psychohistory, psychobiography and the Holocaust. *Psychohistory Review, 13*(1), 40–45.

Kren, G., and Rappoport, L. (1980). *The Holocaust and the crisis of human behavior.* New York: Holmes and Meier.

Langer, W. C. (1972). *The mind of Adolf Hitler: The secret wartime report.* New York: Basic Books.

Lasch, C. (1979). *The culture of narcissism: American life in an age of diminishing expectations.* New York: Norton.

LeVine, R. A. (1973; 2nd ed., 1982). *Culture, behavior, and personality.* Chicago: Aldine.

LeVine, R. A., and Shweder, R. A. (Eds.). (1984). *Culture theory: Essays on mind, self, and emotion.* Cambridge: Cambridge University Press.

LeVine, R. A., and White, M. (1986). *Human conditions: The cultural basis of educational developments.* New York: Routledge and Kegan Paul.

Lewin, R. (1984). *Human evolution.* New York: Freeman.

Lifton, A. J. (1967). *Death in life: Survivors of Hiroshima.* New York: Random House.

Lifton, R. J. (1973). *Home from the war: Vietnam veterans—neither victims nor executioners.* New York: Simon and Schuster.

Lifton, R. J. (1986). *The Nazi doctors.* New York: Basic Books.

Loewenberg, P. (1971). The psychohistorical origins of the Nazi youth cohort. *American Historical Review, 76,* 1457–1502.

Loewenberg, P. (1975). Psychohistorical perspectives on modern German history. *Journal of Modern History, 47*(2), 229–279.

Loewenberg, P. (1977). Why psychoanalysis needs the social scientist and the historian. *International Review of Psycho-Analysis, 4*(3), 305–315.

Loewenberg, P. (1983). *Decoding the past: The psychohistorical approach.* New York: Knopf.

Long, S. (Ed.). (1981). *The handbook of political behavior* (5 vols.). New York: Plenum Press.

Lumsden, C. J., and Wilson, E. O. (1981). *Genes, mind and culture.* Cambridge, Mass.: Harvard University Press.

Lumsden, C. J., and Wilson, E. O. (1983). *Promethean fire: Reflections on the origin of mind.* Cambridge, Mass.: Harvard University Press.

Luria, A. R. (1971). Towards the problem of the historical nature of psychological processes. *International Journal of Psychology, 6*(4), 259–272.

Luria, A. R. (1976). *Cognitive development: Its cultural and social foundations.* Cambridge, Mass.: Harvard University Press.

Mack, J. E. (1976). *A prince of our disorder: The life of T. E. Lawrence.* Boston: Little, Brown.

Magnusson, D., and Endler, N. (Eds.). (1977). *Personality at the crossroads: Current issues in interactional psychology.* Hillsdale, N.J.: Erlbaum.

Maital, S. (1982). *Minds, markets and money: Psychological foundations of economic behavior.* New York: Basic Books.

Manis, M. et al. (1976). Social psychology and history: A symposium. *Personality and Social Psychology Bulletin, 2,* 371–444.

Manuel, F. E. (1972). The use and abuse of psychology in history. In F. Gilbert and S. Graubard (Eds.), *Historical studies today.* New York: Norton.

Manuel, F. E., and Manuel, F. P. (1979). *Utopian thought in the Western world.* Cambridge, Mass.: Harvard University Press.

Marcus, S. (1965). *Dickens: From Pickwick to Dombey.* New York: Basic Books.

Marcus, S. (1974). *Engels, Manchester and the working class.* New York: Random House.

Marcus, S. (1984). *Freud and the culture of psychoanalysis.* Boston: Allen & Unwin.

Martindale, C. (1984). The evolution of aesthetic taste. In K. Gergen and M. Gergen (Eds.), *Historical social psychology.* Hillsdale, N.J.; Erlbaum.

Marwick, A. (1981). *The nature of history* (2nd ed.). London: Macmillan.

Mazlish, B. (1975). *James and John Stuart Mill: Father and son in the nineteenth century.* New York: Basic Books.

Mazlish, B. (1976). *The revolutionary ascetic: Evolution of a political type.* New York: Basic Books.

McClelland, D. C. (1961). *The achieving society.* Princeton, N.J.: Van Nostrand.

McCluskey, K. A., and Reese, H. W. (Eds.). (1984). *Life-span developmental psychology: Historical and generational effects.* New York: Academic Press.

McGuire, W. J. (1976). Historical comparisons: Testing psychological hypotheses with cross-era data. *International Journal of Psychology, 11*(3), 161–183.

Mensch, T. (1979–80). Psychohistory of the Third Reich: A library pathfinder and topical bibliography of English-language publications. *Journal of Psychohistory, 7*(3), 331–354.

Milgram, S. (1974). *Obedience to authority.* New York: Harper & Row.

Miller, A. G. (1986). *The obedience experiments: A case study of controversy in social science.* New York: Praeger.

Miller, J. G. (1978). *Living systems.* New York: McGraw-Hill.

Miller, W. B., and Godwin, K. (1977). *Psyche and Demos: Individual psychology and the issues of population.* New York: Oxford University Press.

Montagu, A. (Ed.). (1980). *Sociobiology examined.* New York: Oxford University Press.

Nesselroade, J. R., and Baltes, P. B. (1974). Adolescent personality development and historical change: 1970–1972. *Monographs of the Society for Research in Child Development 39* (1, Serial No. 154).

Peeters, H., Gielis, M., and Caspers, C. (1985). *Literatuurgids historische gedragswetenschappen.* Baarn, Netherlands: AMBO.

Pervin, L., and Lewis, M. (Eds.). (1978). *Internal and external determinants of behavior.* New York: Plenum Press.

Radding, C. M. (1985). *A world made by men: Cognition and society, 400–1200.* Chapel Hill: University of North Carolina Press.

Riesman, D. (1961). *The lonely crowd: A study of the changing American character.* New Haven, Conn.: Yale University Press.

Roazen, P. (1968). *Freud: Political and social thought.* New York: Knopf.

Rogow, A. A. (1963). *James Forrestal: A study of personality, politics and policy.* New York: Macmillan.

Rosaldo, R. (1980). *Ilongot headhunting, 1883–1974: A study in society and history.* Stanford: Stanford University Press.

Rosenberg, M., and Turner, R. H. (Eds.). (1981). *Social psychology: Sociological perspectives.* New York: Basic Books.

Rosenblatt, P. (1983). *Bitter, bitter tears: Nineteenth-century diarists and twentieth-century grief theories.* Minneapolis: University of Minnesota Press.

Runyan, W. M. (1982). *Life histories and psychobiography: Explorations in theory and method.* New York: Oxford University Press.

Runyan, W. M. (1983). Idiographic goals and methods in the study of lives. *Journal of Personality, 51,* 413–437.

Runyan, W. M. (1984). Diverging life paths: Their probabilistic and causal structure. In K. J. Gergen and M. M. Gergen (Eds.), *Historical social psychology.* Hillsdale, N.J.: Erlbaum.

Runyan, W. M. (1986). Life histories in anthropology: Another view. *American Anthropologist, 88*(1), 181–183.

Runyan, W. M. (1988). Progress in psychobiography. *Journal of Personality, 56*(1), 293–324.

Ryff, C. D. (1987). The place of personality and social structure research in social psychology. *Journal of Personality and Social Psychology, 53*(6), 1192–1202.

Sanford, N. (1973). Authoritarian personality in contemporary perspective. In J. Knutson (Ed.), *Handbook of political psychology.* San Francisco: Jossey-Bass.

Scharfstein, B. (1980). *The philosophers: Their lives and the nature of their thought.* New York: Oxford University Press.

Schlenker, B. R. (1974). Social psychology and science. *Journal of Personality and Social Psychology, 29,* 1–15.

Schoenwald, R. L. (1973). Using psychology in history: A review essay. *Historical Methods Newsletter, 7*(1), 9–24.

Scholl, I. (1983). *The White Rose: Munich, 1942–43.* Middletown, Conn.: Wesleyan University Press.

Scribner, S., and Cole, M. (1981). *The psychology of literacy.* Cambridge, Mass.: Harvard University Press.

Sharaf, M. (1983). *Fury on earth: A biography of Wilhelm Reich.* New York: St. Martin's Press.

Shorter, E. (1975). *The making of the modern family.* New York: Basic Books.

Shorter, E. (1986). Paralysis: The rise and fall of an "hysterical" symptom. *Journal of Social History, 19*(4), 549–582.

Simonton, D. K. (1984). *Genius, creativity, and leadership: Historiometric inquiries.* Cambridge, Mass.: Harvard University Press.

Skocpol, T. (Ed.). (1984). *Vision and method in historical sociology.* Cambridge: Cambridge University Press.

Smelser, N. J., and Smelser, W. T. (Eds.). (1970). *Personality and social systems* (2nd ed.). New York: Wiley.

Smelser, W. T., and Smelser, N. J. (1981). Group movements, sociocultural change, and personality. In M. Rosenberg and R. Turner (Eds.), *Social psychology: Sociological perspectives.* New York: Basic Books.

Smith-Rosenberg, C. (1972). The hysterical woman: Sex roles and role conflict in nineteenth-century America. *Social Research: An International Quarterly of the Social Sciences, 39,* 652–678.

Solomon, M. (1977). *Beethoven.* New York: Schirmer Books.

Spindler, G. (Ed.). (1978). *The making of psychological anthropology.* Berkeley: University of California Press.

Stannard, D. E. (1980). *Shrinking history: On Freud and the failure of psychohistory.* New York: Oxford University Press.

Stearns, C., and Stearns, P. (1986). *Anger: The struggle for emotional control in America's history.* Chicago: University of Chicago Press.

Steiner, J. (1980). The SS yesterday and today: A sociopsychological view. In J. Dimsdale (Ed.), *Survivors, victims, and perpetrators: Essays on the Nazi Holocaust.* Washington, D.C.: Hemisphere.

Stierlin, H. (1976). *Adolf Hitler, a family perspective.* New York: Psychohistory Press.

Stone, L. (1977). *The family, sex, and marriage in England, 1500–1800.* New York: Harper & Row.

Stone, L. (1981). *The past and the present.* Boston: Routledge & Kegan Paul.

Strouse, J. (1980). *Alice James: A biography.* New York: Bantam Books.

Sydnor, C., Jr. (1977). *Soldiers of destruction.* Princeton, N.J.: Princeton University Press.

Szonyi, D. (1985). *The Holocaust: An annotated bibliography and resource guide.* New York: Ktav Publishing House.

Tetlock, P., and McGuire, C. (1986). Cognitive perspectives on foreign policy. In S. Long (Ed.), *Political behavior annual,* Boulder, Colo.: Westview Press.

Trunk, I. (1979). *Jewish responses to Nazi persecution.* New York: Stein and Day.

Tucker, R. C. (1973). *Stalin as revolutionary, 1879–1929: A study in history and personality.* New York: Norton.

Turner, H. A., Jr. (1985). *German big business and the rise of Hitler.* New York: Oxford University Press.

Veroff, J., Douvan, E., and Kulka, R. (1981). *The inner American: A self-portrait from 1957 to 1976.* New York: Basic Books.

Von Wright, G. H. (1971). *Explanation and understanding.* London: Routledge & Kegan Paul.

Waite, R. G. L. (1977). *The psychopathic God: Adolf Hitler.* New York: Basic Books.

Walter, R. G. (1976). *The anti-slavery appeal: American abolitionism after 1830.* Baltimore: Johns Hopkins University Press.

Weinberg, S. (1984). *The first three minutes: A modern view of the origin of the universe.* New York: Bantam Books.

Weinstein, F. (1980). *The dynamics of Nazism: Leadership, ideology, and the Holocaust.* New York: Academic Press.

Weinstein, F., and Platt, G. M. (1973). *Psychoanalytic sociology.* Baltimore: Johns Hopkins University Press.

Wertsch, J. V. (1985). *Vygotsky and the social formation of mind.* Cambridge, Mass.: Harvard University Press.

Westfall, R. S. (1981). *Never at rest: A biography of Isaac Newton.* New York: Cambridge University Press.

Westen, D. (1986). *Self and society: Narcissism, collectivism, and the development of morals.* Cambridge: Cambridge University Press.

White, R. K. (Ed.). (1986). *Psychology and the prevention of nuclear war.* New York: New York University Press.

Wilson, E. O. (1975). *Sociobiology: The new synthesis.* Cambridge, Mass.: Harvard University Press.

Wilson, E. O. (1978). *On human nature.* Cambridge, Mass.: Harvard University Press.

Wyman, D. (1984). *The abandonment of the Jews: America and the Holocaust, 1941–1945.* New York: Pantheon Books.

Yinger, J. M. (1965). *Toward a field theory of behavior.* New York: McGraw-Hill.

Index